## Regule and Summa

The *Regule* of Robertus de Handlo and the *Summa* of Johannes Hanboys are important treatises by Englishmen on the notation of mensural music in the fourteenth century. The *Regule* of 1326 provides one of the two most comprehensive views of late *ars antiqua* notational developments; the other is the nearly contemporaneous *Speculum musicae* of Jacques de Liège. Handlo takes as his point of departure the first part, on notation, of one of those widely circulated, abbreviated versions of the teachings of Franco that begin in most sources with the motto "Gaudent brevitate moderni." To this standard base, he adds a considerable amount of material totaling about twice the size of the Franconian treatise itself. Handlo and the authorities he cites discuss the subdivision of the brevis into as many as nine semibreves, and he makes reference to English music and idiomatic insular notational practices.

The *Summa* of Hanboys, written around 1375, takes Handlo as a point of departure and incorporates an abbreviated redaction of the *Regule*, along with citations of other later English authorities, into an exhaustively systematic survey of *ars nova* forms and rests. Following and building upon an active line of development in English theory, Hanboys undertakes an expansion of the mensural system first codified by Johannes de Muris in the *Notitia artis musicae* to a total of eight figures. A close reading of his numerous digressions provides a wealth of further information about the evolution from the *ars antiqua* to the *ars nova* in England and the distinctive insular notational practices of the fourteenth century.

Both of these texts were edited by Edmond de Coussemaker in the nineteenth century in editions now recognized as seriously deficient. The present critical editions are based on a thorough re-examination and appraisal of the single extant source of each treatise. Full descriptions of these sources are provided, and the sources are illustrated with a plate from each. The critical edition is joined with a fully annotated translation on facing pages. An introduction reviews the available information about the identities of both authors, places the treatises in context with respect to the theoretical traditions of fourteenth-century France and England, and reviews their contents in detail. Indexes for terms, names, and subjects are included. Appendices provide a concordance to the music examples from the *Regule* that are transmitted in the *Summa*, transcriptions of two English motet fragments that exhibit insular notational practices discussed in the treatises, and a brief text that may be derived from another treatise by Hanboys.

Peter M. Lefferts, associate professor of music history at the University of Nebraska-Lincoln, is the author of *The Motet in England in the Fourteenth Century* and of articles in *Early Music History*, *Early Music*, and *L'ars nova italiana del trecento* 6. He is co-editor of several volumes in the series *Polyphonic Music of the Fourteenth Century*.

# Greek and Latin Music Theory

Thomas J. Mathiesen,
General Editor
Indiana University

Jon Solomon,
Associate Editor
University of Arizona

Previously published in this series

Prosdocimo de' Beldomandi, *Contrapunctus*
edited and translated by Jan Herlinger

*The Berkeley Manuscript*, University of California
Music Library, MS. 744 (*olim* Phillipps 4450)
edited and translated by Oliver B. Ellsworth

Sextus Empiricus, ΠΡΟΣ ΜΟΥΣΙΚΟΥΣ,
Against the Musicians (Adversus musicos)
edited and translated by Denise Davidson Greaves

Prosdocimo de' Beldomandi, *Brevis summula
proportionum quantum ad musicam pertinet*
and *Parvus tractatulus de modo
monacordum dividendi*
edited and translated by Jan Herlinger

Gaspar Stoquerus, *De musica verbali*
edited and translated by Albert C. Rotola, S.J.

*Tractatus figurarum*
edited and translated by Philip E. Schreur

# Robertus de Handlo

## REGULE

The Rules

and

# Johannes Hanboys

## SUMMA

The Summa

A new critical text and
translation on facing pages,
with an introduction, annotations,
and *indices verborum*
and *nominum et rerum* by

# Peter M. Lefferts

University of Nebraska Press
Lincoln and London

Copyright © 1991 by the
University of Nebraska Press
All rights reserved
Manufactured in the
United States of America
The paper in this book meets
the minimum requirements of
American National Standard
for Information Sciences—
Permanence of Paper for Printed
Library Materials, ANSI Z39.48–1984.
*Library of Congress
Cataloging-in-Publication Data*
Handlo, Robertus de.
   [Regule. English & Latin]
   Regule / Robertus de Handlo.
And Summa / Johannes Hanboys :
a new critical text and translation
on facing pages, with an introduction,
annotations, and indices verborum
and nominum et rerum / by
Peter M. Lefferts.
      p.   cm.—(Greek and Latin
      music theory)
   English and Latin
   Includes indexes.
   ISBN 0-8032-7934-5 (alk. paper)
   1. Music—Theory—500-1400.
2. Music—Theory—15th century.
I. Lefferts, Peter M. II. Hanboys,
Johannes. Summa. English & Latin.
1991. III. Title. IV. Series.
MT5.5.H3613   1991
781.2—dc20        90–45133
                     CIP
                     MN

To Laura

# CONTENTS

PREFACE .................................................................. ix

INTRODUCTION ........................................................ 1

    The *Regule* of Robertus de Handlo ............................... 4
        The Identity of Robertus de Handlo .......................... 4
        Contents of the *Regule* of Handlo ........................... 8
    The *Summa* of Johannes Hanboys ................................. 30
        The Identity of Johannes Hanboys ............................ 30
        Contents of the *Summa* of Hanboys .......................... 38
    In Summary ..................................................... 64
    The Manuscripts ................................................ 66
    The Edition .................................................... 77

CONSPECTUS CODICUM ET NOTARUM ................................. 79

REGULE ROBERTI DE HANDLO ........................................ 80

    Prima rubrica .................................................. 80
    Secunda rubrica ................................................ 88
    Tertia rubrica ................................................. 92
    Quarta rubrica ................................................. 100
    Quinta rubrica ................................................. 116
    Sexta rubrica .................................................. 120
    Septima rubrica ................................................ 134
    Octava rubrica ................................................. 136
    Nona rubrica ................................................... 142
    Decima rubrica ................................................. 152
    Undecima rubrica ............................................... 158
    Duodecima rubrica .............................................. 160
    Decimatertia rubrica ........................................... 166

SUMMA MAGISTRI JOHANNIS HANBOYS ............................... 180

    Capitulum I .................................................... 182
    Capitulum II ................................................... 184
    Capitulum III .................................................. 194
    Capitulum IV ................................................... 204
    Capitulum V .................................................... 206
    Capitulum VI ................................................... 212
    Capitulum VII .................................................. 220

Capitulum VIII ................................................................. 226
Capitulum IX .................................................................. 232
Capitulum X ................................................................... 236
Capitulum XI .................................................................. 242
Capitulum XII ................................................................. 254
Capitulum XIII ................................................................ 262
Capitulum XIV ................................................................ 274
Capitulum XV ................................................................. 282
Capitulum XVI ................................................................ 298
Capitulum XVII ............................................................... 310
Capitulum XVIII .............................................................. 316
Capitulum XIX ................................................................ 320
Capitulum XX ................................................................. 328
Capitulum XXI ................................................................ 334
Capitulum XXII ............................................................... 342

PLATES ............................................................................ 346

APPENDIX I: EXAMPLES FROM THE *REGULE*
  IN THE *SUMMA* ............................................................. 349

APPENDIX II: TWO MOTET FRAGMENTS
  IN INSULAR NOTATIONS ................................................. 351

APPENDIX III: TEXT POSSIBLY FROM A LARGER
  TREATISE BY HANBOYS .................................................. 361

INDEX VERBORUM TRACTATUS ROBERTI ........................... 367

INDEX VERBORUM TRACTATUS JOHANNIS ......................... 379

INDEX NOMINUM ET RERUM ............................................. 399

## PREFACE

The *Regule* of Robertus de Handlo and the *Summa* of Johannes Hanboys are important treatises by Englishmen on the notation of mensurable music in the fourteenth century. The *Regule* of 1326 takes as its point of departure the first part, on notation, of one of those widely circulated, abbreviated versions of the teachings of Franco of Cologne that begin in most sources with the motto "Gaudent brevitate moderni." To this standard base Handlo adds a considerable amount of material totaling about twice the size of the Franconian treatise itself, providing thereby one of the most comprehensive views of late *ars antiqua* notational developments. The *Summa* of Hanboys, written around 1375, takes Handlo as a point of departure and incorporates an abbreviated redaction of the *Regule*, along with citations of other later English authorities, into an exhaustively systematic survey of *ars nova* forms and rests. A close reading of both treatises provides a wealth of information about the evolution from the *ars antiqua* to the *ars nova* in England (and on the continent) and the distinctive insular notational practices of the fourteenth century.

Both of these texts were edited by Edmond de Coussemaker in the nineteenth century in editions now recognized as seriously deficient. The present critical editions are based on a thorough re-examination and appraisal of the single extant source of each treatise. Full descriptions of these sources are provided, and the sources are illustrated with a plate from each. The critical edition is joined with a fully annotated translation on facing pages. An introduction reviews the available information about the identities of both authors, places the treatises in context with respect to the theoretical traditions of fourteenth-century France and England, and reviews their contents in detail. Appendices provide a concordance to the music examples from the *Regule* that are transmitted in the *Summa*, transcriptions of two English motet fragments that exhibit insular notational practices discussed in the treatises, and a brief text that may be derived from another treatise by Hanboys.

Any volume editor in this series knows what an incalculable debt is owed to general editor Thomas J. Mathiesen for his advice, encouragement, and enormous labors on behalf of his editors and their authors. Special thanks are also due Ernest H. Sanders, who read and recommended numerous improvements to a full draft of this edition and translation. In its preparation I have incurred further debts for scholarly favors both large and small to many individuals, among whom I would like to single out by name Charles Atkinson, Margaret Bent, Roger D. Bowers, Mark Everist, Max Haas, David Howlett, Harry A. Ide, Nicky Losseff, Sandra Pinegar, Klaus-Jürgen Sachs, Dorit Tanay, Thomas Walker, Andrew B. Wathey, and Andrew G. Watson. All had a part in making this work better; none should share responsibility with me for any of its remaining faults.

I would also like to acknowledge the financial support of two Travel-To-Collections grants from the National Endowment for the Humanities (1984; 1987), a Grant-In-Aid from the American Council of Learned Societies (1987), and a Junior Faculty Summer Research Grant from the Division of the Humanities of the University of Chicago (1987). In addition, I should like to thank the Division of Research and the University Graduate School of Indiana University for generous grants in support of Greek and Latin Music Theory.

The British Library kindly granted permission for pages of their manuscripts to be reproduced in this volume.

## INTRODUCTION

The *Regule* of Robertus de Handlo and the *Summa* of Johannes Hanboys are important treatises in the discourse by Englishmen on the notation of mensural music in the fourteenth century,[1] and they provide characteristic examples of the ways in which standard authorities were used as the basis for new works. The *Regule* of 1326 adopts a widespread version of the teachings of Franco of Cologne as a framework for one of the two most substantial accounts of notational practice as it developed in northern Europe between the era of Franco and the era of Philippe de Vitry and Johannes de Muris.[2] The *Summa* of around 1375, which directly incorporates the *Regule* into an ambi-

---

[1] Neither touches on counterpoint. On the considerably better-known insular discant treatises, see Manfred Bukofzer, *Geschichte des englischen Diskants und des Fauxbourdons nach den theoretischen Quellen*, Sammlung Musikwissenschaftlicher Abhandlungen, no. 21 (Strassbourg: Heitz & Co., 1936); Thrasybulos Georgiades, *Englischen Diskanttraktate aus der ersten Hälfte des 15. Jahrhunderts: Untersuchungen zur Entwicklung der Mehrstimmigkeit im Mittelalter* (Munich: Musikwissenschaftliches Seminars der Universität München, 1937); and Sanford B. Meech, "Three Musical Treatises in English from a Fifteenth-Century Manuscript," *Speculum* 10 (1935): 235–69. For more recent discussion of the English discant treatises in a broader context, see also Klaus-Jürgen Sachs, *Der Contrapunctus im 14. und 15. Jahrhundert: Untersuchungen zum Terminus, zur Lehre und zu den Quellen*, Beihefte zum *Archiv für Musikwissenschaft*, vol. 13 (Wiesbaden: Franz Steiner, 1974); and Ernst Apfel, *Diskant und Kontrapunkt in der Musiktheorie des 12. bis 15. Jahrhunderts*, Taschenbücher zur Musikwissenschaft, vol. 82 (Wilhelmshaven: Heinrichshofen's Verlag, 1982).

[2] The only other treatise comparable in its coverage of late *ars antiqua* developments is the nearly exactly contemporary seventh book of the *Speculum musicae* of Jacques de Liège. See *Jacobi Leodiensis Speculum musicae*, 7 vols., ed. Roger Bragard, Corpus scriptorum de musica, no. 3 ([Rome]: American Institute of Musicology, 1973). Ulrich Michels has argued that Book 7 is datable between June 1323 and 1324/25 in *Die Musiktraktate des Johannes de Muris*, Beihefte zum *Archiv für Musikwissenschaft*, vol. 8 (Wiesbaden: Franz Steiner, 1970), pp. 50–55.

tious and rigidly systematic expansion of the mensural system to eight figures, is our primary literary witness to the distinctive insular notational practices of the fourteenth century that appear in numerous musical sources.[3]

The theoretical writings that form the context for these treatises include the following, which are presented in approximate chronological order:

Walter Odington, *Summa de speculatione musicae*.[4]
Robertus de Handlo, *Regule*.[5]
Anonymi of London, British Library (henceforward: **GB**-Lbl), Additional 21455, *Cum de mensurabili musica*.[6]

---

[3]On insular notational practices, see Ernest H. Sanders, "Duple Rhythm and Alternate Third Mode in the 13th Century," *Journal of the American Musicological Society* 15 (1962): 249–91; Margaret Bent, "A Preliminary Assessment of the Independence of English Trecento Notations," in *L'Ars nova italiana del Trecento IV (1975)*, ed. Agostino Ziino (Certaldo: Centro di studi sull'Ars nova italiana del Trecento, 1978), pp. 65–82; Roger Wibberley, "Notation in the Thirteenth and Fourteenth Centuries," in *Fourteenth-Century English Polyphony: A Selection of Facsimiles*, ed. Frank Ll. Harrison and Roger Wibberley, Early English Church Music, vol. 26 (London: Stainer and Bell, 1981), pp. xix–xxviii; and Peter M. Lefferts, *The Motet in England in the Fourteenth Century* (Ann Arbor, MI: UMI Research Press, 1986), pp. 118–54.

[4]Ed. Frederick Hammond, Corpus scriptorum de musica, no. 14 ([Rome]: American Institute of Musicology, 1970); *Scriptorum de musica medii aevi nova series a Gerbertina altera* (henceforward: CS), 4 vols., ed. Edmond de Coussemaker (Paris: Durand, 1864–76; reprint ed., Hildesheim: Olms, 1963), 1:182–250.

[5]CS, 1:383–403; and see this edition *infra*. For a previous translation of the *Regule*, see Luther Dittmer, trans. and ed., *Robert de Handlo*, Music Theorists in Translation, vol. 2 (Brooklyn, NY: Institute of Mediaeval Music, 1959). Dittmer's translation is unreliable and is to be used only in conjunction with its review by Janet Knapp in the *Journal of Music Theory* 3 (1959): 306–10.

[6]"A London Source for the *Ars Nova* of Philippe de Vitry," ed. André Gilles and Gilbert Reaney, in *Philippi de Vitriaco Ars nova*, ed. Gilbert Reaney, André Gilles, and Jean Maillard, Corpus scriptorum de musica, no. 8 ([Rome]: American Institute of Musicology, 1964), pp. 71–78. London, British Library (henceforward: **GB**-Lbl), Additional 21455 is, as Gilles and Reaney have described it (p. 71), "a miscellany of musical tractatuli," some a few pages long, others just a brief paragraph. Its contents are as follows:

1. Cum de mensurabili musica        ff. 3r–4v
2. Modus imperfectus, etc.          f. 5r–v
3. Item secundum antiquos modi      f. 5v

Johannes Torkesey, *Declaratio trianguli et scuti*.[7]
Anonymous, *Tractatus de figuris sive de notis*.[8]
Willelmus, *Breviarium regulare musicae*.[9]
Anonymous, *Quatuor principalia*, Version A.[10]
Anonymous, *Quatuor principalia*, Version B.[11]

---

| | |
|---|---|
| 4. Item sciendum sunt quod octo | f. 5v |
| 5. Falsa musica est | f. 6r |
| 6. Regula discantus | ff. 6r–7r |
| 7. Torkesey, Declaratio | ff. 7r–8v |
| 8. Regula de monachordo | f. 8v |
| 9. It is to wyte that ther are | f. 9r |
| 10. De discantu et contra nota | ff. 9v–11r |
| 11. Septem sunt concordancie | f. 11r |

Gilles and Reaney have edited items 1 and 2 as if they were a single tractatulus, together with item 8. Neither they nor others commenting on this source have observed that item 1 breaks off at the end of f. 4v, in the middle of material on ligatures, with the *reclamans* "sine," which does not match the top of f. 5r. The mensural system of item 1 includes the triplex and duplex longa, longa, brevis, semibrevis, minima, and semiminima. By contrast, the system of item 2 includes the larga, longa, brevis, minor, minima, and semiminima; it also uses *ars nova* terminology for mensuration not employed in item 1: modus perfectus or imperfectus, tempus perfectum or imperfectum, prolatio maior or minor. Furthermore, in the examples of item 2 the longa erecta and brevis erecta appear with a line of text to explain their meaning, the *cauda hirundinis* is used to indicate alteration, and the perfect semibrevis rest has the English form straddling the line. In a discussion of the relationship of the edited items to the other treatises attributed to de Vitry, Sarah Fuller has concluded that "[they] cannot even be considered a witness to the de Vitrian teaching tradition, much less a possible version of the Ars Nova" ("A Phantom Treatise of the Fourteenth Century? The *Ars Nova*," *Journal of Musicology* 4 [1985–86]: 27).

[7][Anonymous of] Ms. Oxford, Bodley 842 (Willelmus), *Breviarium regulare musicae*, ed. Gilbert Reaney; [Anonymous of] Ms. British Museum, Royal 12. C. VI., *Tractatus de figuris sive de notis*, ed. Gilbert Reaney; Johannes Torkesey, *Declaratio trianguli et scuti*, ed. André Gilles and Gilbert Reaney, Corpus scriptorum de musica, no. 12 ([Rome]: American Institute of Musicology, 1966), pp. 58–60.

[8]Ibid., pp. 40–51.

[9]Ibid., pp. 15–31.

[10]Ed. in part (*Quartum principale* only) as Anonymous I of CS, 3:334–64; see also *infra*, pp. 67–68 and 72–73.

[11]CS, 4:200–298.

Johannes Hanboys, *Summa*.[12]
Thomas Walsingham, *Regulae de musica mensurabili*.[13]
Anonymous (the "Wylde anonymous"), *De origine et effectu musicae*.[14]

This tradition is scholastic in its orientation and fairly self-reflective, with much reference by the later treatises to the contents of the earlier.[15]

*The* Regule *of Robertus de Handlo*

The Identity of Robertus de Handlo

The explicit of the *Regule* states that the treatise was completed on the Friday before Pentecost, 1326. Nothing certain is known of its author-compiler, Robertus de Handlo, but from internal evidence in the treatise, it would appear that he was an Englishman active in the first quarter of the fourteenth century who was knowledgeable about contemporary developments in musical notation both at home and on the continent.[16] His treatise appears to have

---

[12]CS, 1:403–48; and see this edition *infra*.

[13]Johannes Hothby, *Opera omnia de musica mensurabili*; Thomas Walsingham, *Regulae de musica mensurabili*, ed. Gilbert Reaney, Corpus scriptorum de musica, no. 31 (Neuhausen-Stuttgart: Hänssler Verlag for the American Institute of Musicology, 1983), pp. 74–98.

[14]Edited in Gilbert Reaney, "The Anonymous Treatise De Origine et Effectu Musicae, an Early 15th Century Commonplace Book of Music Theory," *Musica disciplina* 37 (1983): 101–19.

[15]Just as is true of fourteenth-century French notation theory, these insular materials lack a comprehensive monograph of the kind Gallo has provided for contemporaneous Italian treatises. For the latter, see F. Alberto Gallo, *La teoria della notazione in Italia dalla fine del XIII all' inizio del XV secolo* (Bologna: Tamari Editori, 1966). Gallo has also contributed a notable recent essay that deals at length with the fourteenth-century French and Italian traditions: "Die Notationslehre im 14. und 15. Jahrhundert," in *Die Mittelalterliche Lehre von der Mehrstimmigkeit*, ed. Frieder Zaminer, Geschichte der Musiktheorie, vol. 5 (Darmstadt: Wissenschaftliche Buchgesellschaft, 1984), pp. 257–356. Despite invaluable and detailed work by other modern scholars, including Michels and Sachs, and contributions by Wolf Frobenius, including many significant articles in the *Handwörterbuch der musikalischen Terminologie*, ed. Hans Heinrich Eggebrecht (Wiesbaden: Franz Steiner, 1972– ), the development of French *ars nova* theory still needs considerable clarification.

[16]The only mention of Handlo in the English antiquarian literature is by Thomas Tanner, *Bibliotheca Britannico-Hibernica* (London: David Wilkins,

been written for an audience of singers, or at any rate practical musicians (*cantores*).[17] Handlo's name was not known to the earlier sixteenth-century English antiquarians and literary historians. His treatise is first noted in a 1556 manuscript catalogue of the library of John Dee.[18]

The earliest published reference to Handlo appears in *A Plaine and Easy Introduction to Practicall Musicke* (1597) by Thomas Morley, in which the

---

1748), p. 376. The modern secondary literature on Handlo can be said to begin in 1776 with the publication of two famous British music histories, Charles Burney, *A General History of Music From the Earliest Ages to the Present Period*, ed. Frank Mercer, 4 vols. in 2 (New York: Harcourt, Brace, and Co., 1935), 1:535, 543, and 671; and Sir John Hawkins, *A General History of the Science and Practice of Music*, new ed., 5 vols. in 2 (London: Novello, 1875), 1:176, 221, 230–32, and 252–53. Subsequent literature includes François-Joseph Fétis, "Handlo (Robert de)," *Biographie universelle des musiciens* 4 (1866): 219; W[illiam] B[arclay] S[quire], "Handlo, Robert de," *Dictionary of National Biography* 8 (1890): 1175–76; Oswald Koller, "Handlo, Robertus de," *Quellen-Lexicon der Musiker und Musikgelehrten* 5 (1901): 15; J[ohn] F. R. S[tainer], "Handlo, Robert de," *Grove's Dictionary of Music and Musicians*, 2d ed., 2 (1906): 293–94, an entry reprinted in subsequent editions through the fifth ed. of 1954; R. Alec Harman, "Handlo, Robert de," *Die Musik in Geschichte und Gegenwart* (henceforward: MGG) 5 (1956): 1438–40; and Gordon Anderson, "Robert de Handlo," *New Grove Dictionary of Music and Musicians* 16 (1980): 66–67. There are, of course, references in classic studies of theory and notation based on Coussemaker's text such as Johannes Wolf, *Geschichte der Mensural-Notation von 1250–1460*, 3 vols. (Leipzig: Breitkopf & Härtel, 1904); idem, *Handbuch der Notationskunde*, 2 vols. (Leipzig: Breitkopf & Härtel, 1913–1916); and Hugo Riemann, *Geschichte der Musiktheorie*, 2d ed. (Berlin: M. Hesse, 1920), of which the first two books have been translated and edited by Raymond H. Haggh as *History of Music Theory, Books I and II: Polyphonic Theory to the Sixteenth Century* (Lincoln: University of Nebraska Press, 1962; reprint ed., New York: Da Capo, 1974). See also Jeffrey Pulver, "The English Theorists, III—Robert de Handlo," *Musical Times* 75 (1934): 26; Gustave Reese, *Fourscore Classics of Music Literature* (New York: Norton, 1957), pp. 26–27; Nan Cooke Carpenter, *Music in the Medieval and Renaissance Universities* (Norman: University of Oklahoma Press, 1958; reprint ed., New York: Da Capo, 1972), pp. 60, 70, and 88; Gilbert Reaney, "Questions of Authorship in the Medieval Treatises on Music," *Musica disciplina* 18 (1964): 12; Dittmer, *Robert de Handlo*; and Gallo, "Die Notationslehre."

[17]See Maxim 5 of Rubric IX and the explicit following Maxim 15 of Rubric XIII.

[18]On the complicated history of Dee's library and the *Regule*, see *infra*, pp. 69–71.

*Regule* is cited twice by title and author (where his name is spelled "de Haule") in the annotations to the first part. Handlo's name also appears on the final page among the "Authors Whose Authorities Be Either Cited Or Used In This Book" (where the name is spelled "de Haulo").[19] Morley's acquaintanceship with the *Regule* was evidently quite superficial. He knows its title, referring to it as *Regulae Franchonis cum additionibus Roberti de Haule*,[20] and his explanation of its contents is clearly indebted to the title alone: "One *Roberto de Haule* hath made as it were commentaries upon his [Franco's] rules, and termed them *Additions*."[21] The only excerpt from the *Regule* actually quoted by Morley concerns the raised longa and brevis, which he believed "neither he [Handlo] himselfe, nor any other, ever saw in practice." Since these forms are discussed in the first chapter—or, Rubric—of the *Regule* (they are Rule II, Maxim 2, Rule V, and Maxim 4 of Rubric I), it seems likely that Morley got no further in his scrutiny of the *Regule* than the first page.[22] In view of his reading of the title and the author's name, and his quotation of material before and within the *Regule*, Morley's source could not have been John Dee's manuscript.[23]

The spelling of our author's name varies in its early citations. The 1583 catalogue of John Dee's library spells the name "de Handlo"; however, that part of Dee's volume containing the treatise later became a part of the Cottonian collection, the 1674 manuscript catalogue of which records the name as "de Handle." This reading is followed by Thomas Smith, author of the first published catalog of the Cotton manuscripts (1696), who spells the

---

[19]Thomas Morley, *A Plaine and Easie Introduction to Practicall Musicke* (London: Peter Short, 1597; facsimile edition with an introduction by Edmund Fellowes, Shakespeare Association Facsimiles, no. 14, London: Oxford University Press, 1937), unpaginated annotations to p. 2, ver. 27, and p. 9, ver. 18; final page. These are pp. 108–9, 117, and 319 in the modern second edition by R. Alec Harman (London: Dent, 1963; reprint ed., New York: Norton, 1973), to which for the sake of convenience all subsequent references will be made. Morley's rather than Harman's orthography will be followed in all citations.

[20]Morley (ibid., p. 108) gives the full title of the *Regule* in his description of a gamut that appeared prior to the *Regule* in the vellum manuscript in which they both were preserved.

[21]Ibid., p. 117.

[22]On raised ("erectae") longae and breves, see *infra*, pp. 11–12.

[23]Harman (Morley, *Plaine and Easie Introduction* [ed. Harman], pp. 108–9, n. 5) had proposed the possibility that Morley consulted **GB**-Lbl, Cotton Tiberius B.IX.

name twice, both times as "de Handle."[24] Thomas Tanner, on the other hand, whose entry on Handlo in the *Bibliotheca Britannico-Hibernica* (1748) also cites the Cotton manuscript, reads the name "de Handlo." So does the scribe of **GB**-Lbl, Additional 4909, Dr. Pepusch's eighteenth-century copy that is our sole extant source of the *Regule*. Of course, a direct relationship between the Tanner and Pepusch readings is a likely possibility.

Whatever Morley and the others saw in their respective manuscripts, their readings are sufficiently alike to indicate that the same surname is meant. This derives from a known placename. Handlo and a number of other variants (Haulo, Hanlo, Haudlo, Haudlow, Hadlo, etc.) refer to a medieval manor that is the site of the modern village of Hadlow, northeast of Tonbridge, Kent.[25] A prominent family of the thirteenth and fourteenth centuries from the area bore this name. Its most prestigious member, Sir John de Handlo, was a close personal follower of the Despensers during the reign of Edward II and survived their fall, prospering into the 1340s.[26] He is well attested in the documentary record.[27]

---

[24]See **GB**-Lbl, Harley 694, f. 287r; and Thomas Smith, *Catalogus librorum manuscriptorum bibliothecae Cottonianae* (Oxford: Sheldon Theatre, 1696), p. 24a and its index.

[25]See the forms given under "Hadlow" in Eilert Ekwall, *The Concise Oxford Dictionary of English Place Names*, 4th ed. (Oxford: Clarendon Press, 1960). The name is not recorded in Percy H. Reaney, *A Dictionary of British Surnames*, 2d ed. (London: Routledge and Kegan Paul, 1976), but occurs as "Hadlow" in older authorities such as Charles W. Bardsley, *A Dictionary of English and Welsh Surnames* (London: H. Frowde, 1901), and Henry Harrison, *Surnames of the United Kingdom*, 2 vols. (London: The Eaton Press, 1912). The name, mainly spelled Haudlo, is not uncommon in the Rolls series and other monuments of the fourteenth century.

[26]Both Harman (*MGG*) and Anderson (*New Grove Dictionary*) follow Stainer's earlier *Grove's Dictionary* entries in pointing out that Sir John de Handlo was a prestigious bearer of the name in the early fourteenth century, but there appears to have been no further investigation of the family. References to a Handlo family from a volume of heraldic collections (**GB**-Lbl, Lansdowne 860, no. 124) and from extracts made in the late nineteenth century (**GB**-Lbl, Additional 37122, ff. 82–99) are provided in the *Index of Manuscripts in the British Library*, 10 vols. (Cambridge: Chadwyck-Healey, 1984–86).

[27]On Sir John de Handlo see, *inter alia*, *A Descriptive Catalogue of Ancient Deeds in the Public Records Office*, 6 vols. (London: H. M. Stationery Office, 1890–1915), 2:166; *Calendar of the Patent Rolls Preserved in the Public Record Office* (henceforward: *CPR*), Edward II, v. 1, 1307–1313 (London: H. M. Stationery Office, 1894), pp. 45 and 355; *CPR*,

Another bearer of this name, a Robertus de Haudlo/Handlo, is a potential candidate for identification as the music theorist.[28] This Robertus is perhaps some near relative of Sir John de Handlo, with whom he had property transactions.[29] Robertus is traceable from ca. 1315–1322 in the service of the Despensers. He was, for instance, a participant with Hugh le Despenser the younger in the seizing of Tonbridge Castle in 1315. Later, as a clerk in the service of Hugh le Despenser the elder, Robertus was nominated attorney for Hugh in 1320 when Hugh went overseas. All of this suggests that he was high in the Despenser's trust—an educated, high-ranking administrator. Absence of his name from readily accessible published records after the early 1320s may indicate Robertus's death, but further work in local archives is still required.

### Contents of the *Regule* of Handlo

The *Regule* takes as its point of departure the first part, on notation, of one of those widely circulated, abbreviated versions of the teachings of Franco that begin in most sources either "Gaudent brevitate moderni" or sim-

---

Edward II, v. 2, 1313–1317 (London: H. M. Stationery Office, 1898), pp. 71, 479, 509, 554 and 612; etc. through *CPR*, Edward III, 1343–45 (London: H. M. Stationery Office, 1902). His career is mentioned in passing in detailed studies of the Despensers; see, *inter alia*, Nigel Saul, "The Despensers and the Downfall of Edward II," *English Historical Review* 99, no. 390 (1984): 1–33.

[28] My search of names indexed in the Rolls series turned up this Robertus de Handlo, but I am indebted to Dr. Andrew Wathey for forcefully redrawing my attention to him as a potential candidate for the theorist. On Robert see, *inter alia*, *CPR*, Edward II, v. 3, 1317–1321 (London: H. M. Stationery Office, 1903), pp. 422 and 601; *CPR*, Edward II, v. 4, 1321–1324 (London: H. M. Stationery Office, 1904), p. 189; and *Calendar of Inquisitions Post Mortem*, v. 5, Edward II (London: H. M. Stationery Office, 1908), pp. 331 and 352.

[29] Robertus and John are perhaps both related to the Nicholas de Handlo who was a royal justice in 1260. On Nicholas de Handlo, see, *inter alia*, Hawkins, 1:221; *Calendar of Close Rolls*, 11 Henry III (1259–61) (London: H. M. Stationery Office, 1934), pp. 114–16; *Calendar of Liberate Rolls* (London: H. M. Stationery Office, 1959), v. 4, pp. 264, 317, and 364–65; and *CPR*, Edward II, v. 2, 1313–1317 (London: H. M. Stationery Office, 1898), p. 75.

ply "Quandocunque punctus quadratus vel nota quadrata ...."[30] The various *Gaudent moderni* treatises evidently stem from a single basic tradition but differ significantly in length and in a myriad of details. Stripped of all additional text, those passages attributed in the *Regule* to Franco comprise a complete, coherent, and standard treatise of this sort, occupying about one-third of the total text and determining its large-scale order of contents: simple figures and their combinations, ligatures, plicas, rests, and the rhythmic modes. A collation of the Franconian compendia available in print demonstrates that the version extractable from the *Regule* is most closely related to Coussemaker's Anonymous III.[31] No effort, however, has been made in the present edition to cite parallel passages from this tradition or, in general, to gloss its normal contents.[32]

To this standard base Handlo has added a considerable amount of material totaling about twice the size of the Franconian treatise itself. Although the *Regule* is dated 1326, it discusses none of the radical innovations of Parisian *ars nova* theory of the previous decade. Rather, it presents notational developments, concepts, and terminology that extended and modified the system of Franco of Cologne (ca. 1280) in the late thirteenth and early fourteenth centuries. Indeed, it provides us with one of the two most comprehensive views of the preoccupations of musicians concerned with notational theory in the late *ars antiqua*, the other being the compendious and considerably more garrulous *Speculum musicae* of Jacques de Liège.

Handlo is not the mere compiler of the words of others, as would be suggested by the modesty of the incipit of the *Regule*. He has a great deal of

---

[30]The most comprehensive available accounting of what will be called here the *Gaudent moderni* treatises is a list of seventeen, not including Handlo's *Regule*, that is provided by Heinz Ristory in "Ein Abbreviationstraktat im Umfeld der franconischen und post-franconischen Compendia," *Acta musicologica* 59 (1987): 103–5.

[31]CS, 1:319–27; this treatise was was edited by Coussemaker from Saint-Dié, Bibliothèque Municipale, MS 42, ff. 53r–58v. For a new critical edition, see *Johannes dictus Balloce Abreviatio Magistri Franconis*, ed. Gilbert Reaney; Anonymous, *Compendium musicae mensurabilis artis antiquae* [Anonymous III of CS 1], ed. Gilbert Reaney; Anonymous, *Compendium musicae mensurabilis artis antiquae*, ed. Heinz Ristory; Anonymous, *Tractatus artis antiquae cum explicatione mensurae binariae*, ed. Heinz Ristory, Corpus scriptorum de musica, no. 34 (Neuhausen-Stuttgart: Hänssler Verlag for the American Institute of Musicology, 1987), pp. 23–37.

[32]Coussemaker's edition of the *Regule* is collated with three other *Gaudent moderni* treatises published in CS 1 (those of Johannes Ballox, Anonymous II, and Anonymous III) by Dittmer, pp. 1–2.

importance to say, much of which is delivered as a gloss on the *Gaudent moderni* text. Sometimes this commentary is simply explanatory, amplifying the bare bones of the text with what sounds like a paraphrase of Franco's *Ars cantus mensurabilis*. Handlo also introduces maxims, rules, and larger portions, including whole chapters, of important new material—either his own or drawn from other late thirteenth- and early fourteenth-century musical commentators, some of whom are otherwise unrecorded.[33] These individuals will be further introduced below.

The treatise is not a dialogue per se, though that impression may be left because each contribution is labeled with its author's name, and Handlo's alternation of authorities is clearly modeled on dialogue form. Nor can we assume he is literally quoting his authorities rather than paraphrasing or summarizing them, except in the case of the *Gaudent moderni* text itself.

Handlo divides the *Regule* into thirteen "Rubrics," which are short chapters, each prefaced with an explanatory heading and consisting of a number of "Rules" that may be preceded or followed by commentary in the form of "Maxims." He also provides a limited number of cross references between these. The essential difference between rules and maxims is explained at the very end of the work (in Maxim 15 of Rubric XIII): rules have music examples while maxims do not.

The following paragraphs briefly review some important doctrines of the *Regule*, beginning with what it has to say about individual note-shapes. Cross-references are given to the edition, where fuller documentation is provided in the annotations to the translation.

*Figures and signs*

The note of greatest mensural value discussed by Handlo is an extended longa, used in the old organum, that contains up to nine longae (Rule I and Maxims 1 and 2 of Rubric V).[34] As do a number of continental theorists from around the same time, he recommends forming this note a new way, with strokes through the body of the figure to indicate how many longae it is to contain. Such figures cannot be imperfected, plicated, or ligated and must be pronounced "solido modo" (Maxim 3 of Rubric X). Handlo is preoccupied

---

[33]Citations of authorities in addition to "Franco" are confined to Rubric IV (on semibreves), Rubric IX (on conjunctions of semibreves), and Rubric XII (on rests).

[34]That he stops at nine is of interest in itself. A figure worth nine perfect longae is the largest ever proposed in *ars antiqua* or *ars nova* mensural theory. See *infra*, p. 53.

throughout the *Regule* with the issue of "que figure debent ad invicem associari,"[35] which in fact is the second topic of Rubric V; these extra-long longae, he states, can be mixed with longae and duplex longae.

The duplex longa, like the extended longa, was in the *ars antiqua* a note limited in use to the tenors of motets and organum. In the tradition of the *Ars cantus mensurabilis* and *Gaudent moderni*, the duplex longa has the value of two perfect longae, and nothing is said about its potential for being reduced in value, ligated, or plicated.[36] All of these are possible in the *Regule*, in which the duplex longa can be "imperfected" by a single brevis, retaining a value of five breves (Rule V of Rubric II and Rule III of Rubric V), ligated with one like itself or with a longa (Rules XII–XIII of Rubric VI) or a brevis (Rules VII–X of Rubric VIII) in a binary ligature, and plicated, whether standing alone or in ligature (Rules V–VI of Rubric X). Furthermore, the duplex longa can be mixed with extended longae, integral longae, and breves, as is shown in an example where it is used in a new context: the upper voice of a motet (Rubric V).

The longa may be perfect or imperfect (Maxim 1 of Rubric II), and in Handlo's opinion the imperfect longa is better called the semilonga (Maxim 2 of Rubric II). The latter term appears in the *dicta* of Petrus le Viser (Maxim 4A of Rubric IV *et passim*), from whom Handlo may have adopted it. Although Handlo prefers the term *semilonga*, he grudgingly admits that the term *longa* can be taken to mean either the perfect or the imperfect variety (Maxim 5 of Rubric X).

The brevis may be *recta*, i.e., the normal kind worth one tempus, or *altera*, i.e., the other kind, worth two tempora, when it is the second of a pair (Maxim 2 of Rubric III). Handlo suggests the interesting point that it might be better to call the larger brevis *alterata* (altered), conveying the sense of transformation by context (Maxim 3 of Rubric III). When it is conjoined with semibreves, the brevis will have a stem descending vertically from the left (Rule X of Rubric IX).

The longa erecta, with a single stem ascending from the right, and the brevis erecta, with a single stem ascending from the left, are important insular novelties discussed by Handlo. They are described elsewhere (aside from

---

[35]"Which figures ought to be associated with each other."

[36]Jacques de Liège is particularly adamant that since the duplex longa is not one of Franco's three simple figures, it is not ligable (*Speculum musicae*, Book 7, cap. XXV [ed. Bragard], pp. 53–54). Indeed, his ire about the modern treatment of the duplex longa spills out in a total of four chapters (ibid., cap. XXV–XXVIII).

Hanboys) only in item 2 of **GB-Lbl**, Additional 21455, a brief fragment of a notation treatise with distinctively English contents.[37] When employed in place of the longa (perfect or imperfect) or brevis (normal or altered), these forms raise the notated pitch by a semitone (Maxim 2 of Rubric I). They can never be plicated (Maxim 5 of Rubric I), presumably because it would be impossible to differentiate them from the usual longa plicata and brevis plicata, and because they would be used in melodic situations where there was stepwise motion upward, replacing a whole step with a half step, a context where a plica would be superfluous. In Rule VII of Rubric X, Handlo goes to great lengths to explain just how if a longa is ligated at the end of a ligature or oblique figure and has the ascending stem of a plica, and if there is either a rest immediately following or a note following in the place where one takes the plica to be tending (i.e., a step above), then "by the power of the plica" the longa is turned into a longa erecta. These erect or raised forms of the longa and brevis are found only in a few practical sources, all English.[38]

The semibrevis may be major or minor; *divisa* (separate), ligated, or conjoined; and *nuda* (plain) or plicated. In Rubric IV, Handlo becomes the most informative reporter of all late *ars antiqua* theorists about the subdivision of the brevis beyond three minor semibreves, informing us that Petrus le Viser allowed four equal semibreves and five unequal semibreves per brevis in his *mos mediocris*, Petrus de Cruce permitted up to seven per brevis in the slower tempo that Petrus le Viser called the *mos longus*, and Johannes de Garlandia advanced that number to eight and nine. Garlandia called his smallest value the *semibrevis minima* and named the value worth two minimae the *semibrevis minorata*. These two smaller kinds of semibrevis have the same figure as the minor semibrevis but are differentiated from the latter by the use of a following *signum rotundum* (Rule X of Rubric IV). In addition, the minima always precedes the minorata; they can be mixed with breves and semibreves; they can be conjoined with major and minor semibreves (Rules XII–XIV of Rubric IX); but because they do not have corresponding rests, they cannot participate in hockets (Maxim 7 of Rubric XII). Handlo and Admetus both provide additional commentary on these figures (Rule X, Rule XV, and Rule XVI of Rubric IV; Rules XII–XIV of Rubric IX; and Maxim 1 of Rubric XI). Admetus, in particular, informs us that musicians of Navarre

---

[37] See n. 6 *supra*.

[38] See Lefferts, *The Motet in England*, p. 151; and Bent, "Preliminary Assessment," p. 76, n. 32.

differentiated the minorata and minima by means of signs—in this case, stems.[39]

In the Franconian tradition, pairs of semibreves are normally interpreted as a minor and a major (1+2). There is, however, an alternative tradition supported by both theoretical and musical evidence in which pairs of semibreves are to be interpreted as a major and a minor (2+1).[40] This anti-Franconian (and particularly English) rhythmic preference is accommodated in the practice of Johannes de Garlandia, in which the major semibrevis may precede or follow the minor (Rule X of Rubric IV). When freestanding, the major-minor or minor-major pair can be unambiguously recognized and interpreted (without the help of a punctus) because of the downward stem on the major. The major precedes the minor in ligatures or oblique figures when the stem of opposite propriety is short (Rule XXIII of Rubric VI) and in conjunctions of two semibreves when the first has an oblique stroke—an obvious reference to Garlandia's figure for the major semibrevis (Rule V of Rubric IX).

Since *currentes* or *coniuncturae* are not as common in the notation of late *ars antiqua* music as they had been in the notation of organum, discussions of these figures by authorities such as Franco of Cologne and Walter Odington are mere vestiges, appendixed in the former to a discussion of plicas in ligatures and in the latter to a discussion of the values of ligatures. By contrast, Handlo's Rubric IX is solely devoted to these groups of semibreves, raising the conjunction to a status equivalent to that of the ligature and the oblique figure. His discussion is placed after these figures are surveyed, but before the plica. A conjunction is an aggregate involving melismatic semibreves, either standing by themselves or incorporating other notes, all over a single syllable. Semibreves may be conjoined after a longa, brevis, ligature, or oblique figure. Two, three, or four may be conjoined, having the value of a brevis. In addition, as few as one or as many as five may be conjoined: one, if a related semibrevis follows; five, if grouped three-plus-two, and the two are minors if a related semibrevis follows.[41] This presumably describes situations where there is a change of syllable between related but unconjoined semibreves.[42] Incorporating Garlandia's figures into the discussion, Handlo states that minoratae and minimae can also be conjoined.

---

[39]See pp. 27–28 *infra*.

[40]Lefferts, *The Motet in England*, pp. 118–24.

[41]"Related" semibreves subdivide the same brevis.

[42]For such figures in the musical sources, see Lefferts, *The Motet in England*, pp. 114–15 and example 7.

Oblique figures are normally treated as a subclass of ligatures in thirteenth-century theory, but Handlo distinguishes them as a separate class of figures. They are introduced early in Rubric VI, after the first few rules from the *Gaudent moderni* tradition about propriety at the beginning of a ligature. This chapter has a high degree of redundancy because Handlo's newly introduced material comprises a coherent account of both propriety and obliquity; it may well have been drawn from another treatment of the subject by Handlo. He stresses that an oblique figure, although it is sung as two notes, is not a ligature because it is not to be understood to join two simple figures—it does not tie anything together. Rather, it is a single body, an independent, inseparable figure that stands alone, possessing the capacity to be ligated or plicated.

Handlo's Rubric X on plicas is devoted to their employment at the ends of ligatures and oblique figures, extending significantly the minimal discussion of the *Gaudent moderni* tradition. Most noteworthy in this chapter are discussions of the permitted plication of the duplex longa and the power of the plica to change a longa or semilonga into the raised variety in certain contexts. Rubric XI is a unique discussion of specific temporal values for plicas that incorporates the smaller values of Johannes de Garlandia: the minorata (the value of the plica of normal breves and major semibreves) and the minima (the value of the plica of the minor semibrevis). Instead of taking half the value of the note to which they are attached, as is normally assumed to be the case in modern transcriptions, Handlo's plicas are much quicker and variable in proportion from one third to one ninth of the main note.

In the Franconian theoretical tradition, a sign in the form of a short stroke called the *divisio modi* was used as a *signum perfectionis*[43] to mark off groups of three normal breves or three minor semibreves, or their equivalent, and thus to clarify the rhythms of longae, breves, and semibreves in patterns that were not covered by Franco's default rules. One of the innovations of Petrus de Cruce reported by Handlo (and widely found in continental and English musical sources) is the use of a *punctus divisionis* in place of the *divisio modi*, especially to clarify groups of semibreves that constitute a bre-

---

[43]*Franconis de Colonia Ars cantus mensurabilis*, ed. Gilbert Reaney and André Gilles, Corpus scriptorum de musica, no. 18 ([Rome]: American Institute of Musicology, 1974), p. 32 (cap. 5, sent. 6): "quidam tractulus qui signum perfectionis dicitur, qui etiam alio nomine divisio modi appellatur (a certain little stroke that is said to be a sign of perfection, which is also called by another name a division of the mode)."

vis.⁴⁴ Handlo also reports that it is possible to change or create a mixture of modes, perfection by perfection, by using the *punctus divisionis* for clarification, a practice for which there is precedent in the treatises of both Franco and Odington (Maxim 13 of Rule XIII). A practice unique to Handlo is the use of a punctus in front of an oblique figure lacking propriety; this perfects the first note, a longa (Rule XVII of Rubric VI).

*Genres of mensurable music*

In treatises of the *ars antiqua*, polyphonic genres are usually reviewed in a section devoted to discant, and therefore there is no systematic discussion of them in the *Regule*. Handlo does, however, provide a remarkable and famous list of genres of mensurable music (not all necessarily polyphonic) in his commentary on the fifth mode (the old, pre-Franconian sixth mode): "Ab hoc siquidem modo proveniunt hoketi omnes, rundelli, ballade, coree, cantifractus, estampete, floriture, et universe note brevium et semibrevium que sub celo sunt" (Maxim 10 of Rubric XIII). First in this enumeration are the hockets, about which more will be said below in the discussion about Jacobus de Navernia and Copais. Next are three genres of social dance song with refrain—rondeau, ballade, and round-dance;⁴⁵ the last of these, *corea*, is possibly intended here as synonymous with virelai.⁴⁶ *Cantifractus*, a variant of *cantus fractus* or *fractabilis*, refers to a rapidly moving and rhythmically varied discant over a cantus firmus.⁴⁷ The *estampeta* (estampie) was an

---

⁴⁴Petrus's punctus is particularly useful when four or more semibreves stand in place of a breve. Handlo, however, permits four semibreves to be conjoined in the place of a breve without any sign (Rule VII of Rubric IX).

⁴⁵In the Wylde anonymous, a similar list of dance types adds a fourth jumping dance: "rondellis, baladis, carollis, springis." See Reaney, "De origine," p. 117.

⁴⁶*Corea* or *chorea* is Latin for the Old French and Middle English *carole*, a general term for a kind of sung public ring-dance. See John Stevens, *Words and Music in the Middle Ages: Song, Narrative, Dance and Drama, 1050–1350*, Cambridge Studies in Music (Cambridge: Cambridge University Press, 1986), pp. 159–96; and Christopher Page, *Voices and Instruments of the Middle Ages: Instrumental Practice and Songs in France 1100–1300* (Berkeley: University of California Press, 1986), pp. 77–84.

⁴⁷See Sachs, pp. 38–40 *et passim*. The term is at least as old as the *Liber introductorius* (ca. 1230) of Michael Scot, where *cantus planus* and *cantus fractus* are opposed (see F. Alberto Gallo, "Astronomy and Music in the Middle Ages: The *Liber introductorius* by Michael Scot," *Musica disciplina* 27 [1973]: 6–7). In *De origine et effectu musicae*, the word *cantephato*, which may be an error for *cantifractu*, is listed as a genre of mensurable

instrumental dance melody or an "instrument-related lyric genre."[48] The term *floritura* refers to an embellished or decorated melodic style associated with florid organum over a sustained-tone tenor.[49]

The musical excerpts cited in Rubric XIII as examples of modes are, for the most part, from motets customarily cited in continental treatises of the *Gaudent moderni* tradition. Two items, however, are of insular provenance: a contrafact of the St. Magnus hymn tune *Nobilis humilis* with the text "Rosa primula" (Rule V of Rubric XIII) and a triplum for the often-encountered St.

---

music (Reaney, "De origine," p. 115), and further on, *cantus fractus* is given as a synonym for *cantus coronatus* and described as a kind of discant that can ascend and descend indifferently in perfect and imperfect consonances (Reaney, "De origine," p. 117).

[48]Page, *Voices and Instruments*, p. 252. On this dance form, see Hendrik van der Werf, "Estampie," *New Grove Dictionary of Music and Musicians* 6 (1980): 254–58.

[49]The term *floratura* is used by Franco in the *Ars cantus mensurabilis*, cap. 14, sent. 7 (ed. Reaney and Gilles), p. 81, in reference to florid style in organum duplum: "Item notandum quod quotienscumque in organo puro plures figurae simul in unisono evenerint, sola prima debet percuti, reliquae vero omnes in floratura teneantur (It must be further noted that whenever in organum purum many figures occur together on the same pitch, only the first ought to be struck, while all the remainder should be held *in floratura*)." See also Jacques de Liège, *Speculum musicae*, Book 7, cap. II, sent. 5 (ed. Bragard), pp. 7–8: "Dico autem 'incerta' propter organum duplum quod ubique non est certa temporis mensura mensuratum ut, in fioraturis [*recte* floraturis], in penultimis ubi supra vocem unam tenoris in discantu multae sonantur voces (I say 'uncertain,' moreover, on account of organum duplum, because it is not measured everywhere by a definite measure of time, as *in floraturis*, in penultimates where above one voice of the tenor many voices sound in discant)." I am grateful to Charles Atkinson for this reference and for the information that the manuscripts of the *Speculum* read *floraturis*; see also Atkinson, "Franco of Cologne on the Rhythm of Organum purum," *Early Music History* 9 (1989): 21–23. In both versions of the *Quatuor principalia* (CS, 3:354; CS, 4:278), *floritura* is equated with *copula* ("copula, id est floritura") in a passage glossing Franco. Elsewhere in the *Quatuor principalia* (CS, 3:360–61; CS, 4:294), there is a description of a kind of organal polyphony for five singers in which four perform the chant in parallel at the unison, fifth, octave, and twelfth; all are admonished to decorate their notes ("frangere debent et florere notas") while a fifth singer discants ("discantabit") freely on and between these consonances. On the discussion by Anonymous IV and Jerome of Moravia of the embellishment of the upper voices of organum by "musical flowers," or *florificatio vocis*, see Edward Roesner, "The Performance of Parisian Organum," *Early Music* 7 (1979): 176–84.

Katherine motet on the tenor *Agmina* that survives with exactly the same text elsewhere only as a citation in Odington's treatise (Rule VI of Rubric XIII). Earlier in the *Regule*, the incipit of the notable insular voice-exchange motet on St. Katherine, *Rota versatilis*, is given in the example for Rule II of Rubric V.[50]

### Handlo's authorities

A summary of what can be gleaned about each of the authorities quoted by Handlo is presented below, taking them in rough order of precedence as theorists: Petrus de Cruce, Jacobus de Navernia, Copais, Petrus le Viser, Johannes de Garlandia, and Admetus de Aureliana, with a final word on Handlo himself.

### Petrus de Cruce

Petrus de Cruce is cited in Rules VII and VIIIa of Rubric IV (on semibreves).[51] He is a French composer and music theorist of the *ars antiqua* mentioned by name in the *Speculum musicae* of Jacques de Liège and by at least two treatises in the *Gaudent moderni* tradition, including the *Regule* (a reference carried over into Hanboys's *Summa*).[52] Petrus is credited with

---

[50]On *Rota versatilis*, see Bent, "Rota versatilis," in *Source Materials and the Interpretation of Music*, ed. Ian Bent (London: Stainer and Bell, 1981), pp. 64–98 (I am indebted to this article for drawing my attention to Handlo's quotation); and Lefferts, *The Motet in England*, pp. 145–46 and figure 43.

[51]For a recent review of the achievements of Petrus, see Ernest Sanders, "Petrus de Cruce," *New Grove Dictionary of Music and Musicians* 14 (1980): 598–99. I would also like to acknowledge here the valuable paper of Glenn Pierr Johnson on Petrus de Cruce presented at the 1988 National Meeting of the American Musicological Society in Baltimore: "Petronian Teaching and Petronian Practice: Stylistic Change and the Life and Work of Petrus de Cruce." The paper incorporates material from Mr. Johnson's dissertation-in-progress at Yale University.

[52]Jacques de Liège, *Speculum musicae*, Book 7, cap. XVII, sent. 7–9 (ed. Bragard), pp. 36–37. The other *Gaudent moderni* treatise mentioning Petrus, known as the Faenza anonymous, has been edited as a *Compendium musicae mensurabilis* (Petrus Picardus, *Ars motettorum compilata breviter*, ed. F. Alberto Gallo; Anonymous, *Ars musicae mensurabilis secundum Franconem*, ed. Gilbert Reaney and André Gilles; Anonymous, *Compendium musicae mensurabilis artis antiquae*, ed. F. Alberto Gallo, Corpus scriptorum de musica, no. 15 [(Rome): American Institute of Musicology, 1971]; see p. 69). See also Hanboys, *Summa*, chapter 12 (258.11 and 260.3–17 [numbers given in this form refer to the page and line numbers of this edition]). Petrus is identified as the author of a treatise on mensural music in an anonymous *De*

being a strong singer, an expert on chant, the author of one or more treatises, the creator of various notational innovations, and the composer of two French double motets.[53] There is strong circumstantial evidence that this composer-theorist may have been trained or have worked in Amiens in Picardy. It is highly likely that he is one and the same with the Magister Petrus de Cruce "ambianensis" who wrote a treatise on *musica plana*, the *Tractatus de tonis*;[54] the Petrus de Cruce of Amiens who was paid in 1298 for having written a rhymed office on Saint Louis;[55] and the Master Petrus de Cruce who willed a

---

*musica mensurabili* (Anonymous [dictus Theodoricus de Campo], *De musica mensurabili*, ed. Cecily Sweeney; Anonymous, *De semibrevibus caudatis*, ed. Cecily Sweeney and Gilbert Reaney, Corpus scriptorum de musica, no. 13 [(Rome): American Institute of Musicology, 1971]; see p. 32).

[53]While Handlo only attributes *Aucun ont trouvé chant par usage* to Petrus (Rule VIIIa C of Rubric IV), Hanboys also cites *Novum melos promere* in the same context (*Summa*, chapter 12 [260.15–17]), perhaps considering it to be of the same authorship.

[54]Petrus de Cruce ambianensi(s), *Tractatus de tonis*, ed. Denis Harbison, Corpus scriptorum de musica, no. 29 ([Rome]: American Institute of Musicology, 1976). Immediately following the *Tractatus de tonis* of Petrus in **GB**-Lbl, Harley 281 is the unedited *Tractatus de tonis* of Guido of Saint-Denis. I am indebted to Dr. Anne Walters Robertson for first pointing out to me that Guido several times mentions Petrus de Cruce, who is referred to as a "cantor" and as an authority on the chant of Amiens: "magistrum Petrum de Cruce qui fuit optimus cantor et ambianensis ecclesie consuetudinem specialiter observavit (Master Petrus de Cruce, who was the best singer and particularly observed the custom of the church of Amiens)" (**GB**-Lbl, Harley 281, f. 92[95]r–v; for another reference to Petrus, see f. 78[82]v).

[55]See *Les Journaux du Trésor de Philippe IV, le Bel*, ed. Jules Viard (Paris: Imprimerie nationale, 1940), entries for 3 July 1298 (col. 128), 15 July 1298 (col. 144), and 2 August 1298 (col. 160). Inevitably, doubts can be raised about whether this "Magister Petrus de Cruce de Ambianis" is the composer. Gilbert Reaney, "Petrus de Cruce," *MGG* 10 (1962): 1142, has written, for instance, that: "Ein Petrus de Cruce aus Amiens erhielt im Juli und Aug. 1298 Zahlungen dafür, dass er eine 'hystoriam,' wahrscheinlich ein Officium mit Musik, kompilierte. Ob dieser aber wirklich mit dem Theoretiker und Komp. identisch ist, steht nicht fest." The office in question is not the famous, earlier office for Saint Louis that has recently been shown to have been written by Arnaud du Pré (see Michel Huglo, *Les tonaires* [Paris: Société française de musicologie, 1971], p. 336; and Marcy J. Epstein, "*Ludovicus Decus Regnantium*: Perspectives on the Rhymed Office," *Speculum* 53 [1978]: 283–334).

book of polyphony to the cathedral of Amiens (recorded in inventories of 1347 and 1419).[56]

If theoretical references make it evident that Petrus wrote a treatise on mensurable music, it is not at all clear whether that treatise survives. Michel Huglo and F. Alberto Gallo have recently supported an identification of Petrus de Cruce with the otherwise unknown Petrus Picardus who is named in Jerome of Moravia's *Tractatus de musica* as the author of a short *Ars motettorum* that Jerome transmits.[57] Gilbert Reaney and André Gilles, on the other hand, support the attribution to Petrus de Cruce of a different mensural treatise, an anonymous *Ars musicae mensurabilis secundum Franconem*, on the basis of a suggestion that they claim originated with Coussemaker. Their position has recently been seconded by Heinz Ristory.[58] Neither of these short treatises has language corresponding exactly with that of Petrus as cited by Handlo or Jacques, but this is not immediately disqualifying. Petrus de Cruce's innovations include substitution of a punctus for Franco's *divisio modi*, employment of a punctus to clarify groups of semibreves, and subdivision of the brevis into four, five, six, or seven semibreves, but no more.

---

[56]Michel Huglo, "De Francon de Cologne à Jacques de Liège," *Revue belge de musicologie* 34–35 (1980–1981): 52, n. 47; see also E. Covecque, ed., *Catalogue général des manuscrits des bibliothèques publiques de France, Départements,* Part XIX, Amiens (Paris: Imprimerie nationale, 1953), p. xl. Petrus de Cruce is not recorded in William M. Newman, *La Personnel de la Cathédrale d'Amiens (1066–1306)* (Paris: Picard, 1972).

[57]Simon Cserba, ed., *Hieronymus de Moravia, O.P. Tractatus de musica*, Freiburger Studien zur Musikwissenschaft, no. 2 (Regensburg: Friedrich Pustet, 1935), pp. 259–63. This treatise also survives anonymously in two other sources, for information on which, see *Ars motettorum compilata breviter* (ed. Gallo), pp. 11–15. On the question of authorship, see Huglo, "De Francon de Cologne," pp. 51–52; and Gallo, "Die Notationslehre im 14. und 15. Jahrhundert," pp. 257–356, esp. p. 268. The identification of Petrus Picardus with Petrus de Cruce is rejected by Heinrich Hüschen in "Petrus Picardus," *MGG* 10 (1962): 1144. This possibility is not mentioned by Ernest Sanders ("Petrus de Cruce") or by Albert Seay in "Petrus Picardus," *New Grove Dictionary of Music and Musicians* 14 (1980): 598–99.

[58]*Ars musicae mensurabilis secundum Franconem* (ed. Reaney and Gilles), pp. 31–57, especially p. 33; and Ristory, "Ein Abbreviationstraktat," p. 95. Ristory develops the argument at greater length in *Post-franconische Theorie und Früh-Trecento. Die Petrus de Cruce-Neuerungen und ihre Bedeutung für die italienische Mensuralnotenschrift zu Beginn des 14. Jahrhunderts*, European University Studies, XXXVI (Musicology)/26 (Frankfurt: Peter Lang, 1988), pp. 37–66.

Petrus le Viser observes that the semibreves of Petrus de Cruce would be performed *in more longo*, in which "semibreves, however many there are, can be performed and written down with longae, semilongae, and breves" (Maxim 4B and Maxim 6 of Rubric IV).

Jacobus de Navernia

Jacobus de Navernia is cited for his doctrines about hockets in Maxim 5 of Rubric XII; outside of the *Regule* he is otherwise unattested. He may well be one of the "cantores de Navernia" (or "Naverina") mentioned by Admetus of Orleans. The surname may refer to the country of Navarre, to the College of Navarre in Paris, or perhaps (in a suggestion of Nan Cooke Carpenter) to the historical French province of Nivernais, whose capital was Nevers.[59] It is assumed here that the surname refers to the country.[60]

The kingdom of Navarre was a small but strategically placed country on the Spanish peninsula in the southern foothills of the Pyrenees, lying across the chief pilgrimage route to Santiago de Compostela. It was ruled by a French dynasty after 1234 when Thibaut I (d. 1254), Count of Champagne and Brie, took the throne. Descended from a long and famous line of patrons of music, Thibaut himself was one of the greatest of the trouvères. The sacred and secular musical traditions of northern France were undoubtedly promoted at his court and by his successors.[61] Indeed, the Englishman Anonymous IV, writing around 1275, mentions that there are books of organum and great makers of organa in Navarre as well as in Castile, Aragon, France, and England.[62] Since Handlo's John of Navarre is quoted for information on the

---

[59]Carpenter, p. 60, n. 47.

[60]On the statement that the minima was invented in Navarre and the controversy over whether the kingdom of Navarre or the College of Navarre at the University of Paris is meant in that remark, see the paragraphs on Admetus *infra*, pp. 27–28.

[61]For a general discussion and bibliography on medieval music and musicians in Navarre, see Higinio Anglès, "De cantu organico: tratado de un autor catalan del siglo xiv," *Anuario musical* 13 (1958): 1–3; reprinted in idem, *Scripta musicologica*, 3 vols., ed. José Lopez-Calo (Rome: Edizioni di storia e letteratura, 1976), 3:1321–24. See also idem, *Historia de la música medieval en Navarra* (Pamplona: Diputación Foral de Navarra, Institución Príncipe de Viana, 1970), pp. 105–88, especially pp. 125–26 and 167–71.

[62]Anonymous, "De mensuris et discantu," in Fritz Reckow, ed., *Der Musiktraktat des Anonymus 4*, 2 vols., Beihefte zum *Archiv für Musikwissenschaft*, vols. 4–5 (Wiesbaden: Franz Steiner, 1967), 1:51, lns. 9–15 and 1:60, lns. 10–12.

various forms of hockets, perhaps it is he, or a countryman, to whom Anonymous IV refers in his mention of an *In seculum* hocket, called "the French hocket," which he nonetheless says was composed by "quidam Hyspanus."[63] Though Anonymous IV elsewhere distinguishes Hyspania (presumably Castile) from Navarre and Aragon, it may still be the case that expertise on the hocket is a particularly Iberian accomplishment.

In Maxim 5 of Rubric XII, John of Navarre explains that there are three kinds of hockets, a division based on the rests they use. There are those using breves and rests of either one or two breves, those using minor semibreves and rests of two-thirds of a brevis, and those using minor semibreves and rests of one minor semibrevis. From his description one can alternatively extrapolate four types: a first- or second-mode type using values of normal breves and imperfect longae or altered breves as notes and rests (2+1, 1+2); a sixth-mode type using breves and single brevis rests (1+1+1); a third type corresponding to the long-short rhythms of the first type but moving in the quicker values of major and minor semibreves and their rests ("e converso" seems to imply both the order 1+2 and 2+1 in rhythms); and a fourth type corresponding to the second but running in the quicker values of minor semibreves and their rests. John of Navarre regards the last as the most difficult.

Copais

John of Navarre's description of hockets recalls Walter Odington's examples of hockets in all the modes in a general way, a fact useful in helping to interpret one textual crux. Immediately following Navarre's maxim is a passage (Maxim 6 of Rubric XII) concerned with the confusion of minor semibreves and their rests in groupings by three: the text here is evidently corrupt, even to the name of its author, Copais, which does not sound like a name or any sensible Latin word. The passage does, however, bring to mind Odington's discussion of sixth-mode hockets that move in minor semibreves and their rests. With so many rests involved, all of which look like divisions of the mode, a different sign is needed to indicate clearly the divisions between breves. An amendment to the *Regule*, following Odington's recommendation of the use of a *circulum parvulum*, brings sense to Handlo's text.[64]

---

[63]Ibid., 1:61, ln. 12.

[64]See Maxim 6 of Rubric XII and Odington, *De speculatione musicae*, cap. 17, sent. 15–17 (ed. Hammond), p. 145.

On the *parvum circulum* or *signum rotundum*, see also Lefferts, *The Motet in England*, esp. pp. 124–29 and 150–51. The passage in Odington is

Aside from John of Navarre's information about hockets, Handlo states that in hockets the brevis consists of three semibreves (Maxim 2 of Rubric IV), an observation seconded by Petrus le Viser (Maxim 5E and F of Rubric IV). Johannes de Garlandia mentions that hockets do not use minoratae and minimae because there are no rests corresponding to these smaller values (Maxim 7 of Rubric XII).

Petrus le Viser

The doctrines of Petrus le Viser are presented in Maxim 4, Maxim 5, Rule VIII, and Maxim 6 of Rubric IV (on semibreves).[65] This Petrus, an otherwise unknown figure, is of considerable importance for his codification of binary mensuration of the longa, brevis, and semibrevis, and his recognition of the subdivision of the brevis into three, four, or five semibreves. All of this is brought forward in Handlo's presentation of the three ways or manners of performance of Petrus (the *mos longus*, *mos mediocris*, and *mos lascivus*) and their associated note values.

Petrus's notions have an important counterpart in the *Speculum musicae* of Jacques de Liège. Jacques explains that for better understanding of what the ancients have to say about the longa, brevis, and semibrevis, we must recognize that these figures are used in three mensurations: *morosa*, *media*, and *cita*. And Jacques cites two additional modern authorities to the same effect. One of them, unidentified and not further traceable, writes: "Tripliciter modulamur: aut tractim, aut velociter, aut medie, et quocumque modo fiat, non est mutanda maneries notandi."[66] The other, also unidentified but from the tradition of de Vitry, writes: "Sciendum tempus perfectum esse triplex,

---

not without its own problems, as the text is shared between the main scribe and a marginal addition in a different hand; further, the marginal addition to line 17 mentions "minutis" in a context where "semibrevibus" is more likely to have been intended by the author. See Odington, *De speculacione musicae* (ed. Hammond), p. 145, for the critical commentary; there is a convenient facsimile of the pertinent leaf of Oxford, Corpus Christi College, MS 410 (f. 35v), facing p. 146.

[65]See Ernest Sanders, "Petrus le Viser," *New Grove Dictionary of Music and Musicians* 14 (1980): 600–601; and the earlier discussion by Sanders, with a full translation of Petrus's *dicta*, in "Duple Rhythm," pp. 250–56. See also Jacques Handschin, "The Sumer Canon and Its Background," *Musica disciplina* 3 (1949): 77–78; Lefferts, *The Motet in England*, p. 116; and Bent, "Rota versatilis," pp. 83–84 *et passim*.

[66]"We sing three ways: either slowly or quickly or medium tempo, and whatever way it may be done, the manner of notating must not be changed."

minimum, medium, et maius."[67] All these authorities are acknowledging the development of three different tempos of performance with correspondingly different note values and rhythmic character and with speed measured in relation to the duration of a brevis in inverse proportion to the number of semibreves per brevis.

In the *mos longus* of Petrus le Viser, longae, semilongae, breves, and any number of semibreves are used. He observes that the semibrevis practice of Petrus de Cruce (up to seven per brevis) corresponds to the *mos longus* (Maxim 6 of Rubric IV). The longa here is implicitly perfect and the semibreves implicitly syllabic; Franconian and Petronian rules for the equality and inequality of semibreves obtain.

In the *mos mediocris*, there are two possible notational states: (1) with longae, semilongae, breves, and semibreves, where semibreves (two to five per brevis) are melismatic; and (2) with only semilongae, breves, and semibreves (two to five per brevis), where semibreves are syllabic in groups of two or three and melismatic in groups of four or five. In both, non-Franconian rules for the value of semibreves obtain, i.e., "two semibreves are equal and three unequal, and four equal and five unequal"; hence the brevis is binary. The restriction to semilongae in the second notational state suggests that Petrus le Viser has in mind a regular binary mensuration of the long.

In the *mos lascivus*, there are also two notational states: (1) with (occasional) duplex longae, longae, semilongae, normal breves, and major and minor semibreves; and (2) with only normal breves and major and minor semibreves. In both, there may be no more than three (equal) semibreves per brevis; perhaps it is intended that in the first there be only the alternation of major and minor semibreves, never three minors. It is curious that no use is made of the altered brevis. In the first notational state, the mensuration of the longa may be binary or ternary.

Handlo sustains what might be called an English theoretical tradition, with precedents in the works of Odington and Anonymous IV, by mention of the transmutation of the third and fourth modes, presumably from ternary to binary mensuration, which he associates with the *mos lascivus* of Viser (Maxim 9 of Rubric XIII). It is also the *mos lascivus* in which one finds lively hockets and a great many motets (Maxim 5F and Maxim 2 of Rubric

---

[67]"It must be known that there are three kinds of perfect time: minimum, medium, and major." Jacques de Liège, *Speculum musicae*, Book 7, cap. XVII, sent. 1 (ed. Bragard), p. 35; for the de Vitry tradition, see also the Vatican manuscript version of the *Ars nova*, cap. XX, sent. 3 (ed. Reaney et al.), p. 29.

IV). This coupling of motets and hockets with a mensuration that "runs along" (*currit*) in three semibreves per brevis has a direct parallel in the discussion by Jacques de Liège of the *cita* or *citissima mensuratio brevium*, which the ancients associated with motets and hockets.[68] There is also a parallel in the two notational states of the *mos lascivus* to the notational categories set up for hockets by Jacobus de Navernia.

Johannes de Garlandia

Johannes de Garlandia is cited in Maxim 7, Rule IX, Maxim 8, and Rules XI–XIV and XVII of Rubric IV (on semibreves); and in Maxim 7 of Rubric XII (on rests). Handlo's theorist of this name is only known from the *Regule* (from which he is carried over into the *Summa* of Hanboys). Though he is the most obscure of three or four men of the same name with whom music historians must deal, Handlo's Garlandia was evidently one of the two most significant theorists of the late *ars antiqua* we know by name, the other being Petrus de Cruce. The two best documented of these Johns of Garlànd are a pair active in Paris in the thirteenth century: a music theorist who flourished in the second quarter of the century (ca. 1240) and wrote highly influential treatises on plainchant and polyphony; and a noted English poet-grammarian (ca. 1190/95–ca. 1272) who was an important figure at the universities of Paris and Toulouse. These two men have sometimes been taken to be one and the same person, an identification rejected in most recent musicological literature.[69]

Neither thirteenth-century individual can be equated with Handlo's Garlandia, who must have been active ca. 1300–1320 on the basis of the notational doctrines he espouses. Indeed, it is possible that there were two fourteenth-century Johns of Garland, the authority cited by Handlo and a Parisian master who ran a music school. The Parisian master, however, a "Garlandia the Younger" whose name is associated with treatise materials on intervals and counterpoint, has effectively been shown to be a ghost: "research has proved the latter figure to be both imaginary and unneces-

---

[68]Jacques de Liège, *Speculum musicae*, Book 7, cap. XVII (ed. Bragard), p. 36.

[69]See Erich Reimer, *Johannes Garlandia: De mensurabili musica*, 2 vols., Beihefte zum *Archiv für Musikwissenschaft*, vols. 10–11 (Wiesbaden: Franz Steiner, 1972), 1:12–17. His conclusions are accepted by Rebecca A. Baltzer in "Johannes de Garlandia," *New Grove Dictionary of Music and Musicians* 7 (1980): 662–64.

sary."[70] Skepticism about the fourteenth-century Parisian figure has silently and unfortunately extended to Handlo's man, who goes unmentioned in the article on this name in the *New Grove Dictionary of Music and Musicians*. It is entirely possible that Handlo borrowed the name to identify a theorist who was anonymous to him, but one can also imagine a situation in which the doctrines cited by Handlo were found in a manuscript that paired the thirteenth-century theorist's *musica plana* treatise with an unascribed *musica mensurabilis* treatise that Handlo assumed was by the same author. It is equally possible that there was a later music theorist of this name. The derivation of the name Garlandia does not help us with the question of multiple identities or nationality. Although the earlier English poet-grammarian took his name from the *Clos de Garlande*, the Parisian quarter that housed the schools on the left bank of the Seine, the name Garland or de Garlande is a perfectly good English surname, attested from at least the early thirteenth century.[71] Hence, there is no necessary reason to associate Handlo's Johannes de Garlandia with Paris and its university.

Handlo credits his Johannes de Garlandia with the subdivision of the brevis into as few as three or as many as eight or nine semibreves (Maxim 8 of Rubric IV). It may therefore be plausibly suggested that he is the unnamed musician, clearly subsequent to Petrus de Cruce, who is similarly credited by

---

[70]Baltzer, "Johannes de Garlandia," p. 662. For the complicated source situation that led to the postulation of this Parisian "Garlandia the Younger," see Reaney, "Questions of Authorship," pp. 11–12; Reimer, *Johannes de Garlandia*, 1:8–12; and Sachs, pp. 170–78. Despite their arguments, at least one scholar still gives credence to the possibility that there was a fourteenth-century Johannes Garlandia at Paris who had a singing school (see Fuller, "Phantom Treatise," p. 46).

[71]The *clos de Garlande* was named in honor of Etienne de Garlande, archdeacon of Paris and a protector of the nascent university in the early twelfth century. It had as its principal streets the rue Saint-Jacques, the rue du Fouarre (where the great schools were), and the rue de Garlande (a name that became corrupted to Galande or Gallande). As an English surname, Garland is not a placename (hence not recorded by Ekwall), but rather derives apparently either from garlander, "a maker of garlands," or from the Old English gore-land, hence "a dweller on or by a triangular plot of land." See Bardsley, *A Dictionary of English and Welsh Surnames*, p. 308; Harrison, *Surnames of the United Kingdom*, 1:140; and Reaney, *A Dictionary of British Surnames*, p. 140. In the article on the English poet-grammarian, the *Dictionary of National Biography* 7 (1889–90): 876–79 notes that "The name Garland was also familiar in London: one John Garland was prebendary of St. Pauls in 1200 ... Another was sheriff of London in 1212."

Jacques de Liège with being the "someone else [who] put for a perfect *tempus* not only five, six, or seven semibreves, but also eight and sometimes nine."[72] Garlandia's system is based on the divisibility of the perfect brevis into three (perfect) minor semibreves or nine minimae, therefore roughly equivalent to de Vitry's *tempus perfectum maior* or Marchetto's *novenaria*. In the *Regule*, his major semibrevis is described as having an obliquely descending stem; his smaller semibreves—the minor, minorata, and minima—are identical in figure (lozenge-shaped) and distinguished in context only by a sign, the *signum rotundum*.[73] The major and minor may be paired in either order, but the minima always precedes the minorata.

A weakness of Garlandia's system is the identity in shape of the three smaller semibreves, and it is evidence of Garlandia's influence that musicians attempted to remedy this defect by proposing the use of new signs to distinguish them. Such modifications include those of some musicians of Navarre reported by Admetus of Orleans in the *Regule* (see immediately below) and those of the Englishmen W. de Doncastre and Robertus Trowell as reported by Hanboys.[74] In the musical examples preserved in **GB-Lbl**, Additional 4909 for Rubrics IV and IX (where the discussion of Garlandian notation is concentrated), the consistency with which the major semibrevis is identified with a downward stem implies strongly that this is the form in which the Pepusch scribe found the examples in his exemplar, **GB-Lbl**, Cotton Tiberius B.IX.[75]

The single surviving composition whose notation corresponds closely to that of Handlo's Johannes de Garlandia is found in some leaves of English motets now at Westminster Abbey (London, Westminster Abbey [henceforward: **GB-Lwa**], 12185). This is the motet *Hac a valle–Hostem*

---

[72]Ernest Sanders, "Petrus de Cruce," p. 598, quoting Jacques de Liège, *Speculum musicae*, Book 7, cap. XVII, 11 (ed. Bragard), p. 38 (see also CS, 2:401b): "Unus autem alius pro perfecto tempore non modo quinque semibreves, sex et septem posuit, sed etiam octo et quandoque novem."

[73]Garlandia's semibrevis maior, minor, minorata, and minima are equivalent to the imperfect brevis, perfect semibrevis, imperfect semibrevis, and minima "of the moderns," as we are told by Hanboys (*Summa*, chapter 13 [272.25–28]).

[74]See *infra*, pp. 59–71; and Hanboys, *Summa*, chapter 13 (268.26–272.24).

[75]One significant difference in Hanboys's presentation of Handlo's material on Garlandia is that the stem on his major semibrevis is said to descend directly, as it does in the *Summa* examples (chapter 13 [262.4–5 *et passim*]).

*vicit* (no. 2 in **GB**-Lwa, 12185), which is transcribed in appendix II.[76] In *Hac a valle*, stems on the major semibrevis descend directly, not obliquely, from beneath the lozenge. Moreover, in this motet the major semibrevis always precedes the minor.

Admetus de Aureliana

Admetus de Aureliana is cited in Rules XII–XIV of Rubric IX (on conjunctions of semibreves). He is presumably a Frenchman "of Orleans," otherwise unattested, who may be placed temporally just after Handlo's Johannes de Garlandia, bearing witness to the diffusion of Garlandia's doctrines. His information concerns how musicians of Navarre conjoin minoratae and minimae with each other and with semibreves, "cum signis." If the example of Rule XII is to be believed, these musicians distinguished conjoined minoratae and minimae not by the *signum rotundum* of Garlandia but by the use of other signs: an obliquely descending stem on the minorata and an ascending stem on the minima. This observation by Admetus lends credibility to the remark by the author of the *Quatuor principalia* that the minima was invented in Navarre.[77] Reaney and Gilles, in their edition of the *Ars nova* of Philippe de Vitry, suggest that the latter citation should be interpreted as referring to the Collège de Navarre and thus to its association with de Vitry, but it has more recently been asserted that this suggestion "founders for want of a particle of corroborative evidence."[78] There seems no reason not to

---

[76]See Lefferts, *The Motet in England*, pp. 124–27 and figure 35.

[77]*Quatuor principalia*, quartum principale (CS, 3:337; CS, 4:257): "Minima autem in Navarina inventa erat, et a Philippo de Vitriaco, qui fuit flos totius mundi musicorum, approbata et usitata (The minima was invented in Navarre and was approved and used by Philippe de Vitry, who was the flower of the whole world of music)." It is conceivable that the author drew either on Admetus or on the *Regule* for the first part of this statement. For *ars nova* musicians, the minima was understood to have its own distinct figure, while to these late *ars antiqua* musicians, the semibrevis minima was understood to possess the figure of a semibrevis, which was amended by the addition of a sign.

[78]Sarah Fuller, "Phantom Treatise," pp. 45–46. The College of Navarre, a celebrated college of the University of Paris, was founded in 1304 by the French queen Joanna of Navarre, wife of Philippe IV (le Bel). Though its association with Parisian musical developments of the *ars nova* remains to be demonstrated, one important manuscript in the tradition of de Vitry apparently originated there. See *Ars nova* (ed. Reaney et al.), p. 3; they further suggest (p. 1) that Jacques de Liège may have taught at this college. On this question, see also André Gilles, "Contribution à un inventaire analytique des manuscrits

accept the country of Navarre as an important center of polyphonic practice, as witnessed by the testimony of English theorists—Anonymous IV, Robertus de Handlo, and the author of the *Quatuor principalia*—writing over at least three quarters of a century.

Robertus de Handlo

Many of Handlo's personal contributions to the *Regule* have been detailed above, but three aspects that surface at various points in the treatise will be reviewed here by way of conclusion. First, there is the accumulation of internal evidence by which the *Regule* reinforces its insular origin. This evidence consists of its discussion of notational devices of English provenance such as the notation of Johannes de Garlandia, raised longae and breves, and the anti-Franconian rhythmic interpretation of specially signed pairs of semibreves; its inclusion of several music examples with insular ties, such as the five-section voice-exchange motet *Rota versatilis*, the St. Magnus hymn contrafact *Rosula primula*, and the triplum cited for the *Agmina* motet; and its reference to subject matter also associated with Odington, including topics such as the mixture of modes, the confusion about rests in hockets, the *Agmina* triplum just mentioned, and the transmutation of the third and fourth modes.

Another noteworthy aspect of the *Regule* involves Handlo's use of the term *vox*. This term, oftentimes problematic—or to put it more positively, multidimensional—in medieval music theory, can be successfully rendered here simply as "voice," proffered as sounding voice, withheld as in a musical rest, or completely absent as when the eye alone scrutinizes a notational figure. Handlo's particular orientation to hearing and seeing in respect to musical notation requires him to articulate, however awkwardly, some basic distinctions about the meaning of sound and symbol and the mental and physical activities of a musical score-reader. For him, the proportions of rhythmic durations of notes exist independently of voice but require realization through voice; there is no performance in the mind's ear that is correct in meter and tempo. We are told, for instance, that the longa and semilonga are similar in shape (to the eye) but dissimilar in proportion (to the mind) and by voice[79] (see Rule II of Rubric II). He also cites Petrus le Viser to the effect that longae, breves, and semibreves can be sung ("in voce proferuntur") and written down ("proferri et describi possunt") in three different ways that correspond

---

interessant l'Ars Nova de Philippe de Vitry," *Revue belge de musicologie* 10 (1956): 151; and the references in n. 61 *supra*.

[79]Literally, by use of the mouth: "in proportione et ore secundum vocem."

to rates of speed, mensural organization, and prevalent note values (Maxim 4 of Rubric IV). And Handlo observes that the third and fourth modes may be transmuted into binary mensuration if sung ("per vocem exprimantur") in Petrus le Viser's liveliest fashion (Maxim 9 of Rubric XIII). Perhaps most revealing of the insufficiency of notation alone is Handlo's discussion of the oblique figure (Maxim 2 of Rubric VI). This figure represents two notes, which are found by the voice ("per vocem inveniuntur") at its beginning and end. If the meaning of the figure is investigated without its being sung, then the intention to represent two notes is only understood indirectly, by implication ("sine voce vero subintelliguntur"). Like the medieval reader of the same era, the musician is at a stage in the development of a literate mentality when vocalization is still necessary in order to fully grasp a text because hearing is still more important than seeing.[80]

Handlo's use of *vox* is symptomatic of the refinements of language and conceptualization that he and his authorities introduce into late *ars antiqua* theory. Another instance is the distinction of *figura* and *signum*. In the *ars nova*, new values are represented by new notational figures, but in late *ars antiqua* thought, Franco's three simple figures—the longa, brevis, and semibrevis—continue to suffice. They are amended as necessary by sign, in particular by the use of the punctus, the *signum rotundum*, and the stem in various configurations. A characterisic expression of this mode of thought is credited in the *Regule* to Johannes de Garlandia: "Rectum est ut tam in figura quam in signo semibrevis maior a minore distinguatur"[81] (Rule IX of Rubric IV). But the most pervasive and original distinction that Handlo introduces is his own raising of oblique figures and conjunctions to equivalent status with freestanding notes and ligatures. This concept shapes the division of *Gaudent moderni* material into rubrics and is reinforced in the chapter headings. It furthermore calls forth Handlo's most emphatic language, as he exclaims: "In divisionibus igitur figurarum, in ligaturis et in obliquitatibus et in coniunctionibus earum, hec est ars inventa quam cuilibet cantori habere necesse est"[82]

---

[80]On the medieval reader in general, on vocalization, and on "the literate mentality" and "hearing and seeing," see M. D. Clanchy, *From Memory to Written Record: England, 1066–1307* (Cambridge: Harvard University Press, 1979), pp. 202–30, esp. pp. 214–20.

[81]"It is proper that the major semibrevis be distinguished from the minor not only in shape but also in sign."

[82]"In the divisions of figures, therefore—in ligatures and oblique figures and conjunctions of them—, this is the learned art that is necessary for any singer to have."

(Maxim 5 of Rubric IX). This statement falls at the conclusion of a chapter but has the ring of a peroration suitable to the end of a more significant textual subdivision or perhaps even to a colophon (it is conceivable that Handlo has merged material from a separate treatise of his own into the *Regule*).[83] This fourfold categorization, replacing the dichotomy of *simplex* and *compositus* of Franco,[84] and Handlo's preference for using the term *simplex* in the sequence longa simplex, longa duplex, longa triplex, etc., require him to find another word for *simplex* in Franco's sense. He opts for a complex of new vocabulary including the noun *divisio* (for the condition of being separated from other notes) and these almost synonymous adjectives, virtually always feminine in context: *divisa* (separate), *nuda* (plain, i.e., unsigned and unplicated), and *sola* (solitary). These subtle distinctions bespeak not dry pedantry but rather a lively confrontation of the scholar-teacher with the music of his generation and the active discourse about its notation.

### *The* Summa *of Johannes Hanboys*

### The Identity of Johannes Hanboys

Brian Trowell has made a compelling equation of Johannes Hanboys[85] with the music theorist J. de Alto Bosco who is named in a famous English

---

[83]Evidence for this is to be found particularly in Rubric VI, in which the full *Gaudent moderni* material on propriety in ligatures is interspersed with material by Handlo introducing oblique figures. The interpolated sections by themselves are a coherent discussion of both obliquity and propriety and could well have been drawn from another work. The repetition of the doctrines of Petrus de Cruce in Rubric IV (e.g., Rule IV and Rule VII) likewise suggests that Handlo is adding material to the *Gaudent moderni* base from sources including another text of his own.

[84]See Hanboys, *Summa*, chapter 2 (184.13).

[85]The modern secondary literature on Hanboys begins with Burney (ed. Mercer), 1:673–74 and 678; and Hawkins (new ed.), 1:234 and 291, in both of which, Hanboys is known only through the antiquarian references to be cited below.

Literature taking into account **GB**-Lbl, Additional 8866 includes François-Joseph Fétis, "Hamboys ou Hanboys, (Jean)," *Biographie universelle des musiciens* 4 (1866): 210–11; W[illiam] H. H[usk], "Hamboys, or Hanboys, John," *Grove's Dictionary of Music and Musicians* 1 (1879–89): 647 and A[ugustus] H[ughes]-[Hughes], "Hanboys, John," *Grove's Dictionary of Music and Musicians* 4 [Appendix] (1879–89): 664 (the Husk and Hughes-Hughes entries, joined, were reprinted essentially unchanged in the

"musicians motet" from the 1370s, *Sub arturo plebs*.[86] Many of the Latinized names of musicians cited in the triplum of this motet are recognizable English placenames, and Trowell argues for the likely equivalence of "Alto Bosco" with "Haute Bois" (or in medieval orthography "Hauboys," with variants such as Hautboys, Haultboys, Hoboys). Great and Little Hauboys are a pair of small villages (modern spelling "Hautboys") in Norfolk just northeast of Norwich, and it is likely that this placename is the surname of our music theorist.[87] Trowell was not able to trace this fourteenth-century figure any further, and he observes that in the explicit of the *Summa*, Hanboys "is called 'reverend', which suggests that he may have been a friar or monk, hidden in

---

second through fifth editions); W[illiam] B[arclay] S[quire], "Hanboys or Hamboys, John," *Dictionary of National Biography* 8 (1890): 1153–54; Oswald Koller, "Hanboys, Johannes," *Quellen-Lexicon der Musiker und Musikgelehrten* 5 (1901): 12–13; R. Alec Harman, "Hanboys (Hamboys), John," *MGG* 5 (1956): 1437–38; and Andrew Hughes, "Hanboys [Hamboys], John," *New Grove Dictionary of Music and Musicians* 8 (1980): 80. See also Wolf, *Geschichte der Mensural-Notation* and *Handbuch der Notationskunde*; Riemann, *History of Music Theory*; Jeffrey Pulver, "The English Theorists, VI—John Hanboys," *The Musical Times* 75 (1934): 220–21; Brian Trowell, "A Fourteenth-Century Ceremonial Motet and Its Composer," *Acta musicologica* 29 (1957): 65–75; Carpenter, pp. 60 and 87–88; Reaney, "Questions of Authorship," p. 12; and Roger Bowers, "Fixed Points in the Chronology of English Fourteenth-Century Polyphony," *Music and Letters* 71 (1990): 325–26.

[86]Trowell, "Fourteenth-Century Ceremonial Motet," pp. 69–70. For bibliography on *Sub arturo plebs*, see Lefferts, *The Motet in England*, p. 301. On possible dates that have been suggested for this motet, see ibid., p. 87; and Bowers, "Fixed Points," pp. 320–35.

[87]See the forms given under "Hautboys" in Ekwall, *English Place Names*. Reaney, *British Surnames*, does not record "Hautboys," but it is given in Harrison, *Surnames of the United Kingdom*, and Bardsley, *English and Welsh Surnames*. Alfred B. Emden records a thirteenth-century Franciscan friar Humphrey de Hautboys (*A Biographical Register of the University of Cambridge to 1500* [Cambridge: Cambridge University Press, 1963], p. 293), and the surname is not uncommon in the fourteenth-century monuments and Rolls Series. Trowell ("Fourteenth-Century Ceremonial Motet," p. 69) inadvertently gives the towns' county as Suffolk. See also Roger Bowers, "Fixed Points," p. 325.

As **GB-Lbl**, Additional 8866 consistently spells the author's name with an n and the antiquarian tradition consistently misspells it with an m (perhaps from an incorrect expansion of a contracted form), this edition stays with the spelling Hanboys rather than reverting to Hauboys.

the anonymity of a monastery."[88] It is perhaps more likely that this was merely a term of respect, with no implication of religious vocation or employment.

In the second and third stanzas of the triplum text of *Sub arturo plebs*, J. de Alto Bosco is said to unlock with his theory the unprecedented works of the singer and composer J. de Corbe:[89]

| En milicia cum clero | Behold, the knighthood flourishes |
| floret musicorum vero | with the clergy; the choir of |
| chorus odas iubilat | musicians lift its voices in songs; |
| e quibus modo sincero | among them John of Corby stands out |
| J. de Corbe emicat. | for his purity of delivery. |

| Cuius non previsas posco | I invoke among his unprecedented |
| res quas J. de Alto Bosco | creations the ones which John of Hautbois |
| reserat theorica | unfolds in his theory; |
| qua fulgens vernat ut nosco | by which, as I know, blooms the |
| G. Martini practica. | illustrious practice of G. Martyn. |

This J[ohannes] de Corbe is probably the John de Corby who can be documented in musical service to the Black Prince and Edward III from 1347 until at least 1381. G[ilbertus?] Martini (Gilbert Martyn?), apparently a composer who learned his craft from Hanboys, has proved harder to trace.[90]

Received opinion until recently placed Hanboys and his *Summa* a full century later than Trowell's identification does.[91] The prevalent belief that Hanboys was a later fifteenth-century figure, active ca. 1470 in the reign of Edward IV rather than ca. 1370 in the reign of Edward III, relies on the authority of the earliest English antiquarians and on the repetition of their information by Charles Burney and Sir John Hawkins, who wrote before the

---

[88] Trowell, "Fourteenth-Century Ceremonial Motet," p. 70.

[89] See ibid., pp. 69–70; and the translation provided for *Sub arturo plebs* by A. G. Rigg in Margaret Bent, *Two 14th-Century Motets in Praise of Music[ians]* (North Harton, Devon: Antico Edition, 1977), pp. 2–3.

[90] For biographical data on de Corbe and Martini, see Trowell, "Fourteenth-Century Ceremonial Motet," pp. 69–70; Bowers, "Fixed Points," pp. 323 and 328; and Andrew Wathey, "The Peace of 1360–1369 and Anglo-French Musical Relations," *Early Music History* 9 (1990): 151–52 and 170.

[91] Both fourteenth- and fifteenth-century dates for Hanboys are advocated in the *New Grove Dictionary of Music and Musicians*: Andrew Hughes presents the traditional view, while Margaret Bent dates the treatise to ca. 1375? in "Notation, III, 3—Western, c. 1260–1500," *New Grove Dictionary of Music and Musicians* 13 (1980): 368. Gilbert Reaney ("Questions of Authorship," p. 12) assigns the *Summa* to "about the end of the 14th century."

single known manuscript of the *Summa* came to light and entered the British Library in 1831. This manuscript, **GB**-Lbl, Additional 8866, was probably copied in the second quarter of the fifteenth century. The antiquarian record, important nonetheless, is a tangled web of often repetitive testimony also involving Simon Tunstede and the authorship of the *Quatuor principalia*. It will require some unravelling here.

We must begin with the observation that the explicit of the *Summa* identifies the treatise as "summa ... super musicam continuam et discretam." This differentiation of continuous and discrete music is also found in the *Quatuor principalia*, where these terms correspond respectively to plainsong and mensurable music.[92] It seems likely that the explicit of the *Summa* in **GB**-Lbl, Additional 8866 simply errs by attributing the contents of the whole manuscript—rather than just the rear portion of it—to Hanboys. This may have come about because the scribe believed that Hanboys was in fact the author of a multivolume compendium, a point to which we will return below. It was undoubtedly the erroneous wording of the explicit that led antiquarians, following Bale, to attribute the *Quatuor principalia* to Hanboys.[93]

The earliest of the sixteenth-century English antiquaries, John Leland (ca. 1506–1552), accumulated substantial manuscript notes for a history of English literature. These notes were used by John Bale and other later authors but were not published until the eighteenth century. They included material on Tunstede (not as musician, however) but apparently had nothing about Hanboys.[94] The secondary literature on Hanboys begins with the first published history of English literature, the *Illustrium maioris britanniae scripto-*

---

[92] See the *Quatuor principalia*, quartum principale (CS, 3:335; CS, 4:254): "... plana musica et eius proportiones exordia sumpserunt que in continua consistunt quantitate ... at contra mensurabilis musica que per numeros producitur, in quantitate permanet discreta (... plain chant and its proportions took beginnings that consist in continuous quantity ... to the contrary is mensurable music, which is produced through numbers and abides in discrete quantity)."

[93] On the basis of content, language, and approach, it seems certain that the author of the *Summa* (Hanboys) was not the author of either surviving version of the *Quatuor principalia*. The fact that the *Summa* follows Version B of the *Quatuor principalia* in **GB**-Lbl, Additional 8866 suggests that the scribe either believed it to be the later of the two or considered it to consist of material extending the first treatise (much as many fourteenth-century music theory manuscripts pair *ars antiqua* and *ars nova* treatises on notation).

[94] See Leland, *Commentarii de Scriptoribus Britannicis*, ed. Anthony Hall (Oxford: Sheldon Theatre, 1709); and idem, *Collectanea de rebus britannicis*, ed. Thomas Hearne (Oxford: Sheldon Theatre, 1715).

*rum* (1548) of John Bale (1495–1563). Bale's *Illustrium* has an entry on Iohannes Hamboys (*sic*) in the last hundred of his five "centuries" of biographies.[95] This entry was slightly modified and expanded in the second edition of Bale's work, which appeared as *Scriptorum illustrium maioris brytanniae* (1557–59). Here Ioannes Hamboys is number forty in the eighth of twelve "centuries."[96] According to Bale, he was a celebrated doctor of music who

---

[95]John Bale, *Illustrium maioris britanniae scriptorum* (Ipswich: John Overton, 1548), f. 202v: "Ioanne Hamboys, Anglus, ab adolescentia liberalibus scientiis educatus, arti Musices (ut in qua semper maiorem habuerit delectationem) in fine firmius haerebat. Vocum enim consonantias, proportionum inductiones, & quicquid est quod ad hanc speculationem attinet, perfectissime vir officiosus ac diligens novit, Suppetebat ei non mediocriter, cum eloquio mellito, ingenium facundum & amoenum. Post frequentata igitur suae terrae gymnasia, ob egregie navatam operam, in ea facultate fit doctor, sui temporis plane celeberrimus. Unde tumdemum latine edidit, quo posteris haberetur beneficus, Summam artis musices, li.1 Quemadmodum inter triticum &, Cantica diversi generis, li.1 (John Hanboys, Englishman, educated from adolescence in the liberal sciences, in the end more firmly clung to the art of music, in which he always had more pleasure. The consonances of voices, the introducing of proportions, and whatever it is that concerns this discipline, this diligent and obliging man most perfectly knew; and was present in him not in mediocre fashion, but with lovely eloquence, fluent and pleasant ingenuity. After having attended the school of his land, on account of having succeeded in his endeavors so uncommonly well, in that faculty he was made a doctor, the most widely celebrated of his time. Whence just then he edited in Latin, so that posterity would have the benefit, a *Summa of the Art of Music* in one volume, beginning *Quemadmodum inter triticum* etc.; and *Songs of Various Kinds* in one volume)."

[96]Idem, *Scriptorum illustrium maioris brytanniae* (Basel; I. Oporinum, 1557–59), p. 617 (viii, 40):
"Ioannes Hamboys, elimatae eruditionis homo, ab adolescentia in liberalibus scientiis educatus, musicae, ut illi arti cui prae aliis favebat semper, in finem usque ardentius adhaerebat. Vocum enim consonantias, proportionum inductiones, & quicquid est quod ad eam speculationem attinet, perfectissime vir ille officiosus ac diligens novit. Suppetebat ei non mediocriter, cum eloquio mellito, ingenium facundum & amoenum. Post frequentata igitur multis annis suae terrae gymnasia, ob egregie navatam operam, in ea scientia communi suffragio fit doctor, sui temporis plane in Anglia celeberrimus. Qui demum, ut ex longo labore fructum educeret, ac aliis communem faceret, Latine composuit, Summam artis musicae, Lib.1. Quemadmodum inter triticum & zizan. Cantiones dulcissimas, Lib.1. Caetera eius scripta non vidi, cum tamen alia edidisse feratur. Summa illius, opus elegans est, & eius artis amatoribus gratum. Claruisse vero fertur anno a Christi Domini natali 1470, sub praedicto rege Eduardo quarto (John Hanboys, a man of perfect erudi-

flourished around 1470 during the reign of Edward IV (r. 1461–1483). In both entries, Hanboys is identified as the author of a single-volume work entitled *Summa artis musices*, the incipit of which begins "Quemadmodum inter triticum." This incipit, however, is not that of the *Summa* but rather the beginning of Version B of the *Quatuor principalia*. The error of attribution is most likely the result of a too cursory examination of the manuscript (perhaps **GB**-Lbl, Additional 8866 itself or a closely related source). Hanboys is also said to be the composer of a volume of music.

Bale had no entry for Simon Tunstede in the 1548 edition, but in the 1557 edition, Tunstede is included and identified as the author of a single-volume work, *Quatuor principalia*, for which no incipit is given. The misattribution of the *Quatuor principalia* to Tunstede, another long-lived error, is likely due to a careless reading of its explicit as it appears in Oxford, Bodleian Library (henceforward: **GB**-Ob), Digby 90 or a related copy. Bale's manuscript index (1549/50–1557) corrected part of the problem, providing an entry for Tunstede in which the incipit "Quemadmodum inter triticum" is at least properly associated with the *Quatuor principalia*. This entry provides a cross reference to Hanboys ("Vide Ioannem Hamboys"), but there is in fact no article under his name.[97]

---

tion, educated from adolescence in the liberal sciences, in the end clung more ardently to music, that art which he always favored above the others. The consonances of voices, the introducing of proportions, and whatever there is that concerns this discipline, this diligent and obliging man most perfectly knew; and was present in him not in mediocre fashion, but with lovely eloquence, fluent and pleasant ingenuity. After having attended the school of his land for many years, on account of having succeeded in his endeavors so uncommonly well, he was made a doctor in this science by common suffrage, the most widely celebrated in England of his time. Who then, just as fruit is produced after long labor and is made available to others, composed in Latin a *Summa of the Art of Music* in one volume, beginning *Quemadmodum inter triticum & zizan*; and *Songs Most Sweet* in one volume. I have not seen other works written by him, although he is supposed to have published some. His *Summa* is an elegant work and pleasing to the lovers of his art. He came to fame in the year 1470 after the birth of Our Lord, under the aforesaid king Edward IV)."

[97]Bale's index names sources of information for most entries. The article on Tunstede is cited "Ex Michaele Hobley." Hobley is cited seven other times (e.g., "Ex domo Michaelis Hobley," "Ex officina Michaelis Hobley") but nothing further about him or his relationship to Bale can be gleaned from the index. See Reginald Lane Poole and Mary Bateson, eds., *Index Britanniae scriptorum quos collegit J. Baleus* (Oxford: Clarendon Press, 1902), pp. 415 and 577.

Next to mention Hanboys is the historian Raphael Holinshed (died ca. 1580), in whose *Chronicles of England, Scotland, and Ireland* (1577; 2d ed., 1586–87) Hanboys is placed among "such writers of our nation as lived in his days" (speaking of Edward IV) and is described as follows: "Iohn Hambois an excellent Musician, and for hys notable cunnyng therein, made doctor of Musicke."[98] Holinshed elsewhere acknowledges citation of Bale, and Bale out of Leland; this entry is likely to be merely a brief paraphrase of Bale. After Holinshed, the next traceable reference to Hanboys is by John Pits (1560–1616), who draws on Bale (and perhaps Holinshed) for his article on Hanboys in *De Illustribus Angliae Scriptoribus*, the principal part of *Relationum Historicarum de Rebus Anglicis* (1619).[99]

---

[98]See *Holinshed's Chronicles of England, Scotland, and Ireland*, 6 vols. (London: J. Johnson, 1807–1808), 3:359.

[99]Pits, *Relationum historicarum de rebus Anglicis* (Paris: Thiery and Cramoisy, 1619), p. 662 (no. 870; year, 1470):

"De Ioanne Hambois. Ioannes Hambois natione Anglus, vir humanioribus litteris, imo omnibus liberalibus artibus, & Mathematicis scientiis non vulgariter instructus, ex omnibus tamen Musicam, qua naturaliter valde delectabatur, insolito quodam more quasi unicam elegit, in qua foecundum & facetum ingenium suum potissimum exerceret. In harmoniis igitur & consonantiis concinnandis, in dissonantiis inveniendis & evitandis, in proportionibus perpendendis, denique in omnibus quae ad hanc speculationem pertinent, tam faeliciter laboravit, tantamque in hac tota facultate peritiam consecutus est, ut in illa arte cum praecipuis sui temporis conferri potuerit. Huc accessit elegantia linguae Latinae, qua scriptis hos suos labores mandavit, & hanc artem Angelicam posteris commendavit. Scripsit enim Summam artem musices, Librum unum. Cantionum artificialium diversi generis, Librum unum. Et alia plura. Vixit anno gratiae 1470, sub Angliae Rege Edwardo quarto (John Hanboys, of the English nation, a man not just of average education in the humane letters, indeed in all the liberal arts and mathematical sciences, out of all of which he chose music, which was naturally and strongly pleasing to him, in a certain almost unusual way the one and only for him, in which he exercised his fecund and elegant ingenuity to the maximum. In the sounding together of harmonies and consonances, in the inventing and avoiding of dissonances, in the considering of proportions, and further in everything that pertains to this discipline, so happily he labored, and so much skill did he attain in this whole branch of study, that in that art with the peculiarities of its time he could bring together. To this purpose, elegance befell the language of Latin in which he consigned these his labors to writing and commended this angelic art to posterity. He wrote a *Summa of the Art of Music* in one volume, one volume of artful song of various kinds, and many other things. He lived in the year of grace 1470, under the English king Edward IV)."

The last noteworthy link in this chain of antiquarian citations is the *Bibliotheca Britannico-Hibernica* (1748) of Thomas Tanner (1674–1735).[100] Its entry for Hanboys draws on Bale and Pits, repeating, for instance, the mistaken association of the *Summa artis musicae* with the incipit "Quemadmodum inter triticum." Tanner observes that this is also the beginning of the *Quatuor principalia*, which he attributes not to Tunstede but simply to a Friar Minor of Bristol and Oxford in accord with the explicit of **GB-Ob**, Digby 90, which also exhibits the date 1351. Tanner does not repeat the assertion that Hanboys is a fifteenth-century figure.

Clearly the antiquarian tradition descends from a single authority: Bale (even to the consistent spelling of Hanboys with "m" for "n"). If Bale only knew the *Summa* at second hand or from an earlier fifteenth-century copy such as **GB-Lbl**, Additional 8866, he may simply have erred in the chronological placement of its author. If he knew Hanboys as a "doctor of music" only from a remark such as appears in the explicit of **GB**-Lbl, Additional 8866 ("Johannis Hanboys, doctoris musice reverendi"), his elaboration into "in ea scientia communi suffragio fit doctor,"[101] though unwarranted, is not unnatural in a day when the Mus.B. and Mus.D. degrees were relatively new at Oxford and Cambridge.[102] It may even be that Bale was somehow confusing Hanboys with a prominent itinerant English theorist of the later fifteenth century, the Carmelite monk Johannes Hothby (ca. 1410–1487), whose name does not otherwise appear in the antiquarian literature before Tanner.

---

[100]Tanner, *Bibliotheca Britannico-Hibernica*, p. 373.

[101]"He was made a doctor in this science by common suffrage."

[102]On the strength of the antiquarian testimony, Hanboys was for many years believed to be the first holder of a doctorate in music from a British university. The interest of Burney (ed. Mercer), 1:678–80, and Hawkins (new ed.), 1:291, was particularly strong in this matter. If Hanboys was a fifteenth-century figure and earned a Mus.D., it probably would have come from Cambridge, whose first recorded Mus.B. and Mus.D. degrees date from 1463/1464; the first Oxford degrees in music were granted ca. 1499. In any event, Hanboys is not recorded as a graduate of either university. See Alfred B. Emden, *A Biographical Register of the University of Cambridge to 1500*; idem, *A Biographical Register of the University of Oxford to A.D. 1500*, 3 vols. (Oxford: Clarendon Press, 1957–59); idem, *A Biographical Register of the University of Oxford A.D. 1501–1540* (Oxford: Clarendon Press, 1974).

See also Thurston Dart, "The Origins of Music Degrees," *Musical Times* 105 (1964): 190–91, which suggests that these degrees may perhaps have been initiated at the latter school by royal command of Edward IV.

The relationship between the treatises of Handlo and Hanboys has been observed only infrequently in the literature. Though he published them side by side, Coussemaker did not remark on it in his edition of 1864. Neither do the respective articles in the *New Grove Dictionary*, although the relationship was pointed out at least as early as the signed articles by Oswald Koller for Eitner's *Quellenlexicon*. Gilbert Reaney, who was aware of their relationship, has mentioned the suggestion of Nan Cooke Carpenter that Handlo and Hanboys may be the same man, with one name a corruption of the other.[103] The difference in content and approach of the two treatises, the few clues to biography and chronology that tend to separate them by about half a century, and the distinct etymologies of their author's names make this hypothesis highly unlikely.

## Contents of the *Summa* of Hanboys

The *Summa* of Hanboys takes Handlo as a point of departure, incorporating an abbreviated redaction of the *Regule* into an exhaustively systematic survey of *ars nova* note forms and rests. In its present state, it is not a true *summa* of the art of music in the mold of the *Summa de speculatione musicae* of Walter Odington, the anonymous *Quatuor principalia*, or the *Breviarium regulare musicae* of Willelmus. Nor is it a commentary on Franco's *Ars cantus mensurabilis* as such. Eighty percent of the *Summa* is just a straightforward series of descriptions of the nearly identical properties of eight notes: the larga, duplex longa, longa, brevis, semibrevis, minor, semiminor, and minima. This material is prefaced with text drawn from Franco's *Ars cantus mensurabilis* and followed by discussions of ligatures and rests; it is closed by a vestigial chapter on the rhythmic modes. The resulting presentation is the longest of all the English treatises on notation, nearly twice as long as the corresponding pages in Version B of the *Quatuor principalia*, for instance. Yet in some form, what survives may have been only the final part of a more ambitious multivolume compendium, since at the end of a brief extract on metrics and the *sinemmenon* in the unique manuscript source of the *Summa*, there is a citation to an otherwise unknown book by Hanboys that evidently must have concerned plainchant.[104]

---

[103]Reaney, "Questions of Authorship," p. 12; and Carpenter, p. 60.

[104]See f. 64r of **GB**-Lbl, Additional 8866: "... ut dicit hanboys libro primo capitulo sexto." The *tractatulus* concluded by this statement is edited in appendix III.

Hanboys was clearly working at a later time than Handlo (Handlo's "moderns" are Hanboys's "ancients"), but in many respects his treatise still reveals the tensions between *ars antiqua* and *ars nova* notational and mensural practice. Hanboys stripped out much of what is distinctive in the *Regule* concerning the late *ars antiqua* as he redistributed material from the earlier treatise to suit his own ends.[105] Differences in readings suggest either that Hanboys wielded his editorial pen vigorously or else that Hanboys's exemplar may have differed significantly from the version of the *Regule* in **GB**-Lbl, Additional 4909.[106] About fifty percent of the *Regule* is retained, amounting to under twenty percent of the text of the *Summa*. Rubrics I–V survive more or less intact and in order as part of Hanboys's chapters 7, 10, 11, 12, and 13, except for excision of the doctrines of Petrus le Viser and Admetus de Aureliana. In these sections, Hanboys's version accords closely with the language of the *Regule* in **GB**-Lbl, Additional 4909, and the "dialogue" format is retained (substituting "Hanboys" for "Handlo"), though there is no trace of any labelling and cross-referencing for rubrics, rules, and maxims. On the other hand, the contents of Rubrics VI–VIII, X, XII–XIII are truncated and to a large degree rearranged; missing entirely are Rubric IX (concerning conjunctions of semibreves) and Rubric XI (on the values of plicas). Among the materials excised are remarks about the duplex longa and the semilonga, pairs of semibreves to be read 2+1, the obliquity as a distinct figure, hockets, most other references to conjunctions of semibreves, and Handlo's commentary on the rhythmic modes. Under these circumstances, it is of the greatest interest that references to the raised longa and brevis are retained. In respect to his citation of other authorities, Hanboys quotes Franco directly from the *Ars cantus mensurabilis*; he also cites the Englishmen W. de Doncastre, Robertus Trowell, Robertus de Brunham, and one or more additional anonymous authorities of the early *ars nova*.

---

[105]The present edition's concordance of the music examples from Handlo that appear in Hanboys, given in appendix I, provides a convenient overview of the distribution of material from the *Regule* into the later treatise.

[106]One could extract from the *Summa* a partial version of the *Regule*, taking care to differentiate the Franco of the *Regule* from the Franco of the *Ars cantus mensurabilis* and to distinguish the references where the name Hanboys is a mere substitution for Handlo from Hanboys's own remarks. More troublesome are remarks attributed to Franco that do not originate in either of the sources just named. In part these may be mistakes of the rubricator that ought to be corrected to Hanboys, but some may reflect material in a hypothetical exemplar of the *Regule* (perhaps credited there to Franco) that significantly updates the version in **GB**-Lbl, Additional 4909.

Hanboys's exposition is often mechanical and repetitive. Only a few lumps of material, in many ways the most interesting and revealing, are not well integrated. It is just these passages that provide perspectives on the authorities and doctrines he wishes to uphold or challenge, and they occasionally bespeak a pedantic, syllogistic form of argument that points to the intellectual milieu for which the treatise may have been destined.[107] The following introduction to the *Summa* begins with a review of two topics across the entire range of note values to show the degree to which Hanboys's exposition is standardized and the degree to which the appearance of great uniformity may be deceptive. This will be followed by a review of several of the most important "lumps."

*Imperfection and alteration*

One topic given a great deal of space in the *Summa* concerns what to do when counting by threes to make perfections and one or two notes remain. This is a question, central to the explanation of the workings of imperfection and alteration, where the classic *ars antiqua* treatment occurs in the discussion of the relationship of longa and brevis. In Franco's *Ars cantus mensurabilis*, if more than three breves are found between two longs, they are counted by threes, and if two are left over at the end, then the first is normal and the second is altered. If just one brevis is left over, then the default solution (that is, the solution unclarified or amended by any punctus) is to reconceive the series of breves as a single brevis followed by groups of three, with the single brevis forming a perfection with the preceding longa. If a punctus is employed, it will follow the first longa, forcing the last brevis to be interpreted as the single brevis, thus pertaining to the subsequent longa. It is curious that the *Gaudent moderni* treatises omit discussion of the circumstance in which a single brevis is left over. Handlo, however, treats this situation with care in a series of remarks noteworthy for their direct question-and-answer format (glossed "questio" and "respondeo" in the *Summa*, chapter 11), in which he advocates the Franconian solution (Rules XI, XII, and Maxim 8 of Rubric III).

---

[107]From a remark in chapter 2 (186.4), it would appear the *Summa* was intended for "compositoribus et cantoribus."

Table 1. Concerning chains of the same figure between two of the next higher figure, counted by threes.
  a. If two are left over.[108]
  b. If one is left over (the example uses a punctus but the text does not mention it).
  c. If one is left over (the default solution with no punctus).
  d. If one is left over (the example uses a punctus and the text does mention it).

| Figure | a. | b. | c. | d. |
|---|---|---|---|---|
| Larga | -- | -- | -- | -- |
| Duplex longa | 214.25 | 216.3 | -- | -- |
| Longa | 234.11 | 234.14 | -- | -- |
| Brevis | 248.17 | -- | 248.24 | 250.2 |
|  | 250.8 | -- | -- | 250.10 |
|  | 250.17 | -- | -- | -- |
|  | 250.24 | -- | -- | -- |
| Semibrevis | 286.12 | -- | 292.6 | 292.8 |
| Minor | 302.21 | 302.24 | 304.5 | 304.7 |
| Semiminor | 312.26 | 312.29 | 314.2 | 314.4 |
| Minima | 318.23 | 318.26 | 318.31 | 318.33 |

Table 1 presents all corresponding passages in Hanboys, identified by the pertinent example. It shows first that the larga is not involved in this question. In the case of the duplex longa and longa, Hanboys only covers the situations in which two are left over (column a) and in which the lone value imperfects the subsequent higher value (column b) without any mention of the punctus, which nevertheless appears correctly placed in each example. For the brevis, the initial discussion follows Handlo's *Regule* (column a, c, d: examples 248.17–250.2, 250.8–10). Hanboys continues, however, with three suggestions of his own "for greater understanding when five breves are found between two longae." The first (example 250.17) advocates what might be called overcautious dotting, adding three puncti that are redundant in light of normal Franconian practice as just described.[109] The second (for which no example is given), with its expressions "modus imitatur" and "per colorem differt," resists explanation. The third (example 250.24) proposes that when no puncti are present, the breves should be grouped 1+3+1, corresponding to

---

[108] All examples in column a have an "overcautious" punctus after the first figure, except for 248.17 and 250.8 (the two purely Franconian examples) and 250.24, which is to be read 1+3+1.

[109] See n. 108 *supra*, concerning column a of table 1.

Franco's solution for five when a punctus is employed after the first brevis. For the semibrevis, the presentation in three examples (columns a, c, d) is straightforward and unexceptional. To these standard three examples, the discussions for the minor, semiminor, and minima add a fourth (column b) corresponding to the examples in the treatment of this topic for the duplex longa and longa.

In respect to the imperfection of a larger by a smaller value, a small lump of material relevant to *ars nova* practices is treated briefly by Hanboys in chapters 7 and 19. According to Franconian rules, if an isolated brevis precedes a long, it imperfects it, but Hanboys explains (chapter 7 [224.13–17]) that by the use of a punctus after the longa, it is possible to mix breves with longae, the longa remaining perfect.[110] Hanboys then states the general rule that any two adjacent figures can be mixed this way. A similar, specific observation about breves and semibreves is stimulated by Hanboys's reaction to the statement that no semibrevis can stand alone (chapter 19 [328.3–8]); this was true in the *ars antiqua* but no longer in the *ars nova*. Hanboys is being mildly radical here. In these instances, common continental practice would identify the punctus as one of division. Thus, the smaller value would imperfect the larger, whose perfection could only be guaranteed if it were flanked both fore and aft by *puncti syncopationis*.

For Hanboys's four smaller figures (but not his four larger), discussion of groupings by three and their residues in triple time is followed by discussion of groupings by two and their residues in duple time. Here Hanboys describes a *punctus perfectionis* that is in effect a *punctus additionis* (example 292.16, etc.) and what is in effect a simple form of syncopation within or across the barline (example 292.28, etc.).

*Diminishment*

Another topic that cuts across most of the *Summa* is diminishment. Whereas imperfection concerns the reduction in value of a note by the next smaller note (e.g., the imperfection of a perfect longa by an adjacent brevis), diminishment involves the reduction in value of a note by one two steps smaller (e.g., the diminishment of a longa by an adjacent semibrevis). A note is usually unaffected by more remote figures, that is, those three or more steps away in the mensural hierarchy (e.g., the normal longa is not dimin-

---

[110]The mixing of breves with longae under these circumstances effectively creates displacement rhythms (syncopations) across longa-perfections.

ished by an adjacent minima).[111] The primary topics concerning diminishment are catalogued in table 2, in which columns a–d concern the diminishment of normal notes and columns e–g concern altered notes. From this table, it can be seen that only for the brevis and semibrevis are all possibilities fully aired. The larga cannot be altered, for instance, because nothing can be any larger than it already is. The semiminor and minima cannot be diminished because there are no figures small enough to do so, a circumstance that also curtails possibilities for diminishment of the normal minor and altered semiminor. Discussion of the diminishment of the altered duplex longa and longa is limited to the statement that it is handled like that of the imperfect larga or imperfect duplex longa, respectively.

---

[111]Diminishment in this sense is, of course, a central novelty of the *ars nova*; early discussions regard it as a form of imperfection and center just on the longa-semibrevis and brevis-minima relationships. See, for instance, the treatment by de Muris in the *conclusiones* of the *Notitia artis* (ed. Michels, pp. 93–103) or in the Berkeley theory treatises (*The Berkeley Manuscript*, ed. and trans. Oliver B. Ellsworth, Greek and Latin Music Theory, vol. 2 [Lincoln: University of Nebraska Press, 1984], pp. 154–65). I have chosen to speak of "diminishment" rather than "diminution" to stay as far as possible from other musical uses of the latter word, in respect to ornamentation and proportional reduction.

Table 2. Concerning diminishment.

| Figure | a. | b. | c. | d. |
|---|---|---|---|---|
| Larga | 198.13–202.27 | 204.8 | 204.13 | 204.24 |
| Duplex longa | 208.1–212.3 | 216.11 | 216.15 | 216.24 |
| Longa | 226.12–230.21 | 234.23 | 236.4 | 236.11 |
| Brevis | 238.15–242.17 | 244.23 | 244.26 | 246.6 |
| Semibrevis | 294.26–298.17 | 284.8 | 284.11 | 284.16[112] |
| Minor | 306.18–308.32 | (300.19–23[113]) | | |
| Semiminor | -- | -- | -- | -- |
| Minima | -- | -- | -- | -- |

  a. A note can be worth 9, 8, 7, 6, 5, 4 of the note two steps smaller (the agent).
  b. A recta note can be diminished by a preceding or following agent; if following, the agent can be imperfected by a preceding note one step smaller.
  c. A recta note can be diminished by a following agent; a chain of successively smaller notes, each imperfecting the preceding, can follow the agent.
  d. A recta note can be diminished by a following agent; a chain of successively larger notes can precede the agent, all diminishing the recta note.
  e. An altered note can be diminished by a preceding or following agent; the agent can be followed by a chain of successively smaller notes, each imperfecting the preceding.
  f. An altered note can be diminished by agents preceding and following; both agents can be followed by a chain of successively smaller notes, each imperfecting the preceding.
  g. An altered note can be diminished by agents preceding and following; the preceding agent can be followed by a chain of successively smaller notes, all but the last followed by a dot, and all further diminishing the altered note; the following agent can be preceded by a chain of successively larger notes, all further diminishing the altered note.

---

[112]Example 284.16 is the only one in column d to require a punctus for clarification.

[113]In these three examples the minor is diminished by a preceding minima, by a following minima, and by preceding and following minimae.

| Figure | e. | f. | g. |
|---|---|---|---|
| Larga | -- | -- | -- |
| Duplex longa | (like the imperfect larga[114]) | | |
| Longa | (like the imperfect duplex longa[115]) | | |
| Brevis | 252.8–13 | 252.19 | 254.3 |
| Semibrevis | 294.7–12 | 294.17 | 294.25 |
| Minor | 306.3–7 | 306.11 | 306.17 |
| Semiminor | | | (314.28–316.7[116]) |
| Minima | -- | -- | -- |

There is an interesting asymmetry in the discussions of the diminishment of normal and altered notes. Given the former, a note may be diminished by a preceding or following value, but the diminishing agent itself can be imperfected (by a preceding or following note or a following chain of ever smaller notes) only when it follows the diminished note, as in column b and c. In the case of altered notes, the diminishing agent is never imperfected by a preceding smaller note, only by a following note or chain of decreasing figures, as in columns e and f. But when the altered value is diminished from the front and rear simultaneously, both agents, not just the following one, may be imperfected, as in column f.

There is just one way in which normal and altered notes can be diminished by smaller notes more than two levels below (again, following the normal, or preceding and following the altered note), as in columns d and f. In this instance, all the notes from three steps below the attacked value down to the minima also carve value out of the usually impregnable diminished note.[117] For instance, if a normal perfect longa is followed by a minor and a

---

[114] *Summa*, chapter 6 (216.4–5).

[115] *Summa*, chapter 9 (234.15–16).

[116] In these three examples the altered semiminor is diminished by a preceding minima, by a following minima, and by preceding and following minimae.

[117] "Which notes can be mixed with which" is a characteristic concern of the late *ars antiqua* and early *ars nova*, a concern articulated in the *Regule* by Handlo and by Petrus le Viser. Handlo's rubric on this topic is transmitted by Hanboys (*Summa*, chapter 13 [268.21–23]) who observes that the limits set by Handlo no longer hold regarding the mixtures of larger values (largae,

semibrevis, in that order, the minor has no effect at all on the longa. The semibrevis diminishes the value of the longa from nine to eight semibreves, and it is in turn imperfected by the minor. If, however, the longa is followed directly by a minima, semiminor, minor, and semibrevis, then according to Hanboys, each will erode value from the longa. There is a point of possible ambiguity where the situations in columns b and d of table 2 intersect or, in other words, where the note imperfecting the diminishing agent is itself the smallest possible figure, the minima. This occurs at the level of the semibrevis, where examples 284.8 and 284.16 are identical save for the introduction of a punctus in 284.16 to clarify that the minima is separate from the semiminor and without effect upon it.

## Expansion of the gradus system

The first of the major lumps that interrupt Hanboys's exposition is found in chapter 2, immediately preceding the main presentation on the various properties of his eight figures that occupies chapters 3 through 18. The *Summa* begins with a preface and an initial chapter borrowed literally from the opening pages of Franco's *Ars cantus mensurabilis*. Once Franco's introduction of his three species of simple figures (longa, brevis, and semibrevis) is reached in the first paragraph of chapter 3, Hanboys has arrived at the opening from which he can begin his own argument. He apparently starts by attacking Franco, in a passage that is unfortunately corrupt. It becomes evident, however, that it is not Franco (or at least not the author of the *Ars cantus mensurabilis*) who is his true target at all. In the second paragraph, Hanboys appears to say that he wants to add two figures, one larger and one smaller (namely the larga and the minima) to Franco's system of three, which would result in a system of five figures. But from the final paragraph of the chapter (and the entire ensuing treatise), we know that he wishes to arrive at a total of eight figures. Therefore, his starting point must not actually be the three figures of Franco of Cologne but rather the six figures of someone else's set, a set already including the duplex longa, longa, brevis, semibrevis, minima, and crocheta.[118]

---

duplex longae, longae) with smaller values (breves, semibreves, etc.) on account of this form of repeated diminishment.

[118]Perhaps Johannes Torkesey or Robertus de Brunham; see *infra*, pp. 54–57 and 63. It may be that Hanboys's unnamed authority here used the term *duplex longa*; however, it is possible that he used the term *larga*, as in the *Summa*, chapter 6 (218.1–2).

Paragraph three, which appears in the present context to be an interpolation in an argument that runs from paragraph two directly to paragraph four, is quite probably a vestige of an earlier stage in the development of Hanboys's theories. In it, Hanboys attacks those who use the term *crocheta* for a value smaller than a minima, proposing that the two terms should be reversed so that the term *minima* identifies the smallest value. This suggestion makes sense only in terms of the set of six figures just mentioned. Hanboys appeals to the Philosopher (i.e., Aristotle) for the maxim "impossibile est dare minus minimo,"[119] which encapsulates the fundamental argument against introducing any figure smaller than a minima, or as here, against using any name for the smallest figure other than *minima*. He wishes to change the names only, leaving the figures themselves in the same order, according to the principle "melius est mutare nomen figure quam extra gradum suum ponere (it is better to change the name of a figure than to use it outside of its own rank)." Keeping the order of a sequence of figures or note shapes intact while renaming them if necessary was a major concern of *ars nova* theorists; it was a way to create stability amidst the proliferation of names, shapes, and signs of the late *ars antiqua*. This doctrine is also articulated in the teachings of de Vitry, in regard to the naming of smallest values, in a passage likely known by Hanboys: "Minimae tamen et semiminimae, ad gradum salvandum in quo posita fuit minima, alia nomina imponi possent, ita quod minima vocetur seminimor et semiminima minima nominetur."[120] Hanboys appears to have retained paragraph three from some earlier argument only for the purpose of setting out a principle. In paragraph four, he rejects the term *crocheta* altogether and instead proposes the renaming that he will follow in the treatise, substituting minor for minima and seminimor for crocheta, while adding

---

[119]"It is impossible to give less than the least."

[120]"Minimae and semiminimae, in order to preserve the level at which the minima is placed, can be given other names, so that the minima is called the semiminor and the semiminima is called the minima." The quotation is from the Vatican manuscript version of the *Ars nova*, cap. XV, sent. 14 (ed. Reaney et al.), p. 24; see also the closely related language of a Parisian manuscript version beginning *Sex sunt species principales* (ed. Reaney et al.), p. 65, lns. 49–52: "Minime et semiminime ad gradum superlatum solvendum nominantur, sicut et alie semibreves inposita habentes nomina: alia nomina inponi possunt, ita quod minima vocatur semiminor et semiminima minima (Minimae and semiminimae are named in order to be released from the superlative degree [i.e., to open up an additional level beyond the minima]; just like other semibreves having been given names, they can be given other names, so that the minima is called the semiminor and the semiminima is called the minima)."

a new smallest value for which he reserves the name *minima*. He again invokes the key term *gradus*, the rank or level of the figures ("manente in suo gradu ... mutato nomine") to explain the renaming.

To gain a context for this passage in Hanboys and, more generally, to understand the significance of the term *gradus*, we need to understand the concept of the gradus system and the status of the minima and semiminima at the time of the earliest expositions of *ars nova* mensural theory emanating from Paris: the *Tractatus de musica* of the Anonymous OP,[121] the *Notitia artis musicae* (1321) of de Muris,[122] and the early treatises of the de Vitry tradition. In effect, their discussions of musical time and the role of the minima are a small, peripheral contribution to the lively debate about continuity and infinity that was central to late thirteenth- and fourteenth-century scholastic thought.[123] In the later *ars antiqua*, values smaller than a third of a brevis were conceived as fractions of an infinitely divisible brevis and therefore as kinds of semibrevis.[124] A radical novelty of the new French theory

---

[121] According to Michels, the treatise of the Anonymous OP is the first to use the word *gradus* with the meaning we find more fully worked out in the *Notitia artis musica* of de Muris. See Ulrich Michels, "Der Musiktraktat des Anonymus OP. Ein frühes Theoretiker-Zeugnis der Ars nova," *Archiv für Musikwissenschaft* 26 (1969): 53 and 56. Michels edits this treatise from GB-Ob, Bodley 77, a fifteenth-century English manuscript.

[122] Johannes de Muris, *Notitia artis musicae et Compendium musicae practica*; Petrus de Sancto Dionysio, *Tractatus de musica*, ed. Ulrich Michels, Corpus scriptorum de musica, no. 17 ([Rome]: American Institute of Musicology, 1972).

[123] This most interesting line of thought cannot be pursued at any length here. It is one of the central issues discussed in an important recent dissertation by Dorit Tanay, "Music in the Age of Ockham: The Interrelations between Music, Mathematics, and Philosophy in the 14th Century" (Ph.D. dissertation, University of California at Berkeley, 1989). I am grateful to Dr. Tanay for generously sharing with me her table of contents and a typescript copy of chapter 4, "Infinity and Continuity" (pp. 65–112 of the dissertation).

[124] As these shorter values proliferated, they posed the theoretical question how far the process of subdivision of the brevis could be taken. One late *ars antiqua* answer was provided by the Evesham monk and Oxford scholar Walter Odington, who argued in *De speculatione musicae* (ed. Hammond), p. 128, that because time was a continuum, it was infinitely divisible, and because sounds were measured by time, they were therefore likewise infinitely divisible: "Sed quia continuum est divisibile in infinitum, et tempus continuorum est, voces quidem sunt mensuratae temporibus quare divisibiles erunt in infinitum (But because a continuum is infinitely divisible, and time is of a continuum, the voices that are measured by time therefore are infinitely

was the concept of the minima as a separate figure (not simply a signed semibrevis), indivisible, and the unit from which all else is built. The various mensurations in the mensural hierarchy therefore shared minima equivalence. In such a discrete system, a fraction of the unit value is inconceivable—"non est dare minus minimo," as de Muris puts it in the *Notitia*. Hence, the semiminima is absent from the de Muris tradition even as late as the *Libellus cantus mensurabilis* of around 1340. Nonetheless, the semiminima was alive and well in Paris in the early 1320s. It is mentioned, for instance, both by Jacques de Liège and in the complex of treatises related to Philippe de Vitry.[125] De Vitry is even said to have invented it.[126] There is some discomfort surrounding the term, however, whose legitimacy is questioned in a Parisian manuscript source of de Vitry material ("si dici possunt semiminimae").[127] That fractions of "one" needed to be acknowledged is undoubtedly due to the fact that neither the theory of de Muris nor de Vitry fully encompassed all of the various subdivisions of the brevis that had emerged by the end of the second decade of the century in French music. While their new Parisian theory was an effort to control and standardize a discourse and a practice, it did not make a perfect fit with all the available data.[128]

---

divisible)." Odington (p. 129) himself did not push this tenet beyond the notes immediately subdividing the minor semibrevis while retaining its shape, which he calls "minutae ... quasi minimae seu velocissimae." The author of the *Quatuor principalia*, taking this passage by Odington as his starting point, objected vehemently. From his *ars nova* perspective, musical time is held to be discrete, with the minima as indivisible unit value, and the kind of infinite divisibility of the continuum of time that Odington advocates is said to pertain to astronomy, not music (see CS, 3:352b; CS, 4:275).

[125]For example, Jacques de Liège, *Speculum musicae*, Book 7, cap. XXIII, sent. 11 (ed. Bragard), p. 52: "qui vero ponunt semiminimas vel semiminores"; and *Ars Nova* (ed. Reaney et al.), p. 24: "Illa ... quae vero minimae meditatem, semiminima nominatur (that which is [worth] a half a minima is named the semiminima)."

[126]More accurately, the author of the *Quatuor principalia* disputes someone's claim that de Vitry invented it (CS, 3:336b–37a and CS, 4:257a); see also Fuller, "Phantom Treatise," pp. 40–41.

[127]*Ars nova* (ed. Reaney et al.), p. 63, ln. 24; there is similar language in Anonymous, *De arte musicae breve compendiolum* (Anon. III of CS 3), cap. 3, sent. 11 (*Ars nova* [ed. Reaney et al.], p. 85). In the Vatican manuscript version of the *Ars nova* (ed. Reaney et al.), p. 24, a renaming is proposed that would avoid the locution *semiminima*; see *supra*, p. 47.

[128]Moreover, the figure with a value of two minimae (Latin *dragma*, French *fusiel*), the phenomenon called the *syncope*, and the employment of

The gradus system, as presented by de Muris in his *Notitia artis musicae* of 1321, encompassed and codified in formal language and means of presentation the fundamental theoretical advances of the *ars nova* over the *ars vetus*, presenting in a systematic array most of the proliferation of note values, note names, and note shapes that were a hallmark of late *ars antiqua* and early *ars nova* mensural theory. Table 3 presents the values and names of the gradus system of de Muris, along with the alternative names of which he is aware.[129]

Table 3. The Gradus System of de Muris and its expansion by Phillipotus

| System of de Muris | | | System of Phillipotus | | |
|---|---|---|---|---|---|
| | | | 243 | longissima | |
| | | | 162 | semilongissima | |
| 81 | longissima | | 81 | longior | longior |
| 54 | longior | | 54 | | semilongior |
| 27 | longa | longa perfecta | 27 | longa | longa |
| 18 | | longa imperfecta | 18 | semilonga | |
| 9 | brevis | brevis | 9 | brevis | brevis |
| 6 | brevior | | 6 | | semibrevis |
| 3 | brevissima | parva | 3 | brevior | brevior |
| 2 | | minor | 2 | semibrevior | |
| 1 | | minima | 1 | brevissima (vel minima) | |

four minimae in the time of three are also mentioned in descriptions of early *ars nova* theory. These are not developments of the second half of the century, nor have some early theorists simply invented entities that would only later be put to use. Rather, the semiminima and the rest predate the most formal *ars nova* theory; not finding a place in that theory, they remained outside of it.

[129]De Muris gives a name to every value and presents not only his preferred set of nine names (with potential for confusion because some of the *partes prolacionis* have two names and two values) but also two or three additional sets of names that are used by others. Naming was an important corollary to the fundamental extension of values and figures, and evidently many different systems of names were in circulation. See especially the discussion by de Muris ("De figuris nominandis") in *Notitia artis musicae* (ed. Michels), pp. 78–79; and its repetition in large part by Jacques de Liège in the *Speculum musicae*, Book 7, cap. XXIV (ed. Bragard), pp. 52–53.

| Alternative terminology reported by de Muris | |
|---|---|
| triplex longa or maxima | larga |
| duplex longa or maior | semilarga |
| simplex longa or magna | longa |
| - - - - - | |
| longa perfecta | longa |
| longa imperfecta | semilonga |
| brevis | brevis |
| - - - - - | |
| brevis perfecta | brevis |
| brevis imperfecta | semibrevis |
| semibrevis | minor |
| - - - - - | |
| semibrevis perfecta | minor |
| semibrevis imperfecta | semiminor |
| minima | minima |

From bottom to top, the four levels of this array encompassed nine values, from a single indivisible minima up to eighty-one minimae ("ab unitate ... usque ad 81 ... dicuntur esse termini"), arranged in four groups of three values each that stand in the ratio 1:2:3. These values were represented by a total of five notational figures ("partes prolacionis") and nine names. The system de Muris describes was closed: "sunt igitur quatuor gradus perfectionis neque plures neque pauciores." This closure was insured by the numbering of the levels from one to four beginning with the greatest values at the top as the first level and moving to the smallest values at the bottom as the fourth. Given this numbering, one could imagine expanding the system only downward toward even smaller values, with a fifth level of minima and semiminima values. But of course, for de Muris there was no possibility of introducing a value smaller than the smallest, and therefore a fifth level was entirely precluded.

Fourteenth-century English theorists showed a great preoccupation with the gradus system of de Muris and its expansion.[130] Their relevant contributions can be separated into three main streams. For their principal systems of figures and nomenclature, see table 4. One English line of development is represented by the *Quatuor principalia*; the topic is well developed in Version A and elaborated even more fully in the prolix Version B. This may perhaps be the earliest English contribution, because its discussion of the concept of gradus is in such great measure specifically dependent on the language and

---

[130]The Vatican manuscript version of the *Ars Nova* (ed. Reaney et al.), p. 24, sent. 16, uses the expression *in gradu ternario* for when the semibrevis is perfect, so the minima could be altered; the concept of gradus, however, is not a legacy of de Vitry to the English.

Table 4. Principal systems of figures and nomenclature.

| de Muris | Quatuor principalia | Tractatus (primary) | Tractatus (alternate) | Walsingham (primary) | Walsingham (alternate) |
|---|---|---|---|---|---|
|  |  | largissima | longissima | longissima | [longissima] |
|  |  |  |  | imperf. longissima | imperf. longissima] |
| maxima | triplex longa | larga | longior | longior | longior or larga |
|  | duplex longa |  |  | imperf. longior | semilongior or semilarga |
| longa | longa | longa | longa | longa | longa |
|  |  |  |  | imperf. longa | semilonga |
| brevis | brevis | brevis | brevis | brevis | brevis |
|  |  |  |  | imperf. brevis | semibrevis |
| semibrevis | semibrevis | semibrevis | brevior | brevior | brevior or minor |
|  |  |  |  | imperf. brevior | semibrevior or seminimor |
| minima | minima | minima | brevissima | brevissima | minima |

| de Muris | Torkesey | GB-Lbl 21455 item 2 | Willelmus | Hanboys | Anon. scuto |
|---|---|---|---|---|---|
| maxima | larga | larga | largissima | larga | triplex longa |
|  |  |  |  | duplex longa | duplex longa |
| longa | longa | longa | larga | longa | simplex longa |
| brevis | brevis | brevis | longa | brevis | brevis |
| semibrevis | semibrevis | minor | brevis | semibrevis | simplex medius |
|  |  |  | semibrevis | minor | simplex minor |
| minima | minima | minima | minuta | seminimor | duplex minor |
|  | simpla | [semiminima] | simpla | minima | minima |

concepts of the *Notitia*.[131] The *Quatuor principalia* does, however, depart from de Muris in a number of significant particulars. Only four figures are identified, not five: the longa, brevis, semibrevis, and minima. Together they define just three principal levels, not four, of a mensural hierarchy. At the same time, however, the levels are numbered from the smaller to the larger, so the system is conceptually open ended, and the author declares its capacity for infinite expansion toward larger values "per binarium et ternarium."[132]

A second line of development can be identified with those theorists pressing the expansion of the five figures and four levels of the *Notitia* to six figures and five levels by adding a new largest value. This represents an extension of large values to the farthest limits found in gradus theory—two levels above the longa—to a *longissima* or *largissima* of up to nine perfect longae worth as many as 243 minimae.[133] Versions of this system are described by the anonymous and relatively early *Tractatus de figuris*[134] and by two authorities from the end of the century, Thomas Walsingham and the Wylde Anonymous. It is also described in a fourteenth-century glossing of de Muris's *Notitia* by a certain Petrus of St.-Denis, who gives credit for the innovation to a certain Phillipotus, whose nationality is unknown (there is no reason in particular to think that he was English).[135] For a comparison of the systems of de Muris and Phillipotus, see table 3.

---

[131]See *partes immediates* and *partes mediates*, etc. But the author explicitly rejects the terminology of comparative adjectives (*magnus, maior, maxima* or *parva, minor, minima*) that de Muris uses to label the values of the gradus.

[132]*Quatuor principalia*, quartum principale (CS, 3:340; CS, 4:261–62). In this treatise, the longa can be simplex, duplex, or triplex; these three stand in the 1:2:3 ratio of de Muris. The triplex longa is also known as the maxima, but it is not the largest possible value.

[133]There is a direct correspondence here to Handlo's "longa novem perfectionum," the largest permissible of his "longis qui excedunt valorem longe duplicis" (see Rule I of Rubric V; and see also *supra*, p. 10).

[134]Mention of the *scuto* in the *Tractatus de figuris* (ed. Gilles and Reaney), p. 43, probably indicates that this treatise postdates Torkesey's *Declaratio*.

[135]See Petrus de Sancto Dionysio, *Tractatus de musica* (ed. Michels), p. 154. Exactly when Phillipotus flourished is not known, nor, for that matter, do we know when Petrus of St.-Denis was active, though both seem to be fairly contemporary critics of de Muris. This version of the treatise by Petrus, preserved in Chicago, Newberry Library, Ms. 54.1, ff. 1r–6v, was copied by an Englishman in Italy in 1391 (the contents of this manuscript also include a seven-level Torkesey triangle; see *infra*, pp. 56–57). Its only two

The surviving three chapters of the *Tractatus de figuris* deal with the minima, semibrevis, and brevis, and incorporate important digressions that discuss nomenclature and other relevant topics. The author apparently intended to discuss larger values in the manner of Phillipotus, but though we learn their names and they appear in some examples of notation, they are not discussed in any detail in the surviving chapters. It is not out of the question that the *Tractatus de figuris* is either Phillipotus's missing treatise or derived from it, though the principal set of names of the *Tractatus* is not that of Phillipotus and intermediate values in each level are not named or discussed. Walsingham provides a number of alternative names for the values in his system, including a set close to those of de Muris and Phillipotus. The Wylde anonymous, in a presentation employing the principal names in the *Tractatus*, includes the largior between the larga and largissima, suggesting a closer link between the *Tractatus* and the Phillipotus-Walsingham line than can now otherwise be traced.

The third line of development runs contrary to the expansion toward larger values found in the first two, augmenting de Muris's five figures not with a larger but with a smaller one, a semiminima called the *crocheta* or *simpla*. Its first representative is the *Declaratio trianguli et scuti* of Johannes Torkesey. Torkesey's simpla is impartibilis or indivisibilis; moreover, he specifically declares that the simpla can only be used melismatically, not syl-

---

other sources end just prior to where the Newberry copy begins, and the latter is presented as an integral treatise. Petrus of St.-Denis (ed. Michels), pp. 154–55, regarded the expansion of the gradus system by Phillipotus as unnecessary: "quem gradum non reprobo tamquam impossibilem, sed mihi non videtur necessarius nec regularis .... Primum ex istis modis propter superfluitatem relinquo, quia quatuor ultimi gradus sufficiunt, et secundum istos proceditur in hoc libro (I do not disapprove of this level on account of its impossibility, but it seems to me neither necessary nor proper .... The first of these ways I relinguish on account of its superfluousness, since the four remaining levels suffice, and it is according to them that we will proceed in this book)"; see also Michels, *Die Musiktraktate*, p. 78.

I should add parenthetically that Petrus's Phillipotus is presumably not to be equated with either the unknown Phillipotus [Phillipoctus] Andrea to whom the *Tractatus figurarum* is attributed in Chicago, Newberry Library, Ms. 54.1, or the composer Philippus [Philipoctus] de Caserta to whom the *Tractatus figurarum* is attributed in Faenza, Biblioteca Comunale, Ms. 117 (see the *Treatise on Noteshapes [Tractatus figurarum]*, ed. and trans. Philip E. Schreur, Greek and Latin Music Theory, vol. 6 [Lincoln: University of Nebraska Press, 1989], pp. 3–4 *et passim*).

labically.[136] The *Declaratio*'s set of values, ranging from 1 to 243 simplae, is equivalent to those of Phillipotus and the *Tractatus de figuris*, which range from 1 to 243 minimae, but there is a different orientation and a signal innovation here: a value has been introduced that is smaller than the minima of de Muris and de Vitry. Toward the end of the century, in the treatise of Walsingham, discomfort was still being voiced over the addition of this value to the classic set of five.[137]

In this third line of development, there was an erosion of the full sense of the gradus concept. Rather than referring to a set of relationships involving two figures and three values, the grade or level simply refers to a place in a series held by a notational figure—or in other words to the equation of one name and one figure with a whole set of values. This ultimately stems from such condensations of the gradus system of de Muris as his own *Compendium* of ca. 1322, with its emphasis on the five "partes prolacionis."[138] In the *Declaratio*, Torkesey introduced a potent visual image, the triangle or shield, by which to represent the proportions of the note values of mensurable music, displaying the full array of values in the system. The term *gradus* does not play a central role in Torkesey's treatise, but it would appear from its single use that the various grades or levels are adjacent rows in his diagram.[139] Versions of the triangle exist with six, seven, and eight rows. These may be compared in table 5.

---

[136]Torkesey, *Declaratio*, cap. III, lns. 14–15 (ed. Gilles and Reaney), p. 59.

[137]Walsingham, *Regulae* (ed. Reaney), p. 74: "Et nunc addita est species sexta quae crocheta vocatur, et ad nil deserviret si compositores utique circumspicerentur, quia ultra minimam non est ulterius de iure divisio facienda (And now a sixth species is added, which is called the crocheta, and it is worth nothing, in any case, to survey composers [i.e., they use it, even if they should not], because by right there is no further division making beyond the least [minima])"; and (p. 81): "Sed nunc addita est ulterius, id est ultra minimam, scilicet non per artem sed per placitum, quae dicitur crocheta (And now a further is added, that is, beyond the least [minima], certainly not by art but by preference, which is called the crocheta)."

[138]de Muris, *Notitia artis musicae* (ed. Michels), pp. 111–46.

[139]Torkesey, *Declaratio*, cap. III, ln. 3 (ed. Gilles and Reaney), p. 59.

Table 5. Figures and values in the Triangle of Torkesey.

### Six figures

| | | | | | | |
|---|---|---|---|---|---|---|
| simpla | 1 | | | | | |
| minima | 2 | 3 | | | | |
| semibrevis | 4 | 6 | 9 | | | |
| brevis | 8 | 12 | 18 | 27 | | |
| longa | 16 | 24 | 36 | 54 | 81 | |
| larga | 32 | 48 | 772 | 108 | 162 | 243 |

Cambridge, Trinity College, O.9.29, f. 53v
London, British Library, Additional 21455, f. 8r
London, British Library, Lansdowne 763, f. 89v
Rome, Biblioteca Apostolica Vaticana, Reg. lat. 1146, f. 55v

### Seven figures

| | | | | | | | |
|---|---|---|---|---|---|---|---|
| simpla | 1 | | | | | | |
| minuta | 2 | 3 | | | | | |
| semibrevis | 4 | 6 | 9 | | | | |
| brevis | 8 | 12 | 18 | 27 | | | |
| longa | 16 | 24 | 36 | 54 | 81 | | |
| larga | 32 | 48 | 72 | 108 | 162 | 243 | |
| largissima | 64 | 96 | 144 | 216 | 324 | 486 | 729 |

Oxford, Bodleian Library, Bodley 842, f. 71v
Chicago, Newberry Library, 54.1, f. 9r

### Eight figures

| | | | | | | | | |
|---|---|---|---|---|---|---|---|---|
| minima | 1 | | | | | | | |
| duplex minor | 2 | 3 | | | | | | |
| simplex minor | 4 | 6 | 9 | | | | | |
| simplex medius | 8 | 12 | 18 | 27 | | | | |
| brevis | 16 | 24 | 36 | 54 | 81 | | | |
| simplex longa | 32 | 48 | 72 | 108 | 162 | 243 | | |
| duplex longa | 64 | 96 | 144 | 216 | 324 | 486 | 729 | |
| triplex longa | 128 | 192 | 288 | 432 | 648 | 972 | 1458 | 2187 |

London, British Library, Additional 4909, f. 31r

Torkesey's position was subjected to modification. In the *Breviarium regulare musicae,* Willelmus expanded Torkesey's set of figures from six to seven by the addition of a *largissima* with a maximum value of 729 simplae. Though its inclusion by Willelmus clearly postdates the adoption of the simpla, Willelmus gives the rationale for its addition to the set of six figures of Torkesey that it allows him to have three species of longae and three of breves, plus the simpla, thus isolating the unit value outside a more symmetrical grouping akin to that of the second line of development.[140] The text of the *Breviarium* includes a Torkesey triangle with an added row of values for this figure, which is precisely the same figure that Phillipotus had added to the five-figure system of de Muris. There are just a few traces of a seven-level system in other theoretical sources. The Wylde anonymous describes a seven-figure set identical to that of Willelmus, and a seven-level triangle just like the one in the *Breviarium* exists as an isolated musical illustration later in the same manuscript that preserves the treatise of Petrus of St.-Denis with its passage about Phillipotus (see table 4 and 5).[141]

Like Willelmus, Johannes Hanboys also takes as his point of departure the six-figure system of Torkesey. Hanboys, however, expands it not by one figure but by two—by an additional one at each end—to create a total of eight. His minima sits two levels below de Muris's smallest value, thus extending beyond Torkesey into previously unexplored territory. This new value, for which he adheres to the name minima, is declared to be "simplex" and "individuum," i.e., indivisible. In respect to the longa, his larga (of up to 2187 minimae) is two levels above. It is, therefore, precisely equivalent to the other largest maximum values just discussed, the *longissima* of Phillipotus and the *largissima* of the *Tractatus* or Willelmus. Hanboys's language suggests that he has the image of the triangle in his mind's eye. In a passage such as "Larga si sit perfecta ex omnibus perfectis, continet 3 duplices longas, 9 longas, 27 breves, 81 semibreves, 243 minores, 729 semiminores, 2187 minimas," he could be reading right off the diagonal of such a diagram. The only known representation of an eight-figure system by means of a triangle, however, is an anonymous diagram that apparently was interpolated into Version A of the *Quatuor principalia* (see table 5). This diagram has a unique set of names with only a distant kinship to those of Hanboys.[142]

---

[140]The terminology of Willelmus shows the influence of Torkesey in the use of *simpla* and of Odington in the use of the term *minuta* as a stratagem to avoid the word *minima*.

[141]Chicago, Newberry Library, Ms. 54.1, f. 9r; see Kurt von Fischer, "Eine wiederaufgefundene Theoretikerhandschrift des späten 14. Jahrhunderts," *Schweizer Beiträge zur Musikwissenschaft* 1 (1972): 26. The triangle is not, however, identical to that of Torkesey, as reported (i.e., with six levels), but rather has seven levels. For a facsimile, see *Tractatus figurarum* (ed. Schreur), frontispiece.

[142]Since the diagram is found in **GB-Lbl**, Additional 4909 in association with version A of the *Quatuor principalia*, it might pre-date 1351 (if that may be reliably taken as the date of Version B). It could, however, merely be an interpolation by the scribe of those leaves of **GB-Lbl**, Cotton Tiberius B.IX,

Hanboys's adherence to larga and minima for the absolutely largest and smallest values is noteworthy. He avoids altogether the most frequently encountered terms for semiminima or smallest value favored in English treatises, i.e., simpla or crocheta, and retains the term *larga* for the largest value, thereby avoiding superlatives at the expense of retaining *duplex longa* (which in view of its name might, ironically, represent a ternary value) as the term for the figure between longa and larga. Hanboys is unique in his avoidance of sets of names like longa—longior—longissima or brevis—brevior—brevissima, both in respect to the longa-brevis dichotomy and as a style of naming using comparatives and superlatives. In this light, it is interesting to recall that Willelmus specifically justified his extension to seven figures by the desire to have three kinds of longae and three of breves, with the unit value, the simpla, standing to one side. Hanboys may have added an eighth figure in order to create a symmetry around brevis and semibrevis instead of around longa and brevis, with three levels below (minor, semiminor, minima) and three above (longa, duplex longa, larga). It may also be that these theorists wanted a system in which the irreducible unit value was smaller than whatever smallest value was in widespread use. This would imply that at the time Hanboys wrote, the crocheta or simpla (i.e., semiminima, Hanboys's semiminor) had begun to be employed in musical sources. Though this event does not provide a firm date, it would associate the *Summa* temporally with three important English musical sources of the latter part of the fourteenth century: New York, Pierpont Morgan Library, 978; Oxford, Corpus Christi College, 144; and Cambridge, Gonville and Caius College, 230, in each of which there are large-scale cantilenas employing ornamental flagged semiminimae.

*Concerning puncti*

Having introduced the *punctus perfectionis* at the beginning of chapter 3, Hanboys enters on an explanatory digression beginning with the "modern" observation that there are two kinds of puncti, the *punctus perfectionis* and the *punctus divisionis*, a formulation that he may owe to de Muris's *Libellus cantus mensurabilis* (ca. 1340). He describes a unique, fourfold use of the *punctus perfectionis* (before, after, above, below) that has distant counterparts only in obscure doctrines of the earlier de Muris and Torkesey, and he describes the twofold use of the *punctus divisionis*: either to divide one mode from another (echoing Franco, Odington, and Handlo) or to separate perfections and thus indicate alteration. A punctus may indicate both per-

---

which are reportedly copied in a hand of the second half of the fourteenth century (see the manuscript description *infra*, pp. 66–71).

fection and division, in that order. In chapter 13, there are echoes of Hanboys's fourfold use of the *punctus perfectionis* in another, similar interpolation. This is a paragraph on the use of the circle, stimulated by mention of the *signum rotundum* in Garlandian notation, which describes the employment of a circle not only in front of a note (to indicate perfection of the brevis, i.e., as the typical mensuration sign for *tempus perfectum*), but also above or below it (for reasons that are not so clear).

## Concerning the duplex longa

At the end of chapter 6, there is a kind of coda, appended to the very end of the discussion of the duplex longa, in which a contrast is made between what some say in Hanboys's day about this figure (not, however, including Hanboys himself) and what some formerly said. It is not clear who is being discussed in either case; Hanboys does not identify the contemporaries he has in mind and they could be English or continental. In respect to the older doctrine, he does, however, make specific reference to Franco: "ut patet hic per Franchonem," though it is unclear whether this statement is intended to cover simply the next two or all of the next eight examples. In any event, none of the subsequent text originates in either the *Ars cantus mensurabilis* or the *Gaudent moderni* tradition. It is probably indebted, instead, to some treatment of the duplex longa such as is found in a number of anonymous treatises of the early *ars nova*. The reference to Franco might indicate that this material was to be found in Hanboys's exemplar of the *Regule*.

## Concerning the semibrevis

Hanboys devotes four chapters to the semibrevis (chapters 12–15), only the first and last of which follow his general pattern of exposition. Chapter 12 introduces this figure and discusses its value and effect when mixed with longae and breves, following Handlo's Rubric IV up through the material on Petrus de Cruce (excising reference to Petrus le Viser) with glosses attributable to Hanboys that only slightly modernize Handlo's comments. Chapter 15, a natural continuation of chapter 12, discusses alteration and diminishment of the semibreve according to the moderns. Chapters 13 and 14, on the other hand, are "lumps" in the present sense and could be omitted without doing violence to Hanboys's overall outline. They are, however, of great intrinsic interest, for they describe semibrevis practice "among the ancients" as it developed in England after Johannes de Garlandia, and they discuss notations that appear in insular sources.

Chapter 13 begins as a continuation of chapter 12, in that Hanboys continues to reproduce Handlo's Rubric IV, presenting the material on Johannes de Garlandia lightly edited and glossed. Whereas in the notation of Garlandia according to Handlo, the stem on the major semibrevis descends obliquely, in the *Summa*, Garlandia's major semibrevis stem is said to descend beneath, and the example shows it descending vertically. The Garlandian passage is followed by Handlo's Rubric V in its entirety, with a concluding gloss by Hanboys contradicting Handlo's conclusions on what notes can be mixed with what, based on up-to-date doctrines about diminishment by remote values. The retention of the material on Garlandia must be interpreted as an affirmation of his significance for the English tradition. This is reinforced by the final part of chapter 13, in which Hanboys introduces two more explicit ways to differentiate visually Garlandia's four kinds of semibreves (the major, minor, minorata, and minima) by means of new figures, not simply by signs. These are attributed to the Englishmen W. de Doncastre and Robertus Trowell. Trowell cannot be further identified, and his notation is found in no surviving practical sources.[143]

Doncastre comes a little more clearly into focus, and he may perhaps be identified with a Dominican friar who was at Cambridge in the early 1340s.[144] Whether or not this is our man, there is an intensely scholastic flavor to the chain of syllogisms, with their Aristotelian premises regarding contrariety, that are propounded in defense of his note shapes (chapter 13 [268.26–272.13]). The manner of presentation suggests that Doncastre is a man of the schools or university and that Hanboys is quoting or closely paraphrasing him, either from lecture notes or a treatise now lost.

The sole surviving composition with a notation corresponding to that of Doncastre is the motet *Beatus vir–Benedicamus Domino* (**GB**-Lwa 12185, 3), which immediately follows the Garlandian *Hac a valle* in the same West-

---

[143]The notation of the fourteenth-century English motet *Triumphus patet* may be yet a third attempt to differentiate Garlandia's smaller semibreves by using signs to create distinct figures. See Lefferts, *The Motet in England*, pp. 149–50 and figure 46. It is apparent in all of these post-Garlandian systems that their inventors are not concerned with stabilizing a set of figures and keeping that order, which is so marked a feature of the doctrines of de Muris, de Vitry, and Hanboys.

[144]A William de Doncastre (Dancastre) of about the right age was ordained an acolyte at the Dominican convent at Cambridge in 1345, and records trace his promotion to subdeacon, deacon, and priest at various convents of the Black Friars over the next year and a half. He was probably born ca. 1320/25. See Alfred B. Emden, *A Survey of Dominicans in England Based on the Ordination Lists in Episcopal Registers (1268–1538)* (Rome: Istituto Storico Domenicano Santa Sabina, 1967), p. 326; and idem, *Biographical Register of the University of Cambridge*, p. 177.

minster Abbey manuscript.[145] In *Beatus vir*, as in *Hac a valle*, the stem on the major semibrevis descends directly and the major semibrevis always precedes the minor; in contrast to Garlandian precepts, the minorata precedes rather than follows the minima.[146] In this motet there are *ars nova* notational devices not treated in Hanboys's presentation: the brevis is sometimes perfect and sometimes imperfect, and red notation is used; further, the minor semibrevis is occasionally replaced by four minimae, implying the existence of a semiminima.[147]

Chapter 14 continues the presentation of semibrevis practices according to "some of the ancients," but it is unclear whether Hanboys is glossing an older text at this point or systematically explaining English customs. Throughout this chapter, Hanboys stresses that the practices he is recording are those of the past, to be contrasted with those of today in the new fashion of the moderns. The older authorities are nowhere identified but might be described as of the early *ars nova* period. In respect to division of the brevis, the doctrines of Garlandia, Doncastre, and Trowell discussed in chapter 13 imply a mensural organization akin to that of de Vitry's *tempus perfectum maior* or Marchetto's *novenaria*, since the brevis can be subdivided into three minor semibreves or nine minimae. In chapter 14, Hanboys reviews the English equivalents of the other three French prolations (though this is not his terminology, and conceptually he is still dividing the brevis, not adding up minimae), beginning with the perfect brevis in minor prolation, then the imperfect brevis in major prolation, and finally the imperfect brevis in minor prolation. These mensurations employ major, equal, and minor semibreves of fluctuating value. The perfect brevis of as many as six semibreves can be divided into three semibreves or four semibreves consisting of two majors and two equals or five semibreves consisting of one major and four equals or six equals. This mensuration is akin to de Vitry's *medium tempus perfectum* or Marchetto's *senaria per-*

---

[145]For a transcription of *Beatus vir*, see appendix II.

[146]Doncastre's minoratas have an obliquely descending stem and always precede the unstemmed minima. Thus his minorata-minima pair has the appearance of Garlandia's major-minor pair as described by Handlo. On Doncastre's notation, see also Lefferts, *The Motet in England*, pp. 127–29 and figure 35 (where, it should be noted, the publisher's art staff inadvertently clipped away the shapes of Doncastre's maior, minor, minorata, and minima).

[147]*Beatus vir* also has a relatively sophisticated numerical phrase scheme. All in all, a date in the 1340s for this motet, roughly contemporary with the Dominican Doncastre, seems plausible.

*fecta*.[148] Hanboys spends little time on the imperfect brevis with perfect semibreves akin to de Vitry's *tempus imperfectum maius* or Marchetto's *senaria imperfecta*,[149] devoting but a single example to it. The final mensuration, with an imperfect brevis consisting of imperfect semibreves, is akin to de Vitry's *tempus imperfectum minor* but more comparable to Marchetto's *quaternaria* and *octonaria*, for it is further subdivided depending on whether there are four equals (*curta mensura*) or as many as eight equals per brevis (*longa mensura*).[150] If there are three semibreves per brevis in *curta mensura*, the larger one is simply called a semibrevis and the two smaller ones are "minor equals"; if there are four, all are equals. More complex patterns occur in *longa mensura* when four to seven semibreves replace a brevis. Hanboys describes them in terms of majors (also called simply semibreves, worth two or three of the smallest value), equals (worth one or two of the smallest values), and minors (the smallest values). Hanboys further describes these patterns in terms of their interpretation by the moderns, for whom, "when in *longa mensura*, that which is employed for a brevis comprises the value of a longa (282.1–2)." The very extent of this discussion underlines its evident practical importance in Hanboys's eyes, and indeed, these peculiarly English forms of binary mensuration are frequently found in musical sources of the fourteenth century.

Chapter 15 resumes the normal course of presentation of the *Summa*, with the exception of an interpolation prompted by the discussion of the alteration of semibreves. Robertus de Brunham provides four alternative means of indicating the standard Franconian assignment of alteration to the second of paired semibreves. For each of these four ways, however, Hanboys raises an objection to Brunham, quoting Franco. The first three ways can be understood as involving binary ligatures with propriety and perfection (brevis-longa) to which the stem indicating opposite propriety has been given, reducing both values while retaining the 1:2 proportions (minor semibrevis-major semibrevis). The fourth of Brunham's ways to indicate alteration involves the use of a *cauda yrundinis* (two strokes in the shape of a swallow's tail) to indicate the larger value. This provokes Hanboys's sharpest reproof, couched in a syllogism the major premise of which ("frustra fit per plura quod fieri potest per pauciora"[151])—here attributed to the Philosopher

---

[148]See Group B of the English circle-stem notational complex in Lefferts, *The Motet in England*, pp. 124–31, table 19, and figures 35–36.

[149]See ibid., Group C.

[150]See ibid., Groups D (i) and Group D (ii).

[151]"It is bad to do with more what can be done with less (290.1–2)."

(again, presumably, Aristotle)—is none other than the classic expression of the famous nominalist law of parsimony known as Ockham's razor.

Brunham is perhaps the most influential of the individuals identified by name in the *Summa*.[152] His ligature shapes and *cauda yrundinis* for indicating alteration (chapter 15), and his forms for rests (chapter 21), all appear in the practical sources of fourteenth-century English polyphony. He probably flourished in the second quarter of the century since his name and innovations are not mentioned in Handlo's *Regule* of 1326. On the basis of the rests he proposes, it is apparent that he advocates a six-figure system akin to that of Torkesey, and indeed he is identified as the author of Torkesey's *Declaratio* in one of its sources. Hanboys's disdain for Brunham's *cauda yrundinis* is shared by the author of the *Quatuor principalia*, in a passage appearing in both versions—and strengthened in vehemence in Version B. But the rationale for Brunham's innovations is clear: they were undoubtedly a serious effort to unambiguously specify the Franconian rhythmic alternative for paired semibreves (1+2) in the face of an insular tradition that customarily assumed the opposite rhythm (2+1), and in this light, it is important that they clearly were still worthy of Hanboys's attention and rebuke at the time of the *Summa*. Brunham's ligature shapes and cauda are transmitted anonymously (and with disapproval) at least as late as the *Regulae* of Thomas Walsingham.

*Concerning rests*

After the minima is treated in chapter 18, there follow two condensed and unexceptional chapters on ligatures that draw on the *Regule* and the *Ars cantus mensurabilis*. Hanboys's discussion of rests in chapter 21, however, is far from perfunctory. He reviews a total of four different systems, the first of which is an *ars antiqua* set: the five rests of Franco. The other three sets are of the *ars nova*, beginning with a system of eight rests according to the moderns: the familiar six shapes of de Vitry and de Muris for perfect and imperfect longa, brevis, semibrevis (the perfect semibrevis rest has a peculiarly English form, straddling the line), and minima, plus forms hooked to the right and left

---

[152]Robertus de Brunham is identified as "frater" by Hanboys and by a manuscript of the *Declaratio trianguli et scuti* (ed. Gilles and Reaney, p. 36 and n. 8, with reference to Cambridge, Trinity College, O.9.29, ff. 53v and 94), in which its authorship is ascribed to Brunham rather than to Johannes Torkesey. Brunham is a place-name, a variant of Burnham, the name of a number of towns in Buckinghamshire, Lincolnshire, etc., but this information brings us no closer to an identification. See also Lefferts, *The Motet in England*, pp. 138–39 and 152; and Bent, "A Preliminary Assessment," pp. 68 and 70.

for smaller values. Next to be described is a distinctive set of ten rests for the perfect and imperfect forms of a six-figure system according to Robert of Brunham. Finally, Hanboys proposes his own system, with eight rests corresponding to his eight figures; in a radical departure from custom, each rest is subject in the same way as its corresponding figure to perfection and imperfection, alteration and diminution.[153]

### In Summary

Hanboys is emphatic about his modernity. He speaks of today (*hodie*), of the new (*de novo modo*), of what the "moderni" do and what the "antiqui" did. His is essentially a French *ars nova* posture, a modernity of the mid-fourteenth century (not of the mid-fifteenth), with preoccupations that include the extension of note forms by the addition of new figures instead of signs; the indivisibility of the minima and the concept of gradus; the importance of the duplex longa and even bigger values; rests for all these new figures; alteration and imperfection; diminishment by remote values; *puncti perfectionis* that are, in effect, *puncti additionis*; binary mensuration; mensuration signs; and syncopation in binary and ternary mensurations. There is no explicit acknowledgement of French theorists in the *Summa*, but the concept of gradus, the argument for renaming figures, and the quotation of some common maxims associate Hanboys with the earlier authorities Johannes de Muris, Philippe de Vitry and even Jacques de Liège. These characteristics are indicative, at the very least, of a shared intellectual culture.

The *Summa* documents the extent to which English musicians went their own way—or rather a plurality of ways—after Petrus de Cruce, guided by the ultimate authority of Franco and the multiplication and subdivision of breves. These fourteenth-century English notational systems are roughly equivalent to the developments of Parisians and Italians but independent of them. Hanboys's text yields references to at least two or three previous generations of musicians and four or more systems, not necessarily strung chronologically one after the other along a single track. In particular, we learn about Johannes de Garlandia (through Handlo's *Regule*) and the extension of his concepts by W. de Doncastre and Robertus Trowell; we encounter more indirectly the six-figure systems of Johannes Torkesey and the innovative Robertus de Brunham; and we are taken through the four mensurations of the brevis in perfect and imperfect time (including *curta* and *longa mensura*) of certain unidentified *antiqui*. The paragraphs in chapter 2 about renaming the

---

[153]See Lefferts, *The Motet in England*, pp. 151–52 and figure 47.

crocheta and minima in a six-figure system seem to draw upon previous theoretical work by Hanboys himself; some other lumps in the text may also be from this posited earlier work. The *Summa* is rich in original formulations of many sorts, the most obscure of which include certain workings of the *punctus perfectionis* (chapters 7 and 19), the fourfold placement of puncti (chapter 3), the threefold use of the circle (chapter 13), certain ways to interpret mixtures of breves and longae (chapters 7 and 11), various systems of rests (chapter 21), and the diminishment of altered values by extensive chains of ever-smaller notes.

It is by no means clear that Hanboys is representative of an insular mainstream. He is certainly writing after the abandonment by his moderns of most distinctive English notations and the general adoption of French *ars nova* practices, including use of the syllabic minima and ornamental semiminima. But his moderns may be in the minority—an avant-garde. The very intensity with which he argues certain points indicates that these are issues of relevance and debate. At four moments of most rigorous argument, Hanboys launches into syllogisms and quotes his most telling maxims. These moments are the renaming of minima and crocheta in chapter 2, the shapes of Doncastre's figures in chapter 13, the refutation of Brunham's ligatures and *cauda* in chapter 14, and the justification of Hanboys's minima-shape in chapter 18. It is evident that music using older notations was still being written, or at any rate performed, and quite likely there were treatises representative of the older generations that still had to be addressed, even if they had been superseded.[154]

This prompts the following hypothesis: if Hanboys was an associate of an elite company of musicians in service to Edward III and the Black Prince in the middle years of the century, and if the *Summa* may be tentatively put at ca. 1370, then perhaps he was born ca. 1310–20, was an adult in the early years of the development of gradus theory by the English, and produced the *Summa* as a mature late work with earlier formulations behind it. If he was indeed the contemporary of J. de Corbe and G. Martini honored by mention in the motet *Sub arturo plebs* for his *theorica*, then the *Summa* may well be a

---

[154]Despite the hostility to the *cauda yrundinis* in the *Quatuor principalia*, in the *Summa*, and probably also in Walsingham's *Regule*, it continues to appear in sources up to the end of the century (see Lefferts, *The Motet in England*, pp. 138–39 and table 21). Similarly, despite the diatribe by Hanboys against Brunham's ligature shapes, they also appear in late fourteenth-century sources contemporaneous with or later than the *Summa* (see Lefferts, *The Motet in England*, p. 138 and figure 40).

part of this discourse, and its most immediate audience of *moderni*, the musicians named in that motet so remarkably advanced for its day.

## The Manuscripts

Descriptions of all three manuscripts will appear in the forthcoming RISM volume (B/III/v) devoted to music treatises in English libraries, edited by Michel Huglo and Christian Meyer. Extensive, excellent descriptions of **GB-Lbl**, Cotton Tiberius B.IX and Additional 4909, which are corrected or augmented here only in small details, are given in Fritz Reckow, ed., *Der Musiktraktat des Anonymus 4*, 2 vols., Beihefte zum *Archiv für Musikwissenschaft*, vols. 4–5 (Wiesbaden: Franz Steiner, 1967), 1:7–18.

### C

London, British Library, Cotton Tiberius B.IX

Parchment; 237 fragmentary leaves, greater than 210x150 mm
England, 14th–early 15th century; foliated 1–236 with 118*

1. *Tabulae planetarum de radicibus et motibus.*[155] *Inc.*: "Tabulae chronologicae continentes annos expansos et reductos Latinorum, Aegyptiorum, Graecorum, Arabum, et Persarum, cum eorundem mensium nominibus et mensuris, et motu solis, lunae, aliorumque planetarum." (ff. 1r–4v)
2. Registers of W. Cratfield (1390–1415) and W. Exeter (1415–1429), abbots of Bury St. Edmunds.[156] (ff. 5r–203v)
3. Robertus de Handlo, *Regule.*[157] *Inc.*: "Incipiunt Regulae cum Maximis Magistri Franconis cum additionibus aliorum Musicorum compilatae a roberto de Handlo ..." *Exp.*: "... Expliciunt Regulae cum additionibus, finitae die Veneris proximo ante Pentecost Anno Domini Millesimo Tricentesimo Vicesimo Sexto et caetera. Amen." (once prior to f. 204)

---

[155]Dee M95, item p; Smith, *Catalogus*, no. 1 (for Dee numbers, see n. 170 *infra*).

[156]Smith, *Catalogus*, no. 2. Listed in Godfrey R. Davis, *Medieval Cartularies of Great Britain: A Short Catalogue* (London: Longmans, 1958), no. 128.

[157]Dee M72, item a; Smith, *Catalogus*, no. 3. See **GB-Lbl**, Additional 4909, item 1.

4. Anonymous, *Tractatus figurarum*.[158] *Inc*.: "Alius Tractatulus de Musica Incerto Authore. Incipit Tractatus diversarum Figurarum per quas dulces modi discantantur et ideo sequendo ordinem tenoris scilicet alterius temporis secundum Magistrum Egidium de Muris vel de Morino ..." *Exp*.: "... quia non potest dividi nisi in duas partes, et si quatuor ascenderent usque octo et unus sic deficeretis. Sic itaque ad completionem hujus operis consecutus sum, et ideo refero gratias Deo. Amen." (once prior to f. 204)

Additional section (epilogue on *traynour*, etc.) *Inc*.: "Superius dictum est de Diminutione et augmentatione Figurarum, Nunc videndum est qualiter ipsas ordinabis ad discantandum ..." *Exp*.: "... de tempore imperfecto minore et de semibrevibus perfectis."

5. Anonymous, *De modo componendi tenores motettorum*.[159] *Inc*.: "primo accipe Tenorem acutus antiphone vel responsorii ..." *Exp*.: "... Si majores Subtilitates habere volueris quam in isto volumine continentur, tunc stude fortiter in Musica, et forte Deus dabit tibi per suam gratiam majorem intellectum atque Subtilitatem." (once prior to f. 204)

6. Anon., *Quatuor principalia*.[160] (ff. 204r–214r)

Introduction and *Primum principale* (Version A). *Inc*.: "Alius Tractatulus de Musica, Incerto Authore. Pro aliquali notitia de Musica habenda. Primo, videndum est quid sit Musica, et unde dicatur. Secundo, quae ejus partes ..." *Exp*.: "... vide Orphei et Amphionis modulationes, ac alias Musicae virtutes quas ponit Macrobius de sompno Scipionis, libro $2^{do}$. Ex hiis omnibus praecedentibus colligo hanc divisionem sequentem: ⟨exemplum sequitur⟩." (once prior to f. 204)

Fragment of *Secundum principale* (Version A), from near the beginning.[161] *Inc*.: "Secundo. Principaliter videndum est, primo, de Arte Musicae ac Elementorum sive Literarum quae Claves vocantur inventione ..." *Exp*.: "... sesquetertius est tunc sequitur quinarius numerus minor est quaternario et quaternarius ternario et ternarius numerus binario et binarius numerus minor est unitate et sic sequitur quod in

---

[158]Not separately numbered by Smith. See **GB**-Lbl, Additional 4909, item 2.

[159]Not separately numbered by Smith. See **GB**-Lbl, Additional 4909, item 3.

[160]Smith, *Catalogus*, no. 4. See **GB**-Lbl, Additional 4909, item 4. Reckow, ed., *Der Musiktraktat des Anonymus 4*, 1:11, judges the hand to be of the late fourteenth century.

[161]By comparison with the copy in **GB**-Lbl, Additional 4909, ff. 20v–26v, it can be determined that the surviving text corresponds to that on ff. 21v–24v.

majoribus numeris minor est proportio et in minoribus numeris minor proportio continetur." (ff. 204r–204v)

Fragment of *Tertium principale* (Version A), including the end.[162] *Inc.*: "In superioribus particulis dictum est de divisione Musicae, de ejus etiam inventione ac de proportionibus ad Monacordi divisionem pertinentibus, in ista parte declarandum est de plano cantu qui in quinque consistit. Prima est ..." *Exp.*: "... Ex praedictis vero Tredecim speciebus nulla in numerorum Musicalium proportione recipitur praeter Tonum quae est in Sesqueoctava proportione, et dyatessaron quae est in sesquetertia proportione, et diapente quae est in sesquealtera proportione et diapason quae semper duplam proportionem, ut superius in Secundo principali Capitulo et cetera." (ff. 205r–v)

Text in a second hand.[163] *Inc.*: "⟨exemplum trianguli⟩. 1a. Omnis nota praeter simplam carent puncto omnino imperfecta est. ..." *Exp.*: "... Omnis nota quae post se punctum habet omnimo perfecta dicitur, quia et ipsa perfecta est, et omnes partes ipsam oblique componentes omnino perfecte sunt excepta sola simpla quae est inpartibilis." (f. 205v)

*Quartum principale* (Version A), nearly intact from beginning to end and in large measure legible. *Inc.*: "Dictis aliquibus circa planum cantum, restat aliud dicendum de cantu sive Musica mensurabili, circa quod primo dicendum est de quantitate Musicae mensurabilis, secundo de divisione ..." *Exp.*: "... Et haec de Musicae continuae et etiam discretae principiis sufficiant ad praesens, que tanto ut credo acceptiora sunt quanto aliorum dictis concordiam habent nam in isto libello nichil apposui quod non ab auctoritatibus et a Magistris peritis et approbatis mediante gratia Dei addici. Explicit." (ff. 206r–214r; f. 214v blank)

7. Anonymous, *De mensuris et discantu*.[164] *Inc.*: "Cognita modulatione melorum secundum viam octo troporum et secundum usum consuetudinem Fidei Catholicae ..." *Exp.*: "... In nomine et honore sanctissimi mediatoris omnium, qui est verus salvator, Jesus Christus, filius

---

[162]By comparison with the copy in **GB**-Lbl, Additional 4909, ff. 26v–31r, it can be determined that the surviving text corresponds to that on ff. 28v–31r.

[163]From what is legible of the surviving charred fragments, it is apparent that the accompanying diagram (now lost) must have been entered on a blank page, which suggests that the four *principalia* were written in independent gatherings. See also *infra*, n. 177.

[164]Smith, *Catalogus*, no. 5. Reckow, ed. *Der Musiktraktat des Anonymus 4*, 1:11, reports that Neil R. Ker dated the hand of items 7 and 8 (ff. 215r–224v) to the third quarter of the fourteenth century. See also **GB**-Lbl, Additional 4909, item 5.

dei vivi, et qui est corona et gloria omnium sanctorum ad quam gloriam possumus omnes pervenire cum sanctissimo." (ff. 215r–224r)

8. Anonymous, *De sinemenis*.[165] *Inc.*: "Sequitur de sinemenis sic ..." *Exp.*: "... Omnis spiritus laudet Dominum etc. cuncta bona etc. Explicit." (ff. 224r–224v)

9. *Liber Divisionum Mahumeti Bag-dadini*.[166] (ff. 225v–229r)

10. *Rogeri Baconi liber de speculis comburentibus cum figuris*.[167] (ff. 230v–235r; f. 235v blank)

11. Moralizing leoninian hexameters (f. 236r–v); f. 236v overwitten with "De loquacitate."[168]

This composite manuscript, which passed into the British Museum with the Cotton collection in 1753, was greatly damaged in the fire that engulfed the Cottonian Library at Ashburnham House in Westminster on 23 October 1731. As bound by Cotton, the manuscript had 272 folios; the portion prior to f. 204v that contained the *Regule* of Handlo was entirely lost in the fire. The contents of the manuscript, however, are traceable from the sixteenth century and—bound together as they were subsequently preserved in Cotton's library—were catalogued in the seventeenth century.[169] The musical portions were transcribed for Dr. Johann Christoph Pepusch (1667–1752) before the fire. That transcription survives in **GB**-Lbl, Additional 4909, which is inventoried below.

The prior history of some of the components of **GB**-Lbl, Cotton Tiberius B.IX can be traced back to the middle of the sixteenth century, at which time they were bound in two different manuscripts (M72 and M95) in the library of John Dee (1527–1608), the great Elizabethan mathematician, astronomer, alchemist, and astrologer.[170] Dee's manuscript M72 contained the musical

---

[165]Not separately numbered by Smith, but rather subsumed under his no. 5. See also **GB**-Lbl, Additional 4909, item 6.

[166]Dee M95, item q; Smith, *Catalogus*, no. 6.

[167]Dee M95, item s; Smith, *Catalogus*, no. 7.

[168]See Reckow, ed., *Der Musiktraktat des Anonymus 4*, 1:11–12.

[169]For **GB**-Lbl, Harley 694 and Smith, *Catalogus*, see n. 24 *supra*.

[170]For these manuscript reference numbers and the information in this paragraph, I am indebted to Richard J. Roberts and Andrew G. Watson, *John Dee's Library Catalogue* (London: The Bibliographical Society, forthcoming). Professor Watson graciously shared information with me from this monograph prior to its publication. On Dee's library catalogues in general, see also James O. Halliwell, *The Diary of Dr. John Dee*, Camden Society, o.s. 19 (London: Camden Society, 1842); and Montague R. James, *Lists of Manuscripts Formerly Owned by Dr. John Dee*, Supplement to the Biblio-

treatises listed as items 3–8 of the present inventory, along with a group of scientific treatises. It was apparently acquired by him from William Dussing and was in his possession by 1556, when it appeared in a list of the contents of his library as "De musica Libri varii." In a later inventory of Dee's library, compiled in 1583, the identification of the contents of M72 begins "Magistri Franconis Regulae Musicales cum additionibus aliorum musicorum, collectis a Roberto de Handlo." After Dee's death, litigation prevented dispersal of his library until 1625/26. Upon its sale, M72 was probably acquired directly either by Sir Robert Cotton, who then gave the scientific treatises (which survive as **GB**-Lbl, Harley 80) to the antiquarian and collector Sir Simonds D'Ewes (1602–1650), or by D'Ewes, who then gave the music treatises to Cotton. Other items bound into **GB**-Lbl, Cotton Tiberius B.IX (items 1, 9, and 10) were to be found earlier in Dee's library as a part of his manuscript M95, an Oxford book once owned by Simon Bredon of Merton College that Bredon bequeathed to Merton in 1372. At the dispersal of Dee's library in 1625/26, M95 was probably acquired directly either by Cotton, who then gave parts of it to D'Ewes and Thomas Allen (1542–1632), or it went directly to D'Ewes, who detached and kept one part and gave the remainder to Cotton.

The composite manuscript **GB**-Lbl, Cotton Tiberius B.IX was assembled by Cotton from parts of M72 and M95, with the addition of the Bury St. Edmunds registers (item 2), at some time between 1625/26 and his death in 1631. The fascicle of musical treatises may have borne some evidence of an association with Bury St. Edmunds that caused Cotton to have it bound with the Bury registers. This is pure speculation, though—slim grounds for suggesting a Bury origin for the treatises. Another composite manuscript, however, that contains items 7 and 8 (**GB**-Lbl, Royal 12.C.vi) was apparently procured for Bury St. Edmunds in the fourteenth century by Henry of

---

graphical Society's Transactions, vol. 1 (Oxford: Bibliographical Society, 1921). For the particularly convoluted histories of M72 and M95, see also Andrew G. Watson, "Sir Robert Cotton and Sir Simonds D'Ewes: An Exchange of Manuscripts," *British Museum Quarterly* 30 (1962): 19–24; idem, "The Provenance of J. Dee's MS of the *De superficienum divisionibus* of Machometus Bagdedinus," *Isis* 64, no. 223 (1973): 382–83; idem, "A Merton College MS. Reconstructed: Harley 625; Digby 178, ff. 1–14, 88–115; Cotton Tib. B.IX, ff. 1–4, 225–35," *Bodleian Library Record* 9 (1976): 207–17; and idem, "Thomas Allen of Oxford and His Manuscripts," in *Medieval Scribes, Manuscripts and Libraries: Essays Presented to N. R. Ker*, ed. Malcolm B. Parkes and Andrew G. Watson (London: Scolar Press, 1978), pp. 279–314.

Kirkestede (fl. 1338–78). The Cotton manuscript version of item 7 (copied in a hand that has been dated to the third quarter of the fourteenth century) can be shown to be descended from the Royal manuscript version (copied in a hand of the late thirteenth century). If the relationship is direct, it perhaps therefore originated at Bury.[171]

## A1

### London, British Library, Additional 4909

Paper; 106 leaves (originally paginated 1–211), 384x244 mm
England, early 18th century

1. Robertus de Handlo, *Regule*.[172] *Inc.*: "Incipiunt Regulae cum Maximis Magistri Franconis cum additionibus aliorum Musicorum compilatae a Roberto de Handlo ..." *Exp.*: "... Expliciunt Regulae cum additionibus, finitae die Veneris proximo ante Pentecost Anno Domini Millesimo Tricentesimo Vicesimo Sexto et caetera. Amen." (ff. 1r–11r)
2. Anonymous, *Tractatus figurarum*.[173] *Inc.*: "Alius Tractatulus de Musica Incerto Authore. Incipit Tractatus diversarum Figurarum per

---

[171]The second half of this paragraph is dependent on Edward Roesner, "The Origins of W1," *Journal of the American Musicological Society* 29 (1976): 379, n. 199. See also Reckow, ed., *Der Musiktraktat des Anonymus 4*, 1:1–18.

[172]CS, 1:383a–403b, and this edition. Copied from now lost folios of **GB-Lbl**, Cotton Tiberius B.IX.

[173]CS, 3:118a–123b, where it is called *Tractatus de diversis figuris* and attributed to Philippus de Caserta; for a new edition, see *Treatise on Noteshapes (Tractatus figurarum)* (ed. Schreur). Our manuscript identifies the treatise as "secundum Magistrum Egidium de Muris vel de Morino," which may indicate a confusion between Johannes de Muris and Egidius de Morino; Egidius is credited with its authorship in a number of other sources. Wulf Arlt concluded that the question of authorship must remain open ("Der Tractatus figurarum—ein Beitrag zur Musiklehre der 'ars subtilior,'" *Schweizer Beiträge zur Musikwissenschaft* 1 [1972]: 35–53). Philip Schreur, in his new edition in the present series (pp. 3–9), has reaffirmed the ambiguity of the evidence concerning attribution. Wathey ("The Peace of 1360–1369") has shown that when Louis de Male, the Count of Flanders, was in England in 1364 to negotiate a marriage contract for his daughter, one of the clerks in his chapel was Egidius de Murino. His presence provides one possible route of transmission for items 2 and 3 into England and for their association with Egidius. By not numbering this item or the next separately in the *Catalogus*,

quas dulces modi discantantur et ideo sequendo ordinem tenoris scilicet alterius temporis secundum Magistrum Egidium de Muris vel de Morino ..." *Exp.*: "... quia non potest dividi nisi in duas partes, et si quatuor ascenderent usque octo et unus sic deficeretis. Sic itaque ad completionem hujus operis consecutus sum, et ideo refero gratias Deo. Amen." (ff. 11v–14v)

Additional section (epilogue on *traynour*, etc.).[174] *Inc.*: "Superius dictum est de Diminutione et augmentatione Figurarum, Nunc videndum est qualiter ipsas ordinabis ad discantandum ..." *Exp.*: "... de tempore imperfecto minore et de semibrevibus perfectis." (f. 14v)

3. Anonymous, *De modo componendi tenores motettorum*.[175] *Inc.*: "primo accipe Tenorem acutus antiphone vel responsorii ..." *Exp.*: "... Si majores Subtilitates habere volueris quam in isto volumine continentur, tunc stude fortiter in Musica, et forte Deus dabit tibi per suam gratiam majorem intellectum atque Subtilitatem." (ff. 14v–17v)

4. Anonymous, *Quatuor principalia* (Version A).[176] (ff. 17v–56r)

---

Smith evidently held the impression from their presentation in **GB**-Lbl, Cotton Tiberius B.IX that they were a continuation of Handlo's treatise. The Pepusch scribe recognized this item as separate from the *Regule* but treated the next (*De modo componendi*) as its direct continuation, following his copy text in (now lost) folios of **GB**-Lbl, Cotton Tiberius B.IX. Several other sources of the *Tractatus figurarum* also conjoin it with the epilogue on *traynour* and the treatise on motets (see *Treatise on Noteshapes [Tractatus figurarum]* [ed. Schreur], p. 3 *et passim*).

[174]CS, 3:123b–124b; for a new edition, see *Treatise on Noteshapes (Tractatus figurarum)* (ed. Schreur), pp. 20–24 and 98–114.

[175]CS, 3:124a–128a, where it is called *Tractatus cantus mensurabilis* and attributed to Egidius de Morino. In several manuscripts, including the present one (whose copy text was [now lost] folios of **GB**-Lbl, Cotton Tiberius B.IX), this treatise is directly conjoined with item 2 and its epilogue on *traynour*, and associated with Egidius (see n. 173 *supra*). Here it lacks the appendix on secular songs that appears in other sources, for an edition of which, see CS, 3:128b.

[176]Copied from folios of **GB**-Lbl, Cotton Tiberius B.IX, some of which are now lost. Only the fourth and final part has been printed by Coussemaker from **GB**-Lbl, Additional 4909, as *De musica antiqua et nova* (Anonymous I of CS, 3:334a–364b). The anonymous *Pro aliquali notitia* and the subsequent *De musica antiqua et nova*, however, together comprise a complete early redaction, Version A, of the *Quatuor principalia*. Only the early cataloguers of the Cotton manuscripts and a few modern scholars, including Coussemaker, Hughes-Hughes, and Gilbert Reaney, have recognized that these items belong together. See, for instance, Gilbert Reaney, "Tunstede, Simon," *MGG* 13 (1966): 980. Lawrence Gushee's opinion that their relationship is questionable ("Anonymous Theoretical Writings," *New Grove Dictionary of*

*Inc.*: "Alius Tractatulus de Musica, Incerto Authore. Pro aliquali notitia de Musica habenda. Primo, videndum est quid sit Musica, et unde dicatur. Secundo, quae ejus partes ..." *Exp.*: "... vide Orphei et Amphionis modulationes, ac alias Musicae virtutes quas ponit Macrobius de sompno Scipionis, libro 2$^{do}$. Ex hiis omnibus praecedentibus colligo hanc divisionem sequentem: [example]." (ff. 17v–20r)

*Inc.*: "Secundo. Principaliter videndum est, primo, de Arte Musicae ac Elementorum sive Literarum quae Claves vocantur inventione ..." *Exp.*: "... sesquetertius est tunc sequitur quinarius numerus minor est quaternario et quaternarius ternario et ternarius numerus binario et binarius numerus minor est unitate et sic sequitur quod in majoribus numeris minor est proportio et in minoribus numeris minor proportio continetur." (ff. 20v–26v)

*Inc.*: "In superioribus particulis dictum est de divisione Musicae, de ejus etiam inventione ac de proportionibus ad Monacordi divisionem pertinentibus, in ista parte declarandum est de plano cantu qui in quinque consistit. Prima est ..." *Exp.*: "... Ex praedictis vero Tredecim speciebus nulla in numerorum Musicalium proportione recipitur praeter Tonum quae est in Sesqueoctava proportione, et dyatessaron quae est in sesquetertia proportione, et diapente quae est in sesquealtera proportione et diapason quae semper duplam proportionem, ut superius in Secundo principali Capitulo et cetera." (ff. 26v–31r)

Diagram of a triangle. *Inc.*: "1a. Omnis nota praeter simplam carent puncto omnino imperfecta est. ..." *Exp.*: "... Omnis nota quae post se punctum habet omnimo perfecta dicitur, quia et ipsa perfecta est, et omnes partes ipsam oblique componentes omnino perfecte sunt excepta sola simpla quae est inpartibilis."[177] (ff. 31r–v)

*Inc.*: "Dictis aliquibus circa planum cantum, restat aliud dicendum de cantu sive Musica mensurabili, circa quod primo dicendum est de quantitate Musicae mensurabilis, secundo de divisione ..." *Exp.*: "... Et haec de Musicae continuae et etiam discretae principiis sufficiant ad praesens, que tanto ut credo acceptiora sunt quanto aliorum dictis concordiam habent nam in isto libello nichil apposui quod non ab auctoritatibus et a Magistris peritis et approbatis mediante gratia Dei addici. Explicit." (ff. 31v–56r)

---

*Music and Musicians* 1 [1980]: 445) apparently follows the authority of Reckow's edition of Anonymous IV, in which the manuscript descriptions fail to make the association between them.

[177] The diagram and short text that were interpolated between the third and fourth *principalia* by a later hand in **GB-Lbl**, Cotton Tiberius B.IX can be identified as a version of the Torkesey triangle with, however, eight levels instead of six. See *supra*, pp. 55–57 and table 5.

5. Anonymous, *De mensuris et discantu*.[178] *Inc*.: "Cognita modulatione melorum secundum viam octo troporum et secundum usum consuetudinem Fidei Catholicae ..." *Exp*.: "... In nomine et honore sanctissimi mediatoris omnium, qui est verus salvator, Jesus Christus, filius dei vivi, et qui est corona et gloria omnium sanctorum ad quam gloriam possumus omnes pervenire cum sanctissimo." (ff. 56v–93r)

6. Anonymous, *De sinemenis*.[179] *Inc*.: "Sequitur de sinemenis sic ..." *Exp*.: "... Omnis spiritus laudet Dominum etc. cuncta bona etc. Explicit." (ff. 93r–94v)

7. Anonymous, *De discantu*.[180] *Inc*.: "Est autem Unisonus ..." *Exp*.: "... Item si descendat per diatessaron sta in eodem." (ff. 94v–96r)

8. Guidonian hand and musical notation.[181] (ff. 96v–97v)

9. Anonymous, *Tractatus de figuris sive notis*.[182] *Inc*.: "Cum in isto tractatu de Figuris sive de Notis quae sunt ..." *Exp*.: "... et sic finitur Capitulum tertium etc." (ff. 98r–104v)

10. Anonymous, *Faus semblaunt* [French rondeau a2].[183] (f. 104v)

---

[178]Anonymous IV of CS, 1:327a–364b. For a new edition, see Reckow, ed., *Der Musiktraktat des Anonymus 4*; and for a translation of this edition, see Jeremy Yudkin, trans., *The Music Treatise of Anonymous IV. A New Translation*, Musicological Studies and Documents, vol. 41 (Neuhausen-Stuttgart: Hänssler Verlag for the American Institute of Musicology, 1985). This text was copied from **GB**-Lbl, Cotton Tiberius B.IX, ff. 215r–224r; for a concordance, see **GB**-Lbl, Royal 12.C.vi, ff. 59r–80v.

[179]CS, 1:364a–365b. For a new edition, see Prosdoscimo de' Beldomandi, *Brevis summula proportionum quantum ad musicam pertinet* and *Parvus tractatulus de modo monacordum dividendi*, ed. and trans. Jan Herlinger, Greek and Latin Music Theory, vol. 4 (Lincoln: University of Nebraska Press, 1987), appendix B: "The Fragment 'Sequitur de synemenis,'" pp. 123–35. This text was copied from **GB**-Lbl, Cotton Tiberius B.IX, f. 224r–v; for a concordance, see **GB**-Lbl, Royal 12.C.vi, ff. 80v–81v.

[180]Anonymous V of CS, 1:366a–368b. This text was copied from **GB**-Lbl, Royal 12.C.vi, ff. 50r–51v.

[181]This text was copied from **GB**-Lbl, Royal 12.C.vi, ff. 52v–53v.

[182]Anonymous VI of CS, 1:369a–377b. For a new edition, see *Tractatus de figuris* (ed. Reaney and Gilles), pp. 40–51. This text was copied from **GB**-Lbl, Royal 12.C.vi, ff. 54r–58r.

[183]For editions of this song, see Wolf, *Geschichte der Mensural-Notation*, 2:15–16 and 3:27–28; and Gordon K. Greene, ed., *French Secular Music: Rondeaux and Miscellaneous Pieces*, Polyphonic Music of the Fourteenth Century, vol. 22 (Paris and Monaco: Editions de L'Oiseau Lyre,

11. Walter Odington, *De speculatione musicae*. [3 excerpts] (ff. 105r–106r).

   a. *Inc.*: "Notum quod est unum genus cantus organici ..." *Exp.*: "... et hujusmodi cantus Truncatus dicitur a rei convenientia qui et Hoequets dicitur—haec Odyngton."[184]

   b. *Inc.*: "Longa perficitur cum longa praecedit ..." *Exp.*: "... vel valor brevis resolute in semibreves sic (ex. sequ.)."[185]

   c. *Inc.*: "De modis quibus procedunt cantus organici. Modus in hac parte est ..." *Exp.*: "... Primus itaque secundi imperfectus."[186]

This manuscript consists of copies of the portions of **GB**-Lbl, Cotton Tiberius B.IX and Royal 12.C.vi concerning music.[187] The transcriptions were made for Dr. Pepusch some time before 1731. At the death of Pepusch in 1752, **GB**-Lbl, Additional 4909 passed into the hands of Sir John Hawkins (1719–1789), who presented it to the British Museum on 30 May 1778.[188]

---

1989), pp. 64 and 175. This chanson was copied from **GB**-Lbl, Royal 12.C.vi, f. 58r.

[184]Cap. 11: *De generibus cantuum organicum*, in full (ed. Hammond), pp. 139–40; see also CS, 1:245b–246a.

[185]Cap. 3: *Quot modis longa perfecta vel imperfecta dicitur*, in full (ed. Hammond), pp. 129–30; see also CS, 1:236b–237a.

[186]Cap. 6: *De modis de quibus procedunt cantus organici*, in full, and cap. 7: *De perfectione modorum et imperfectione et eorum mutatione*, lns. 1–12 (ed. Hammond), pp. 131–32; see also CS, 1:238a–239b.

[187]For an overview of the shared and separate musical contents of **GB**-Lbl, Royal 12.C.vi, Cotton Tiberius B.IX, and Additional 4909, see Reckow, ed., *Der Musiktraktat des Anonymus 4*, 1:18.

[188]On the Hawkins collection of fifteen manuscripts relating to music (now **GB**-Lbl, Additional 4909–4923), see Augustus Hughes-Hughes, *Catalogue of Manuscript Music in the British Museum*, 3 vols. (London: The Trustees of the British Museum, 1906–1909), 3:x; and *Catalogue of Additions to the Manuscripts 1756–1782* (London: British Museum Publications, 1977), pp. 283–84.

## A 2

London, British Library, Additional 8866

Parchment; 3+83 folios (one leaf is missing after f. 22, two are missing after f. 48), 215x145 mm
England; early 15th century

1. Anon., *Quatuor principalia* (Version B).[189] (ff. 4r–64r).
   *Inc.*: "Quemadmodum inter triticum et zizaniam quamdiu herba est et nec dum venit ad spicam ..." *Exp.*: "... Sed etiam quicquid loquimur vel venarum pulsibus commovetur armonia probatur esse virtutibus sociatum. Explicit primum principale." (ff. 4r–11r)
   *Inc.*: "Incipit secundum principale. Ante inventionem huius artis naturaliter cantibus utebantur canebat homines ..." *Exp.*: "... Cetera vero que pertinent ad numeros musicales in musica Boecii satis tractantur et ideo ad planam musicam transeamus. Explicit secundum principale." (ff. 11r–19v)
   *Inc.*: "Nunc incipit tertium principale. In superioribus particulis dictum est de divisione musice et de eius inventione ac de proportionibus ..." *Exp.*: "... igitur naturam eius demonstrare ordo nunc postulat. Explicit tertium principale in quo terminatur musica que dicatur continua." (ff. 19v–40r)
   *Inc.*: "Incipit Quartum principale in quo consistit musica que dicatur discreta. Cum omnis quantitas aut est continua aut est discreta ut ait Boicius in sua musica ..." *Exp.*: "... quod incepi ad honorem dei et sancte matris ecclesie atque proximorum utilitate in scriptis apposui. Explicit cuius quidem finis primo erat pridie Nonas Augusti Anno domini 1351°." (ff. 40r–64r)
2. Anonymous, *Sciendum est tamen et neupme loco sunt pedum*.[190] *Inc.*: "Sciendum est tamen et neupme loco sunt pedum et distinctiones loco versuum utpote ista neupma Dactilico ..." *Exp.*: "... Sinemmenon est figura quedam et dicitur commutacio sive defectio tonorum vel semitoniorum et est in alphabeto 2 ut dicit Hanboys li° p° c° 6°." (f. 64r)
3. Hanboys, *Summa*.[191] *Inc.*: "Hic incipit musica magistri Franco cum additionibus et opinionibus diversorum. Cum de plana musica quidam philosophi sufficienter tractaverant ..." *Exp.*: "... Sciendum est quod

---

[189]CS, 4:200–298, following the text of **GB**-Ob, Digby 90.

[190]This *tractatulus* by Hanboys is unrelated either to the *Quatuor principalia* that precedes it or the *Summa* of Hanboys that follows. Its explicit refers to an otherwise unknown work. For an edition, see appendix III.

[191]CS, 1:403–48, and this edition.

modus est representatio soni longis brevibusque temporibus mensurati. Explicit summa magistri Johannis Hanboys doctoris musice reverendi super musicam continuam et discretam." (ff. 64v–86v)

This manuscript, an integral codex, was not known to music historians before it passed into the British Museum collections in 1831, and its previous whereabouts have not been traced. Nevertheless, either this manuscript or one very closely related in contents (i.e., containing both the *Summa* and Version B of the *Quatuor principalia*, and with the same incipit for the *Summa*) was probably known to Bale.

At its acquisition, museum authorities judged the manuscript to date from the fourteenth century, a date revised in later references to the fifteenth century.[192] The main hand that copied the manuscript (and a secondary one that can be distinguished, which does not show much difference in type) is decidedly a mixed one, describable as a Bastard Anglicana with secretary features or perhaps as an Anglicana formata with some Bastard Anglicana (i.e., the more formal modification of the script) and secretary elements. It can probably be dated to the second quarter of the fifteenth century (see plate 2).[193]

*The Edition*

The edition of Handlo's *Regule* is based on the readings of its single source, the eighteenth-century copy in **GB**-Lbl, Additional 4909. It reverts, however, to medieval orthography rather than preserving the classicizing forms of Pepusch's scribe in respect to the ae diphthong and the use of j for i. The Pepusch scribe is suspect as a reader of the hand he encountered. Some abbreviations stumped him (e.g., the abbreviation for *e converso*, rendered consistently as *aequo*, and *recte stat* rendered as *recescat*). Yet he evidently attempted to preserve many aspects of his exemplar, particularly in respect to the use of red rubrics and the marginal identification of rules and maxims. The copied text was proofread by another eighteenth-century scribe who understood the hand of the treatise better than the principal copyist and caught

---

[192]See *A List of Additions Made to the Collections in the British Museum in the Year 1831* (London: Trustees of the British Museum, 1833), p. 25; *Catalogue of the Manuscript Music in the British Museum*, compiled by Thomas Oliphant and revised by Frederick Madden (London: Trustees of the British Museum, 1842), p. 75, no. 209; and Hughes-Hughes, *Catalogue of Manuscript Music in the British Museum*, 3:305 and 311.

[193]For their generous advice on the classification and dating of the scribal hands of **GB**-Lbl, Additional 8866, I would like to thank Professor Andrew G. Watson and Dr. Andrew Wathey of the University of London.

a number of lacunae and errors; some remaining errors can be corrected from Hanboys. Where necessary, the *Regule* has been made consistent with regard to the labelling and attributions of authorship of rules and maxims. Plate 1 (**GB**-Lbl, Additional 4909, f. 8r) was chosen to illustrate typical rubrication and corrections, and it also provides facsimiles of some of the more complex examples of Rubric IX.

The edition of Hanboys's *Summa* retains medieval orthography, with standardization of inconsistent spellings and normalization of i/j, u/v, c/t before i plus vowel (keeping -cio), double consonants, and assimilations. Numbers are spelled out or given as numerals and may be converted from one form to the other without editorial mention. The *Summa* was copied mainly by a single hand, with the major exception of about half of one page, which has been entered in a second, similar hand. Plate 2 (**GB**-Lbl, Additional 8866, f. 66r) provides a facsimile of this page (the second hand takes over twelve text lines from the bottom), which includes text from chapter 3. Incipit and explicit of the *Summa* were added after the main body of text was entered, and the text was proofread and corrected at least twice, once by a thick pen probably of the principal scribe and once by the finer pen of the hand that made the marginal notes for the rubricator. Some marginal notes comment on deficiencies in the text.

The rubrication of the *Summa* was never completed, and marginal annotations were not always accurately placed. These have been made consistent in respect to the intended division into chapters, which has been judged according to the location of large initials. The identification of quotations is more problematic, as "Hanboys" not only replaces "Handlo," but also occasionally substitutes for another of the earlier author's authorities; "Franco" may represent Franco of Cologne or the "Franco" of some version of the *Regule*. Without attempting to fully provide all possible ascriptions, but in light of the fact that the rubrication was never completed, a number have been provided editorially in the main text (and others in the notes), especially in those sections most dependent on Handlo or that quote Franco directly from the *Ars cantus mensurabilis*.

The Latin text is found on the verso of each opening of the edition, with an indication in the interior margin of the corresponding page in the earlier edition of Coussemaker. Critical commentary appears at the bottom of each verso. An English translation of the main text appears on facing recto pages. Annotations are footnoted to the English. These serve to explain the text, trace quotations and source materials, provide cross-references for the *Regule* and the *Summa*, and link their content with that of other treatises and practical musical sources.

# CONSPECTUS CODICUM ET NOTARUM

## Manuscripts

A1    London, British Library, Additional 4909, **GB**-Lbl
A2    London, British Library, Additional 8866, **GB**-Lbl

## Earlier Editions or References

CS    *Scriptorum de musica medii aevi nova series a Gerbertina altera*, 4 vols., ed. Edmond de Coussemaker (Paris: Durand, 1864–1876; reprint ed., Hildesheim: Olms, 1963), 1:383–403 and 403–48.
D    The 1583 inventory of Dr. John Dee's library (see Introduction, pp. 69–70).
M    Thomas Morley, *A Plaine and Easy Introduction to Practicall Musicke* (1597) (see Introduction, pp. 5–6).
S    Thomas Smith, *Catalogus librorum manuscriptorum bibliothecae Cottonianae* (Oxford: Sheldon Theatre, 1696) (see Introduction, pp. 6–7).
T    Thomas Tanner, *Bibliotheca Britannico-Hibernica* (London: David Wilkins, 1748) (see Introduction, p. 7)

## Notes

| | | | |
|---|---|---|---|
| *add.* | added | *ter.* | third |
| *ante* | before | *tractus* | tail |
| *ante corr.* | before correction | *ult.* | last |
| *ascendens* | ascending | *una* | one |
| *bis* | twice | *ut* | like |
| *clavis* | clef | *vacua* | hollow |
| *corr.* | corrected | | |
| *del.* | deleted | | |
| *descendens* | descending | | |
| *exemplum* | example | | |
| *fig.* | noteshape | | |
| *fort.* | perhaps | | |
| *fort. recte* | perhaps correctly | | |
| *idem* | the same | | |
| *in marg.* | in the margin | | |
| *inter* | between | | |
| *m. sec.* | in a second hand | | |
| *om.* | omits, omitted | | |
| *post* | after | | |
| *pr.* | first | | |
| *rep.* | repeated | | |
| *sec.* | second | | |
| *sine* | without | | |
| *sup. lin.* | above the line | | |

< > enclose letters, words, or longer passages added by the editor's conjecture.
⟦ ⟧ indicate deletion by the scribe.
{ } indicate text transposed to a different location.

Variants in the musical notation are given in the critical apparatus by numbering each symbol (including clefs and puncti) in the example. The names of the noteshapes are given in italics. Ligatures are considered as single symbols. If there is more than one line of notation, the symbols in each line are numbered separately. Editorial additions appear in [ ].

## REGULE ROBERTI DE HANDLO

 Incipiunt regule cum maximis magistri Franconis cum additionibus aliorum musicorum, compilate a Roberto de Handlo.
 I. Incipit prima rubrica. De longis, brevibus et semibrevibus, et qualiter
5 in divisione se habent.
Maxima 1
 Franco: Gaudent brevitate moderni, etc.
⟨Regula I⟩
 Idem: Quandocunque punctus quadratus vel nota quadrata, quod idem

---

2–3 Incipiunt ... Handlo]Magistri Franconis Regulae Musicales cum additionibus aliorum musicorum, collectis a Roberto de Handlo D Regulae Franchonis cum additionibus Roberti de Haule M Regulae, cum maximis, Magistri Franconis, cum additionibus aliorum musicorum, compilatae a Roberto de Handle S Regulas musicas cum maximis magistri Franconis T Hic incipit musica magistri Franconis cum additionibus et opinionibus diversorum A2 ‖ 3 compilate]compositae CS ‖ 9 quandocunque]quandocumque A1 ‖

## THE RULES OF ROBERTUS DE HANDLO

Here begin the rules with maxims of Master Franco with the additions of other learned musicians, compiled by Robertus de Handlo.
 I. Here begins the first rubric. Concerning longae, breves, and semibreves, and in what ways they are arranged in division.[1]
Maxim 1
 Franco: The moderns rejoice in brevity, etc.[2]
Rule 1
 The same: Whenever a square notehead[3] or a square note, which is the

---

[1]The expression "in divisione" occurs again ("in divisionibus") only in Maxim 5 of Rubric 9, while the related adjective *divisus* is more common; these seem to be a coinage of Handlo. In the *Regule*, figures in this condition are contrasted with ligatures, oblique figures, and conjunctions, thus clarifying that the expression refers to a sequence of separate notes.

[2]This opening motto "is a device frequently and variously used by medieval authors," as F. Alberto Gallo has observed in the introduction to his edition of an anonymous *Compendium musicae mensurabilis artis antiquae* (Petrus Picardus, *Ars motettorum compilata breviter*, ed. F. Alberto Gallo; Anonymous, *Ars musicae mensurabilis secundum Franconem*, ed. Gilbert Reaney and André Gilles; Anonymous, *Compendium musica mensurabilis artis antiquae*, ed. F. Alberto Gallo, Corpus scriptorum de musica, no. 15 [(Rome): American Institute of Musicology, 1971], p. 63, n. 3). There Gallo makes reference to numerous occurrences cited in Hans Walther, *Lateinische Sprichwörter und Sentenzen des Mittelalters*, 9 vols. (Göttingen: Vandenhoeck & Ruprecht, 1963–86); see Walther, nos. 1853, 13942, 14824, 22446, 32520, 37102. Of particular relevance here is the fact that this expression opens a number of related music treatises in a tradition transmitting abbreviated doctrines of Franco of Cologne. The statements credited by Handlo to Franco in the *Regule*, taken together, coherently comprise one such *Gaudent moderni* treatise. See the Introduction, pp. 8–10.

[3]The term *punctus* has two meanings, depending on whether the language of the *Gaudent moderni* tradition or of Petrus de Cruce is being followed. In the former, the punctus is a notehead, and in this sense the term will be translated as "notehead." In the doctrine of Petrus, the punctus is equivalent to Franco's *divisio modi*, and this technical sense will be preserved in the translation by retaining "punctus" with appropriate modifiers.

est, tractum habet a parte dextra descendentem, longa vocatur, ut hic: ‖

⟨Regula II⟩
⟨Handlo⟩: Si tractum habeat a parte dextra solumodo ascendentem, erecta
5   longa vocatur, ut hic:

---

4 solumodo *om.* M ‖ 5 longa *sup. lin., m. sec.* A1 *om.* M ‖

same thing, has a stem descending from the right side,[4] it is called a longa, as here:[5]

Rule II

Handlo: If it has a stem ascending only from the right side, it is called a longa erecta, as here:[6]

---

[4]In Franco's *Ars cantus mensurabilis*, the stem on the longa only descends (*Franconis de Colonia Ars cantus mensurabilis*, ed. Gilbert Reaney and André Gilles, Corpus scriptorum de musica, no. 18 [(Rome): American Institute of Musicology, 1974], p. 30). Handlo reserves the form of the longa with an ascending stem for the longa erecta. In many treatises of the *Gaudent moderni* tradition, however, the stem of the longa is described as either ascending or descending from the right ("tractum habens descendentem vel ascendentem a parte dextra"). See, for example, an anonymous *Compendium musicae mensurabilis artis antiquae* (ed. Gallo), p. 66; the *Abbreviatio* attributed to Johannes Balloch (*Johannes dictus Balloce Abreviatio Magistri Franconis*, ed. Gilbert Reaney; Anonymous, *Compendium musicae mensurabilis artis antiquae* [Anonymous III of CS 1], ed. Gilbert Reaney; Anonymous, *Compendium musicae mensurabilis artis antiquae*, ed. Heinz Ristory; Anonymous, *Tractatus artis antiquae cum explicatione mensurae binariae*, ed. Heinz Ristory, Corpus scriptorum de musica, no. 34 [Neuhausen-Stuttgart: Hänssler Verlag for the American Institute of Musicology, 1987], p. 13); another anonymous *Compendium musicae mensurabilis artis antiquae* (ed. Ristory), p. 49; and an anonymous *Tractatus artis antiquae cum explicatione mensurae binariae* (Ristory ed., p. 69). See also the anonymous treatise once attributed to Theodoricus de Campo (Anonymous [dictus Theodoricus de Campo], *De musica mensurabili*, ed. Cecily Sweeney; Anonymous, *De semibrevibus caudatis*, ed. Cecily Sweeney and Gilbert Reaney, Corpus scriptorum de musica, 13 [(Rome): American Institute of Musicology, 1971], p. 33). Walter Odington mentions the form with ascending stem as a variant form of the longa plicata (*Summa de speculacione musicae*, ed. Frederick Hammond, Corpus scriptorum de musica, no. 14 [(Rome): American Institute of Musicology, 1970], p. 129).

[5]Hanboys, *Summa*, chapter 7 (220.5–9 *infra*). The contents of this chapter are transmitted fully in the *Summa*, chapters 7 (on the longa), 10 (on the brevis), and 12 (on the semibrevis), except for Maxims 1 and 3 and Rule VI.

[6]Hanboys, *Summa*, chapter 7 (220.9–10 *infra*). The brevis erecta is introduced in Rule V and Maxim 4 of this rubric. Outside of Handlo and the corresponding passages transmitted by Hanboys, there is theoretical mention of the longa and brevis erecta, with notated examples, only in a fragmentary tractatulus of English origin (London, British Library [henceforward: GB-Lbl], Additional 21455, item 2, f. 5r–v): "Sciendum quod ubicumque longe erecte inveniuntur, per solum semitonum eriguntur et nunquam plicari pos-

⟨Maxima 2⟩

⟨Idem⟩: Ponuntur enim iste longe erecte ad differenciam longarum precedentium, que sunt recte. Et vocantur erecte, quia ubicunque inveniuntur, per semitonium eriguntur.

5 ⟨Regula III⟩

Franco: Longa vero duos tractus possedens ‖ quorum dexter longior est sinistro, plicata longa vocatur, ut hic:

CS1: 384a

⟨Maxima 3⟩

10 Handlo: Erecte longe, sive perfecte sint sive imperfecte, nunquam plicari possunt.

⟨Regula IV⟩

Franco: Quandocunque punctus quadratus invenitur qui caret omni tractu, brevis dicitur, ut hic:

15 ⟨Regula V⟩

Handlo: Si tractum habeat a parte sinistra solumodo ascendentem, erecta brevis vocatur, ut hic:

---

2 differenciam A2M dextram A1 ‖ 2–3 precedentium *om.* M ‖ 3 quia]quod M ‖ 4 semitonium A2M semitonum A1 ‖ 6 possidens A1 ‖ 7 plicati A1 ‖ 10 sit A1 I nusquam A1 ‖

Maxim 2

The same: These longae erectae are employed to differentiate them from the preceding longae, which are rectae.[7] And they are called "erectae" because wherever they are found, they are raised by a semitone.[8]

Rule III

Franco: The longa possessing two stems, of which the right is longer than the left, is called a longa plicata, as here:[9]

Maxim 3

Handlo: Longae erectae, whether they are perfect or imperfect, can never be plicated.[10]

Rule IV

Franco: Whenever a square notehead is found that lacks any stem, it is said to be a brevis, as here:[11]

Rule V

Handlo: If it has an ascending stem on the left side only, it is called a brevis erecta, as here:[12]

---

sunt. Item sciendum est de brevibus erectis" (see *Philippi de Vitriaco Ars nova*, ed. Gilbert Reaney, André Gilles, and Jean Maillard, Corpus scriptorum de musica, no. 8 [(Rome): American Institute of Musicology, 1964], p. 78). On the source **GB**-Lbl, Additional 21455, and on the appearance of the longa and brevis erecta in the practical musical sources, see the Introduction, pp. 2–3, 11–12. Rule II and Maxim 2 (on the longa erecta) are quoted in full in Latin, and Rule 5 and Maxim 4 (on the brevis erecta) are briefly paraphrased in English, in Thomas Morley, *A Plaine and Easie Introduction to Practicall Musicke (1597)*, ed. R. Alec Harman, 2d ed. (London: Dent, 1963; reprint ed., New York: Norton, 1973), p. 117.

[7] The term *recta* is taken here in the sense of "usual, common, standard, ordinary, proper," that is, according to rule, but not with the sense of correct as opposed to incorrect.

[8] Hanboys, *Summa*, chapter 7 (220.11–13 *infra*).

[9] Hanboys, *Summa*, chapter 7 (222.1–3 *infra*).

[10] Hanboys, *Summa*, chapter 7 (222.4–5 *infra*). See Rule VII of Rubric X, however, where Handlo explains circumstances under which a longa, plicated upward at the end of a ligature, is interpreted as a longa erecta.

[11] Hanboys, *Summa*, chapter 10 (236.17–18 *infra*).

[12] Hanboys, *Summa*, chapter 10 (236.19–21 *infra*). Without reference to the name or properties of the brevis erecta, this shape of brevis also is described in an anonymous *De musica mensurabili* (ed. Sweeney), pp. 33 and 50; and in Thomas Walsingham, *Regulae de musica mensurabili*, ed.

⟨Maxima 4⟩
   ⟨Idem⟩: Et etiam per semitonium eriguntur veluti longe erecte.
⟨Regula VI⟩
   Franco: Brevis vero duos tractus habens, quorum sinister longior est
5 dextro, plicata brevis vocatur, ut hic:

⟨Maxima 5⟩
   Handlo: Sicut erecte longe non plicantur, ita nec erecte breves.
⟨Regula VII⟩
10   Franco: Semibreves vero ad modum losonge formantur, ut hic:

⟨Regula VIII⟩
   Idem: Plicari non possunt, nisi quando tres super unam sillabam ordinantur:
15
⟨Maxima 6⟩
   ‖ Handlo: Que quidem quando sic ordinantur suo modo, coniungi dicuntur, ultima manente plicata sursum, non deorsum.

CS1: 384b

---

2 semitonum A1 ‖ 6 *omnes tractus descendentes* 6.3–4 A1 ‖ 15 *tractus om.* 15.3 A1 ‖

Maxim 4

The same: And they are also raised by a semitone, just as are longae erectae.[13]

Rule VI

Franco: A brevis having two stems, of which the left is longer than the right, is called a brevis plicata, as here:[14]

Maxim 5

Handlo: Just as longae erectae are not plicated, so neither are breves erectae.[15]

Rule VII

Franco: Semibreves are formed in the manner of a lozenge, as here:[16]

Rule VIII

The same: They cannot be plicated, except when three are ordered over one syllable:[17]

Maxim 6

Handlo: When some of these are so ordered in this manner, they are said to be conjoined,[18] with the last remaining one plicated upwards, not downwards.[19]

---

Gilbert Reaney, Corpus scriptorum de musica, no. 31 (Neuhausen-Stuttgart: Hänssler Verlag for the American Institute of Musicology, 1983), p. 75.

[13]Hanboys, *Summa*, chapter 10 (236.22 *infra*).

[14]Hanboys, *Summa*, chapter 10 (236.23–25 *infra*).

[15]Hanboys, *Summa*, chapter 10 (236.26 *infra*).

[16]Hanboys, *Summa*, chapter 12 (254.5–7 *infra*).

[17]Hanboys, *Summa*, chapter 12 (254.8–10 *infra*).

[18]The conjunction of semibreves is fully treated as the topic of Rubric IX. See also the Introduction, p. 13.

[19]Hanboys, *Summa*, chapter 12 (254.11–12 *infra*). See also Rule IV and Maxim 3 of Rubric X.

88

　　　　II. Incipit secunda rubrica. De longa, etiam semilonga et earum valore, et de longa duplici.
　　　　⟨Regula I⟩
　　　　Franco: Longa ante longam valet tria tempora, ut hic:
5
　　　　⟨Maxima 1⟩
　　　　Idem: Longa perfecta vocatur longa trium temporum, imperfecta duorum.
　　　　⟨Maxima 2⟩
10　　　Handlo: Longa, quando imperfecta est, semilonga magis proprie, et si perfecta, longam dici oportebit.
　　　　⟨Regula II⟩
　　　　Idem: Semilonga vero et longa similes sunt in figura, dissimiles vero in proportione et ore secundum vocem, ut hic: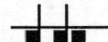
15
　　　　⟨Regula III⟩
　　　　Idem: Hec que dicenda sunt de longis et semilongis erectis, ut hic:

---

17 de]in A1 ‖

II. Here begins the second rubric. Concerning the longa and semilonga and their values, and concerning the duplex longa.
Rule I
Franco: A longa before a longa is worth three tempora, as here:[20]

Maxim 1
The same: A longa of three tempora is called a perfect longa, one of two tempora, imperfect.[21]
Maxim 2
Handlo: A longa, when it is imperfect, more properly will have to be said to be a semilonga, and if perfect, a longa.[22]
Rule II
The same: The semilonga and the longa are similar in shape but indeed dissimilar in proportion and delivery of the voice, as here:[23]

Rule III
The same: This also must be said of longae and semilongae erectae, as here:[24]

---

[20]Hanboys, *Summa*, chapter 7 (222.6–7 *infra*). The material on longae (Rule I through Rule III, except for Maxim 2) is fully transmitted in the *Summa*, chapter 7, while the material on duplex longae (Rule IV through Rule V) is not to be found. For Hanboys's citation of material on the duplex longa that may have been drawn from a modified form of the *Regule*, see the *Summa*, chapter 6 (218.1–220.2 *infra*), and see also the Introduction, pp. 11 and 59. The term *tempus* (time; pl. *tempora*) refers to the customary unit of time measurement in *ars antiqua* music, the duration of a normal brevis.

[21]Hanboys, *Summa*, chapter 7 (222.19–20 *infra*).

[22]Petrus le Viser also uses the term *semilonga*, and as he is the earlier authority, he may be Handlo's source for it. See Maxim 5 of Rubric X.

[23]Hanboys, *Summa*, chapter 7 (222.21–22 *infra*). On first encounter, this seems like an unnecessarily complex way of stating something quite obvious. Handlo, though, is characteristically concerned with distinguishing these figures not only conceptually or mentally (using the term *proportio* [proportion or size], which is more or less synonymous with *valor* [value or equivalent]) but also practically, in a vocal rendition (the term *vox* means "voice" throughout the *Regule*). For another instance, see Maxim 2 of Rubric VI and its note.

[24]Hanboys, *Summa*, chapter 7 (222.24 *infra*).

⟨Regula IV⟩
Franco: Duplex longa valet sex tempora et formatur sic:

⟨Maxima 3⟩
Handlo: Sic non est de longa erecta, quia simplex est.
⟨Regula V⟩
Idem: Longa vero duplex est quinque temporum ⟨quando imperficitur⟩ per brevem precedentem vel sequentem, vel per brevis valorem, ut patet in regula tertia quinte rubrice et in eius exemplo. ‖

---

2 format (ur *sup. lin., m. sec.*) A1 ‖

Rule IV
Franco: The duplex longa is worth six tempora and is so formed:

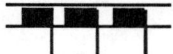

Maxim 3
Handlo: This does not apply to the longa erecta, because it is simplex.²⁵
Rule V
The same: The duplex longa is of five tempora when it is imperfected by a preceding or following brevis, or by the value of a brevis, as is shown in Rule III of Rubric V and in its example.²⁶

---

²⁵That is, it is worth three breves. This is apparently a caution against confusing the duplex longa with a longa erecta. In the *Regule*, the adjective *simplex* most frequently modifies longa as part of the series simplex longa, duplex longa, triplex longa, etc. In Franco's *Ars cantus mensurabilis* or in Hanboys's *Summa*, the word has another meaning: that simple figure stands alone and unadorned, neither plicated nor compounded with any other figure in a ligature or conjunction; here the opposite of *simplex* is *compositus*. Handlo introduces a unique and more varied vocabulary to convey this second sense through the use of the adjectives *nuda* (plain), *solus* (solitary), and *divisa* (separate). For a single example of Handlo's use of simplex according to this second meaning, see Maxim 7 of Rubric VI.

²⁶*Ars antiqua* terminology is strained here because, strictly speaking, the duplex longa is not perfect to begin with (it is worth two longs, not three), and the loss of the value of one brevis is what *ars nova* theorists would call diminishment by a remote value, not imperfection. In the Franconian tradition of the *Ars cantus mensurabilis* and the *Gaudent moderni* treatises, the shortening of value of the duplex longa is not discussed. Hanboys refers to an unnamed authority, according to whom the duplex longa can be "imperfected" not only from six to five breves but also to four breves (*Summa*, chapter 6 [220.1–2 *infra*]).

III. Incipit tertia rubrica. Ad cognoscendum longas a semilongis et e converso per breves et semibreves et pausas eis appositas, et de equalitate brevium et de brevi altera.

Regula I

Franco: Quandocunque sola brevis vel valor precedit ⟨longam⟩, imperficit eam, ut hic:

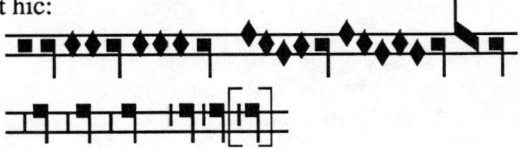

Regula II

Idem: Si autem sola brevis vel valor sequatur longam, imperficit eam, ut hic: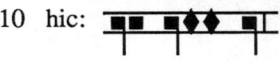

Regula III

Idem: Nisi per divisionem modi aliter distinguantur, ut hic:

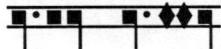

Maxima 1

Idem: Tunc prima longa habebit tria tempora, et brevis sequens vel valor refertur ad longam sequentem, et imperficit eam.

Maxima 2

Idem: Sciendum est quod omnes breves sunt inequales tribus modis, quorum primus est ‖ quandocunque inter duas longas due breves inveniuntur. Prima brevis valet unum tempus vel valor, ultima brevis valet duo tempora, et vocatur altera brevis.

Maxima 3

Handlo: Que magis proprie potest dici brevis alterata, quia a sua recta proportione alteratur.

---

9 eam causa A1 ‖ 14 *longa post* 14.9 A1 ‖

III. Here begins the third rubric. On understanding longae compared to semilongae (and conversely), by means of breves and semibreves and rests placed next to them; and concerning the equality of breves and the brevis altera.

Rule I

Franco: Whenever a solitary brevis or its value precedes a longa, it imperfects it, as here:[27]

Rule II

The same: If, moreover, a solitary brevis or its value follows a longa, it imperfects it, as here:[28]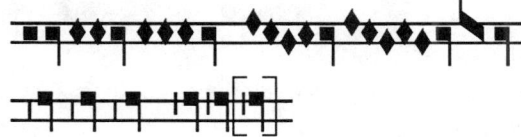

Rule III

The same: Unless they are otherwise distinguished by a division of the mode, as here:[29]

Maxim 1

The same: Then the first longa will have three tempora, and the following brevis or value is related to the following longa and imperfects it.[30]

Maxim 2

The same: It must be known that all breves are unequal in three manners, of which the first is whenever two breves are found between two longae.[31] The first brevis or its value is worth one tempus; the last brevis is worth two tempora and is called a brevis altera.[32]

Maxim 3

Handlo: This more properly can be said to be an altered brevis, because it is altered from its normal proportion.[33]

---

[27]Hanboys, *Summa*, chapter 7 (224.10–11 *infra*). The contents of this chapter are fully transmitted in the *Summa*, chapters 7 and 11, except for Rule XV.

[28]Hanboys, *Summa*, chapter 7 (224.1–3 *infra*).

[29]Hanboys, *Summa*, chapter 7 (224.4–5 *infra*).

[30]Hanboys, *Summa*, chapter 7 (224.6–7 *infra*).

[31]For the second and third manners, see Maxim 7 and Rule X.

[32]Hanboys, *Summa*, chapter 11 (246.14–16 *infra*).

[33]Hanboys, *Summa*, chapter 11 (246.12–13 *infra*). The term *altera* refers to another kind of brevis, occurring as the second of a pair of two, that is identical in figure to the brevis recta (normal) but is understood to possess

Regula IV
Franco: Ambe autem longe erunt perfecte, ut hic:

Regula V
Idem: Nisi brevis sola vel valor precedat vel subsequatur, ut hic: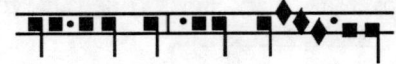

Maxima 4
Handlo: Due breves igitur inter duas longas inequales manent.
Regula VI
Franco: Nisi per divisionem modi aliter distinguantur, ut hic:

Maxima 5
Idem: Tunc ambe breves erunt equales, et prima primam longam imperficit, secunda secundam. ‖
Regula VII
Idem: Si autem tres breves inveniantur inter duas longas, predicte breves erunt equales. Ambe autem longe erunt perfecte, ut hic:

Rule IV
   Franco: Moreover, both longae will be perfect, as here:[34]

Rule V
   The same: Unless a solitary brevis or its value precedes or follows, as here:[35]

Maxim 4
   Handlo: Therefore, two breves between two longae remain unequal.[36]
Rule VI
   Franco: Unless they are otherwise distinguished by a division of the mode, as here:[37]

Maxim 5
   The same: Then both breves will be equal, and the first imperfects the first longa, while the second imperfects the second longa.[38]
Rule VII
   The same: If, moreover, three breves are found between two longae, the aforesaid breves will be equal. Moreover, both longae will be perfect, as here:[39]

---

twice its value; it has the duration of an imperfect longa or semilonga. Handlo points out that a better adjective for this brevis of greater duration might be the more dynamic *alterata* (altered), thus viewing the brevis altera as a brevis recta that has been actively changed by its context rather than simply as a specific note value—represented by the same figure as the brevis recta—that is found in certain contexts. The English *Tractatus de figuris* once uses the expression "altera sive alterata minima"; see [Anonymous of] Ms. Oxford, Bodley 842 (Willelmus), *Breviarium regulare musicae*, ed. Gilbert Reaney; [Anonymous of] Ms. British Museum, Royal 12. C. VI., *Tractatus de figuris sive de notis*, ed. Gilbert Reaney; Johannes Torkesey, *Declaratio trianguli et scuti*, ed. André Gilles and Gilbert Reaney, Corpus scriptorum de musica, no. 12 ([Rome]: American Institute of Musicology, 1966), p. 41.

[34]Hanboys, *Summa*, chapter 11 (246.17–18 *infra*).
[35]Hanboys, *Summa*, chapter 11 (246.19 *infra*).
[36]Hanboys, *Summa*, chapter 11 (246.20 *infra*).
[37]Hanboys, *Summa*, chapter 11 (246.21–22 *infra*).
[38]Hanboys, *Summa*, chapter 11 (246.23–24 *infra*).
[39]Hanboys, *Summa*, chapter 11 (248.1–4 *infra*).

Regula VIII
Idem: Nisi predictas longas brevis vel valor precedat vel subsequatur, ut hic:

Maxima 6
Handlo: Tres ergo breves inter duas longas equales manent.
Regula IX
Franco: Nisi per divisionem modi aliter distinguantur, ut hic:

Maxima 7
Idem: Tunc prima brevis primam longam imperficit, secunda brevis valet unum tempus, et tertia duo tempora, et est altera brevis. Et hic modus est secundus quod breves fiunt inequales.
Regula X
Idem: Tertius autem modus est si plures quam tres inveniantur inter duas longas, vel etiam sine prima longa, ita quod semper ultima longa || remaneat. Computentur ergo tres et tres pro perfectione, et si in fine due remaneant, tunc ultima brevis duo tempora habebit, ut hic: CS1: 386b

Regula XI
Handlo: Sed quid si quatuor breves inter duas longas inveniantur? An manebit prima longa perfecta, et tres breves computabuntur pro perfectione, et ultima brevis imperficiet longam ultimam, vel prima brevis primam longam imperficiet, et tres computabuntur pro perfectione, manente ultima perfecta? Respondeo: Prima quamvis via abolenda est, secunda tenenda, ut hic:

---

8 distinguatur A1 || 17 duo A1 || 19 *brevis post* 19.7 A1 || 25 quavis A1 ||

Rule VIII

The same: Unless a brevis or its value precedes or follows the aforesaid longae, as here:⁴⁰

Maxim 6

Handlo: Three breves, therefore, between two longae remain equal.⁴¹

Rule IX

Franco: Unless they are otherwise distinguished by a division of the mode, as here:⁴²

Maxim 7

The same: Then the first brevis imperfects the first longa, the second brevis is worth one tempus, and the third is worth two tempora and is a brevis altera. And this is the second manner that breves are made unequal.⁴³

Rule X

The same: Moreover, the third manner is if more than three are found between two longae, or even without a first longa, so that the last longa always remains. They are therefore counted by threes as a perfection, and if two remain at the end, then the last brevis will have two tempora, as here:⁴⁴

Rule XI

Handlo: But what if four breves are found between two longae? Will the first longa remain perfect, three breves be counted as a perfection, and the last brevis imperfect the last longa? Or will the first brevis imperfect the first longa, and three be counted as a perfection, with the last longa remaining perfect? I answer: the first way must be abolished as much as possible, and the second way must be held fast, as here:⁴⁵

---

⁴⁰Hanboys, *Summa*, chapter 11 (248.4–6 *infra*).

⁴¹Hanboys, *Summa*, chapter 11 (248.7 *infra*).

⁴²Hanboys, *Summa*, chapter 11 (248.8–9 *infra*).

⁴³Hanboys, *Summa*, chapter 11 (248.10–11 *infra*).

⁴⁴Hanboys, *Summa*, chapter 11 (248.13–17 *infra*). See also Rule XIII of this rubric.

⁴⁵Hanboys, *Summa*, chapter 11 (248.18–24 *infra*). It is curious that treatises in the *Gaudent moderni* tradition do not normally relate what happens when four breves are found between two longs; hence, Handlo must provide his own discussion, which is conventional enough. See Franco, *Ars cantus mensurabilis*, cap. 5, sent. 17–20 (ed. Reaney and Gilles), pp. 36–38.

Regula XII
    Idem: Fallit tantum modi divisione apposita, ut hic:

Maxima 8
    Idem: Tunc prima tenenda est via.
Regula XIII
    Idem: Si etiam inter duas longas quinque breves inveniantur, recurrendum est ad Franconem, dicentem longam primam perfectam fieri, manentibus tribus equalibus et duabus ultimis inequalibus, quia ultima brevis alterata manet, ut hic:

‖ Regula XIV
    Idem: Fallit tantum modi divisione apposita, ⟨ut hic⟩:

CS1: 387a

Maxima 9
    Idem: Et tunc prima brevis primam longam imperficit, manentibus tribus equalibus, et ultimam longam ultima ⟨brevi⟩ imperficiente.
Regula XV
    Idem: Sciendum est quod brevis alterata potest fieri erecta veluti brevis recta, ut hic:

---

6 si]sed A1 ‖ 13 *brevis* 13.1 A1 ‖ 16 ultima]ultimam A1 ‖ 19 erecta A1 ‖

Rule XII

The same: This fails when there is the introduction of a division of the mode, as here:[46]

Maxim 8

The same: Then the first way must be held fast.[47]

Rule XIII

The same: If five breves are found between two longae, reference must be had to Franco,[48] who says that the first longa is made perfect, with the remaining three equal and the last two unequal, because the last brevis remains altered, as here:[49]

Rule XIV

The same: This fails when there is the introduction of a division of the mode, as here:[50]

Maxim 9

The same: And then the first brevis imperfects the first longa, with the remaining three equal and the last brevis imperfecting the last longa.[51]

Rule XV

The same: It must be known that the altered brevis can be made erecta just like the brevis recta, as here:

---

[46]Hanboys, *Summa*, chapter 11 (250.1–2 *infra*).
[47]Hanboys, *Summa*, chapter 11 (250.3 *infra*).
[48]See Rule X of this rubric.
[49]Hanboys, *Summa*, chapter 11 (250.4–8 *infra*).
[50]Hanboys, *Summa*, chapter 11 (250.9–10 *infra*).
[51]Hanboys, *Summa*, chapter 11 (250.11–12 *infra*).

IV. Incipit quarta rubrica. De semibrevibus et de earum equalitate et inequalitate et modi divisione, et quot pro brevi et longa debeant sumi.
Regula I
   Franco: Quandocunque due semibreves inter duas longas vel breves, vel longam et brevem vel e converso inveniantur, prima semibrevis habebit unum tempus semibrevis, id est tertiam partem unius temporis, secunda vero duo, ut hic:

Regula II
   Idem: Si autem tres semibreves inveniantur, erunt equales, ut hic:

‖ Maxima 1

CS1: 387b

   Handlo: Equales vocantur, quando tres pro una brevi ponuntur. Et etiam dicuntur minores. Minor enim semibrevis tertiam partem unius brevis habet.
Regula III
   Franco: Si autem quatuor semibreves inter duas longas vel breves inveniantur, tunc semper due et due pro recta brevi computantur, ut hic:

Maxima 2
   Handlo: Regula Franconis precedens, que est tertia in hac quarta rubrica, locum habet quando valor brevis non currit nisi ad proportionem trium semibrevium, que siquidem vera est in hoketis et in quampluribus motetis.
Regula IV
   Idem: Securius tamen et verius in motetis et in aliis cantibus ubi semibreves sunt, addatur punctus inter duas et duas, vel inter tres et tres, vel inter

---

4 duo A1 ‖ 5 e converso]aequo A1 ‖ 6 semibreve A1 ‖ 14 dicuntur *m. sec.* A1 ‖

IV. Here begins the fourth rubric. Concerning semibreves, their equality and inequality, and the division of the mode; and how many ought to be taken for a brevis and a longa.

Rule I

Franco: Whenever two semibreves are found between two longae or breves or between a longa and a brevis (or conversely), the first semibrevis will have one semibrevis tempus, that is, the third part of one tempus; the second will have two, as here:[52]

Rule II

The same: If, moreover, three semibreves are found, they will be equal, as here:[53]

Maxim 1

Handlo: They are called equal when three are employed for one brevis. And they are also said to be minor. A minor semibrevis has the third part of one brevis.[54]

Rule III

Franco: If, moreover, four semibreves are found between two longae or breves, then they are always counted by twos for a brevis recta, as here:[55]

Maxim 2

Handlo: The preceding rule of Franco, which is the third in this fourth rubric, obtains when the value of the brevis does not run beyond the proportion of three semibreves, which at any rate is true in hockets and in a great number of motets.[56]

Rule IV

The same: It is, nevertheless, safer and more suitable in motets and in other songs where there are semibreves for a punctus to be added between

---

[52]Hanboys, *Summa*, chapter 12 (256.5–10 *infra*). The contents of this chapter are fully transmitted in the *Summa*, chapters 12 and 13, except for Maxims 2, 4, 5, 6, and 7. The expression "semibrevis tempus" (in other words, the third part of the duration of a brevis) is the harbinger of a major conceptual change in the status of the brevis, whose duration was heretofore the unchallenged unit of measurement in mensural music.

[53]Hanboys, *Summa*, chapter 12 (256.14–17 *infra*).

[54]Hanboys, *Summa*, chapter 12 (258.1–3 *infra*).

[55]Hanboys, *Summa*, chapter 12 (258.4–6 *infra*).

[56]The term *currit* (run) is obviously chosen to suggest the liveliness of motets and hockets with this division of the brevis, corresponding to the *mos*

duas et tres, vel inter tres et duas, ut ponit Petrus de Cruce. Hoc idemque faciunt moderni cantores, ut hic:

### Regula V

Franco: Sciendum est quod quando plures semibreves quam tres inveniuntur inter duas longas vel breves, vel longam et brevem vel e converso, predicte semibreves erunt inequales, nisi tres in fine remaneant. Ille erunt equales, ut hic: ‖

### Regula VI

Idem: Nisi per divisionem modi aliter distinguantur, ut hic:

### Maxima 3

Handlo: Tunc punctus inter tres et tres positus facit eas equales. Et si due in fine remaneant, ille erunt inequales.

### Regula VII

Petrus de Cruce: In semibrevibus est evidens nostra intentio. Ponimus, ut prius dictum est, inter duas et duas punctum, et tunc erunt inequales; hoc est, prima erit minor et secunda maior. Vel inter tres et tres, et tunc erunt equales; hoc est, omnes erunt minores. Vel inter duas et tres, et tunc erunt

---

6 e converso]aequo A1 ‖ 9 *brevis* 9.1 A1 ‖

two and two or between three and three or between two and three or between three and two, as Petrus de Cruce employs it.⁵⁷ Modern singers do the same, as here:⁵⁸

Rule V

Franco: It must be known that when more than three semibreves are found between two longae or breves or between a longa and a brevis (or conversely), the aforesaid semibreves will be unequal, unless three remain at the end. Those will be equal, as here:⁵⁹

Rule VI

The same: Unless they are otherwise distinguished by a division of the mode, as here:⁶⁰

Maxim 3

Handlo: Then the punctus employed between three and three makes them equal. And if two remain at the end, they will be unequal.⁶¹

Rule VII

Petrus de Cruce: In the semibreves, our concept is clear. We employ, as was previously said, a punctus between two and two, and then they will be unequal—that is, the first will be minor and the second major; or between three and three, and then they will be equal—that is, all will be minors; or

---

*lascivus* of Petrus le Viser (see Maxim 5F of this rubric, and Maxims 5C and 6 of Rubric XII). On quick-moving motets and hockets, see also the Introduction, pp. 23–24; and *Jacobi Leodiensis Speculum musicae*, 7 vols., ed. Roger Bragard, Corpus scriptorum de musica, no. 3 ([Rome]: American Institute of Musicology, 1973), 7:35–36 (Book 7, cap. XVII).

⁵⁷On Petrus de Cruce, see the Introduction, pp. 17–20.

⁵⁸Hanboys, *Summa*, chapter 12 (258.9–12 *infra*). For Handlo, writing in 1326, Petrus is not one of the moderns. Moreover, when this passage is quoted by Hanboys, even Handlo's moderns have become Hanboys's ancients.

⁵⁹Hanboys, *Summa*, chapter 12 (258.13–17 *infra*).

⁶⁰Hanboys, *Summa*, chapter 12 (258.18–19 *infra*).

⁶¹Hanboys, *Summa*, chapter 12 (260.1–2 *infra*).

⟨due⟩ inequales et tres equales. Vel inter tres et duas, et tunc tres equales et due inequales, ut hic:
Maxima 4

Petrus le Viser: A. Triplici vero more longe, semilonge, breves et semibreves in voce ‖ proferuntur, scilicet more longo, ⟨more⟩ mediocri et more lascivo.

B. More vero longo, semibreves, quotquot sunt, cum longis, semilongis et brevibus proferri et describi possunt.

C. More vero mediocri proferuntur tres, vel quatuor, vel quinque semibreves pro brevi cum semilongis et brevibus, et aliquando cum longis, et tunc has semibreves oportet coniungi, non dividi, et si dividi debeant, sint tres et non plures divise.

Maxima 5

D. Idem: In hoc vero more due semibreves equales sunt, et tres inequales, et quatuor equales, et quinque inequales. More tamen longo omnes precedentes regule tangentes de equalitate et inequalitate semibrevium locum habent; more tamen mediocri nequaquam.

E. More vocato lascivo proferuntur longe, semilonge et breves cum semibrevi minori et maiori, divisis, ligatis, vel obliquis, et aliquando cum eis proferuntur longe duplices. Sed nec tres, nec quatuor, nec quinque semibreves in hoc more inveniuntur, nisi omittantur longe et semilonge, et tunc, eis omissis, proferuntur breves et semibreves, scilicet due vel tres pro brevi, non plures.

F. Ex hiis itaque semibrevibus proveniunt hoketi lascivi quamplures in hoc more. Et sic regula tertia in hac rubrica locum habet, teste maxima secunda sequente.

CS1: 388b

---

8 brevibus *sup. lin., m. sec.* A1 ‖ 15 longae A1 ‖ 18 vocatae lasciva A1 ‖

between two and three, and then two will be unequal and three equal; or between three and two, and then three will be equal and two unequal, as here:⁶²

Maxim 4

Petrus le Viser:⁶³ A. Longae, semilongae, breves, and semibreves are performed by the voice⁶⁴ in three fashions, namely in the *mos longus*, the *mos mediocris*, and the *mos lascivus*.⁶⁵

B. In the *mos longus*, semibreves, however many there are, can be performed and written down with longae, semilongae, and breves.

C. In the *mos mediocris*, three or four or five semibreves replacing a brevis can be performed with semilongae and breves, and sometimes with longae; and then these semibreves must be conjoined and not separate; and if they ought to be separate, then there should be three separate notes and no more.⁶⁶

Maxim 5

D. The same: In this *mos*, two semibreves are equal, three unequal, four equal, and five unequal. In the *mos longus*, however, but never in the *mos mediocris*, all the preceding rules touching on the equality and inequality of semibreves obtain.

E. In the *mos* called *lascivus*, longae, semilongae, and breves are performed with the minor and major semibrevis, whether separate, ligated, or oblique, and sometimes duplex longae are performed with them. But in this *mos*, three or four or five semibreves are never found unless longae and semilongae are omitted, and then, since they are omitted, breves and semibreves (two or three per brevis but no more) are performed.

F. And so from these semibreves in this *mos* issue a great many lively hockets. And thus Rule III in this rubric obtains, as the following Maxim 2 attests.

---

⁶²Hanboys, *Summa*, chapter 12 (260.3–9 *infra*).

⁶³On the doctrines of the otherwise unknown Petrus le Viser, see the Introduction, pp. 22–24.

⁶⁴It is characteristic of Handlo (and here, Petrus le Viser) to observe that only when performed by the voice as sounding music are these distinct rates of speed and styles of performance actualized.

⁶⁵These fashions, or ways of singing, apparently have to do with tempo (slow, medium, fast), available note values, and perhaps style of delivery (see the Introduction, pp. 22–23). The *mos lascivus* is a "lively," not a "wanton" way of singing, but at this time, "lascivus" would not have been without a touch of moral opprobrium (private communication from Dr. David Howlett).

⁶⁶The separate semibrevis, not conjoined or ligated to other semibreves, will carry a syllable of text.

Regula VIII

⟨Idem⟩: A. In hoc vero more denegamus omnem brevem alteram et omnes brevium inequalitates, quarum equalitatem affirmamus.

B. Due igitur breves inter duas longas posite in hoc more sunt equales, ambe longe imperfecte; et sic deneganda est regula quarta tertie rubrice que tamen locum habet in longo more. ‖

C. Si tamen in hoc more lascivo tres breves inter duas longas inveniantur, ambe longe erunt perfecte, nisi brevis vel valor eas precedat vel sequatur, ut patet supra in regula quinta tertie rubrice.

D. Breves vero inter ipsas longas posite sunt equales, ut patet supra in regula septima tertie rubrice.

⟨Regula VIIIa⟩

Petrus de Cruce: A. Quatuor semibreves, divise sive coniuncte, brevem valent unam ⟨quando inter longas et breves⟩ vel inter breves et semibreves ligatas vel obliquas posite sunt.

B. Si inter semibreves divisas semibreves quatuor divise inveniantur, et punctus post eas sequatur, tunc unius brevis valorem habebunt.

C. Idem: Etiam est dicendum si quinque, vel sex, vel septem inveniantur, cum punctu eas sequente, ut patet in hoc moteto:

*Aucun ont trouvé chant par usage*

Rule VIII
The same: A. In this *mos*, we reject every brevis altera and all inequalities of breves, the equality of which we affirm.

B. Therefore, two breves employed between two longae in this *mos* are equal; both longae are imperfect. And thus Rule IV of Rubric III must be rejected, which nevertheless obtains in the *mos longus*.

C. Nevertheless, if three breves are found between two longae in this *mos lascivus*, both longae will be perfect, unless a brevis or its value precedes or follows them, as is shown above in Rule V of Rubric III.

D. The breves employed between these longae are equal, as is shown above in Rule VII of Rubric III.

Rule VIIIa
Petrus de Cruce: A. Four semibreves, separate or conjoined,[67] are worth one brevis when they are employed between longae and breves or between breves and ligated or oblique semibreves.

B. If four separate semibreves are found between separate semibreves, and a punctus follows after them, then they will have the value of one brevis.

C. The same: This also must be said if five, six, or seven are found with a punctus following them, as is shown in this motet:[68]

*Aucun ont trouvé chant par usage*

---

[67]This expression ("divise sive coniuncte") is probably an interpolation by Handlo.

[68]Hanboys, *Summa*, chapter 12 (260.10–14 *infra*). The example quotes the opening of the triplum of the French double motet *Aucun ont trouvé chant-Lonc tens-T.Annuntiantes,* whose full music survives anonymously in two sources: Montpellier, Bibliothèque Interuniversitaire, Section de Médecine, H 196 (MO), ff. 273r–275r (RISM no. 237; Rok no. 254) and Turin, Biblioteca Reale, Vari 42 (Tu), ff. 14r–15v (RISM no. 14). In citations of the motet incipit by Handlo (repeated in Hanboys), by Jacques de Liège (*Speculum musicae*, Book 7, cap. XVII [ed. Bragard], p. 37), and in the Faenza Anonymous (ed. Gallo), p. 69, another *Compendium musicae mensurabilis artis antiquae* of the *Gaudent moderni* tradition, we learn that it is a composition by Petrus de Cruce. The incipit is also cited without attribution in an anonymous *De cantu organico* edited by Higinio Anglès (*Anuario musical* 13 [1958]: 21; reprinted in idem, *Scripta musicologica*, 3 vols., ed. José Lopez-Calo [Rome: Edizioni di storia e letteratura, 1976], 3:1352), and a passage from the triplum (not the opening) is cited anonymously in an anonymous *Ars musicae mensurabilis secundum Franconem* (ed. Reaney and Gilles), p. 42; see also Edmond de Coussemaker, *Histoire de*

Maxima 6
   Petrus le Viser: Hec omnia vera sunt, ubi semibreves more longo proferuntur.
Maxima 7
5   Johannes de Garlandia: De semibrevibus autem verum et iudicium bonum dabimus in hoc opere sequente.
Regula IX
   ⟨Idem⟩: Rectum est ut tam in figura quam in signo semibrevis maior a minore distinguatur sic: si maior, sic formabitur, ad modum losonge habens

Maxim 6

Petrus le Viser: All of these things are true when semibreves are performed in the *mos longus*.

Maxim 7

Johannes de Garlandia:[69] Concerning semibreves, we will give true and good judgment following in this work.

Rule IX

The same: It is proper that the major semibrevis be distinguished from the minor not only in shape but also in sign.[70] If a major, it will be so formed in the manner of a lozenge having a stem extending obliquely below it.[71] If

---

*l'Harmonie au Moyen Age* (Paris: Didron, 1852), Doc. VI, p. 277. The motet has been edited most recently by Hans Tischler in *The Montpellier Codex*, Part III: *Fascicles 6, 7, and 8*, Recent Researches in the Music of the Middle Ages and Early Renaissance, vols. 6–7 (Madison, WI: A-R Editions, 1978), no. 254 (fasc. 7, no. 2) with an edition and translation of the texts in Susan Stakel and Joel C. Relihan, *The Montpellier Codex*, Part IV: *Texts and Translations*, Recent Researches in the Music of the Middle Ages and Early Renaissance, vol. 8 (Madison, WI: A-R Editions, 1985). On this motet, see also Wolf Frobenius, "Petrus de Cruces Motette 'Aucun ont trouvé chant par usage/Lonc tans me sui tenu de chanter/Annuntiantes': Französische Motettenkomposition um 1300," in *Analysen. Festschrift für Hans Heinrich Eggebrecht*, ed. Werner Breig, Reinhold Brinkmann, and Elmar Budde, Beihefte zum *Archiv für Musikwissenschaft*, vol. 23 (Wiesbaden: Franz Steiner, 1984), pp. 29–39; and Heinz Ristory, "Ein Abbreviationstraktat im Umfeld der franconischen und post-franconischen Compendia," *Acta musicologica* 59 (1987): 97–100 and 107–10.

[69]Concerning Johannes de Garlandia, see the Introduction, pp. 24–27.

[70]Here the term *recta* is taken as correct, proper, or appropriate rather than simply normal. Johannes de Garlandia's distinction between *figura* (shape) and *signum* (sign) is informative. For him, a *figura* is one of the simple shapes of Franco—the longa, brevis, or semibrevis. The added stem or stroke is a sign, an additional means of distinction. The punctus and the *signum rotundum* are further signs that help distinguish notes sharing the same figure.

[71]Handlo's example in **GB-Lbl**, Additional 4909, with its vertically descending stems, is in direct conflict with the text. The corresponding passage in Hanboys (*Summa*, chapter 13 [262.3–5 *infra*]) says merely "formabitur ad modum losonge habens sub se tractum," and in the accompanying example the stem of the major semibrevis descends vertically. The latter is the most commonly encountered form of the major semibrevis in continental sources; in the *Summa*, its use may reflect the influence of W. de Doncastre, who advocates this form for the major semibrevis and uses the lozenge with descending oblique stem as the figure for the minorata (Hanboys, *Summa*,

subtus se tractum in obliquum; si minor, nudo modo ad modum losonge formabitur, ut hic: ‖ ◆◆◆◆◆◆◆◆◆

CS1: 389b

Regula X

5   Handlo: Et ideo aliquando maior precedit minorem, et e converso, puncto deposito, ut hic: ◆◆◆◆ ◆◆◆

Maxima 8

Johannes de Garlandia: Pro valore brevis sumuntur tres semibreves, vel
10 quatuor, vel quinque, vel sex, vel septem, vel octo, vel novem, ad quas pertinet unius brevis proportio.

Regula XI

Idem Johannes: Minimas et minoratas agnoscere oportet. Nam minor semibrevis tres minimas valet, brevis valet tres minores, ergo brevis novem
15 minimas valebit. Et formari debent ut semibreves minores, sed per signum rotundum distinguntur, ut hic: ◆◆ o ◆◆◆ o ◆◆◆ o

Regula XII

Idem: Sunt etiam minorate semibreves. Unde minorata una duas minimas valet, et formatur veluti minima. Naturaliter vero precedit minima
20 minoratam, quando ambe post se signum rotundum habent, ut hic:

---

1 inobliquum *fort.* A1 ‖ 3 *recte cum tractibus obliquis hic et sequens* ‖ 5 e converso]aequo A1 ‖ 6 deposito *sup. lin., m. sec.* A1 dempto A2 ‖ 7 *semibrevis maior, semibrevis, semibrevis maior, semibrevis* 7.5–8 A1 ‖ 16 *brevis post* 16.6 A1 ‖ 16–114.10 *multae losongae habent tractatulum descendentem* A1 ‖ 19 minima (*pr.*) *sup. lin.* A1 ‖ 20 ambo A1 ‖

a minor, it will be formed in a plain manner in the manner of a lozenge, as here:[72]

Rule X

Handlo: And sometimes the major precedes the minor, and conversely, with the punctus unemployed, as here:[73]

Maxim 8

Johannes de Garlandia: For the value of a brevis, three semibreves are taken—or four, five, six, seven, eight, or nine, to which the proportion of one brevis pertains.[74]

Rule XI

The same Johannes: One must recognize minimae and minoratae. For the minor semibrevis is worth three minimae, while the brevis is worth three minors; therefore, the brevis will be worth nine minimae. And they ought to be formed like minor semibreves, but they are distinguished by a *signum rotundum*, as here:[75]

Rule XII

The same: There are also semibreves minoratae, where one minorata is worth two minimae and is formed like a minima. The minima naturally precedes the minorata when the two of them have a *signum rotundum* after themselves, as here:[76]

---

chapter 13 [268.27–270.14 *infra*]). A short stem is also employed to indicate the major semibrevis preceding the minor in ligatures (Rule XXIII of Rubric VI) and conjunctions (Rule V of Rubric IX), most likely in both cases with the practice of Johannes de Garlandia in mind. In all subsequent examples, this edition follows the manuscript in giving major semibreves vertical downstems. See also the Introduction, pp. 27 and 59–61.

[72]Hanboys, *Summa*, chapter 13 (262.6 *infra*). For Garlandia, the term *nuda* (plain) clearly means something like "unsigned." See p. 91, n. 25 *supra*.

[73]Hanboys, *Summa*, chapter 13 (262.9–11 *infra*). Pepusch's main scribe evidently had trouble here, leaving the reading of the word *deposito* to the proofreader; the proofreader also may have mistaken the word, which in the *Summa* is *dempto*. In any event, the point seems to be that the punctus is not necessary, i.e., when a minor is found with a major, whether preceding or following, the two must belong together.

[74]Hanboys, *Summa*, chapter 13 (262.13–15 *infra*).

[75]Hanboys, *Summa*, chapter 13 (262.15–18 *infra*).

[76]Hanboys, *Summa*, chapter 13 (264.1–4 *infra*). The Latin could be read to imply that each ought to have a *signum rotundum* following it, but the examples make clear that one small circle should follow both. The Latin

### Regula XIII

Idem: Si autem sola semibrevis habeat post se signum rotundum, minor dicetur, et tunc misceri debet inter minimas et minoratas. Due etiam semil|breves minores duo signa rotunda habebunt inter minimas et minoratas, quando tertia deest, ut hic:

CS1: 390a

### Regula XIV

⟨Idem⟩: Et si inter minimas et minoratas tres semibreves minores continentur, punctum habebunt post se, ut hic:

### Regula XV

Handlo: Minorata nunquam poni potest sine minima ipsam precedente, ut hic:

### Regula XVI

Idem: A. Tot igitur modis dicuntur semibreves, scilicet maior et minor vel equalis, minorata et minima.

B. Brevis denique maiorem et minorem ⟨valet⟩, vel tres minores, et tunc sunt equales, vel tres ⟨minimas et tres⟩ minoratas mixtim se habentes, vel novem minimas.

---

2 sola]sona A1 ‖ 18 maiorem et minorem]maiores (et minores *sup. lin.*) A1 ‖

Rule XIII

The same: If, moreover, a solitary semibrevis should have after itself a *signum rotundum*, it is said to be a minor, and then it ought to be mixed between minimae and minoratae. Two minor semibreves will have two *signa rotunda* between minimae and minoratae, when a third one is lacking, as here:[77]

Rule XIV

The same: And if three minor semibreves are contained between minimae and minoratae, they will have a punctus after themselves, as here:[78]

Rule XV

Handlo: A minorata can never be employed without a minima preceding it, as here:[79]

Rule XVI

The same: A. Therefore, semibreves are defined in so many manners, namely, major and minor, or equal, minorata, and minima.

B. Finally, a brevis is worth a major and a minor, or three minors (and then they are equals), or three minimae mixed with three minoratae, or nine minimae.

---

also might be read to suggest that without a following *signum rotundum*, the minorata might precede the minima; this is impossible, however, as without the use of the circle, they would never be identified as such small values in the first place. Handlo clarifies the precedence of the minima in Rule XV of this rubric. In **GB-Lbl**, Additional 4909, the scribe has given each minorata a slight downward stem.

[77]Hanboys, *Summa*, chapter 13 (264.8–12 *infra*).

[78]Hanboys, *Summa*, chapter 13 (264.13–15 *infra*).

[79]Hanboys, *Summa*, chapter 13 (264.16–18 *infra*). In effect, Handlo is simply repeating Rule XII of this rubric; however, he makes emphatic what was only implicit in Johannes de Garlandia's statement.

C. Tres breves se habent in perfectione; ergo perfectio habet 27 minimas, vel novem minimas et totidem minoratas mixtim se habentes, vel novem minores, vel tres maiores et totidem minores mixtim se habentes, vel e contrario, ut hic: ‖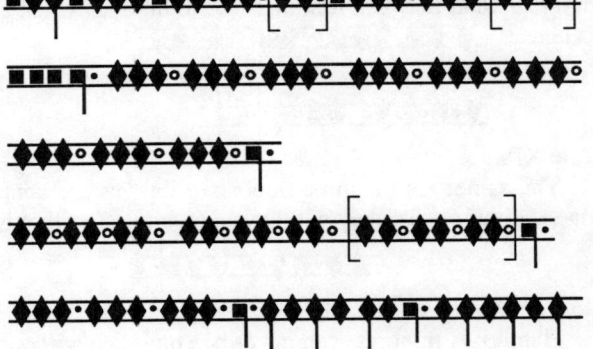

⟨Regula XVII⟩

Johannes de Garlandia: Semibreves itaque maiores atque minores divisim et coniunctim inter minimas et minoratas concomitari possunt, ut hic: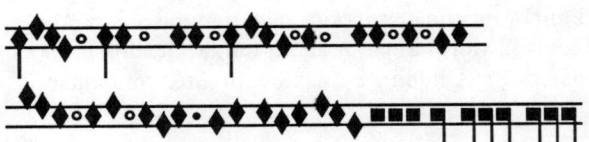

---

4 e contrario] ⟦aequo⟧ (e contrario *sup. lin., m. sec.*) A1 ‖ 5 *punctus om.* lin. 3.14 | *brevis post* lin. 4.12 A1 | *semibrevis maior, semibrevis, longa, punctus* lin. 5.21–24 A1 ‖ 7 Gerlandia A1 ‖

C. Three breves are arranged in a perfection; therefore, a perfection has twenty-seven minimae, or nine minimae mixed with just as many minoratae, or nine minors, or three majors mixed with just as many minors, or contrariwise, as here:[80]

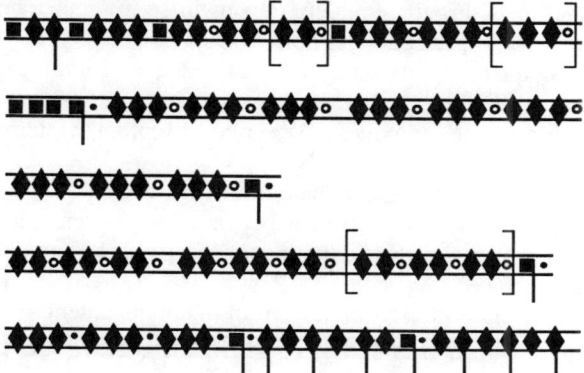

Rule XVII

Johannes de Garlandia: And so, semibreves, both major and minor, can be accompanied separately and conjoinedly by minimae and minoratae, as here:[81]

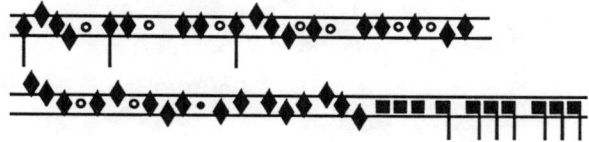

---

[80]Hanboys, *Summa*, chapter 13 (264.19–27 *infra*).
[81]Hanboys, *Summa*, chapter 13 (266.15–17 *infra*).

V. Incipit quinta rubrica. De longis que excedunt valorem longe duplicis, et que figure debent adinvicem associari.

Regula I

Handlo: A. Figura siquidem habens in se tres quadrangulos longa triplex, id est trium perfectionum nota, vocatur.

B. Si quatuor habeat, quadruplex, id est quatuor perfectionum nota, dicetur.

C. Si quinque, quinque; si sex, sex; si septem, septem; si octo, octo; si novem, novem.

D. Nec ultra debet longa maiorari.

E. Quia sic longa simplex habet in valore novem semibreves minores, sic longa novem || perfectionum novem longas in valore debet habere et non plures. CS1: 391a

F. Ecce omnium istarum longarum figure hic patent:

Maxima 1

Idem: Talibus vero longis utitur vetus organum purum, sed non formantur sic. He itaque sic figurantur, ut melius et securius agnoscantur.

Maxima 2

Idem: He longe prefigurate nunquam imperfici possunt, quia inter breves

---

15 *figurae in exemplum currit de quatuor brevibus ad decem breves* || 17–18 formatur A1 || 18 heae A1 || 20 he]heae et | inperfici A1 ||

V. Here begins the fifth rubric. Concerning longae that exceed the value of a duplex longa; and which shapes ought to be associated with each other.
Rule I

Handlo: A. A shape having in itself three squares is called a triplex longa, that is, a note of three perfections.

B. If it has four, it is said to be quadruplex, that is, a note of four perfections.

C. If five, five; if six, six; if seven, seven; if eight, eight; if nine, nine.

D. But the longa ought not to be made larger beyond this.

E. Because just as a longa simplex has nine minor semibreves in value, so a longa of nine perfections ought to have nine longae in value and no more.[82]

F. Behold the shapes of all these longae shown here:[83]

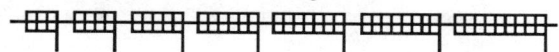

Maxim 1

The same: The old organum purum uses such longae, but they are not thus formed. And these are thus shaped so that they can be better and more safely recognized.[84]

Maxima 2

The same: These longae written above can never be imperfected because

---

[82]A figure worth nine longae is the largest ever proposed in late medieval mensural theory; see the Introduction, pp. 10 and 53.

[83]Hanboys, *Summa*, chapter 13 (266.20–268.3 *infra*). The contents of this chapter are fully transmitted in Hanboys, *Summa*, chapter 13.

[84]Hanboys, *Summa*, chapter 13 (268.4–5 *infra*). At least four other early *ars nova* treatises discuss such longae "that exceed the value of a duplex longa" and, as here, indicate by some notational means how many longae or breves are contained in the figure. These are a *Compendium musicae mensurabilis tam veteris quam novae artis* (Anonymous, *De valore notularum tam veteris quam novae artis*; Anonymous, *Compendium musicae mensurabilis tam veteris quam novae artis*; Anonymous, *De diversis manieribus in musica mensurabili*, ed. Gilbert Reaney, Corpus scriptorum de musica, no. 30 [Neuhausen-Stuttgart: Hänssler Verlag for the American Institute of Musicology, 1982], p. 34; see also Anonymous IV of *Scriptorum de musica medii aevi nova series a Gerbertina altera* [henceforward: CS], 4 vols., ed. Edmond de Coussemaker [Paris: Durand, 1864–76; reprint ed., Hildesheim: Olms, 1963], 3:376b); the quotations by Jacques de Liège from a source closely related to the preceding, in *Speculum musicae*, Book 7, cap. XXVII, sent. 1–2 (ed. Bragard), pp. 55–56; Anonymous, *De musica mensurabili* (ed. Sweeney), pp. 46–47; and Anonymous, *De cantu organico* (ed. Anglès, *Anuario musical* 13), p. 23 (= *Scripta musicologica*, 3:1354). For remarks on the performance practice of these longae, see Maxims 3B and 3C of Rubric X.

non ponuntur, nec inter semibreves. Decet enim eas inter longas simplices et duplices poni.

Regula II

Idem: Longe vero simplices cum brevibus misceri debent, cum semi-
brevibus et maioribus et minoribus concomitari possunt, sed cum minimis et minoratis nequaquam. Breves vero cum longis duplicibus misceri possunt, cum semibrevibus etiam et obliquis, ut hic patet consequenter:

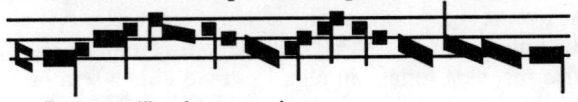

*Rota versatilis rubens versucia*

⟨Regula III⟩

Idem: Ideo longa duplex, id est sex temporum, imperficitur per brevem precedentem vel subsequentem vel per pausam unius temporis, et ⟨tunc⟩ est longa quinque temporum, ut hic:

‖ Maxima 3

Idem: A. Breves etiam cum semibrevibus minoribus et maioribus, cum minimis et minoratis, associari debent.

B. Et si alia mixtura sit, inconsona est.

C. Patet igitur que note cum quibus ⟨mixtim se⟩ habere possunt.

CS1: 391b

---

1 longa A1 ‖ 7 consequenter]quanter A1 ‖ 8

*Rota versatilis rubens versucia*

A1 ‖ 10 imperficitur per *sup. lin., m. sec.* A1 ‖ 13 *duplices longae*]simplices longae A1 ‖ 16 decent A1 ‖ 17 sit]sic A1 ‖ 18 haberi A1 ‖

they are not employed between breves or between semibreves. They should be employed between simplex and duplex longae.[85]

Rule II

The same: Simplex longae ought to be mixed with breves; they can be accompanied by major and minor semibreves, but never by minimae and minoratae. Breves can be mixed with duplex longae or with semibreves and oblique figures, as is consequently shown here:[86]

*Rota versatilis rubens versucia*

Rule III

The same: The duplex longa, that is, of six tempora, is imperfected by a preceding or following brevis or by a rest of one tempus, and then it is a longa of five tempora, as here:[87]

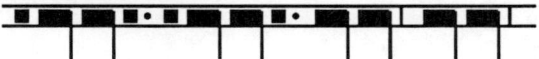

Maxim 3

The same: A. Breves ought to be associated with minor and major semibreves, with minimae and minoratae.

B. And if there should be another mixture, it is unsuitable.

C. It is therefore evident which notes can be mixed with which.[88]

---

[85]Hanboys, *Summa*, chapter 13 (268.5–8 *infra*).

[86]Hanboys, *Summa*, chapter 13 (268.9–13 *infra*). Handlo's example is the only source of the opening of one upper voice of *Rota versatilis*, a five-section, large-scale English voice-exchange motet in four voices. I am indebted to Margaret Bent for drawing the citation to my attention. For a transcription and extensive commentary, see Margaret Bent, "Rota versatilis: Towards a Reconstruction," *Source Materials and the Interpretation of Music*, ed. Ian Bent (London: Stainer and Bell, 1981), pp. 65–98; and see also Peter M. Lefferts, *The Motet in England in the Fourteenth Century* (Ann Arbor, MI: UMI Research Press, 1986), pp. 145–46 and figure 43.

[87]Hanboys, *Summa*, chapter 13 (268.14–17 *infra*). See also Rule V of Rubric II. Rule III interrupts Handlo's presentation on what figures go with each other; its addition was probably triggered by the remark that breves can be mixed with duplex longae.

[88]Hanboys, *Summa*, chapter 13 (268.18–20 *infra*).

VI. Incipit sexta rubrica. Ad cognoscendum principia ligaturarum, obliquitatem et obliquitates, et quemadmodum obliquitates in ligaturis se habent.

Maxima 1

Handlo: Tribus modis noscuntur principia ligaturarum, scilicet cum proprietate, sine proprietate, et cum proprietate opposita.

Regula I

Franco: Quandocunque secundus punctus altior est primo, et primus punctus caret omni tractu, cum proprietate dicitur, ut hic:

Regula II

Handlo: Si etiam primus punctus habeat super eum obliquitatem ascendentem vel descendentem, si tractu careat, cum proprietate etiam dicitur, ut hic:

Regula III

Franco: Quandocunque primus punctus altior est secundo, et ille primus habet tractum a || parte sinistra descendentem, cum proprietate dicitur, ut hic:

CS1: 392a

Maxima 2

Handlo: Ligatura est congeries figurarum in notis rectis et obliquis apte formata. Obliquitas est annexio solida in qua due note per vocem inveniun-

---

1 cognoscend A1 || 6 sine propritate A1 || 15 *brevis supra obliquitatem* 15.1 A1 || 20 *tractus pr. om.* 20.6 A1 || 23 firmata A1 ||

VI. Here begins the sixth rubric. On understanding the beginnings of ligatures, the oblique figure and figures, and in what way oblique figures are arranged in ligatures.[89]

Maxim 1

Handlo: The beginnings of ligatures are identified in three manners: with propriety, without propriety, and with opposite propriety.[90]

Rule I

Franco: Whenever the second notehead is higher than the first and the first notehead lacks any stem, the latter is said to be with propriety, as here:[91]

Rule II

Handlo: If the first notehead has above it an ascending or descending oblique figure, if it lacks a stem, it is also said to be with propriety, as here:

Rule III

Franco: Whenever the first notehead is higher than the second, and the first one has a stem descending from the left side, it is said to be with propriety, as here:[92]

Maxim 2

Handlo: A ligature is an aggregate of shapes suitably formed with normal and oblique notes. An oblique figure is a solid link in which two notes

---

[89]In Rubric VI, the full *Gaudent moderni* material on propriety in ligatures is interspersed with material by Handlo introducing oblique figures (e.g., Maxims 2, 3, 4, 7, and Rule VI). The interpolated sections by themselves are a coherent discussion of both oblique figures and propriety, and thus a considerable amount of repetition is introduced (e.g., Maxim 6 and Rules IV, V, and VII in respect to Rules I and III; or Rule XIV in respect to Rules VIII and IX). The interpolated material may, for this reason, come from a previous treatment of the subject by Handlo.

[90]See Franco, *Ars cantus mensurabilis*, cap. 7, sent. 6 (ed. Reaney and Gilles), p. 44; and see also Hanboys, *Summa*, chapter 19 (322.1–3 *infra*). This chapter is transmitted only in part in the *Summa*, chapter 19, in readings clearly derived from the *Regule* but usually differing in details of language from the present version.

[91]Hanboys, *Summa*, chapter 19 (322.6–9 *infra*).

[92]Hanboys, *Summa*, chapter 19 (322.10–12 *infra*).

tur, sine voce vero subintelliguntur, in eius principio et in fine. De cuius medio nichil est curandum.
Maxima 3
Idem: Obliquitatem vero distinguere oportet a ligatura, quando per se sola est.
Maxima 4
Idem: Precedentibus tribus modis dictis in prima maxima huius rubrice utitur obliquitas nuda, vel quando ligata est in principio ligature.
Maxima 5
Franco: In ligatura cum proprietate brevis est prima.
Maxima 6
Handlo: Hoc idem dicendum est in principio nude obliquitatis vel ligate, tractum ⟨descendentem⟩ habentis a parte sinistra.
Regula IV
Idem: Ad hanc animadvertendum est, quod duobus modis fit ligatura cum proprietate: uno modo, si ligatura sit ascendens, nec in sinistra primi puncti parte aliquis tractus invenitur, tunc est cum proprietate, ut in exemplo regule prime huius rubrice. ‖
Regula V
Idem: Alio modo, si ligatura sit descendens, vel per punctus quadratos vel per obliquitatem, habens in principio unum tractum descendentem, cum proprietate etiam dicetur, ut hic:

CS1: 392b

---

18 prima A1 ‖

are found by the voice (in fact, without the voice, they are implied) at the beginning of it and at the end. Concerning its middle, no attention must be paid it.[93]

Maxim 3

The same: One must distinguish an oblique figure from a ligature when it is solitary in itself.

Maxim 4

The same: The plain oblique figure makes use of the preceding three manners stated in Maxim 1 of this rubric, or when it is ligated at the beginning of a ligature.

Maxim 5

Franco: In a ligature with propriety, the first note is a brevis.[94]

Maxim 6

Handlo: This same thing must be said about the beginning of a plain or ligated oblique figure that has a stem descending on its left side.[95]

Rule IV

The same: On this, it must be considered that a ligature with propriety occurs in two manners: in one manner, if the ligature is ascending without some stem found on the left side of its first notehead, then it is with propriety, as in the example of Rule I of this rubric.

Rule V

The same: In the other manner, if the ligature is descending, whether by square noteheads or by an oblique figure, and has at its beginning a descending stem, it is also said to be with propriety, as here:[96]

---

[93]After Handlo formally defines the ligature, he must formally define the oblique figure, which he regards as a distinct, unitary entity, not a combination of figures. Just as a literary text exists for the medieval reader when spoken aloud, so the oblique figure has greatest reality when the singer sings it—gives voice to it, as it were. When read without singing, its meaning is merely implicit, because it looks like one note but sounds as two. The rather elementary caution that no note is indicated by the middle of this figure may simply indicate Handlo's pedantic caution, but it may also suggest he anticipated an audience containing individuals not familiar with basic plainchant neumes. For another instance in the *Regule* of an implicit meaning made explicit in sound, see Rule II of Rubric II.

[94]See also Hanboys, *Summa*, chapter 19 (322.13 *infra*).

[95]Hanboys, *Summa*, chapter 19 (322.14–16 *infra*).

[96]Hanboys, *Summa*, chapter 19 (322.10–12 *infra*).

**Maxima 7**

Idem: Nulla nuda obliquitas per se ligatura dici debet. Et est ratio, quia oblique breves dummodo in sola obliquitate manent, vel semibreves non sunt nisi in uno corpore. Inconveniens igitur est dicere eas ligari, cum ligatura duo corpora ad minus requirat. Maneat ergo obliquitas nuda per se simplex in qua breves et semibreves obliquantur, et non ligantur.

**Regula VI**

Idem: Plures tamen obliquitates ligate ligaturam adinvicem constituunt, ut hic:

**Regula VII**

Idem: Obliquitas descendens habens in principio tractum descendentem cum proprietate dicetur, et si ascendens fuerit habens tractum in principio descendentem, obliquitas etiam cum proprietate dicetur, ut hic:

⟨**Maxima 7a**⟩

Franco: Quandocunque secundus punctus altior est primo, et ille primus punctus habet a ‖ parte dextra tractum descendentem, sine proprietate dicitur.  CS1: 393a

**Regula VIII**

Handlo: Licet super primum punctum ligetur obliquitas ascendens vel descendens, ut hic:

---

15 *tractus pr. om.* 15.3 A1 | *tractus ultimus ascendens* 15.4 A1 ‖ 18 ascendentem A1 ‖

Maxim 7

The same: No plain oblique figure in itself ought to be said to be a ligature.⁹⁷ And the reason is because oblique breves remain always in a solitary oblique figure, and there cannot be semibreves except in one body. Therefore, it is improper to say they are ligated, since a ligature requires at least two bodies. A plain oblique figure, therefore, in which breves and semibreves are joined obliquely and not ligated, remains simplex in itself.⁹⁸

Rule VI

The same: Nevertheless, several oblique figures ligated to each other constitute a ligature, as here:⁹⁹

Rule VII

The same: A descending oblique figure having a descending stem at the beginning is said to be with propriety, and if it were ascending having a descending stem at the beginning, the oblique figure also is said to be with propriety, as here:¹⁰⁰

Maxim 7a

Franco: Whenever the second notehead is higher than the first, and the first notehead has a descending stem on its right side, it is said to be without propriety.¹⁰¹

Rule VIII

Handlo: It is permitted to ligate an ascending or descending oblique figure above the first notehead, as here:¹⁰²

---

⁹⁷This repeats Maxim 3, but now reasons are given.

⁹⁸Hanboys, *Summa*, chapter 19 (322.17–21 *infra*). Here simplex carries the meaning "integral, separate, unincorporated with any other figure" (see p. 91, n. 25 *supra*).

⁹⁹Hanboys, *Summa*, chapter 19 (322.21–23 *infra*). These can only be descending oblique figures (see Maxim 9).

¹⁰⁰Hanboys, *Summa*, chapter 19 (324.1–3 *infra*). In Handlo's example, there is no reason why the descending oblique figures should have plica-like stems on the right, though the ascending figure requires one (see Maxim 9 of this rubric). Such apparently superfluous stems are, however, a frequently encountered (purely calligraphic?) feature of oblique figures in fourteenth-century English musical sources.

¹⁰¹Hanboys, *Summa*, chapter 19 (324.4–7 *infra*).

¹⁰²Hanboys, *Summa*, chapter 19 (324.8–10 *infra*).

126

Regula IX
Franco: Quandocunque vero primus punctus altior est secundo, et ille primus punctus caret omni tractu, sine proprietate dicitur, ut hic:

5 Regula X
Handlo: Si etiam descendendo plures punctus primum sequantur in ligatura vel obliquitate, et primus punctus omni tractu caret, ligatura sine proprietate dicetur, ut patet hic consequenter:

10 Maxima 8
Franco: In ligatura sine proprietate prima longa est.
Regula XI
Handlo: Non plures longe quam due in una ligatura ligari possunt descendendo vel ascendendo. Sic ligari dicunt, ut hic patet:
15

|| Regula XII
Idem: Longa vero simplex precedens cum longa duarum perfectionum ligatur in descensu et e converso, ut hic:

CS1: 393b

20 Regula XIII
⟨Idem⟩: In ascensu vero longa simplex supra longam duarum perfectionum recte stat sed non e converso, ut hic:

Regula XIV
25 Idem: Tribus atque modis noscitur ligatura sine proprietate quorum primus est, si ligatura sit ascendens habens tractum a parte dextra primi puncti

---

14 ligari]longari A1 || 15  A1 || 18 e converso]aequo A1 || 22 recte stat]recescat A1 | e converso]aequo A1 || 23 *omnes longae ultimae sine tractibus* A1 ||

Rule IX

Franco: Whenever the first notehead is higher than the second and the first notehead lacks any stem, it is said to be without propriety, as here:[103]

Rule X

Handlo: If in descending several noteheads follow the first, whether in ligature or as an oblique figure, and the first notehead lacks any stem, the ligature is said to be without propriety, as is consequently shown here:[104]

Maxim 8

Franco: In a ligature without propriety, the first note is a longa.[105]

Rule XI

Handlo: No more than two longae can be ligated in one ligature, descending or ascending.[106] They are thus said to be ligated, as is shown here:

Rule XII

The same: In descent, a preceding longa simplex can be ligated with a longa of two perfections (or conversely), as here:[107]

Rule XIII

The same: In ascent, a longa simplex stands normally above a longa of two perfections (but not conversely), as here:[108]

Rule XIV

The same: A ligature without propriety is identified in three manners, of which the first is: if the ligature ascends, it has a descending stem on the

---

[103]Hanboys, *Summa*, chapter 19 (324.11–14 *infra*).

[104]Hanboys, *Summa*, chapter 19 (324.15–17 *infra*).

[105]Hanboys, *Summa*, chapter 19 (324.18 *infra*).

[106]See also Franco, *Ars cantus mensurabilis*, cap. 10, sent. 2 (ed. Reaney and Gilles), p. 59. Handlo's interpolation of Rules XI–XIII on ligatures of simplex and duplex longae was clearly triggered by Maxim 8, concerning how a longa can appear at the beginning of a ligature. For ligatures of breves and duplex longae, discussed in the context of lack of perfection, see Rules VII–X of Rubric VIII.

[107]Hanboys, *Summa*, chapter 20 (334.3–5 *infra*).

[108]Hanboys, *Summa*, chapter 20 (332.14–16 *infra*).

descendentem, ut supra dictum est. Secundus est, si ligatura sit descendens et primus punctus caret omni tractu. Tertius est, si ligatura incipiat per descendentem obliquitatem, eadem omni tractu carente, dicetur ligatura sine proprietate, ut hic patet in exemplo:

Regula XV

Idem: Obliquitas ascendens sola manet, nisi eam precedant longa vel brevis, vel plures breves, vel obliquitas vel obliquitates, ut hic:

‖ Maxima 9                                                                                      CS1: 394a

Idem: Post ascendentem vero obliquitatem nichil potest ei ligari nec adiungi, nisi plica. Superfluum vero est imponere obliquitatem ascendentem, plica carente.

Regula XVI

Idem: Obliquitas autem, ascendens et descendens, carens in sinistra parte tractu, longa dicetur, ut hic:

⟨Regula XVII⟩

Idem: Principium vero obliquitatis sine proprietate perficitur quando punctus preest; finis quoque ad id quod sequitur pertinebit, ut hic:

---

9 *punctus pr. cum tractu descendente ad dexteram* 9.2 A1 ‖ *tractus pr. om.* 9.5 A1 ‖ 13 carentem A1 ‖ 15 et descendens *sup. lin.* A1 ‖ 20 quod *m. sec.* A1 ‖ sequitur *sup. lin.* A1 ‖ 21 *punctus om.* 21.5, 7 A1 ‖

right side of the first notehead, as was said above. The second is: if the ligature descends, the first notehead also lacks any stem. The third is: if the ligature begins with a descending oblique figure, lacking any stem, it is said to be a ligature without propriety, as is shown here in an example:[109]

### Rule XV

The same: An ascending oblique figure remains solitary unless a longa or a brevis, many breves, or an oblique figure or oblique figures precede it, as here:[110]

### Maxim 9

The same: After an ascending oblique figure, nothing can be ligated or added to it except a plica. It is superfluous to employ an ascending oblique figure lacking a plica.[111]

### Rule XVI

The same: An oblique figure, ascending or descending, lacking a stem on the left side, is said to be a longa, as here:[112]

### Rule XVII

The same: The beginning of an oblique figure without propriety is perfected when a punctus is put before, and then the end will pertain to what follows:[113]

---

[109]Hanboys, *Summa,* chapter 19 (324.19–21 *infra*).

[110]Hanboys, *Summa,* chapter 19 (326.1–3 *infra*).

[111]Hanboys, *Summa,* chapter 19 (324.22–24 *infra*). See also Rule XVIII of this rubric, and Rule III of Rubric X. This technical point, not transmitted in the *Gaudent moderni* tradition, is made in Franco, *Ars cantus mensurabilis,* cap. 8, sent. 9 (ed. Reaney and Gilles), p. 53: "Imperfectio tamen obliqua ascendens non est ponenda sine plica, nam positio imperfectionis rectae sufficit ubicumque non est plica, et proprior est et magis usitata"; and the Franconian language persists, for instance, in the *Quatuor principalia* (CS, 3:340; 4:260–61): "Item, brevis obliqua ascendens sine plica non est ponenda, nam positio recte brevis sufficit ubicumque non est plica, et proprior est et magis usitata."

[112]The Latin text may be faulty here. It is clearly intended to say that the initial element of such a ligature is a longa.

[113]There is no precedent for this interesting rule, in which the punctus functions as a *punctus perfectionis* when placed just in front; it is to be read,

⟨Regula XVIII⟩
Idem: Obliquitas quoque descendens, si sola sit, cum plica vel sine semper potest poni; ascendentes autem nequaquam, ut hic patet in exemplo:

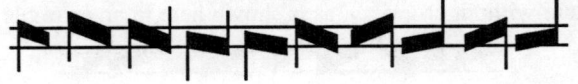

⟨Regula XIX⟩
Franco: Opposita proprietas est quandocunque in primo punctu ligature tractus ascendens invenitur, vel in uno corpore obliquo, ut hic:

Maxima 10
Handlo: Et sunt semibreves, scilicet minor precedens maiorem, que vero obliquantur per se solumodo, non ligantur.
⟨Regula XX⟩
Idem: Recta semibrevis precedens cum obli‖quitate ligari potest ascendendo et descendendo, ut hic:    CS1: 394b

⟨Regula XXI⟩
Idem: Plures semibreves quam due nunquam ligantur vel obliquantur; coniungi tamen possunt adinvicem, ut hic:

---

4 *tractus om.* 4.10 A1 ‖ 7 oblico A1 ‖ 19 *tractus pr. om.* 19.4, 7, 13 A1 ‖

Rule XVIII

The same: A descending oblique figure, if it is solitary, always can be employed with or without a plica; but ascending ones, by no means, as is shown here in an example:[114]

Rule XIX

Franco: There is opposite propriety whenever an ascending stem is found on the first notehead of a ligature or on an oblique body, as here:[115]

Maxim 10

Handlo: And they are semibreves, namely a minor preceding a major, which are in themselves oblique, not ligated.

Rule XX

The same: A preceding normal semibrevis can be ligated with an oblique figure, ascending or descending, as here:

Rule XXI

The same: More than two semibreves can never be ligated or made oblique; nevertheless, they can be conjoined to each other, as here:[116]

---

therefore, not as a division between figures but as a sign of the perfection of the first note in the oblique figure.

[114]Hanboys, *Summa*, chapter 19 (326.6–8 *infra*). This says that if without propriety, the ascending form can only be used with a plica; see Maxim 9 of this rubric.

[115]Hanboys, *Summa*, chapter 19 (326.9–11 *infra*).

[116]Hanboys, *Summa*, chapter 20 (330.10–12 *infra*). The conjunction of semibreves is dealt with fully as the topic of Rubric IX (especially in Rule VI); and see also the Introduction, p. 13.

⟨Regula XXII⟩
Idem: Ligarique possunt semibreves recte et oblique cum brevibus rectis et obliquis, semilongis et longis, ut hic:

5 ⟨Regula XXIII⟩
Idem: Si tractus autem ascendens, qui causat oppositam proprietatem, fiat curtus, tunc in hac obliquitate sive ligatura maior semibrevis minorem precedit, ut hic patet: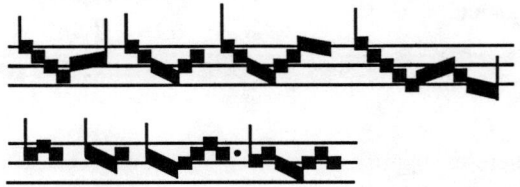

10 ⟨Maxima 11⟩
Franco: Omnis opposita proprietas signum est semibrevitatis duorum.

---

4 *tractus pr. om.* 4.1, 2, 4, 5, 7 A1 | *punctus cum tractu ascendente ad dexteram* 4.3 A1 ‖ 7 sive]sine A1 ‖ 9 *tractus pr. om.* 9.1, 5 A1 ‖

133

Rule XXII

The same: Normal and oblique semibreves can be ligated with normal and oblique breves, semilongae, and longae, as here:

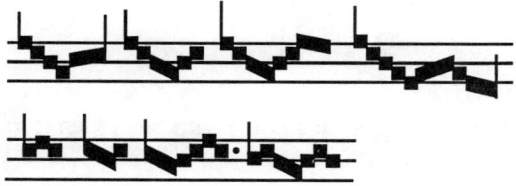

Rule XXIII

The same: If the ascending stem, which causes opposite propriety, is short, then in this oblique figure or ligature the major semibrevis precedes the minor, as is shown here:[117]

Maxim 11

Franco: Every opposite propriety is the sign of the semibrevity of two.[118]

---

[117]Handlo describes an "anti-Franconian" (2+1) interpretation of paired semibreves in a ligature or oblique figure; the abbreviated stem may derive from the notation of the major semibrevis by Johannes de Garlandia. See Rule IX of Rubric IV and also Rule V of Rubric IX.

[118]Hanboys, *Summa*, chapter 19 (326.12 *infra*).

VII. Incipit rubrica septima. Ad cognoscendum ligaturarum mediales.
Regula I
Franco: Omnes medie sunt breves, nisi per oppositam proprietatem defendantur, et tunc media est semibrevis, ut hic: ǁ

Regula II
Handlo: Et ratio ⟨est, quia⟩ due prime semibreves sunt; id quod sequitur nequaquam. Sic patet in exemplo regule prime huius rubrice.
⟨Maxima 1⟩
Franco: Ratio est quia nulla semibrevis sola potest esse.
⟨Regula III⟩
Handlo: Ligature obliquitatum quarum medie breves sunt, sic formantur:

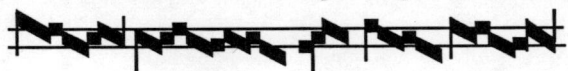

⟨Regula IV⟩
Idem: Recte breves cum eis ligantur quarum etiam medie sunt breves, ut hic:

⟨Maxima 2⟩
Idem: Obliquitas in medio ligature descendens semper est, non ascendens.

---

1 mediales]terminationes A1 ǁ 17 *tractus pr. om.* 17.3, 4 A1 ǁ

VII. Here begins the seventh rubric. On understanding the middle of ligatures.
Rule I
Franco: All middle notes are breves, unless this is prevented by opposite propriety, and then the middle note is a semibrevis, as here:[119]

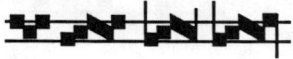

Rule II
Handlo: And the reason is because the first two are semibreves, but never that which follows.[120] This is shown in the example of Rule I of this rubric.
Maxim 1
Franco: The reason is because no semibrevis can be solitary.[121]
Rule III
Handlo: Ligatures of oblique figures, of which the middle notes are breves, are so formed:[122]
Rule IV
The same: Normal breves are ligated with these, of which the middle notes are breves, as here:

Maxim 2
The same: An oblique figure in the middle of a ligature is always descending, not ascending.[123]

---

[119]Hanboys, *Summa*, chapter 19 (326.13–16 *infra*). This chapter is transmitted only in part the *Summa*.
[120]Hanboys, *Summa*, chapter 19 (326.12 *infra*).
[121]Hanboys, *Summa*, chapter 19 (326.16–17 *infra*).
[122]Hanboys, *Summa*, chapter 19 (328.13–14 *infra*).
[123]See Maxim 9 of Rubric VI.

VIII. Incipit octava rubrica. Ad cognoscendum ligaturarum terminationes.
Regula I
Franco: Quandocunque ultimus punctus recte stat super penultimam, cum perfectione dicitur, ut hic:

Regula II
⟨Idem⟩: Quandocunque in fine ligature ultimus punctus quadratus sub penultima invenitur, cum perfectione dicitur, ut hic: ‖

CS1: 395b

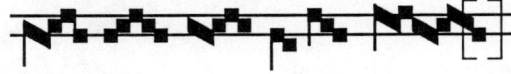

Regula III
Handlo: Ascendendo vero longa super longam, vel super brevem, vel super plures breves, super semibreves penitusque super omnem obliquitatem descendentem recte stari potest, et fiunt ligature cum perfectione, ut hic:

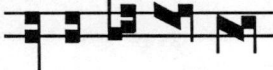

Maxima 1
Franco: Omnis perfecta longa.
Regula IV
Handlo: Si ligatura desinat descendendo, et habeat ultimam quadratam, ultima erit longa, licet sub longa vel brevi, vel sub pluribus brevibus, vel sub semibrevibus inveniatur, ut hic:

Regula V
Franco: Quandocunque ultimus punctus stat indirecte super penultimam, brevis est, ut hic:

---

4 recte stat]recescat A1 ‖ 14 recte stari]recescari A1 ‖ 21 sub semibrevibus]⟦pluribus brevibus vel sub⟧ semibrevibus A1 ‖ 22 *tractus pr. om.* 22.4, 5 A1 ‖

VIII. Here begins the eighth rubric. On understanding the ends of ligatures.

Rule I

Franco: Whenever the last notehead stands normally above the penultimate, it is said to be with perfection, as here:[124]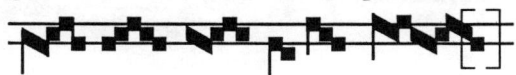

Rule II

The same: Whenever at the end of a ligature the last square notehead is found below the penultimate, it is said to be with perfection, as here:[125]

Rule III

Handlo: In ascending, a longa normally can be stood above a longa, above a brevis, above many breves, above semibreves, or entirely above every descending oblique figure, and these will become ligatures with perfection, as here: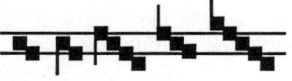

Maxim 1

Franco: Everything perfect is a longa.[126]

Rule IV

Handlo: If a ligature ends by descending and has a square as the last note, the last note will be a longa, whether it is found below a longa or brevis, below many breves, or below semibreves, as here:[127]

Rule V

Franco: Whenever the last notehead stands indirectly above the penultimate, it is a brevis, as here:[128]

---

[124]Hanboys, *Summa*, chapter 20 (328.19–21 *infra*). This chapter is transmitted only in part in the *Summa*.
[125]Hanboys, *Summa*, chapter 20 (330.1–3 *infra*).
[126]Hanboys, *Summa*, chapter 20 (330.7 *infra*).
[127]See Rule II *supra* and Hanboys, *Summa*, chapter 20 (330.1–3 *infra*).
[128]Hanboys, *Summa*, chapter 20 (330.4–6 *infra*).

Regula VI
    Idem: Quandocunque due note in uno corpore obliquo in fine ligature inveniuntur, ultima erit brevis, ut hic: ‖

CS1: 396a

5  Regula VII
    Handlo: In ligatura descendente brevis cum longa duarum perfectionum ligari potest, sed non e converso, ut hic: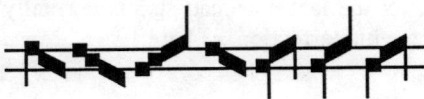

Regula VIII
10    Idem: Similiter duplex longa cum se ipsa deorsum ligari potest, ut in exemplo regule proxime precedentis.
Regula IX
    Idem: In ascendente vero ligatura longa duplex precedens ligatur cum brevi et cum se ipsa, ut patet hic:
15

⟨Regula X⟩
    ⟨Idem⟩: Una brevis vel plures inter duas duplices longas ligari possunt, ut hic:

20 Regula XI
    Idem: Sciendum est etiam quod brevis altera latet aliquando in ligatura rectarum brevium et in obliquitate, ut hic:

---

3 invenitur A1 ‖ 4 *tractus ult. om.* 4.3, 6 A1 ‖ 7 e converso *m. sec.* A1 ‖ 20 Regula 10ª A1 ‖

Regula VI

The same: Whenever two notes are found in one oblique body at the end of a ligature, the last will be a brevis, as here:[129]

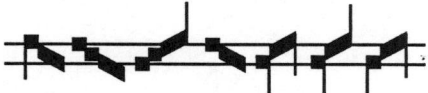

Rule VII

Handlo: In a descending ligature, a brevis can be ligated with a longa of two perfections, but not conversely, as here:[130]

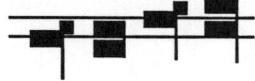

Rule VIII

The same: Similarly, a duplex longa can be ligated downwards with one like itself, as in the example of the rule just preceding.

Rule IX

The same: In an ascending ligature, a preceding duplex longa can be ligated with a brevis or with one like itself, as here:[131]

Rule X

The same: One or more breves can be ligated between two duplex longae, as here:[132]

Rule XI

The same: It must be known that a brevis altera sometimes lies concealed in a ligature of breves rectae and in an oblique figure, as here:

---

[129]Hanboys, *Summa*, chapter 20 (330.13–19 *infra*).

[130]Rules VII–X, an interpolation on ligatures of breves and duplex longae that was triggered by the discussion of lack of perfection, correspond to the rules about ligatures of single and duplex longae following the discussion about lack of propriety in Rules XI–XIII of Rubric VI. The "imperfection" of a duplex longa by a brevis is one of the novel doctrines of the *Regule* (see Rule V of Rubric II and Rule III of Rubric V), which is undoubtedly why these ligatures warrant specific inclusion here.

[131]Hanboys, *Summa*, chapter 20 (334.6–8 *infra*).

[132]Hanboys, *Summa*, chapter 20 (334.9–12 *infra*).

⟨Maxima 2⟩
Idem: Denique viciosum est notas ligabiles non ligare, ligareque nonligabiles. ‖

CS1: 396b

Maxim 2

The same: Lastly, it is defective not to ligate notes that can be ligated or to ligate notes that cannot be ligated.[133]

---

[133]Hanboys, *Summa*, chapter 20 (330.20–21 *infra*). See Franco, *Ars cantus mensurabilis*, cap. 10, sent. 1 (ed. Reaney and Gilles), p. 59: "Item sciendum quod figura ligabilis non ligata vitiosa est, sed magis non ligabilis ligata"; and see also Maxim 4 of Rubric IX.

IX. Incipit nona rubrica. De coniunctionibus semibrevium, et quibus figuris seu ligaturis semibreves debeant coniungi.
Regula I
Handlo: Notandum est quod tres semibreves minores ordinatim coniun-
5  guntur sursum et deorsum, cum punctu divisionis quando necesse est, ut hic:

Regula II
Idem: Minime et minorate simili modo cum figuris rotundis coniungi possunt, ut hic:
10
Regula III
Idem: Due vero semibreves cum longa vel brevi coniungi decet, ut hic:

Regula IV
15  Idem: Quando due semibreves similes sunt in coniunctione, prima erit minor, alia maior, ut supra in exemplo regule tertie huius rubrice.
Regula V
Idem: Nisi tractum obliquum sit impedimentum; et tunc erit semibrevium dissimilitudo, et fiet prima maior, altera minor, ut hic: ‖
20

CS1: 397a

Regula VI
⟨Idem⟩: In fine siquidem cuiuslibet ligature vel obliquitatis, semibreves due vel tres vel quatuor deorsum vel sursum, vel partim deorsum vel partim

---

5 neccesse A1 ‖ 20 *recte semibreves cum tractibus obliquis* ‖

IX. Here begins the ninth rubric. Concerning conjunctions of semibreves and the shapes or ligatures with which semibreves ought to be conjoined.[134]

Rule I

Handlo: It must be noted that three minor semibreves are conjoined in a row upwards and downwards, with a *punctus divisionis*[135] when necessary, as here:

Rule II

The same: In similar manner, minimae and minoratae can be conjoined with round shapes, as here:

Rule III

The same: Indeed, two semibreves should be conjoined with a longa or a brevis, as here:

Rule IV

The same: When two similar semibreves are in conjunction, the first will be minor, the second major, as above in the example of Rule III of this rubric.

Rule V

The same: Unless an oblique stem is an obstacle, and then there will be a dissimilarity of the semibreves, and the first will become major, the other minor, as here:[136]

Rule VI

The same: At the end of any ligature or oblique figure, two or three or four semibreves can be conjoined downwards or upwards, or partly down-

---

[134]This chapter is not transmitted in the *Summa* of Hanboys. It corresponds to a brief passage in Franco, *Ars cantus mensurabilis*, cap. 8, sent. 11–14 (ed. Reaney and Gilles), pp. 53–54, but represents a vast expansion upon and formalization of it. See the Introduction, p. 13.

[135]This is the first use by Handlo of the expression *punctus divisionis*, essentially the punctus of Petrus de Cruce, in place of the *Gaudent moderni* tradition's *divisio modi*.

[136]Handlo describes an anti-Franconian interpretation (2+1) of paired semibreves in conjunction. The oblique stem prescribed for the major derives from the notation of the major semibrevis by Johannes de Garlandia (see Rule IX of Rubric IV), and as there, the manuscript example shows a

sursum, coniungi possunt, si ligature vel obliquitates non plicentur, ut hic:

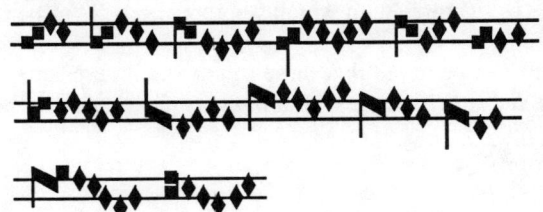

Regula VII
    Idem: Quatuor semibreves adinvicem coniunguntur sine signo, valorem habentes unius brevis, ut hic:

Regula VIII
    Idem: Fallit tamen modi divisione opposita, ut hic:

Maxima 1
    Idem: Et tunc tres pro brevi computantur. Ultima vero ad id quod sequitur pertinebit, scilicet ‖ ad divisam semibrevem proximam sequentem vel eius valorem.  CS1: 397b

Regula IX
    Idem: Tres vero semibreves vel quatuor cum brevi vel longa coniungi possunt et e converso, ut hic:

Regula X
    Idem: Brevis vero precedens quando semibreves duas vel tres vel quatuor in coniunctione se habent, nuda non potest esse, sed tractum a parte

---

16 e converso]aequo A1 ‖ 19 quando]que A1 ‖

wards and partly upwards, if the ligatures or oblique figures are not plicated, as here:[137]

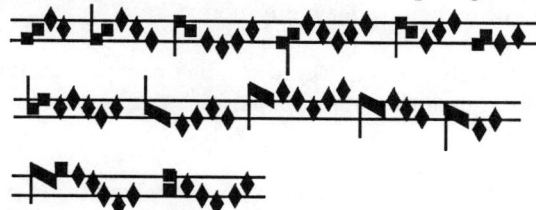

### Rule VII

The same: Four semibreves that have the value of one brevis are conjoined to each other without a sign, as here:[138]

### Rule VIII

The same: This fails when there is the employment of a division of the mode, as here:

### Maxim 1

The same: And then three are counted as a brevis. The last will pertain to what follows, namely to the next following separate semibrevis or its value.

### Rule IX

The same: Three or four semibreves can be conjoined with a brevis or longa (and conversely), as here:

### Rule X[139]

The same: A preceding brevis, when two or three or four semibreves are arranged in conjunction, cannot be plain but will have a stem descending

---

directly descending stem. For paired semibreves in ligature read 2+1, see Rule XXIII of Rubric VI.

[137]Hanboys, *Summa*, chapter 20 (330.10–12 *infra*). See also Rule XXI of Rubric VI.

[138]This differs from the practices of both Franco of Cologne and Petrus de Cruce. For Franco, four semibreves not distinguished by a *divisio modi* are worth two breves; Petrus de Cruce uses a punctus either to distinguish two and two or to indicate four in the place of a brevis. See Rule II of Rubric IV and Rule VIIIa of this rubric.

[139]Plate 1 illustrates a passage beginning in the middle of this rule and extending to the end of the rubric (146.1–150.14).

sinistra habebit descendentem, et dicetur brevis coniungens, ut patet supra in exemplo regule tertie et regule none huius rubrice.
Regula XI
   Idem: Semibreves etiam oblique et recte adinvicem possunt coniungi sub perfectionis valore, quarum coniunctio patet in exemplo regule vigesime prime sexte rubrice.
Regula XII
   Admetus de Aureliana: Cantores de Navernia minoratas et minimas per se sic coniungunt adinvicem cum signis, et coniunguntur deorsum non sursum, ut hic:

|| Regula XIII                                                                CS1:
   Idem: Semibrevis maior vel minor precedens aliquando minoratas et  398a
minimas coniungit, ut hic:

---

5–6 21ᵐᵉ *sup. lin., m. sec.* A1 || 8 Navernia *fort.* Naverina A1 || 11 *vide* Plate 1 || 15 *vide* Plate 1 ||

from the left side, and it is said to be a conjoined brevis, as is shown above in the examples of Rule III and Rule IX of this rubric.[140]

Rule XI

The same: Oblique and semibreves rectae can be conjoined to each other under the value of a perfection, the conjunction of which is shown in the example of Rule XXI of Rubric VI.

Rule XII

Admetus of Orleans:[141] Singers of Navarre[142] conjoin minoratae and minimae to each other by themselves with signs, and they are conjoined downwards but not upwards, as here:

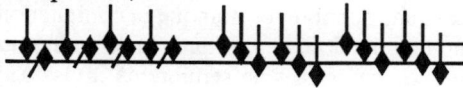

Rule XIII

The same: A preceding major or minor semibrevis sometimes conjoins minoratae and minimae, as here:

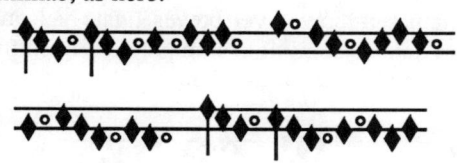

---

[140]The conjoined brevis is probably a punctus quadratus with a stem descending vertically from its left side. Walter Odington discusses figures similar to Handlo's, with a stemmed square brevis conjoined to semibreves, in *De speculatione musicae*, cap. 9, sent. 8–10 and cap. 10, sent. 5–6, 18 (ed. Hammond), pp. 137 and 138–39. One wonders whether this shape may be indebted to the earlier "English coniunctura" figure whose first element was a lozenge with a stem descending either obliquely or directly from its left shoulder. See Lefferts, *The Motet in England*, pp. 104–11, esp. pp. 108–9 and figure 30.

[141]Admetus is known only through this reference. The signs used by the musicians of Navarre include the obliquely descending stem on the minorata and the upward stem on the minima. On the invention of the minima (or at least of this shape for it) in Navarre, see the Introduction, pp. 27–28.

[142]Either the kingdom of Navarre or the College of Navarre may be intended. A John of Navarre is cited in this treatise as an authority on hockets; see Maxim 5 of Rubric XII and the Introduction, pp. 20–21.

Regula XIV

Idem: Et e contrario, minime et minorate, semibrevem minorem vel maiorem vel utramque, ligatam vel obliquam, coniungunt, ut hic:

Regula XV

Handlo: Si vero nude semibreves quinque in coniunctione inveniantur, et post tres fit punctus divisionis, tres pro brevi computantur; due vero sequentes minores iudicantur, si sola semibrevis divisa sequens inveniatur, ut hic: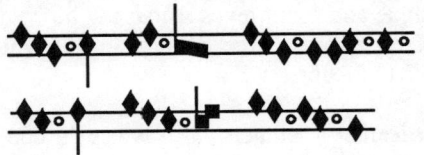

Regula XVI

Idem: Due etiam semibreves vel breves ligate vel oblique, cum tribus minoribus vel cum duabus et minima et minorata sequentibus, coniungi possunt, et e converso, ut hic patet in exemplo:

---

2 e contrario] [[aequo]] (e contrario *sup. lin., m. sec.*) A1 ‖ 4 *vide* Plate 1 ‖ 10 *vide* Plate 1 ‖ 12 vel (*pr.*)]ad A1 ‖ 14 e converso]aequo A1 ‖ 15 *vide* plate 1 ‖

## Rule XIV

The same: And conversely, minimae and minoratae are conjoined with a minor or major semibrevis, or either one of these ligated or oblique, as here:

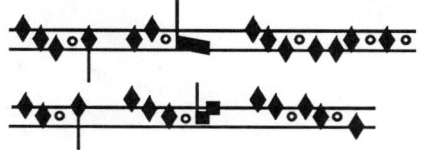

## Rule XV

Handlo: If five plain semibreves are found in conjunction and after three there is a *punctus divisionis*, the three are counted as a brevis; the following two are judged to be minors, if a solitary following separate semibrevis is found, as here:[143]

## Rule XVI

The same: Two semibreves or breves, ligated or oblique, can be conjoined to three minors or to two following a minima and a minorata, and conversely, as is shown here in an example:

---

[143]Examples of the practice described here, drawn from English motets, can be found in Lefferts, *The Motet in England*, pp. 114–15 and example 7 of figure 32. Johannes Wolf mistakenly interpreted this passage as referring to syncopation; see his *Geschichte der Mensural-Notation von 1250–1460*, 3 vols. (Leipzig: Breitkopf & Härtel, 1904), 1:132; and idem, *Handbuch der Notationskunde*, 2 vols. (Leipzig: Breitkopf & Härtel, 1913–1916), 1:342.

⟨Maxima 2⟩

‖ Idem: Sola vero semibrevis post omnem ligaturam vel obliquitatem coniungi potest; referri vero debet ad proximam semibrevem sequentem vel eius valorem.

CS1: 398b

Maxima 3

Idem: Coniunctio est conglutinatio figurarum debito modo supra sillabam ordinata.

Maxima 4

Idem: Optimum est denique notas iungibiles iungere, disiungereque noniungibiles.

Maxima 5

Idem: In divisionibus igitur figurarum, in ligaturis et in obliquitatibus et in coniunctionibus earum, hec est ars inventa quam cuilibet cantori habere necesse est.

---

2 semibrevis]brevis A1 ‖ 9 iungibiles]iniungibiles A1 ‖ 12 obliquitatibus]obliquibus A1 ‖

Maxim 2

The same: A solitary semibrevis can be conjoined after every ligature or oblique figure; it ought to be related to a semibrevis immediately following or its value.

Maxim 3

The same: A conjunction is a cementing together of shapes ordered in proper manner over a syllable.

Maxim 4

The same: Finally, it is best to join notes that are joinable and to disjoin notes that are not joinable.[144]

Maxim 5

The same: In the divisions of shapes, therefore—in ligatures and oblique figures and conjunctions of them—, this is the learned art that is necessary for any singer to have.

---

[144]Handlo has borrowed his syntax from the earlier rule about ligatures; see Maxim 2 of Rubric VIII.

X. Incipit decima rubrica. Quomodo se plice habent in ligaturis et in obliquitatibus, et qualiter simplex longa plicata transit a vi plice in erectam longam ⟨et qualiter longa ad perfectionem et ad imperfectionem⟩ equivocatur.

Maxima 1

Handlo: In ligaturis vel obliquitatibus nunquam ponitur plica, nisi in fine.

Regula I

Franco: Quandocunque in fine ligature plicatur, punctus quadratus pro longa tenetur.

Handlo: Sive sit ascendens ligatura sive descendens, sive partim ascendens vel partim descendens, ut hic:

‖ Regula II

Franco: Quandocunque in fine ligature due note in uno corpore obliquo sunt, et in fine sit tractus ascendens vel descendens, ultima pro brevi plicata tenetur, ut hic:

CS1: 399a

Regula III

Handlo: Et si in fine ligature, obliquitas ascendens utitur plica; aliter vitiosum esset eam imponere, ut supra patet in maxima nona sexte rubrice.

⟨Regula IIIa⟩

Idem: Obliquitas duarum semibrevium habet ascendentem plicam et descendentem, ut hic:

Regula IV

Idem: Tres etiam semibreves minores habent in fine plicam solumodo ascendentem, ut patet in exemplo regule octave et in maxima sexta sequente prime rubrice.

---

2 obliquitatibus]obliquibus A1 ‖ 11 sit]sic A1 ‖ 13 *tractus per plicam om.* lin. 1.2, 3, 4 et lin. 2.5, 6 A1 ‖ 15 obliquo]obliquae A1 ‖ 18 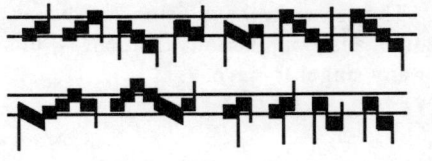 A1 ‖ 21 imponere]inponere A1 ǀ sexte]quinte A1 ‖

X. Here begins the tenth rubric. How plicas are arranged in ligatures and oblique figures, and how a plicated simplex longa changes into a longa erecta through the power of a plica, and how a longa has two meanings, referring to perfection and imperfection.

Maxim 1

Handlo: A plica is never employed in ligatures and oblique figures except at the end.[145]

Rule I

Franco: Whenever a square notehead is plicated at the end of a ligature, it is held to be a longa.[146]

Handlo: Whether the ligature is ascending or descending, or whether ascending in part or descending in part, as here:

Rule II

Franco: Whenever at the end of a ligature there are two notes in one oblique body and at the end there is a stem ascending or descending, the last is held to be a brevis plicata:[147]

Rule III

Handlo: And if at the end of a ligature there is an ascending oblique figure, it uses a plica. It would be wrong to employ it otherwise, as is shown above in Maxim 9 of Rubric VI.

Rule IIIa

The same: An oblique figure of two semibreves has an ascending or descending plica, as here:

Rule IV

The same: Three minor semibreves have at the end only an ascending plica, as is shown in the example of Rule VIII and Maxim 6, which follows in Rubric I.[148]

---

[145]Hanboys, *Summa*, chapter 20 (330.22 *infra*). The *Summa*, in chapter 20, quotes only selectively from this rubric.
[146]Hanboys, *Summa*, chapter 20 (332.1–3 *infra*).
[147]Hanboys, *Summa*, chapter 20 (332.4–6 *infra*).
[148]See also Maxim 3 of this rubric.

## Regula V

Idem: Duplex vero longa ascendendo et descendendo plicari potest, ut hic:

## Regula VI

Idem: Et si sit in fine ligature, et ascendendo et descendendo, perplicari potest, ut hic: ||

CS1: 399b

## Regula VII

Idem: Sciendum est quod longa vel semilonga ligata in fine ligature vel obliquitatis habens tractum ascendentem transit a vi plice in erectam longam quando nota vel pausa sequens invenitur ibi quo plica tendit, et dicetur erecta longa, ut hic patet in exemplo:

## Maxima 2

Idem: Omnis igitur ligatura, sive ex longis, brevibus vel semibrevibus, obliquitatibusve constituta sit, in fine plicari potest sursum similiter et deorsum.

## Maxima 3

Idem: A. Omnis etiam coniunctio semibrevium minorum et in fine perplicari potest sursum, non deorsum; minimarum vero et minoratarum nequaquam.

B. Ille etiam magne longe, que mensuram excedunt unius longe duplicis, nunquam perplicantur neque ligantur.

C. Decet enim eas solido modo pronunciari.

---

4 *omnes tractus om.* 4.1–3 A1 || 6 si *sup. lin.* A1 || 8 *duplices longae*]*obliquitates descendentes* A1 || 21 potest]possunt A1 ||

Rule V

The same: A duplex longa can be plicated ascending and descending, as here: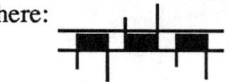

Rule VI

The same: And if it is at the end of a ligature, it can be plicated either ascending or descending, as here:[149]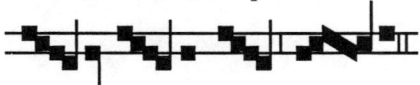

Rule VII

The same: It must be known that a longa or a semilonga ligated at the end of a ligature or an oblique figure that has an ascending stem changes into a longa erecta through the power of the plica when a following note or rest is found in the place where the plica is tending, and it is said to be a longa erecta, as is shown here in an example:[150]

Maxim 2

The same: Therefore, every ligature, whether constituted of longae, breves or semibreves, or oblique figures, can be similarly plicated at the end, rising or falling.

Maxim 3

The same: A. Every conjunction of minor semibreves can be plicated upwards but not downwards at the end, but never one of minimae and minoratae.[151]

B. Those large longae that exceed the measure of one duplex longa can never be plicated nor ligated.

C. They should be uttered in a firm manner.[152]

---

[149]Hanboys, *Summa*, chapter 20 (332.17–19 and 334.1–2 *infra*).

[150]See also Hanboys, *Summa*, chapter 20 (332.17–19 *infra*). On the longa erecta, see Maxim 3 of Rubric I. Franco, *Ars cantus mensurabilis*, cap. 8, sent. 8 (ed. Reaney and Gilles), p. 53, observes that a plica after a square note at the end of an ascending ligature without perfection perfects that note. Walter Odington comments on the same phenomenon in *De speculatione musicae*, cap. 8, sent. 18 and cap. 10, sent. 25 (ed. Hammond), pp. 136 and 139.

[151]See Maxim 1F of Rubric XI; and see also Rule IV of this rubric and Rule VIII and Maxim 6 of Rubric I.

[152]Maxims 3B and 3C belong with Handlo's principal discussion of extra-long longae in Rubric V. The recommendation to sing them firmly or

Maxima 4

Idem: Alterata vero brevis in fine ligature ⟨vel⟩ in obliquitate perplicari potest, dummodo cum longa a se divisa sequatur seu semilonga.

Maxima 5

5   Idem: Hic terminus longa equivocari potest ad perfectionem, videlicet et ad imperfectionem. Et ‖ sic longa pro se ipsa et aliquando pro semilonga sumi potest, ut patet supra in regula prima, et in maxima prima et in secunda secunde rubrice.

CS1: 400a

Maxim 4

The same: An altered brevis at the end of a ligature or in an oblique figure can be plicated so long as a separate longa or semilonga follows it.

Maxim 5

The same: This term "longa" can have two meanings: referring to perfection and to imperfection. And thus a longa can be taken for itself and sometimes for a semilonga, as is shown above in Rule I and Maxims 1 and 2 of Rubric II.

---

straightforwardly ("solido modo pronunciari"), presumably meaning with no plica or sag in pitch or volume, is important evidence for vocal performance practice in the old organum purum ("vetus organum purum"). It recalls Edward Roesner's suggestion (in "The Performance of Parisian Organum," *Early Music* 7 [1979]: 176) that a difficult passage in Franco's *Ars cantus mensurabilis* (cap. 14, sent. 5 [ed. Reaney and Gilles], pp. 80–81) might be recommending the same thing, if "se in concordantiam fingat (shape itself into a consonance)" can be glossed as "holding the note as though it were consonant by singing it forthrightly." See also Walter Odington, *De speculatione musicae*, cap. 12, sent. 10 (ed. Hammond), p. 141.

XI. Incipit undecima rubrica. De valore plicarum.
Maxima 1
   Handlo: A. Sciendum est quod plica unius longe duplicis valorem unius semibrevis maioris habet.
5  B. Simplicis vero longe et semilonge plica unam semibrevem minorem valet.
   C. Brevis vero plica unius minorate valorem habet, et si alterata sit, eius plica semibrevem minorem valebit.
   D. Plica etiam semibrevis maioris unam minoratam valebit.
10  E. Semibrevis quoque minoris unam minimam.
   F. Recta semibrevis ligata, sed nec minime, nec minorate, perplicari possunt.

---

2 1]unica A1 ‖ 7 brevis]brevi A1 ‖ 9 maioris]valoris A1 ‖

XI. Here begins the eleventh rubric. Concerning the value of plicas.[153]
Maxim 1

Handlo: A. It must be known that the plica of one duplex longa has the value of one major semibrevis.

B. The plica of a simplex longa or semilonga is worth one minor semibrevis.

C. The plica of a brevis has the value of one minorata, and if the brevis is altered, its plica will be worth a minor semibrevis.

D. The plica of a major semibrevis will be worth one minorata.

E. That of a minor semibrevis, one minima.

F. A ligated semibrevis recta, but neither minimae nor minoratae, can be plicated.[154]

---

[153]This chapter is not transmitted by Hanboys, and, in fact, nowhere outside the *Regule* is there a discussion of the length of plicas. The language here (and perhaps the concept) is obviously indebted to Handlo's Johannes de Garlandia on account of its reference to major and minor semibreves, minoratae and minimae. Unusual English attention to plicas is not limited to Handlo. A figure showing the pitch resolution of plicas, likewise unique, is found in the British source **GB**-Lbl, Royal 12.C.vi, f. 53v.

[154]On the plication of semibreves, see Rule VII and Maxim 6 of Rubric I, and see also Maxims 2 and 3A of Rubric X.

XII. Incipit duodecima rubrica. De pausis que vocem omissam faciunt.
Maxima 1
    Franco: Pausationum sex sunt species.
    A. Prima est trium temporum.
    B. Secunda, duorum.
    C. Tertia, unius.
    D. Quarta, duarum partium unius.
    E. Quinta, tertie partis unius.
    F. Sexta et ultima nullius temporis, sed potius immensurabilis pausa appellatur. Causa inventionis cuius, ut ubicunque inveniretur, penultimam notam designaret esse longam, licet penultima brevis vel semibrevis foret.
Maxima 2
    Handlo: Minorate vero nec minime pausam non habent correspondentem. ‖
Regula I
    Franco: A. Pausa trium temporum tria spatia vel valorem trium tegit, scilicet cum duobus integris et duobus semis. Pausa vero duarum temporum duo spatia tegit vel unum integrum et duo semis.
    B. Pausa vero unius temporis unum spatium tegit vel etiam duo semis.
    C. Pausa vero duarum partium unius temporis duas partes unius spatii tegit tantum.
    D. Pausa vero tertie partis unius temporis tertiam partem unius spatii tegit.
    E. Pausa vero que immensurabilis dicitur, finis punctorum appellatur, quatuor spatia tegens.

CS1: 400b

---

1 pausis]pasis A1 ‖ 9 immensurabilis]inmesurabilis A1 ‖ 12 Maxima 2] Regula I A1 ‖ 15 Regula I]Maxima III A1 ‖ 20 partium]perfectionum A1 ‖ 24 immensurabilis]inmensurabilis A1 ‖

XII. Here begins the twelfth rubric.[155] Concerning rests, which make a withheld voice.[156]

Maxim 1

Franco: There are six kinds of rests.

A. The first is of three tempora.

B. The second, of two.

C. The third, of one.

D. The fourth, of two thirds of one.

E. The fifth, of a third of one.

F. The sixth and last is of no tempus, but rather is named an immensurable rest. The reason for its invention is that wherever it might be found, it would designate the penultimate note to be a longa, though the penultimate may be a brevis or a semibrevis.[157]

Maxim 2

Handlo: Neither minoratae nor minimae have corresponding rests.

Rule I

Franco: A. The rest of three tempora covers three spaces or the value of three, namely two entirely and two halves. The rest of two tempora covers two spaces, or one entirely and two halves.[158]

B. The rest of one tempus covers one space, or else two halves.

C. The rest of two thirds of one tempus covers just two thirds of one space.

D. The rest of a third of one tempus covers one third of one space.

E. The rest that is said to be immensurable is named the endline, covering four spaces.

---

[155]This chapter is transmitted in part by Hanboys, *Summa*, chapter 21.

[156]The voice is withheld or omitted during a musical rest, just as a reader of a literary text withholds sound during the break between sentences. A rest is not "without" sound (*sine voce*) unless it is being interpreted by a score reader who is conceptualizing but not vocalizing. See Maxim 2 of Rubric 6 and its note.

[157]Hanboys, *Summa*, chapter 21 (334.15–336.4 *infra*). The final type of rest is the *finis punctorum* (endline), literally "the end of notes" and therefore a kind of note; the penultimate note is actually the last to be sounded. Concerning this figure, which might also be translated "double bar," see Klaus-Jürgen Sachs, "Punctus, IV.(2)," in *Handwörterbuch der musikalischen Terminologie*, ed. Hans Heinrich Eggebrecht (Wiesbaden: Franz Steiner, 1972– ).

[158]The remark "or two halves" in Rules 2A and 2B is not from Franco's *Ars cantus mensurabilis* or the *Gaudent moderni* tradition but allies Handlo's text with the passage concerning rests in Petrus Picardus, *Ars motettorum compilata breviter* (ed. Gallo), p. 23.

Et apparent forme suarum hic quinte:

⟨Maxima 3⟩
....
5 Maxima 4
⟨Handlo vel Garlandia⟩: Sepius per pausam vero duarum partium unius et tertie partis unius semibrevis minoris se maiori adiunctam causatur.
Maxima 5
Hoketi.
10 Jacobus de Navernia: Et tribus diversificantur hoketi.
A. Primo modo, per brevem et pausam unius vel duarum sibi adiunctam, vel e converso.

---

1 suarum hic quinte]earum hic quinto A1 ‖ 2 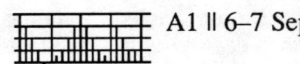 A1 ‖ 6–7 Sepius ... causatur *sup. lin., m. sec.* A1 Unius et tertie partis unius semibrevis sepius; per pausam vero duarum partium minoris majori adjunctam causatur CS ‖ 7 semibrevis]semibrevi A1 ‖ 10 Navernia *fort.* Naverina ‖ 11 duarum] duorum A1 ‖ 12 e converso]aequo A1 ‖

And the five forms of these appear here:[159]

Maxim 3

....[160]

Maxim 4

Handlo or Garlandia: More frequently, by the rest of two-thirds of one tempus and a third of one tempus, the minor semibrevis is caused to be adjoined to the major.[161]

Maxim 5

Hockets.

Jacobus de Navernia:[162] And hockets are differentiated in three manners.[163]

A. In the first manner, by a brevis and a rest of one or of two adjoined to it, or conversely.

---

[159]Hanboys, *Summa*, chapter 21 (336.5–15).

[160]Something is confused about the numbering of maxims and rules at this point in the rubric. Maxim 2 was called Rule I and Rule I was called Maxim 3, which implies at the very least one missing maxim before the present Rule I and perhaps also a missing rule. In context, however, the continuity of the presentation at this point is smooth; where something most seems to be lacking is between Rule I and Maxim 4.

[161]The proofreader who added this text in the manuscript did not record to whom it was attributed. Most likely, it is Handlo's maxim, since it is along the same lines as his remarks about rests that are added to the commentary on the modes in Rubric XIII. Its sense seems to convey a response to the missing material directly above. The thrust of the remark would seem to be that if one writes the rest of a major semibrevis plus the rest of a minor semibrevis in place of a brevis rest, then the prevailing subdivision of the brevis into a major plus a minor is made more evident. Of course, it could be merely a caution to write rests in their proper order in a subdivision of two perfect breves such as the following: minor semibrevis, rest of a major semibrevis, rest of a minor semibrevis, major semibrevis. The use of *adiunctam* (adjoined) also associates it with the remarks immediately following on the typology of hockets.

[162]Nothing more is known of Jacobus de Navernia, though he may be one of the musicians of Navarre cited by Admetus in Rule XII of Rubric IX. See also the Introduction, pp. 20–21.

[163]On hockets in general, see William Dalglish, "The Hocket in Medieval Polyphony," *Musical Quarterly* 55 (1969): 344–63; Ernest Sanders, "The Medieval Hocket in Theory and Practice," *Musical Quarterly* 60 (1974): 246–56 (a slightly longer version of his article "Hocket" in *New Grove Dictionary of Music and Musicians* 8 [1980]: 605–8); and Peter Jeffery, "A Four-Part In seculum Hocket and a Mensural Sequence in an Unknown Source," *Journal of the American Musicological Society* 37

B. Secundo modo, per semibrevem minorem et pausam duarum partium unius etiam sibi adiunctam, vel e converso.

C. Tertio modo, per pausam tertie partis unius semibrevibus minoribus attributam. Quorum trium modorum is ultimus difficilis est. ‖

5  Maxima 6

Copais: Quando siquidem hoketus currit super tres semibreves minores, cum pausis tertie partis unius, iocundum post se et post earum pausas ⟨parvulum circulum⟩ habebit, ut pausarum et semibrevium minorum fallacia deleatur.

10  ⟨Maxima 7⟩

Johannes de Garlandia: Super minimas et minoratas nunquam currit hoketus, quia de sua natura pausas non habebunt in hoketo. Tantum in hoketis contineri possunt.

---

2 e converso]aequo A1 ‖ 3 unius *sup. lin., m. sec.* A1 ‖ 6 Copiiis A1 Corpus CS ‖ 11 Gerlandia A1 ‖

B. In the second manner, by a minor semibrevis and a rest of two thirds of one tempus adjoined to it, or conversely.

C. In the third manner, by a rest of a third of one tempus assigned to minor semibreves. Of these three manners, this last is difficult.[164]

Maxim 6

Copais:[165] When a hocket runs upon three minor semibreves with rests of a third of one tempus, it will be pleasing to have a small circle after them and after their rests, so that the confusion of rests and minor semibreves might be eliminated.[166]

Maxim 7

Johannes de Garlandia: A hocket never runs upon minimae and minoratae because by their nature, they will not have rests in a hocket. Only so much can be comprised in hockets.

---

(1984): 1–48. An article "Hoquetus" by Wolf Frobenius has been announced as forthcoming in the *Handwörterbuch der musikalischen Terminologie*.

[164]See also Maxim 11 of Rubric XIII. The use of the phrase "or conversely" makes this description of rest-writing in the fifth mode more varied than below.

[165]Coussemaker did not interpret this word as the name of an authority, but rather as *corpus*, a noun at the beginning of the sentence. The eighteenth-century scribe of **GB**-Lbl, Additional 4909, however, clearly thought this was the name of a theorist. Nonetheless, it would seem he could not make sense of the text and wrote "Copiiis."

[166]I have introduced the reference to a "small circle" (*parvulus circulus*) to bring sense to the passage; this follows Walter Odington, *De speculatione musicae*, cap. 17, sent. 15–18 (ed. Hammond), p. 145. The point is taken to be that with so many rests, which look like Franconian divisions of the mode, a different sign is needed to clearly indicate the divisions between breves. See also Maxim 2 of Rubric IV and the Introduction, pp. 21–22.

XIII. Incipit decimatertia rubrica. Quot modi cantus sive mensurarum fiunt.
Maxima 1
Franco: Modi cantus quinque ponuntur a modernis.
5 ⟨Regula I⟩
Idem: Primus modus constat ex omnibus longis perfectis, ut patet in hoc moteto:
*In Bethleem*

Maxima 2
10 Handlo: Perfectissimus is modus est, qui modis omnibus mensurabilibus deservit.

XIII. Here begins the thirteenth rubric. How many modes of song or measuring there are.

Maxim 1

Franco: Five modes of song are employed by the moderns.[167]

Rule I

The same: The first mode consists of all perfect longae, as is shown in this motet:[168]

*In Bethleem*

Maxim 2

Handlo: This mode, which serves all mensurable modes, is most perfect.

---

[167]Hanboys, *Summa*, chapter 22 (342.23 *infra*). This chapter is transmitted only in truncated form in the *Summa* and quotes just the rules attributed here to Franco (i.e., the bare bones of the *Gaudent moderni* text). The *Gaudent moderni* treatises typically say that there are five modes "secundum magistrum Franconem," but Handlo's dialogue-format presumably precluded the use of that formula; some also use the phrases "secundum antiquos plures essent" (e.g., Petrus Picardus, *Ars motettorum compilata breviter* [ed. Gallo], p. 24) or "sint plures apud antiquos" (e.g., Johannes dictus Balloce, *Abbreviatio magistri Franconis* [ed. Reaney], p. 20), which may have stimulated Handlo's use of "a modernis." In the older modal tradition of the *Discantus positio vulgaris* and the *De mensurabili musica* of Johannes de Garlandia, the number of rhythmic modes was set at six (Magister Lambertus and Anonymous IV posit even more), but the Franconian tradition reckoned there to be five, combining in the first mode the mode that moves by perfect longae (the old fifth mode) and the mode that moves by longae and breves (the old first mode).

[168]Hanboys, *Summa*, chapter 22 (342.23–25 *infra*). Handlo's example quotes the duplum of the double motet *In Bethleem Herodes iratus-T*. *In Bethleem* (Friedrich Gennrich, *Bibliographie der ältesten französischen und lateinischen Motetten* [Darmstadt: By the author, 1958], no. 98). It is cited as an example of first mode by the Anonymous of St. Emmeram (Heinrich Sowa, *Ein anonymer glossierter Mensuraltraktat 1279*, Königsberger Studien zur Musikwissenschaft, no. 9 [Kassel: Bärenreiter, 1930], p. 87 and 105), by Franco in the *Ars cantus mensurabilis* (ed. Reaney), p. 31, and by at least nine subsequent treatises in the *Gaudent moderni* tradition. The motet itself has been edited recently by Gordon A. Anderson, with extensive bibliography, in *Motets of the Manuscript La Clayette*, Corpus mensurabilis musicae, no. 68 ([Rome]: American Institute of Musicology, 1975), no. 31 (with triplum *Amours mi font rejoir*); and again by Anderson, with additional bibliography, in *Compositions of the Bamberg Manuscript*, Corpus mensurabilis musicae, no. 75 ([Rome]: American Institute of Musicology, 1977), no. 44 (with triplum *Chorus innocentium*).

⟨Regula II⟩
Franco: Vel primus modus constat ex longa et brevi et longa, ut patet hic in exemplo:
[O Maria maris stella plena gratie]

5  ⟨Maxima 3⟩
Handlo: Ad hunc modum primum pertinet trium temporum pausa, longa precedente, vel pausa duorum temporum cum pausa unius, brevi precedente, vel pausa unius, semilonga precedente, vel pausa unius duorum et unius, etiam semilonga precedente. ‖

CS1: 401b

10  Maxima 4
Idem: A. In hoc primo modo, si in loco semilonge figurarum ligatura, vel obliquitas, vel semibrevium coniunctio, vel duorum pausa insit, et brevis sequens divisa maneat et de substantia primi modi dici oportebit.

B. Sed et si loco huius brevis divise sit semibrevium ligatura, vel obli-
15  quitas, vel coniunctio, vel unius pausa, idem erit dicendum.

⟨Regula III⟩
Franco: Secundus modus constat ex brevi et longa et brevi, ut patet in hoc exemplo:
[Mane prima sabbati surgens dei filius]

---

4 *secunda pars de* 166.8 A1 ‖

Rule II

Franco: Or the first mode consists of a longa and a brevis and a longa, as is shown here in an example:[169]

[*O Maria maris stella plena gratie*]

Maxim 3

Handlo: To this first mode pertains a rest of three tempora, when there is a preceding longa; or a rest of two tempora with a rest of one, when there is a preceding brevis; or a rest of one tempus, when there is a preceding semilonga; or a rest of one, of two, and again of one tempus, when there is a preceding semilonga.[170]

Maxim 4

The same: A. In this first mode, if in place of a semilonga there is a ligature of shapes or an oblique figure or a conjunction of semibreves or a rest of two tempora, and a following separate brevis remains, it will be necessary to speak of the substance of the first mode.

B. And if in place of the separate brevis there is a ligature of semibreves or an oblique figure or a conjunction or a rest of one tempus, the same will have to be said.

Rule III

Franco: The second mode consists of a brevis and a longa and a brevis, as is shown in this example:[171]

[*Mane prima sabbati surgens dei filius*]

---

[169]Hanboys, *Summa*, chapter 22 (342.26–27 *infra*). Handlo's example quotes the duplum of the double motet *O Maria virgo davitica-O Maria maris stella-T. In veritatem* (Gennrich, *Bibliographie*, no. 448). It is cited as an example of first mode in at least seven treatises in the *Gaudent moderni* tradition. The motet itself has been edited most recently by Gordon A. Anderson, with extensive bibliography, in *Compositions of the Bamberg Manuscript*, no. 75.

[170]To the *Gaudent moderni* statements on the modes, Handlo adds two kinds of gloss: first, about the rests that pertain; and second, on figures that might replace the longa or brevis in the modal pattern. For the former there is a precedent in Franco, *Ars cantus mensurabilis*, cap. 9, sent. 17 (ed. Reaney and Gilles), p. 56.

[171]Hanboys, *Summa*, chapter 22 (342.28–29 *infra*). It is probable that Handlo's second-mode example is drawn from the tenor of an otherwise unknown motet; it sets the first verse of a Resurrection sequence for St.

Maxima 5

Handlo: Ad hunc modum secundum pertinet duorum pausa ⟨brevi⟩ precedente vel unius pausa cum pausa duorum, semilonga ⟨precedente⟩.

Maxima 6

Idem: A. In hoc modo secundo, si loco brevis sit ligatura, vel obliquitas, vel semibrevium coniunctio, vel unius pausa, et semilonga sequens divisa maneat de substantia secundi modi convenienter dici oportet.

B. Sed et si loco semilonge figurarum ligatura, vel obliquitas, vel semibrevium coniunctio, vel duorum pausa insit, idem dicendum erit.

Regula IV

Franco: Tertius modus constat ex longa et duabus brevibus et longa, ut patet in hoc moteto:

*Quid miraris partum virgineum*

‖ Maxima 7

Handlo: Ad hunc tertium modum pertinet trium temporum pausa, precedente longa.

Maxim 5

Handlo: To this second mode pertains a rest of two tempora, when there is a preceding brevis, or a rest of one tempus with a rest of two tempora, when there is a preceding semilonga.

Maxim 6

The same: A. In this second mode, if in place of the brevis there is a ligature or oblique figure or a conjunction of semibreves or a rest of one, and a following separate semilonga remains, it is necessary to speak appropriately of the substance of the second mode.

B. And if in the place of the semilonga there is a ligature of shapes or an oblique figure or a conjunction of semibreves or a rest of two units, the same will have to be said.

Rule IV

Franco: The third mode consists of a longa and two breves and a longa, as is shown in this motet:[172]

*Quid miraris partum virgineum*

Maxim 7

Handlo: To this third mode pertains a rest of three tempora, when there is a preceding longa.

---

Mary Magdalene, *Mane prima sabbati*. This chant is used as the tenor of two related thirteenth-century Latin-texted motets: (1) the two-voice English fragment *Conditio nature-[T. Mane prima]* (Worcester, Cathedral Library, fragment 35, f. 33v [WF, 65]), whose eightfold pes in alternate-third-mode rhythms is based on a paraphrase of the opening of the sequence; and (2) the continental double motet *Conditio nature-O natio nephandi-T. Mane prima* (Gennrich, *Bibliographie*, nos. 598–99 for tenor M 83), whose tenor is notated in the third rhythmic mode. The latter motet is cited in examples by the Anonymous of St. Emmeram (ed. Sowa), pp. 85 and 105, and it is also cited in the *Discantus positio vulgaris* (CS, 1:97, with no music) as an instance of a motet with a tenor in the third mode. It has been edited recently by Gordon A. Anderson, with extensive bibliography, in *Compositions of the Bamberg Manuscript*, no. 77.

[172]Hanboys, *Summa*, chapter 22 (344.1–3 *infra*). Handlo's example is an upper voice of an otherwise unknown motet (Gennrich, *Bibliographie*, no. 1180).

Regula V

Franco: Quartus modus ⟨constat ex⟩ duabus brevibus et una longa et duabus brevibus, ut hic:

*Rosula primula salve Jesse virgula*

5 Maxima 8

Handlo: Ad hunc quartum modum pertinet trium temporum pausa.

Maxima 9

Idem: Tertius et quartus modus transmutari debent, si more lascivo per vocem exprimantur, ⟨ut supra⟩ in maxima quinta quarte rubrice.

---

2 modus]modus est A1 ‖ 9 quinta quarte]quinte A1 ‖

Rule V
Franco: The fourth mode consists of two breves and one longa and two breves, as here:[173]

*Rosula primula salve Jesse virgula*

Maxim 8
Handlo: To this fourth mode pertains a rest of three tempora.

Maxim 9
The same: The third and fourth modes ought to be transmuted if expressed by voice in the *mos lascivus* (as above in Maxim 5 of Rubric IV).[174]

---

[173]Hanboys, *Summa*, chapter 22 (344.4–6 *infra*). This isolated voice-part is not specifically identified by Handlo as part of a motet, but it has been listed as such by Gennrich (*Bibliographie*, no. 1181). Its melody is identical to the lower voice of *Nobilis humilis*, the famous two-voice hymn in praise of St. Magnus (d. 1115), patron saint of the Orkney Islands, which is found in the late thirteenth-century source Uppsala, Universitetsbiblioteket, MS C.233, ff. 19v–20r (see RISM B/IV/1, pp. 811–12). For a facsimile of the polyphonic setting, see Rev. John Beveridge, "Two Scottish Thirteenth Century Songs," *Music and Letters* 20 (1939): 353 (facing). Manfred Bukofzer was apparently the first to observe the concordance with Handlo's example, which he announced a year later in the same journal (*Music and Letters* 21 [1940]: 203). A convenient edition of the St. Magnus hymn appears in Archibald Davison and Willi Apel, eds., *Historical Anthology of Music*, rev. ed., 2 vols. (Cambridge: Harvard University Press, 1964), 1:no. 25c. The polyphonic hymn has raised a great deal of discussion about its date and place of origin and about its musical style (the hymn tune is doubled above throughout in parallel thirds). See the bibliography cited in RISM B/IV/1; and Ingrid de Geer, *Earl, Saint, Bishop, Skald—and Music* (Uppsala: Uppsala Universitet Institutionen for Musikvetenskap, 1985). The appearance of the tune in Handlo's *Regule* suggests the possibility that the melody was relatively widespread and that the St. Magnus hymn text is not the original, but a contrafact made in the later thirteenth century.

[174]Handlo's cross-reference is to the *mos lascivus* of Petrus le Viser; again, his stress on vocal realization is noteworthy. On the transmutation of the third and fourth modes from ternary to binary mensuration, see Ernest Sanders, "Duple Rhythm and Alternate Third Mode in the 13th Century," *Journal of the American Musicological Society* 15 (1962): 257–60, where attention is drawn to earlier precedents in English theory: Walter Odington, *De speculatione musicae*, cap. 10, sent. 19–20 (ed. Hammond), p. 139 (see also CS, 1:245a); and Anonymous IV, *De mensuris et discantu*, cap. 7 (Fritz Reckow, ed., *Die Musiktraktat des Anonymus 4*, 2 vols., Beihefte zur Archiv für Musikwissenschaft, vols. 4–5 [Wiesbaden: Franz Steiner, 1967], 1:85, lns. 1–7; see also CS, 1:361b–62a).

## Regula VI

Franco: Quintus modus constat ex brevibus et omnibus semibrevibus, ut patet in exemplis sequentibus:

---

2 ex]et A1 ‖ 4 *clavis* (*sec.*) *vacua* lin. 2 A1 ‖

Rule VI
Franco: The fifth mode consists of breves and all types of semibreves, as is shown in the following examples:[175]

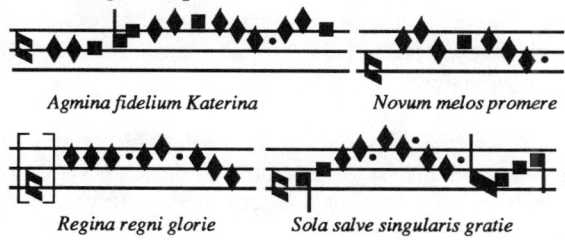

*Agmina fidelium Katerina*  *Novum melos promere*

*Regina regni glorie*  *Sola salve singularis gratie*

[175]Hanboys, *Summa*, chapter 22 (344.7–9 *infra*). The first of Handlo's examples quotes the triplum of the Latin double motet *Agmina fidelium Katerine-Agmina milicie celestis-T. Agmina* (Gennrich, *Bibliographie*, no. 534). This voice is identical, as far as it goes, to the triplum of a motet quoted by Walter Odington in his *De speculatione musicae* (ed. Hammond), p. 143 (a facsimile of the corresponding page from Cambridge, Corpus Christi College, MS 410, f. 35v, follows p. 146). One manuscript of Franco's *Ars cantus mensurabilis* (Milan, Biblioteca Ambrosiana, MS D.5.inf., ff. 110v–118v) cites as its example for the fifth mode a version basically identical in music and only slightly different in text (see Franco, *Ars cantus mensurabilis* [ed. Reaney and Gilles], p. 28). There is an extensive complex of double motets with tenor *Agmina* and duplum *Agmina milicie celestis*, to which this excerpt belongs. For a recent edition of another member of the family, with extensive bibliography, see Gordon A. Anderson, *Motets of the Manuscript La Clayette*, no. 22; there is a further relevant edition by Anderson, with additional bibliography, in *Compositions of the Bamberg Manuscript*, no. 6.

*Novum melos promere* is the opening of the duplum or triplum of an otherwise unknown motet in the notational and declamatory style of Petrus de Cruce (Gennrich, *Bibliographie*, no. 1176). Outside of Handlo (and Hanboys, *Summa*, chapter 12 [260.16–17 *infra*], where it is cited in a different context), it survives only in a more extended quotation in another treatise of the *Gaudent moderni* tradition, an anonymous *Ars musicae mensurabilis secundum Franconem* (ed. Reaney and Gilles), p. 42 (see also Coussemaker, *Histoire de l'Harmonie*, Doc VI, p. 277). In the latter, it immediately precedes a quotation from *Aucun ont trouvé*, while in Hanboys, it immediately follows the same quotation. In the anonymous source, the C clef is written a step below the first note, thus pitching the entire example a third below its level in the *Regule* and the *Summa*.

*Regina regni glorie* and *Sola salve singularis gratie* are presumably the openings of two further motets in the notational and declamatory style of Petrus de Cruce. Aside from citation here, they are otherwise unknown. Gennrich (*Bibliographie*, no. 1182) lists them as a single item.

‖ Maxima 10

Handlo: Ad hunc quintum modum pertinet trium temporum pausa, precedente longa, vel unius pausa, semilonga precedente, vel duorum pausa, brevi precedente, vel pausa duarum partium unius, semibrevi minori precedente, vel pausa tertie partis unius, semibrevi maiori precedente vel duabus minoribus precedentibus.

Maxima 11

Idem: A. Ab hoc siquidem modo proveniunt hoketi omnes, rundelli, ballade, coree, cantifractus, estampete, floriture, et universe note brevium et semibrevium que sub celo sunt, que semibreves, breves, atque longe in hoc modo quinto comprehenduntur.

B. Et hoc modo quinto computabuntur tres breves pro una perfectione, vel trium valores.

C. Et aliquando due breves pro una perfectione computande sunt, quando una duarum brevis altera est.

D. Ad quarum computationem evidens est Franconis intentio.

Maxima 12

Idem: Hic vero modus quintus ad omnes modos precedentes omnesque mensuras convenienter habet reduci.

⟨Maxima 13⟩

Idem: Hii prefati quinque mixtim se habere possunt. Cum igitur modus unus se habet in perfectione una, vel in pluribus, et ipsum sequatur modus alius, demum inter modos illos divisionis punctus addatur, ut melius noscatur mixtura modorum. ‖

---

3 duorum]unius A1 ‖ 10 que (*sec.*)]*fort.* quia A1 ‖ 21 haberi A1 ‖

Maxim 10

Handlo: To this fifth mode pertains a rest of three tempora, when there is a preceding longa, or a rest of one tempus, when there is a preceding semilonga, or a rest of two tempora, when there is a preceding brevis, or a rest of two thirds of one tempus, when there is a preceding minor semibrevis, or a rest of a third of one tempus, when there is a preceding major semibrevis or two preceding minor semibreves.[176]

Maxim 11

The same: A. From this mode come forth all hockets, rondeaux, ballades, round dances, diminished counterpoints, estampies, florid melodies, and all notes of breves and semibreves that are under heaven, for semibreves, breves, and longae are included in this fifth mode.[177]

B. And in this fifth mode, three breves or the value of three are counted as one perfection.

C. And sometimes two breves must be counted as one perfection, when one of the two is a brevis altera.

D. The intention of Franco is evident in this counting.

Maxim 12

The same: This fifth mode has to be reduced appropriately to all preceding modes and all measures.[178]

Maxim 13

The same: These aforesaid five can be mixed. When one mode is arranged in one or more perfections and another mode follows this one, then between those modes a *punctus divisionis* should be added so that the mixture of modes might better be recognized.[179]

---

[176] See Maxim 5 of Rubric XI.

[177] For a discussion of this important list of musical genres, see the Introduction, pp. 15–16.

[178] See Franco, *Ars cantus mensurabilis*, cap. 9, sent. 26 (ed. Reaney and Gilles), p. 59: "Et vide quod quintus modus maxime cum aliis omnibus potest sumi." On the compatibility of fifth mode with either first or second mode, Franco uses the term *accipere*, as in "quintus modus cum primo vel secundo accipere" (to paraphrase p. 57 [ed. Reaney and Gilles]). Handlo's verb, *reducere*, is also Franconian vocabulary. See Maxim 14 and also *accipere* and *reducere* in the *index verborum* to Erich Reimer, *Johannes Garlandia: De mensurabili musica*, 2 vols., Beihefte zum *Archiv für Musikwissenschaft*, vols. 10–11 (Wiesbaden: Franz Steiner, 1972) and Reckow, *Die Musiktraktat des Anonymus 4*.

[179] On the transmutation of one mode into another by means of rests and the acknowledgement that all the modes could run together in a single line of discant, see Franco, *Ars cantus mensurabilis*, cap. 9, sent. 16–23 (ed.

{Maxima 14
Idem: Omnis modus mensurarum et omnis mensura cantuum ad prefatos quinque modos re‖duci habent.}
Maxima 15

5   Idem: Maxime vero a regulis differunt pro tanto, quia regule exemplis utuntur, maxime vero nudo modo sine exemplis intelliguntur, notitiam regulis exhibentes.

Et ideo faciendi plures regulas sive maximas nullus est finis. Verumtamen, kare mi, id modicum volumen cerne et vestigia eius serva. Hic est
10  omnis cantor.

     Et pro vita scriptoris
     Deum intente ora.
     Amen. Finito libro,
     reddatur gloria Christo.

15  Expliciunt regule cum additionibus finite die veneris proximo ante Pentecoste Anno Domini millesimo trecentesimo vicesimo sexto et cetera. Amen.

---

1 14]15 A1 ‖ 1–3 *inter* 7–8 A1 ‖ 4 15]14 A1 ‖ 8 faciendi]facendi A1 ‖ 16 Pentecost A1 ǀ tricentesimo A1 ‖

Maxim 14

The same: Every mode of measures and every measure of song has to be reduced to the aforesaid five modes.[180]

Maxim 15

The same: Maxims differ from rules to some degree, since rules use examples.[181] Maxims are perceived in a plain manner without examples, drawing out knowledge from the rules.

And thus there is no end to making more rules or maxims.[182] For now, my dear one, discern this unassuming volume and keep to its tracks. This is the complete singer!

> And intently pray God
> for the life of the writer.
> Amen. This book being finished,
> let the glory redound to Christ.

Here end the rules with additions, finished the Friday just before Pentecost in the year of our Lord 1326, etc. Amen.

---

Reaney and Gilles), pp. 56–58. The phrase *divisio modi* literally anticipates this function, and indeed, Odington discusses the use of the *divisio modi* to create what he calls *modi secundarii*, related conceptually to Handlo's mixture of modes (*De speculatione musicae*, cap. 6, sent. 8–10 [ed. Hammond], p. 131). Like Handlo, though in a different context, Hanboys also remarks on the use of a *punctus divisionis* to divide one mode from another (*Summa*, chapter 3, [196.7 *infra*]). For mixtures of modes in the practical sources, see Lefferts, *The Motet in England*, pp. 99, 151, and table 14.

[180]See Franco, *Ars cantus mensurabilis*, cap. 3, sent. 4 (ed. Reaney and Gilles), p. 27: "Nos autem quinque tantum ponimus, quia ad hos quinque omnes alii reducuntur."

[181]Some rules only have a cross-reference to an example elsewhere.

[182]See Ecclesiastes 12:12: "faciendi plures libros nullus est finis (there is no end to the making of more books)."

## ⟨SUMMA MAGISTRI JOHANNIS HANBOYS⟩

Hic incipit musica magistri Franconis cum additionibus et opinionibus diversorum.
Prohemium
5 ⟨Franco⟩: Cum de plana musica quidam philosophi sufficienter tractaverunt, ipsam quoque nobis tam theorice quam practice efficaciter illucidaverunt, theorice precise Boetius, practice vero Guydo monachus, et maxime de tropis ecclesiasticis Gregorius; idcirco nos de mensurabili musica quam ipsam plana precedit tanquam principalis subalternam, ad preces quorundam
10 magnorum tractare proponentes; non pervertendo ordinem, ipsam ‖ planam  CS1: musicam perfectissime a predictis philosophis supponimus esse propalatam.  403b

Nec dicat aliquis nos hoc opus propter arrogantiam, vel forte propter propriam tantum commoditatem incepisse, sed vere propter evidentem necessitatem et auditorum facillimam apprehensionem necnon et omnium
15 notatorum ipsius mensurabilis musice perfectissimam instructionem. Quoniam cum videmus multos tam novos quam antiquos in artibus suis de mensurabili musica multa bona dicere, et e contrario in multis et maxime in accidentibus ipsius musice deficere et errare, opinionem eorum forte

## THE SUMMA OF MASTER JOHANNES HANBOYS

Here begins the Musica of Master Franco, with additions and opinions of diverse others.[1]

Introduction[2]

Franco: Since certain philosophers have sufficiently treated plainsong and have effectively clarified it for us both theoretically and practically—Boethius accurately with respect to theory, Guido the Monk with respect to practice, and especially Gregory concerning ecclesiastical chants—we, therefore, at the request of certain great men, propose to treat mensural music, which plainsong precedes just as a leader precedes a subordinate; we do not intend to pervert this order since we suppose plainsong to have been most perfectly supported by the aforesaid philosophers.

Nor let anyone say we began this work out of arrogance or perchance merely for our own advantage, but rather on account of evident necessity, the easier comprehension of pupils, and the most perfect instruction of all of those who write down this mensurable music. For when we see many, both young and old, say many worthy things in their teaching texts[3] on mensurable music and contrariwise fall short and err in many respects, and especially in the details of this music, we have considered their opinions per-

---

[1] This rubric, added by the primary scribe above the main text block, is clearly related to the statement that opens Handlo's *Regule*, though here Franco's treatise is cited as his *Musica* rather than his *Regule*. The modification is significant in light of the fact that Hanboys cites Franconian doctrines not just through Handlo but directly from the *Ars cantus mensurabilis* itself, which he may well have known as the *Musica magistri franconis*. That is its title in a surviving insular copy: Oxford, Bodleian Library, Bodley 842, ff. 49r–62v.

[2] The introduction quotes Franco, *Ars cantus mensurabilis* (ed. Reaney and Gilles), "Prologus" (pp. 23–24) in its entirety.

[3] An "ars," as for instance Franco's own *Ars cantus mensurabilis*, is a teaching text, especially in one of the disciplines of the seven liberal arts. A "summa," as Hanboys's treatise is called in the explicit, aspires to be a more major contribution to learning.

estimavimus succurrendum, ne forte propter defectum et errorem predictorum ‖ dicta scientia detrimentum pateretur.

Proponimus ergo ipsam mensurabilem musicam sub compendio declarare; bene dictaque aliorum non recusabimus interponere, errores quoque
5 destruere et effugare, et si quid novi a nobis inventum fuerit, bonis rationibus sustinere et probare.

## CAPITULUM I

⟨Franco⟩: Mensurabilis musica est cantus longis brevibusque temporibus mensuratus. Gratia huius diffinitionis, videndum est quid sit mensura et quid
10 tempus. Mensura est habitudo quantitativa longitudinem et brevitatem cuiuslibet cantus mensurabilis manifestans. Mensurabilis dico, quia in plana musica non attenditur talis mensura. Tempus est mensura tam vocis prolate quam eius contrarii, scilicet vocis omisse, que pausa communiter appellatur. Dico autem pausam tempore mensurari, quia aliter duo cantus diversi, quo-
15 rum unus cum pausis, alius sine pausis canerentur, non possent adinvicem coequari.

Dividitur autem mensurabilis musica in mensurabilem simpliciter et partim. Mensurabilis simpliciter est discantus, eo quod in omni parte sua tempore mensuratur. Partim mensurabilis dicitur organum pro tanto quod non in
20 omni parte sua tempore mensuratur. Et sciendum est quod organum dupliciter dicitur, scilicet proprie et communiter. Est enim organum proprie sumptum organum duplum, quod purum organum appellatur. Communiter vero organum appellatur quilibet cantus ecclesiasticus tempore mensuratus. Sed quia simplex precedit compositum, ideo primo de discantu dicendum
25 est.

Discantus est aliquorum diversorum cantuum consonantia, in qua illi diversi cantus per voces longas, breves et semibreves proportionaliter adequantur, et in scripto per debitas figuras proportionari ‖ adinvicem designan-

chance as in need of help, lest on account of the shortcomings and errors of the aforesaid, the said science suffer detriment.

Therefore, we propose to expound on this mensural music in the form of a handbook, and though we will not decline to interpose the things well said by others, we will try to eradicate or put to flight errors, and if anything new is found by us, to uphold and prove it with good reasons.

## CHAPTER 1

Franco: Mensurable music is song measured by long and short tempora. Because of this definition, it must be seen what is measure and what is tempus. Measure is a quantitative attribute indicating the longness and shortness of some mensurable song. I say "mensurable" because in plainsong, such a measure is not observed. Tempus is the measure both of sustained voice[4] and of its contrary, namely withheld voice, which is commonly called a rest. I say that a rest is measured by tempus because otherwise two different songs, one of which is sung with rests and the other without, could not be accommodated to each other.

Mensurable music is separated into wholly and partly measurable. Wholly measurable music is discant, because it is measured by tempus in every part. Organum is said to be partly measurable, inasmuch as it is not measured by tempus in every part. And it must be known that organum is spoken of in two ways: properly and commonly. Organum, properly taken, is organum duplum, which is called organum purum. Commonly, however, any ecclesiatical song measured by tempus is called organum. But because the whole precedes the composite, something must therefore be first said concerning discant.[5]

Discant is the consonance of some separate songs in which these separate songs are proportionately matched by long, short, and shorter voices; and in writing, they are designated by means of suitable shapes proportioned to each other. Moreover, discant can be separated thus: some discant is wholly

---

[4]The term *vox* is used in the sense of "sung voice" and is therefore virtually synonymous with pitch or sound.

[5]Franco, *Ars cantus mensurabilis*, cap. 1 (ed. Reaney and Gilles), pp. 24–25. For Franco here, *simplex* (whole) and *compositus* (composite) have the meaning "all of one sort" and "mixing several kinds."

tur. Discantus autem dividitur sic: discantus alius simpliciter prolatus, alius truncatus qui hoketus dicitur, alius copulatus qui copula nuncupatur.

Sed cum omnis discantus tam voce recta quam omissa reguletur et ita sunt diversa, horum erunt diversa significancia, quia diversorum signa sunt
5 diversa. Sed tamen prius sit vox recta quam omissa, nam habitus precedit privationem, prius dicendum est de figuris que vocem rectam significant, quam de pausis que vocem omissam significant.

Figura est representatio vocis sive soni in aliquo modorum ordinate, per quod patet quod figure significare debent modos, et non e contrario, que-
10 madmodum quidam posuerunt.

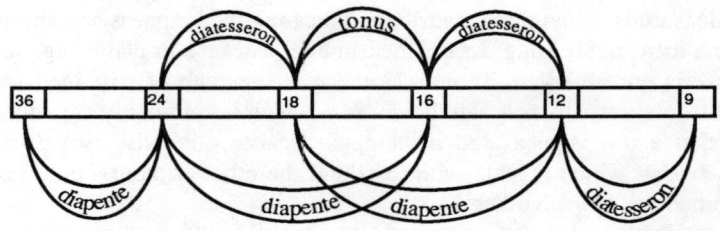

## CAPITULUM II

⟨Franco⟩: Figurarum alie simplices, alie composite nominantur. Simplices sunt ille que non ligantur. Composite sunt ille que ligantur per tractus

---

1 discantuum alius A2 ‖ 8 ordinate]ordinato A2 ‖

spun out; some is broken up, which is said to be hocket; and some is linked, which is referred to as copula.⁶

But since all discant is regulated as much by normal voice as by withheld voice, and they are thus separate, so will their signifiers be separate, because the signs of separate things are separate. But nevertheless, as normal voice is prior to withheld voice—as possession precedes privation⁷—something must first be said concerning the shapes that signify normal voice, then concerning the rests that signify withheld voice.⁸

A shape is the representation of voice or sound ordered according to one or another of the modes, from which it is evident that shapes ought to signify modes, but not contrariwise in the manner some have proposed.⁹

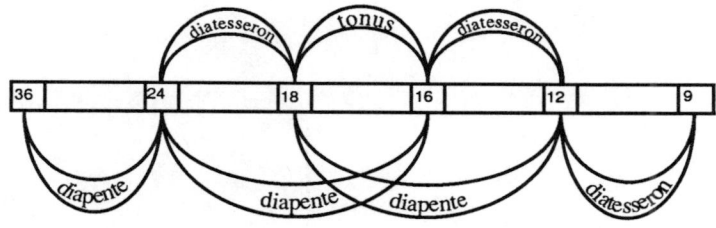

## CHAPTER 2

Franco: Some of the shapes are named "whole," others "composite." Whole shapes are those that are not ligated. Composite shapes are those that

---

⁶Franco, *Ars cantus mensurabilis*, cap. 2, sent. 1–2 (ed. Reaney and Gilles), p. 26.

⁷This pairing invokes Aristotle's teachings on opposition, as in the *Categories* 11b15: "Things are said to be opposed to one another in four ways: as relatives or as contraries or as privation and possession or as affirmation and negation" (J. L. Ackrill, trans. and ed., *Aristotle's Categories and De Interpretatione*, Clarendon Aristotle Series [Oxford: Clarendon Press, 1963], p. 31).

⁸Franco, *Ars cantus mensurabilis*, cap. 3, sent. 12–13 (ed. Reaney and Gilles), pp. 28–29. Excised from Franco's text are all references to mode.

⁹Franco, *Ars cantus mensurabilis,* cap. 4, sent. 1 (ed. Reaney and Gilles), p. 29. The example does not come from Franco; it is perhaps a holdover from an earlier section of a larger treatise by Hanboys, of which the present text devoted to mensural music was merely the final part.

debitos. Harum tres sunt species, scilicet longe, breves, et semibreves.

⟨Hanboys⟩: Et quia Francho, doctor noster venerabilis in hac arte liberali, sufficienter non dixit ut figuras in regulis suis composuit prout nunc decet compositoribus et cantoribus, ideo magnus est error. Ad succurrendum et errores de‖struendos, addo duas figuras, scilicet largam et minimam.

CS1: 405a

---

2 noster ⟦liberalis⟧ venerabilis A2 ‖ 5 addo]addendo A2 | minima A2 ‖

are ligated by suitable stems. Of these, there are three types: longae, breves, and semibreves.[10]

Hanboys: And because Franco, our revered teacher in this liberal art, did not say enough as he composed the shapes in his rules[11] for them now to be appropriate for composers and singers, on that account the error is great. To be helpful and destroy the errors, I add two shapes: the larga and the minima.[12]

---

[10]Abbreviated from Franco, *Ars cantus mensurabilis*, cap. 4, sent. 2–5 (ed. Reaney and Gilles), p. 29.

[11]The reference to rules (*regulis*) suggests that Hanboys may have the *Gaudent moderni* tradition in mind (perhaps specifically as encountered through Handlo's *Regule*) rather than Franco's *Ars cantus mensurabilis*. In the following line, however, Hanboys pointedly alludes to Franco through the use of vocabulary ("to be helpful and destroy the errors [ad succurrendum et errores destruendos]") that Franco employed for his own justification in the *Ars cantus mensurabilis* ("succurrendum ... errores ... destruere"), as quoted in Hanboys's introduction.

[12]Something is wrong here, and changing the participle (addendo) into an active form (addo) solves only a part of the problem. In light of the next sentence and the following paragraph, it becomes clear that Hanboys wants to add these two figures to a set of six, not to Franco's original set of three. Rather than Franco, he has in mind Johannes Torkesey, Robertus de Brunham, or someone else of their theoretical line of development (this person may nonetheless have been known to him as Franco because of the transmission of his theories in a modified *Gaudent moderni* treatise—perhaps even Handlo's *Regule* in the form in which it reached Hanboys). These are individuals who propose an expansion beyond the five figures of Johannes de Muris to a set of six by adding the equivalent of the duplex longa, minima, and crocheta to Franco's set of three. See the Introduction, pp. 46–55.

Nomina duarum figurarum, scilicet minime et crochete, volo mutare, quia melius est mutare nomen figure quam eam extra gradum suum ponere. Minima sic formatur: 

5  Crocheta sic formatur: 

Que quidem crocheta minor est minima. Quidem hoc sit vitiosum primo, nam pars minor est toto. Sed crocheta est pars minime, ergo minor ea, quod est contra Philosophum, dicentem impossibile est dare minus minimo. Maior

I wish to change the names of two shapes, namely, of the minima and the crocheta,[13] because it is better to change the name of a shape than to employ it outside its own rank.[14] The minima is formed thus:

The crocheta is formed thus:
And indeed, the crocheta is smaller than the minima. Indeed, this is defective in the first place, for the part is smaller than the whole. But the crocheta is part of a minima, therefore smaller than it, which is contrary to the Philosopher, who says it is impossible to give less than the least.[15] But the greater

---

[13]In fourteenth-century English mensural theory, the two most prevalent terms for semiminima are crocheta and simpla. For other references to crocheta, see Willelmus, *Breviarium regulare musicae* ([Anonymous of] Ms. Oxford, Bodley 842 [Willelmus], *Breviarium regulare musicae*, ed. Gilbert Reaney; [Anonymous of] Ms. British Museum, Royal 12. C. VI., *Tractatus de figuris sive de notis*, ed. Gilbert Reaney; Johannes Torkesey, *Declaratio trianguli et scuti*, ed. André Gilles and Gilbert Reaney, Corpus scriptorum de musica, no. 12 [(Rome): American Institute of Musicology, 1966]), p. 24: "simpla sive crocheta"; the *Quatuor principalia* (CS, 3:349b): "semiminimam id est crochutam"; Walsingham, *Regulae de musica mensurabilis* (ed. Reaney), p. 75 *et passim*; and the Wylde anonymous (Gilbert Reaney, "The Anonymous Treatise De Origine et Effectu Musicae, an Early 15th Century Commonplace Book of Music Theory," *Musica disciplina* 37 [1983]: 114): "crocheta vel simpla."

[14]On gradus, an important word in *ars nova* theory, conceptualizing as it does the extension of the relationship of longa and brevis to adjacent figures higher and lower in a strict mensural hierarchy, see the Introduction, pp. 47–51.

[15]Hanboys's proximate source for the maxim "it is impossible to give less than the least (impossibile est dare minus minimo)" is unknown. In music theory treatises, it can be traced back to its probable source in the *Notitia artis musicae* (1321) of de Muris (see Johannes de Muris, *Notitia artis musicae et Compendium musicae practica*; Petrus de Sancto Dionysio, *Tractatus de musica*, ed. Ulrich Michels, Corpus scriptorum de musica, no. 17 [(Rome): American Institute of Musicology, 1972], pp. 102 and 117): "Quia philosophus dicit, non est minimo dare minus (as the philosopher says, it is not possible to give less than the least)." This is one of two distinctive scholastic maxims (the other being Ockham's razor: "frustra fit per plura," on which, see chapter 15 [290.1–2]) that can also be found in Book 7 of the *Speculum musicae* of Jacques de Liège (ed. Bragard), 7:35: "Minimo autem non est dare minus, nec minimum divisibile est (it is not possible to give less than the least, nor is the least divisible)" and 7:66: "Minimo autem non est dare minus." Additional English and continental theorists citing this maxim include Anonymous, *Tractatus de figuris* (ed. Gilles and Reaney), p. 40: "cum nulla vox sit minor minima, quia minus minimo non est dandum in

manifesta est de se minor primo. Crocheta aut est dimidia pars minime aut tertia, ergo minor ea. Ideo mutanda sunt nomina, scilicet minime et crochete.

is shown in the first place as less in itself. The crocheta is a half or a third of a minima, and therefore smaller than it. Thus the names of the minima and

---

rerum natura (no voice is less than a minima, for less than the least must not be given in the nature of things)"; Anonymous dictus Theodoricus de Campo, *De musica mensurabili* (ed. Sweeney and Reaney), appendix I, p. 51): "Nota quod, secundum suum vocabulum, inproprie dicerentur minimae, quia secundum diffinitionem Philosophi, non est dare minimum minimo (Note that according to his noun, they are improperly said to be minimae, because according to the definition of the Philosopher, it is not possible to give the least to the least)" and p. 54: "nec propter hoc est contra diffinitionem Philosophi positum, ubi dicit: quod non est dare minimum minimo (nor on account of this is it employed contrary to the definition of the Philosopher, where he says that it is not possible to give the least to the least)"; *Tractatus figurarum*, ed. Philip Schreur, Greek and Latin Music Theory, vol. 6 (Lincoln: University of Nebraska Press, 1989), p. 80 (see also CS, 3:120): "Et licet aliqui magistri dicunt quod non est dare ultra minimam (Granted, some masters say that there is nothing smaller than a minima)"; and Johannes Hothby, *Regulae cantus mensurati* (Johannes Hothby, *Opera omnia de musica mensurabili*; Thomas Walsingham, *Regulae de musica mensurabili*, ed. Gilbert Reaney, Corpus scriptorum de musica, no. 31 [Neuhausen-Stuttgart: Hänssler Verlag for the American Institute of Musicology, 1983]), p. 20: "unde ultra minimam non datur minimum (wherefore, not the least thing is given beyond the minima)."

Though certainly Aristotelian in spirit, "non est dare minus minimo" cannot be found in the Latin corpus of Aristotle's works, nor does it occur, for example, in Aquinas's commentaries (exhaustively indexed in the *Index Thomisticus: Sancti Thomae Aquinatis operum omnium indices et concordantiae*, ed. Roberto Busa, 49 vols. [Stuttgart: Frommann Verlag, 1974–80]). Neither was it such a commonplace that it made its way into an earlier-fourteenth-century florilegium like the *Auctoritates Aristotelis* (see *Les Auctoritates Aristotelis. Un florilège médiéval. Etude historique et édition critique*, ed. Jacqueline Hamesse [Louvain: Publications Universitaires, 1974]). Willelmus, who is the most heavily and explicitly Aristotelian in orientation among English theorists, does not cite this maxim in the *Breviarium regulare musicae* (ed. Gilles and Reaney), p. 23 and 25, but rather has the following to say: "Unde hic notandum secundum Aristotilem quod minimum in quolibet genere est mensura omnium eiusdem generis; sic minimus sonus in musica est mensura omnium aliorum sonorum seu vocem (whence it must be noted according to Aristotle that the minimum in any genus is the measure of all that genus; thus the minimum sound in music is the measure of all other sounds or the voice)" and "minima nulla est minor (nothing is smaller than a minima)." Perhaps a model for his thought is to be found in the *Metaphysics* of Aristotle (1052b18–19), as quoted in the florilegium (ed. Hamesse), p. 135, noted above: "In unoquoque genere est dare aliquod primum et minimum quod fit metrum et mensura omnium illorum quae sunt in illo genere (In every single genus, there is given something that is first and least, which becomes the meter and measure of all of the things that are in

Nam minima manente in suo gradu ut prius, mutato nomine, minor vocatur. Et vocatur minor eo quod minor est semibrevi. Sic crocheta formaliter manente ut prius in suo gradu, nomine mutato, semiminor vocatur. Et dicitur semiminor a semis, quod est imperfectum, eo quod minorem imperficit.

5   Et sicut sunt octo toni sive modi, sic sunt octo species figurarum, scilicet larga, duplex longa, longa, brevis, semibrevis, minor, semiminor, minima.

crocheta must be changed.¹⁶

For the minima, remaining at its own rank as before but changing its name, is called a minor. And it is called a minor since it is smaller than a semibrevis. Thus the crocheta, remaining in shape as before in its own rank but changing its name, is called a semiminor. And it is called a semiminor from "semis," which is "imperfect," since it imperfects the minor.¹⁷

And just as there are eight tones or modes, so there are eight types of shapes: the larga, duplex longa, longa, brevis, semibrevis, minor, semiminor, and minima.

---

the genus)." Another fairly significant parallel passage occurs in William of Ockham's *Sententias* 1.17.8: "Non est dare minimum quin, quocumque dato, potest fieri minus per divinam potentiam (there is not the least thing given—wherever given—that cannot become less by divine power)." Many other parallels could be cited from the extensive fourteenth-century scholastic literature on infinity and continuity generated by Aristotle's *Physics* and *Metaphysics*. See also the Introduction, pp. 47–48.

¹⁶This third paragraph makes a point that is important for Hanboys but essentially parenthetical. It is not directly relevant to the main thrust of his argument, which moves from paragraph two to four, where Hanboys returns to his main theme, the addition of the larga and minima, renaming the minima and crocheta in a manner different than he had proposed in paragraph three, but following the same principle.

¹⁷Hanboys is repeating an old maxim that confounds two different words in a false etymology. One is the Latin "semis," related to the Greek "hemis," meaning a half of any unit (see, *inter alia*, Oxford Latin Dictionary, ed. P. G. W. Clare [Oxford: Clarendon Press, 1976]). The other is the Latin adjective "semus." This, too, has been recorded as meaning half or half-full (see *A Glossary of Later Latin to 600 A.D.*, ed. Alexander Souter [Oxford: Clarendon Press, 1949]), but in later medieval usage, it more commonly means incomplete, deficient, or unfinished (see *Mediae latinitatis lexicon minus*, ed. J. F. Niermeyer [Leiden: E.J. Brill, 1976]); hence, it is virtually synonymous with "imperfectus" (Hanboys also confounds two forms of "imperfect," namely, the adjective just mentioned and the verb "imperficio," which in musical terminology means "to take away a third of the value"). This etymology is also applied to the tone and semitone in the *Quatuor principalia*, tertium principale, cap. XIII (CS, 4: 227a): "Et dicitur semitonium a 'semis, sema, semum', quod est imperfectum, et tonus quasi imperfectus tonus (And "semitonium" is so called from "semis, sema, semum," which is "imperfect," and "tonus"—as if an imperfect tone)." In respect to the brevis and semibrevis, it is at least as old as two continental music treatises of the 1270s: those of Magister Lambertus and the St. Emmeram Anonymous (see Wolf Frobenius, "Semibrevis," in *Handwörterbuch der Musikalischen Terminologie* [1971], p. 3). And it is repeated in the tradition of Philippe de Vitry (*Ars nova* [ed. Reaney et al.], p. 23), to quote a final instance: "Semi-

## ⟨CAPITULUM III⟩

⟨Hanboys⟩: Forma largarum talis est. Quandocunque nota formatur ad modum duplicis longe habens tractum ascendentem et descendentem a parte dextra dicitur larga, ut hic:

Et simplex est, quia ligari non potest. Sed perfici potest; ideo potest facere de se perfectam trinitatem. Hoc est, potest continere in se tres duplices longas, ut larga ante largam vel ante punctum est perfecta. ⟨Larga ante largam⟩, ut hic patet: ||

Tenet regula veluti de modo perfecto, sed de modo imperfecto nequaquam. Larga ante punctum perfectionis, si sit de modo perfecto sive de modo imperfecto, semper perficitur, ut hic:

Ita est de longis duplicibus et de omnibus aliis figuris que perfici possunt. Et nota quod quelibet nota maior alia perfici potest.

CS1: 405b

---

1 larga *add. in marg., m. sec.* A2 || 4 ut hic]ut hic larga A2 || 8 perfecta] perfecta id est continet in se tres duplices longas A2 ||

## CHAPTER 3

Hanboys: The form of largae is thus. Whenever a note is formed in the manner of a duplex longa having a stem ascending and descending on its right side, it is said to be a larga, as here:

And it is whole, for it cannot be ligated.[18] But it can be perfected; hence it can make in itself a perfect trinity. That is, it can comprise in itself three duplex longae, so that a larga before a larga or before a punctus is perfect. A larga before a larga, as is shown here:

This rule holds just as in the perfect mode, but never for the imperfect mode. A larga before a *punctus perfectionis*, whether in a perfect or imperfect mode, is always perfected, as here:[19]

This also holds for duplex longae and all other shapes that can be perfected. And note that any note greater than some other note can be perfected.[20]

---

brevis vero quae quinque vel quatuor, semimaior nuncupatur, a semus, -a, -um, quod est imperfectus (in truth, the semibrevis that is worth five or four [minimae] is referred to as a semimaior, from semus, -a, -um, which means imperfect)."

[18]Of Hanboys's eight figures, four are declared to be whole (simplex) in the sense that they cannot be ligated: the larga, minor (298.22), semiminor (310.6), and minima (316.24).

[19]The *punctus perfectionis*, when used in the imperfect mode, is in effect a *punctus additionis*. Hanboys's use of the phrases perfect and imperfect mode at a level of the mensural hierarchy well above that of the longa, is also noteworthy.

[20]This is the introduction of perfection, and thus a general statement of principle is provided by Hanboys. There is an introduction to alteration in the corresponding discussion of the duplex longa in chapter 6 (212.6–7).

Sciendum est quod punctus dicitur dupliciter, scilicet punctus perfectionis et punctus divisionis. Punctus perfectionis secundum quosdam dicitur quatripliciter, scilicet post notam et ante et sub et supra. Punctus perfectionis postpositus proximam perficit notam precedentem. Punctus suprapositus primam speciem illius figure denotat perfectam. Si ante ponatur, perfectio in secunda verificatur. Si suppositus, perfectio in tertia demonstratur.

Punctus divisionis dicitur dupliciter. Aut dividit modum a modo aut perfectiones, et ibi est alteratio.

Et quando ponitur punctus in medietate, primus denotat perfectionem, secundus vero divisionem.

---

3 perfectionis ⟦secundum quosdam⟧ A2 ‖ 6 verificatur]versificatur (s *sup. lin., m. sec.*) A2 ‖

It must be known that the punctus is said to be of two kinds: the *punctus perfectionis* and the *punctus divisionis*.[21] A *punctus perfectionis*, according to some, is said to be of four kinds: after, before, below, and above a note.[22] A *punctus perfectionis* employed after a note perfects the next preceding note. A punctus employed above denotes that the first part of the figure is perfect. If it is employed before, it verifies perfection in the second part. If it is employed below, it shows perfection in the third part.

A *punctus divisionis* is said to be of two kinds: either it separates one mode from another,[23] or it separates perfections, and that is where there is alteration.

And when the punctus is employed between two notes, the first denotes perfection; the second, division.[24]

---

[21]Having just introduced the *punctus perfectionis,* Hanboys begins an explanatory digression. Though the notion that a small stroke (later a dot) might function as a sign of perfection or division goes back at least as far as Franco's *Ars cantus mensurabilis*, cap. 5, sent. 6 (ed. Reaney and Gilles), p. 32, the straightforward assertion that there are two kinds of punctus, the *punctus divisionis* and *punctus perfectionis*, is a formulation that can be traced back no further than the *Libellus cantus mensurabilis* (ca. 1340) of Johannes de Muris (CS, 3:53a–b): "Duplex est punctus, scilicet perfectionis et divisionis (the punctus is of two kinds, namely, of perfection and of division)." See Klaus-Jürgen Sachs, "Punctus, V.(1)," in *Handwörterbuch der musikalischen Terminologie* (1974). See also Handlo, *Regule*, Rule IV of Rubric IV (100.24–102.1).

[22]The fourfold employment of a *punctus perfectionis* (after, above, below, or before a note), though not with Hanboys's meaning, is found in de Muris, *Notitia artis musicae* (ed. Michels), pp. 99–100. Another such system, similar in concept and impulse to that of de Muris, although not identical, is described in Johannes Torkesey, *Declaratio trianguli et scuti* (ed. Gilles and Reaney), pp. 58–61. Neither of these two doctrines corresponds to what Hanboys reports "according to some," which is the use of a punctus to indicate the perfection either of the entirety or of the first third, middle third, or final third of a ternary note. For Hanboys's discussion in similar language of the threefold use of the circle by the moderns (i.e., before, above, or below a note), see chapter 13 (266.1–9). Handlo's use of a punctus before the first element in an oblique figure without propriety in order to perfect the beginning (*Regule*, Rule XVII of Rubric VI [128.19–21]) is unrelated to the present context.

[23]On the use of the punctus to separate modes, see also Handlo, *Regule*, Maxim 13 of Rubric XIII (176.21–24); and the Introduction, pp. 14–15.

[24]For an extended passage with examples of a punctus that simultaneously indicates perfection and division, see Thomas Walsingham, *Regulae de musica mensurabili*, cap. 15 (ed. Reaney), pp. 94–96; and see also an

Et nota de qualibet perfecte perfecta, pre et post, tertia pars imperfici potest. Sed pars que in medio est, non modo imperfici potest.

Et potest larga, cum sit de modo perfecto, imperfici per duplicem longam precedentem vel subsequentem, vel per valorem. Per duplicem longam
5 precedentem, ut hic:

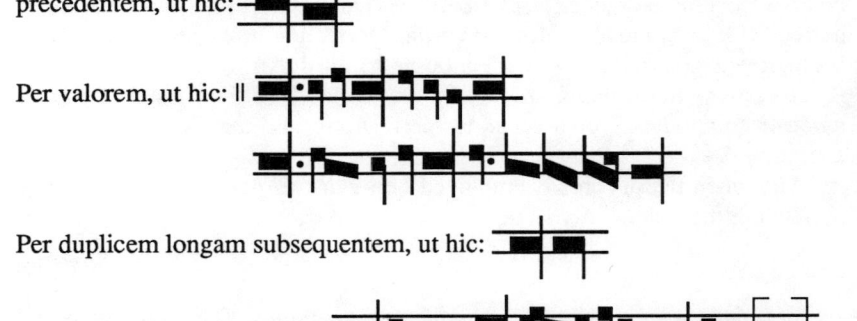

CS1: 406a

Per valorem, ut hic: ‖

Per duplicem longam subsequentem, ut hic:
10
Per valorem, ut hic sequitur:

Larga aliquando valet novem longas, aliquando octo, aliquando septem, aliquando sex, aliquando quinque, aliquando quatuor. Novem longarum,
15 quando larga de largis et duplicibus longis perfectis ponitur ante largam vel ante punctum. Ante largam, ut hic:

Ante punctum, ut hic:

20 Octo longarum, quando longa vel valor antecedit largam, ut hic:

Vel subsequitur, ut hic patet in hoc exemplo: ‖

CS1: 406b

---

3–202.5 *vide* Plate 2 ‖ 8 *duplex longa, duplex longa, larga: figurae del. ante* lin. 1.1 A2 | x *pro punctus* lin 1.2 A2 | *longa* lin. 1.9 A2 ‖ 14 largarum A2 ‖

And note concerning any note perfectly perfected, before and after, that its third part can be imperfected. But the part that is in the middle cannot be imperfected in any manner.

And the larga,[25] when it is in the perfect mode, can be imperfected by a preceding or following duplex longa or its value. By a preceding duplex longa, as here:

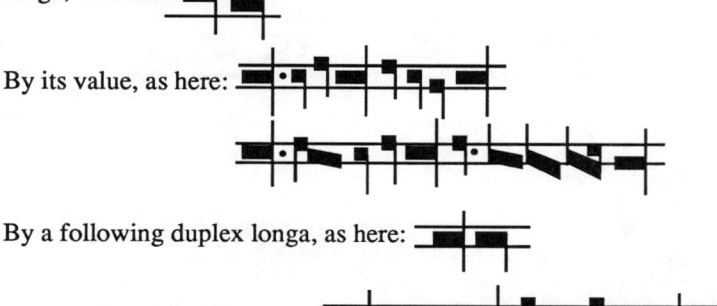

By a following duplex longa, as here:

By its value, as follows here:

The larga sometimes is worth nine longae, sometimes eight, sometimes seven, sometimes six, sometimes five, sometimes four. It is worth nine longae when the larga (consisting of perfect largae and duplex longae) is employed before a larga or a punctus. Before a larga, as here:

Before a punctus, as here: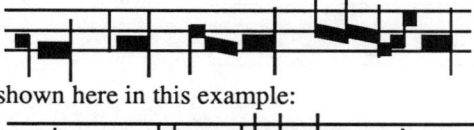

Eight longae when a longa or its value precedes a larga, as here:

Or follows, as is shown here in this example:

---

anonymous medieval commentary on Johannes de Muris's discussion of the punctus in the *Libellus cantus mensurabilis* that has been printed by Wolf in *Geschichte der Mensural-Notation*, 1:105–7.

[25]Plate 2 presents a facsimile of **GB**-Lbl, Additional 8866, f. 66, which reproduces 198.3–202.5.

Septem longarum, quando larga ponitur inter duas longas vel inter valorem, ut patet in exemplo sequenti lucide:

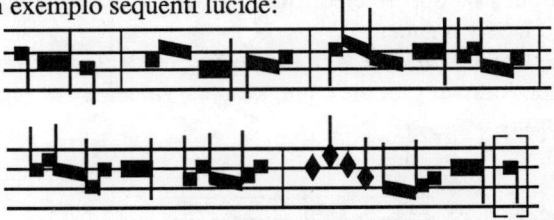

Tunc prima longa vel valor imperficit primam duplicem longam, secunda vero ultimam.
Sex longarum, quando duplex longa vel valor ponitur ante largam, ut hic:

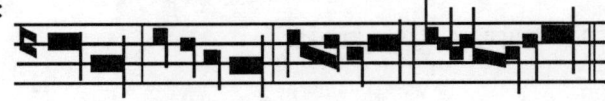

Vel subsequitur, ut hic patet in exemplo:

Quinque longarum, quando longa vel valor precedit largam, et duplex longa perfecta vel valor subsequitur, ut hic patet:

Tunc longa vel valor precedens largam imperficit primam duplicem longam, duplex longa subsequens largam imperficit eam. Vel quando duplex longa vel valor precedit largam, et longa vel valor sequitur, ut hic: ||

CS1: 407a

---

3 *sec. tractus om.* lin. 1.9 A2 || 7 ⟦hic⟧ A2 || 8 *sec. et ter. tractus om.* 8.14 A2 || 11–202.5 *m. sec.* A2 ||

Seven longae when the larga is employed between two longae or between their value, as is clearly shown in the following example:

Then the first longa or value imperfects the first duplex longa; the second imperfects the last.

Six longae when a duplex longa or its value is employed before a larga, as here:

Or follows after, as is shown here in an example:

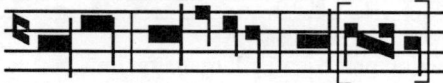

Five longae when a longa or its value precedes a larga and a perfect duplex longa or its value follows, as is shown here:

Then the longa or its value preceding the larga imperfects the first duplex longa, and the duplex longa following the larga imperfects it. Or when a duplex longa or its value precedes the larga, and a longa or its value follows, as here:

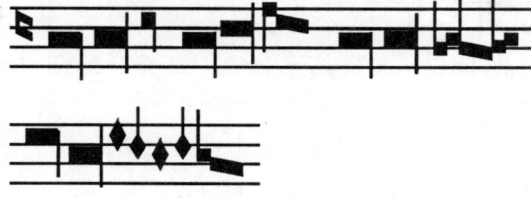

Tunc duplex longa vel valor precedens largam imperficit eam. Longa vero vel valor subsequens eam imperficit ultimam duplicem longam.

Quatuor longarum, quando duplex longa perfecta cum longa sequente vel valor precedit largam et longa vel valor subsequitur, ut hic: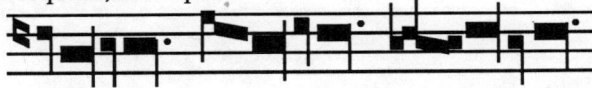

Vel quando longa vel valor largam precedit, et longa cum duplici longa perfecta vel valor sequitur, ut hic patet:

Tunc duplex longa perficitur per punctum; longa recta vel valor precedens largam primam duplicem longam imperficit; longa vero subsequens ultimam imperficit duplicem longam.

Vel quando quatuor longe vel valor precedunt largam et longa vel valor subsequitur:

Tunc tres longe vel valor precedentes largam faciunt perfectionem; quarta longa vel valor primam duplicem longam large imperficit; longa vero vel valor subsequens largam secundam duplicem longam imperficit. Vel quando longa vel valor precedit largam et quatuor longe vel valor sequuntur, ut hic: ‖ CS1: 407b

Tunc longa vel valor precedens largam primam duplicem longam imperficit; longa vero vel valor subsequens imperficit secundam duplicem longam; tres longe sequentes vel valor faciunt perfectionem.

Vel quando larga constat de duabus duplicibus longis imperfectis, ut hic patet: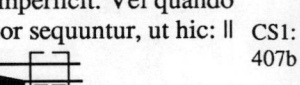

Quia sicut larga ante largam de largis perfectis est perfecta, ita larga ante largam de largis imperfectis est imperfecta, hoc est puncto carente.

---

5 *una figura* 5.12–13 A2 ‖ 8 *punctus om.* 8.11 A2 | *sec. tractus om.* 8.12 A2 | *punctus om.* 8.16 A2 ‖ 19 *tractus om.* 19.11–12 A2 ‖ 23 longis *in marg., m. sec.* A2 ‖

Then the duplex longa or its value preceding the larga imperfects it. The longa or its value following it imperfects the last duplex longa.

Four longae when a perfect duplex longa with a following longa or its value precedes the larga and a longa or its value follows, as here:

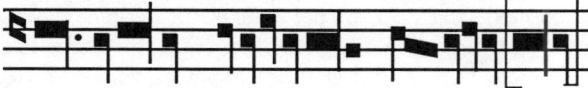

Or when a longa or its value precedes the larga and a longa with a perfect duplex longa or its value follow, as is shown here:

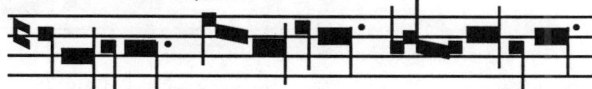

Then the duplex longa is perfected by a punctus; the longa recta or its value preceding the larga imperfects the first duplex longa; the longa following imperfects the last duplex longa.

Or when four longae or their value precede the larga and a longa or its value follows:

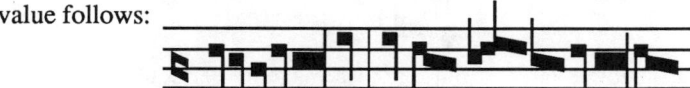

Then the three longae or their value preceding the larga make a perfection; the fourth longa or its value imperfects the first duplex longa; the longa or value following the larga imperfects the second duplex longa. Or when a longa or its value precedes the larga and four longae or their value follow, as here:

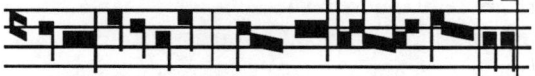

Then the longa or its value preceding the larga imperfects the first duplex longa; the longa or its value following imperfects the second duplex longa; the three subsequent longae or their value make a perfection.

Or when the larga consists of two imperfect duplex longae, as is shown here:

Just as a larga before a larga (consisting of perfect largae) is perfect, so a larga before a larga (consisting of imperfect largae) is imperfect, when it lacks a punctus.

## CAPITULUM IV

⟨Hanboys⟩: Larga perfecta ex omnibus perfectis diminui potest per longam precedentem vel subsequentem, vel per longam precedentem et subsequentem, manente perfecta. Si per longam precedentem vel subsequentem
5 sive per longam precedentem et subsequentem predicta larga diminuatur, longa subsequens largam imperfici potest per brevem precedentem, si brevis vel valor eam sequatur:

Et utraque longa, scilicet precedens largam et subsequens, imperfici potest
10 per brevem subsequentem; brevis etiam per semibrevem; semibrevis per minorem; minor autem per semiminorem; et semiminor per minimam, ut patet in exemplo sequenti apertissime: ‖

CS1: 408a

Alio modo predicta larga diminui potest, manente perfecta. Nam ultima
15 duplex longa imperfici potest per longam subsequentem, manente de duabus longis. Secunda longa imperfici potest per brevem subsequentem, manente de duabus brevibus. Secunda brevis imperfici potest per semibrevem subsequentem, manente de duabus semibrevibus. Secunda semibrevis imperfici potest per minorem subsequentem, manente de duabus minoribus. Secunda
20 minor imperfici potest per semiminorem subsequentem, manente de duabus semiminoribus. Secunda semiminor imperfici potest per minimam subsequentem, manente de duabus minimis, ut hic patet:

Larga, si sit perfecta ex omnibus perfectis, continet 3 duplices longas, 9
25 longas, 27 breves, 81 semibreves, 243 minores, 729 semiminores, 2187 minimas. Et si larga sit imperfecta ex omnibus imperfectis, continet 2 duplices longas, 4 longas, 8 breves, 16 semibreves, 32 minores, 64 semiminores, 128 minimas.

Dictum est de largis, dicendum est de longis duplicibus.

---

1 IV]3ᵐ A2 ‖ 3 vel (pr.)]et A2 ‖ 13 *semiminor* 13.6, 13 A2 ‖ 19 duabus] duobus A2 ‖ 20 de]de⟦d⟧ A2 ‖ 23 *semiminor* 23.2 A2 ‖ 29 longis]longis ⟦simplicibus⟧ A2 ‖

## CHAPTER 4

Hanboys: A larga perfect on all levels can be diminished by a preceding or following longa or by a preceding and following longa, while remaining perfect. If the aforesaid larga is diminished by a preceding or following longa or by a preceding and following longa, the longa following the larga can be imperfected by a preceding brevis if the brevis or its value follows the larga:

And both longae, namely those preceding and following the larga, can be imperfected by a following brevis; the brevis by a semibrevis; the semibrevis by a minor; the minor by a semiminor; and the semiminor by a minima, as is most clearly shown in the following example:

The aforesaid larga can be diminished in another manner while remaining perfect. Its last duplex longa can be imperfected by a following longa, remaining as two longae. The second longa can be imperfected by a following brevis, remaining as two breves. The second brevis can be imperfected by a following semibrevis, remaining as two semibreves. The second semibrevis can be imperfected by a following minor, remaining as two minors. The second minor can be imperfected by a following semiminor, remaining as two semiminors. The second semiminor can be imperfected by a following minima, remaining as two minimae, as is shown here:

The larga, if perfect on all levels, contains 3 duplex longae, 9 longae, 27 breves, 81 semibreves, 243 minors, 729 semiminors, 2187 minimae. And if the larga is imperfect on all levels, it contains 2 duplex longae, 4 longae, 8 breves, 16 semibreves, 32 minors, 64 semiminors, 128 minimae.

Having said something concerning largas, there must now be said something concerning duplex longae.

## CAPITULUM V

⟨Hanboys⟩: Forma longarum duplicium talis est. Quandocunque invenitur punctus magnus et grossus continens quantitatem longarum duarum, duplex longa dicitur, ut hic: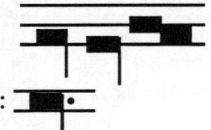

|| Et potest perfici et imperfici. Perfici potest, ut duplex longa ante duplicem longam simplicem vel compositam, vel ante punctum. Duplex longa ante duplicem longam simplicem vel compositam, ut hic: CS1: 408b

Vel ante punctum, ut hic:

Et imperfici potest per longam precedentem vel subsequentem, vel per valorem. Per longam precedentem, ut hic:

Per valorem, ut hic patet:

Per longam subsequentem, ut hic:

Per valorem, ut hic patet:

---

1 V]4ᵐ A2 || 10 ut hic *sup. lin., m. sec.* A2 || 14 *longa post* 14.2 || 16 *ultimus punctus descendens del. in* 16.3 | *punctus post* 16.4 A2 ||

# CHAPTER 5

Hanboys: The form of duplex longae is thus. Whenever a large and thick notehead is found containing the quantity of two longae,[26] it is said to be a duplex longa, as here: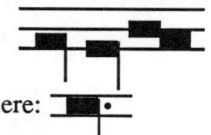

And it can be perfected and imperfected. It can be perfected, as a duplex longa before a whole or composite duplex longa[27] or before a punctus. A duplex longa before a whole or composite duplex longa, as here:

Or before a punctus, as here:

And it can be imperfected by a preceding or following longa or by its value. By a preceding longa, as here: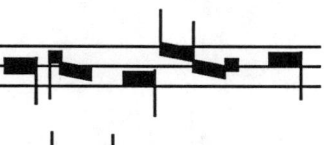

By its value, as is shown here:

By a following longa, as here:

By its value, as is shown here:

---

[26]Here quantity (*quantitas*) refers to physical size, not mensural value; this figure has the shape of two longae joined horizontally end to end, but it may have the value of three longae.

[27]The duplex longa may be whole or composite, in contrast to the larga, which is only whole (chapter 3 [194.6]); Hanboys's longa is similarly whole or composite (chapter 7 [222.6]).

‖ Longa duplex aliquando valet novem breves, aliquando octo, aliquando septem, aliquando sex, aliquando quinque, aliquando quatuor. Novem brevium, quando duplex longa perfecta de longis perfectis ponitur ante duplicem longam vel ante punctum. Ante duplicem longam, ut hic:

Vel ante punctum, ut hic:

Octo brevium, quando brevis antecedit longam duplicem, ut hic:
Vel subsequitur, ut hic:

Septem brevium, quando longa duplex ponitur inter duas breves, ut hic patet:

Vel inter valorem duarum brevium, ut hic:

Tunc prima brevis vel valor imperficit primam longam, secunda vero ultimam.

Sex brevium, quando longa perfecta precedit longam duplicem, ut hic:

‖ Vel subsequitur, ut hic:

Vel valor longe perfecte precedit duplicem longam, ut hic patet:

Tunc duplex longa imperficitur per longam precedentem vel subsequentem vel per valorem.

Quinque brevium, quando brevis vel valor precedit longam ⟨duplicem⟩ et longam perfectam vel valor subsequitur, ut hic in exemplo sequenti patet:

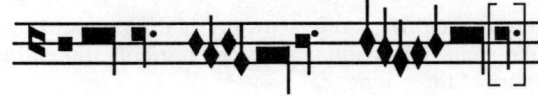

---

4 punctum. Ante]punctum a⟦1⟧n A2 ‖ 14 inter]per (*corr. in marg., m. sec.*) A2 ‖

The duplex longa sometimes is worth nine breves, sometimes eight, sometimes seven, sometimes six, sometimes five, sometimes four. It is worth nine breves when the perfect duplex longa (consisting of perfect longae) is employed before a duplex longa or before a punctus. Before a duplex longa, as here:

Or before a punctus, as here:

Eight breves when a brevis precedes a duplex longa, as here:
Or follows, as here:

Seven breves when a duplex longa is employed between two breves, as is shown here:
Or between the value of two breves, as here:

Then the first brevis or value imperfects the first longa; the second imperfects the last.

Six breves when a perfect longa precedes a duplex longa, as here:

Or follows, as here:

Or the value of a perfect longa precedes a duplex longa, as is shown here:

Or follows, as here:

Then the duplex longa is imperfected by the preceding or following longa or by its value.

Five breves when a brevis or its value precedes a duplex longa and a perfect longa or its value follows, as is shown here in the following example:

⟨Tunc brevis vel valor precedens duplicem longam primam longam imperficit; longa vero vel valor subsequens duplicem longam imperficit eam. Vel quando longa perfecta vel valor precedit duplicem longam et brevis vel valor subsequitur, ut hic⟩:

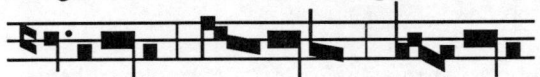

Tunc brevis vel valor subsequens duplicem longam ultimam longam imperficit; longa vero vel valor precedens duplicem longam imperficit eam.

Quatuor brevium, quando longa perfecta cum brevi sequente vel valor precedit duplicem longam et brevis vel valor subsequitur, ut hic patet:

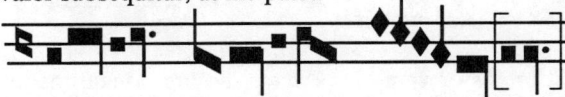

Vel quando brevis vel valor precedit longam duplicem et brevis cum longa perfecta vel valor subsequitur, ut hic patet:

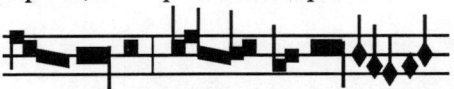

‖ Tunc longa perficitur per punctum; brevis vel valor precedens duplicem longam primam longam imperficit; brevis vero subsequens duplicem longam imperficit secundam longam.

CS1: 410a

Vel quando quatuor breves precedunt duplicem longam vel valor, et brevis vel valor subsequitur, ut hic patet in exemplo:

Tunc tres breves precedentes faciunt perfectionem, quarta brevis primam longam imperficit, brevis subsequens duplicem longam imperficit secundam longam. Vel quando brevis vel valor precedit duplicem longam et ⟨quatuor⟩ breves vel valor sequuntur, ut patet in hoc exemplo:

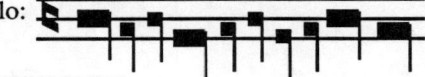

Tunc brevis vel valor precedens duplicem longam imperficit primam longam; brevis vero vel valor subsequens secundam longam imperficit; tres breves sequentes vel valor faciunt perfectionem.

Vel quando duplex longa constat de duabus longis imperfectis, ut hic patet in exemplo:

---

10 *longa* 10.14 A2 ‖ 17 quatuor breves quando A2 ‖ 20 Tunc ... perfectionem *bis* A2 ‖

Then the brevis or its value preceding the duplex longa imperfects the first longa; the longa or its value following the duplex longa imperfects it. Or when a perfect longa or its value precedes a duplex longa and a brevis or its value follows, as here:

Then the brevis or its value following the duplex longa imperfects the last longa; the longa or its value preceding the duplex longa imperfects it.

Four breves when a perfect longa with a following brevis or its value precedes a duplex longa and a brevis or its value follows, as is shown here:

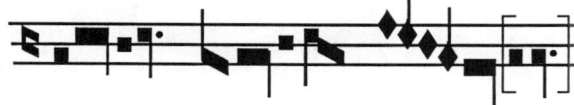

Or when a brevis or its value precedes a duplex longa and a brevis with a perfect longa or its value follows, as is shown here:

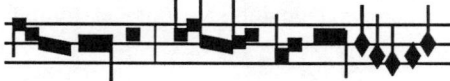

Then the longa is perfected by a punctus; the brevis or value preceding the duplex longa imperfects the first longa; the brevis following the duplex longa imperfects the second longa.

Or when four breves or their value precede a duplex longa and a brevis or its value follows, as is shown here in an example:

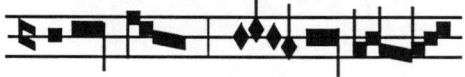

Then the three preceding breves make a perfection; the fourth brevis imperfects the first longa; the brevis following the duplex longa imperfects the second longa. Or when a brevis or its value precedes a duplex longa and four breves or their value follow, as is shown in this example:

Then the brevis or value preceding the duplex longa imperfects the first longa; a following brevis or its value imperfects the second longa; three following breves or their value make a perfection.

Or when the duplex longa consists of two imperfect longae, as is shown here in an example:

Nam sicut duplex longa ante duplicem longam de longis duplicibus perfectis est perfecta, sic duplex longa ante duplicem longam de longis duplicibus imperfectis est imperfecta, hoc ⟨est⟩ puncto carente. ‖

## CAPITULUM VI

5   Hanboys: Longarum duplicium quedam sunt duplices longe que recte vocantur, et quedam sunt duplices longe que altere nominantur. Et nota quod quelibet nota minor alia alterari potest. Recta duplex longa fit tripliciter: ante largam, post largam, et inter largas. Ante largam, ut hic:

10  Post largam, ut hic patet:

Inter largas, ut in hoc exemplo: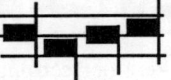

Longa duplex altera duas duplices longas in se includit in valore licet
15  non in forma, quia in qualibet nota que alteratur, valor duplicatur. Et nota quod ubicunque fit alteratio, in maiori constat perfectio.

Fit autem altera duplex longa tribus modis. Primo modo, quando due duplices longe tantum vel valor unius duplicis longe et una duplex longa inveniuntur inter duas largas. Due duplices longe tantum, ut hic:
20

Tunc prima duplex longa recta vocatur, secunda vero alteratur. ‖ Vel valor unius duplicis longe et una duplex longa, ut hic:

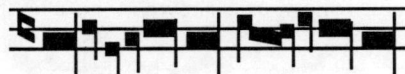

---

3 hoc *in marg., m. sec.* A2 ‖ 4 VI]5ᵐ A2 ‖ 5 hᶜ *in marg., m. sec.* A2 | Hanboys *in marg., m. sec.* A2 ‖

Now just as a duplex longa before a duplex longa (consisting of perfect duplex longae) is perfect, so a duplex longa before a duplex longa (consisting of imperfect duplex longae) is imperfect, that is, when it lacks a punctus.

## CHAPTER 6

Hanboys: Some duplex longae are the duplex longae that are called rectae, and some are the duplex longae that are called alterae. And note that any note smaller than another can be altered.[28] The duplex longa recta occurs in three ways: before a larga, after a larga, and between largae. Before a larga, as here:

After a larga, as here:

Between largae, as in this example: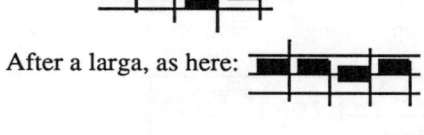

The duplex longa altera includes in itself two duplex longae in value but not in form, for whenever a note is altered, its value is doubled. And note that wherever there is alteration, the greater value is perfect.

Moreover, the duplex longa altera occurs in three manners. In the first manner, when just two duplex longae or the value of one duplex longa and one duplex longa are found between two largae. Just two duplex longae, as here: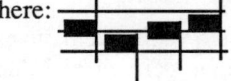

Then the first duplex longa is called recta, the second is altered. Or the value of one duplex longa and one duplex longa, as here:

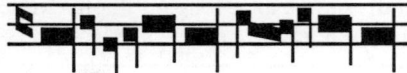

---

[28]This is the introduction of alteration, and thus a brief general statement of principle is provided by Hanboys. There is a comparable sentence when perfection is introduced in chapter 3 (194.15–16). The primary scribe of **GB**-Lbl, Additional 8866 used *altera* and *alterata* interchangeably; it is impossible to tell if one or the other reading was preferred by Hanboys. The distinction was made by Handlo; see the *Regule*, Maxim 2 and Maxim 3 of Rubric III (92.22–25).

Tunc valor duplicis longe pro recta habeatur, et duplex longa subsequens alteratur, nisi per punctum divisionis aliter distinguantur, ut patet in exemplo:

5 Tunc enim due erunt equales et prima duplex longa vel valor ⟨primam⟩ largam imperficit; secunda vero ultimam.

Vel quando due duplices longe tantum vel valor unius duplicis longe et una duplex longa invenitur ante largam. Due duplices longe tantum, ut hic:

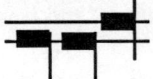

10 Vel valor unius duplicis longe et una duplex longa, ut hic patet in exemplo:

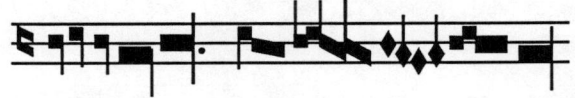

Secundo ⟨modo⟩, quando tres duplices longe vel valor duarum duplicium longarum et una duplex longa inveniuntur inter duas largas, et si inter primam duplicem longam et secundam vel post valorem prime duplicis 15 longe fit punctus divisionis, ut hic:

‖ Tunc prima duplex longa vel valor primam largam imperficit; secunda vero vel valor pro recta habeatur et tertia alteratur.

CS1: 411b

Tertio modo, quando plures duplices longe vel valor adinvicem inve-
20 niuntur. Computandus est tertius numerus pro perfectione vel valor; si due duplices longe vel valor unius duplicis longe et una duplex longa in fine remanserit, prima duplex longa vel valor pro recta teneatur, secunda vero alteratur, et punctum divisionis ante longam duplicem penultimam vel ante valorem habere tenetur, ut hic:

25

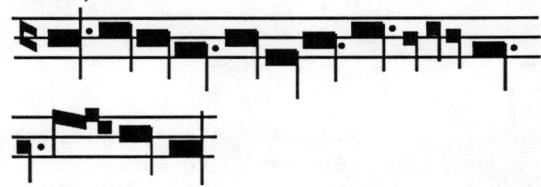

---

2 distinguatur A2 ǀ patet *bis* A2 ‖ 25 *punctus supra* lin. 1.11 A2 ǀ *punctus post* lin. 1.18 A2 ‖

Then the value of the duplex longa is taken as recta, and the following duplex longa is altered, unless by a *punctus divisionis* they are otherwise distinguished, as is shown in an example:

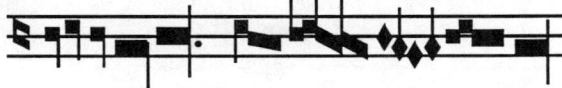

For then the two will be equal and the first duplex longa or its value imperfects the first larga; the second imperfects the last.

Or when just two duplex longae or the value of one duplex longa and one duplex longa are found before a larga. Just two duplex longae, as here:

Or the value of one duplex longa and one duplex longa, as is shown here in an example:

In the second manner, when three duplex longae or the value of two duplex longae and one duplex longa are found between two largae, and if between the first duplex longa and the second or after the value of the first duplex longa, a *punctus divisionis* occurs, as here:

Then the first duplex longa or its value imperfects the first larga; the second or its value is taken as recta, and the third is altered.

In the third manner, when several duplex longae or their value are found together. Three of them or their value must be counted as a perfection. If two duplex longae or the value of one duplex longa and one duplex longa should remain at the end, the first duplex longa or value should be held as recta, the second is altered, and it is held to have a *punctus divisionis* before the penultimate duplex longa or its value, as here:

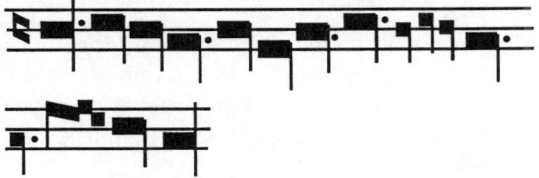

Et si una duplex longa in fine remanserit, recta vocatur et ad perfectionem large subsequentis pertinet, ut sequitur in sequenti formula:

Et potest duplex longa alterata diminui veluti larga imperfecta sibi corre-
5  spondens, manente alterata.

Et potest duplex longa perfecta ex omnibus perfectis diminui per brevem precedentem vel per brevem subsequentem sive per brevem precedentem et subsequentem. ⟨Si per brevem precedentem⟩ predicta duplex longa diminuatur, brevis duplicem longam sequens per semibrevem precedentem imperfici
10 potest si se∥mibrevis vel valor eam sequatur, ut hic patet in exemplo:

CS1: 412a

Si brevis utraque, scilicet ante duplicem longam et post, imperfici potest per semibrevem subsequentem, semibrevis per minorem, minor autem per semiminorem et semiminor per minimam, ut hic patet in exemplo:
15

Longa duplex predicta alio modo potest diminui. Ultima longa imperfici potest per brevem subsequentem, manente de duabus brevibus. Secunda brevis imperfici potest per semibrevem subsequentem, manente de duabus semibrevibus. Secunda semibrevis imperfici potest per minorem subsequentem,
20 manente de duabus minoribus. Secunda minor imperfici potest per semiminorem subsequentem, manente de duabus semiminoribus. Secunda semiminor imperfici potest per minimam, manente de duabus minimis, ut hic patet in exemplo:

25  Longa duplex, cum sit perfecta ex omnibus perfectis, valet 3 longas, 9 breves, 27 semibreves, 81 minores, 243 semiminores, 729 minimas. Et si duplex longa sit imperfecta ex omnibus imperfectis, 2 longas valet, 4 breves, 8 semibreves, 16 minores, 32 semiminores, 64 minimas.

---

11 *semibrevis* 11.9 A2 ǀ *pausa semibrevis perfectae post* 11.15 A2 ‖ 12 brevis ⟦*itaque*⟧ (brevis *sup. lin., m. sec.*) utraque A2 ‖ 25 valet]viz A2 ‖ 27 valet]viz A2 ‖

And if one duplex longa should remain at the end, it is called recta and pertains to the perfection of the following larga, as follows in the following formula:

And the altered duplex longa can be diminished like the imperfect larga to which it corresponds, remaining altered.

And the duplex longa perfect on all levels can be diminished by a preceding brevis or by a following brevis or by preceding and following breves. If the aforesaid duplex longa is diminished by a following brevis, the brevis following the duplex longa can be imperfected by a preceding semibrevis if a semibrevis or its value follows the duplex longa, as is shown here in an example:

If both are breves (namely before the duplex longa and after), each can be imperfected by a following semibrevis, the semibrevis by a minor, the minor by a semiminor, and the semiminor by a minima, as is shown in an example:

The aforesaid duplex longa can be diminished in another manner. Its last longa can be imperfected by a following brevis, remaining as two breves. The second brevis can be imperfected by a following semibrevis, remaining as two semibreves. The second semibrevis can be imperfected by a following minor, remaining as two minors. The second minor can be imperfected by a following semiminor, remaining as two semiminors. The second semiminor can be imperfected by a minima, remaining as two minimae, as is shown in an example: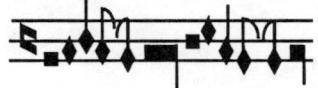

The duplex longa, if it is perfect on all levels, is worth 3 longae, 9 breves, 27 semibreves, 81 minors, 243 semiminors, 729 minimae. And if the duplex longa is imperfect on all levels, it is worth 2 longae, 4 breves, 8 semibreves, 16 minors, 32 semiminors, 64 minimae.

Predicta duplex longa hodie perficitur et imperficitur, et a quibusdem larga vocatur. Olim || tamen dicebatur imperfecta, ut patet hic per Francho- CS1: nem. Duplex longa sic formatur: 412b

5 Sciendum est quod duplex longa duas longas in se includit. Et plicari potest, ut hic patet:

Et sciendum est quod duplicium longarum quedam habent sex tempora, quedam quinque, quedam quatuor. Sex temporum, quando duplex longa stat
10 inter duas longas, ut hic:

Vel ante longam, ut hic:

Vel ante longe pausam, ut hic patet:
15
Quinque temporum, quando brevis antecedit longam duas longas includentem, ut hic patet:

Vel subsequitur, ut hic:
20

---

9 longa *in marg., m. sec.* A2 || 16 longam]longa[[i]] A2 || 18 *exemplum bis* A2 ||

Today, the aforesaid duplex longa is perfected and imperfected and is called by some the larga.[29] Nevertheless, it was formerly said to be imperfect, as is shown here according to Franco.[30] The duplex longa is formed thus:[31]

It must be known that the duplex longa includes in itself two longae. And it can be plicated, as is shown here:

And it must be known that some duplex longae have six tempora, some five, some four.[32] Six tempora when the duplex longa stands between two longae, as here:

Or before a longa, as here:

Or before a longa rest, as is shown here:

Five tempora when a brevis precedes a longa including two longae, as is shown here:

Or follows, as here:

---

[29]It is unfortunate that Hanboys does not identify those he has in mind who call the duplex longa a larga. Jacques de Liège mentions this use of the term larga in Book 7 of the *Speculum musicae* (ed. Bragard), p. 53 *et passim*. From the English tradition see, for instance, the anonymous item 2 in **GB**-Lbl, Additional 21455 (f. 5r–v) (de Vitry, *Ars nova* [ed. Reaney et al.], p. 74); Johannes Torkesey, *Declaratio trianguli et scuti* (ed. Gilles and Reaney), p. 58; and Robertus de Brunham (*Summa*, chapter 20 [338.5–6]).

[30]Though according to Hanboys, the following passage is Franconian, it is from neither the *Ars cantus mensurabilis* nor the *Gaudent moderni* tradition. Hanboys may, of course, be referring specifically to the "Franco" of the *Regule*, and the passage here may have originated in Hanboys's exemplar of Handlo.

[31]See Handlo, *Regule*, Rule IV of Rubric II (90.2).

[32]Handlo only allows the duplex longa to be "imperfected" (rather than "diminished") to a value of five breves by a single preceding or following brevis; see the *Regule*, Rule V of Rubric II (90.7–9) and Rule III of Rubric

Quatuor temporum, quando duplex longa stat inter duas breves, ut hic:

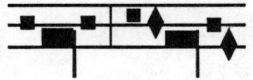

⟨CAPITULUM VII⟩

‖ Sequitur de longis.

Franco: Forma longarum simplicium talis est. Quandocunque punctus quadratus vel nota quadrata, quod idem est, habet tractum a parte dextra descendentem, longa dicitur, ut hic: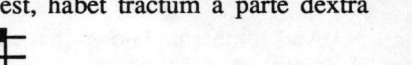

Hanboys: Si tractum habeat a parte dextra ascendentem, erecta vocatur:

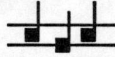

Ponuntur enim iste longe erecte ad differentiam longarum precedentium, que sunt recte. Et vocantur erecte, quia ubicunque inveniuntur per semitonium eriguntur.

CS1: 413a

---

11 d⟦e⟧fferentiam *corr. sup. lin.* A2 ‖

Four tempora when a duplex longa stands between two breves, as here:

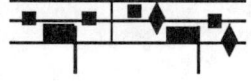

## CHAPTER 7

What follows concerns longae.[33]

Franco: The form of whole longae is thus. Whenever a square notehead or a square note, which is the same thing, has a stem descending from the right side, it is said to be a longa, as here:[34]

Hanboys: If it has a stem ascending from the right side, it is called erecta:[35]

These longae erectae are employed to differentiate them from the preceding longae, which are rectae. And they are called erectae because wherever they are found, they are raised by a semitone.[36]

---

V (118.10–12). The reduction of its value to four breves by both preceding and following breves, as here, is one characteristic doctrine of several anonymous early *ars nova* treatises. See the version of de Vitry's *Ars nova* with the incipit "Sex sunt species principales" (ed. Reaney et al.), p. 57; item 1 of **GB**-Lbl, Additional 21455 (ibid.), p. 74; the anonymous *De musica mensurabili* (ed. Sweeney), p. 46; the anonymous *De valore notularum tam veteris quam novae artis* (ed. Reaney), p. 19 (see also Anonymous II of CS, 3:367a); the anonymous *Compendium musicae mensurabilis tam veteris quam novae artis* (ed. Reaney), p. 34 (see also Anonymous IV of CS, 3:378b); and the attack on the immediately preceding theorist by Jacques de Liège, *Speculum musicae*, Book 7, cap. XXVII (ed. Bragard), p. 56.

[33]This vestige of a rubric in Handlo's style opens the first chapter of the *Summa* that is drawn primarily from the *Regule*.
[34]Handlo, *Regule*, Rubric I, Rule I (80.9–82.3).
[35]Handlo, *Regule*, Rubric I, Rule II (82.4–6).
[36]Handlo, *Regule*, Rubric I, Maxim 2 (84.2–4).

Franco: Longa plicata cum duobus tractibus ascendentibus vel descendentibus dextra parte longiore sinistra, ut hic patet in exemplo:

Hanboys: Erecte longe, sive perfecte sive imperfecte, nunquam plicari possunt.

Franco: Longa ante longam simplicem vel compositam, vel ante valorem, vel ante longam pausam, vel ante punctum valet tria tempora.

Hanboys: Id est, tres breves, ut de modo perfecto.

Franco: Longa ante longam simplicem vel compositam, ut hic:

‖ Vel ante valorem, ut hic: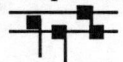

CS1: 413b

Vel ante longam pausam, ut hic: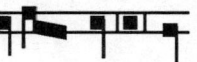

Vel ante punctum, ut hic:

Hanboys: Si sit de modo perfecto sive de modo imperfecto, semper longa ante punctum est perfecta; id est, valet tres breves.

Franco: Longa perfecta vocatur trium temporum, imperfecta vero duorum.

Hanboys: Et habent eandem figuram, scilicet punctum quadratum cum tractu descendente a dextra parte, ut patet hic:

Hanboys: Idem est iudicium de longis erectis, ut hic:

---

3 *omnes tractus descendentes* A2 ‖ 4 nunquam]nuncquam A2 ‖ 7 pausam]pausam ut hic *et exemplum de linea 10* A2 ǀ punctum]punctum ⟦ut hic⟧ A2 ‖ 18 est (*pr.*) *m. sec.* A2 ‖ 24 Hanboys]Franco A2 ‖

Franco: The longa plicata has two stems ascending or descending with the one on the right side longer than the one on the left, as is shown here in an example:[37]

Hanboys: Longae erectae, whether perfect or imperfect, can never be plicated.[38]

Franco: A longa before a whole or composite longa, before its value, before a longa rest, or before a punctus is worth three tempora.[39]

Hanboys: That is, three breves, as in the perfect mode.

Franco: A longa before a whole or composite longa, as here:

Or before its value, as here:

Or before a longa rest, as here: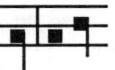

Or before a punctus, as here:

Hanboys: Whether in perfect or imperfect mode, a longa before a punctus is always perfect; that is, it is worth three breves.

Franco: A longa of three tempora is called perfect; one of two tempora, imperfect.[40]

Hanboys: And they have the same shape, namely a square notehead with a stem descending from the right side, as is shown here:[41]

Hanboys: And the same is true for longae erectae, as here:[42]

---

[37]Handlo, *Regule*, Rubric I, Rule III (84.6–8). Hanboys's Latin is sufficiently clear but lacks a verb.

[38]Handlo, *Regule*, Rubric I, Maxim 3 (84.10–11).

[39]Handlo, *Regule*, Rubric II, Rule I (88.4–5).

[40]Handlo, *Regule*, Rubric II, Maxim 1 (88.7–8).

[41]Handlo, *Regule*, Rubric II, Rule II (88.13–15).

[42]Handlo, *Regule*, Rubric II, Rule III (88.17–18).

Franco: Quandocunque sola brevis vel valor sequitur longam, imperficit eam, ut hic: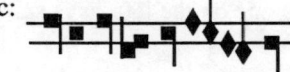

Nisi per divisionem modi aliter distinguantur, ut hic patet: ||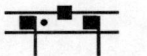

CS1: 414a

Tunc prima longa habebit tria tempora et brevis sequens refertur ad longam sequentem.

Hanboys: Regula predicta habet intelligi in primo moderatorio et non in secundo, et ita potest regula salvari.

Franco: Si autem sola brevis vel valor unius brevis precedit longam, imperficit eam, ut hic patet in exemplo:

Hanboys: Ista regula hodie fallit, quia aliquando tres breves vel valor cum tribus longis misceri possunt. Et quelibet harum trium longarum est perfecta, et punctum perfectionis immediate postpositum habere tenetur; tres breves vel valor faciunt perfectionem, ut hic patet:

Vel possunt poni quatuor breves vel valor mixtim cum quatuor longis; et prima brevis vel valor imperficit primam longam, tres breves sequentes

---

4 distinguatur A2 || 12 *tractus descendens* 12.2 A2 | *pausa brevis post* 12.9 A2 || 14 tribus]duabus A2 || 17 *puncti om.* A2 || 19 imperficit]imperficit secundam A2 ||

Franco: Whenever a solitary brevis or its value follows a longa, it imperfects it, as here:[43]

Unless they are otherwise distinguished by a division of the mode, as is shown here:[44]

Then the first longa will have three tempora and the following brevis is related to the following longa.[45]

Hanboys: The aforesaid rule has to be understood in the first moderation and not in the second, and so the rule can still be made to apply.[46]

Franco: If, moreover, a solitary brevis or the value of one brevis precedes a longa, it imperfects it, as is shown in the example:[47]

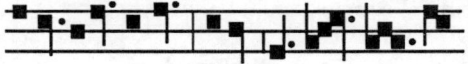

Hanboys: This rule fails today, because sometimes three breves or their value can be mixed with three longae. And each of these three longae is perfect and is held to have a *punctus perfectionis* immediately following; the three breves or their value make a perfection, as is shown here:[48]

Or four breves or their value can be employed, mixed with four longae. And the first brevis or its value imperfects the first longa; the three following

---

[43]Handlo, *Regule*, Rubric III, Rule I (92.5–7).

[44]Handlo, *Regule*, Rubric III, Rule III (92.13–14).

[45]Handlo, *Regule*, Rubric III, Maxim 1 (92.16–17).

[46]This does not make any sense as it stands. If "in the first moderation" (in primo moderatio) is an error for "in first mode" (in primo modo), then it would seem to mean that the rule applies in first mode but not in second mode; but that is not likely. It is also possible that Hanboys intends the difference to be between perfect and imperfect time or that in some other way the difference between *ars antiqua* and *ars nova* practices is being noted. A similarly obscure statement (not helpful in this context) is interpolated by Hanboys into a related discussion about the use of puncti to clarify the relationships of longae and breves (chapter 11 [250.21–22]).

[47]Handlo, *Regule*, Rubric III, Rule II (92.9–11).

[48]The second half of this example essentially anticipates the two following examples.

faciunt perfectionem, secunda longa, tertia longa et quarta sunt perfecte et punctum perfectionis habere tenentur, ut hic patet:

Vel potest ultima brevis imperficere ultimam longam, et tres breves prece-
5   dentes faciunt perfectionem, manentibus tribus longis perfectis, ut hic: ∥   CS1: 414b

Et sicut breves misceri possunt cum longis, manentibus perfectis, ita duplices longe cum largis, longe cum duplicibus longis, semibreves cum brevibus, minores cum semibrevibus, semiminores cum minoribus et
10  minime cum semiminoribus.

### ⟨CAPITULUM VIII⟩

Hanboys: Longa aliquando valet novem semibreves, aliquando octo, aliquando septem, aliquando sex, aliquando quinque, aliquando quatuor. Novem semibrevium, quando ponitur longa ante longam vel ante longam
15  pausam, ut de modo et de tempore perfecto, vel ante punctum. Longa ante longam simplicem vel compositam, ut hic: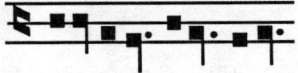

Vel ante longam pausam, ut hic: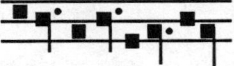

20  Vel ante punctum, ut hic:

---

9 brevibus]semibrevibus A2 | semibrevibus]semiminoribus A2 ∥ 19 *brevis post* 19.4 A2 ∥

breves make a perfection; the second, third, and fourth longae are perfect and are held to have a *punctus perfectionis*, as is shown here:

Or the last brevis can imperfect the last longa, and the three preceding breves make a perfection, with three perfect longae remaining, as here:

And just as breves can be mixed with longae that remain perfect, likewise duplex longae with largae, longae with duplex longae, semibreves with breves, minors with semibreves, semiminors with minors, and minimae with semiminors.[49]

## CHAPTER 8

Hanboys: The longa is sometimes worth nine semibreves, sometimes eight, sometimes seven, sometimes six, sometimes five, sometimes four. It is worth nine semibreves when a longa is employed before a longa or before a longa rest (when the mode and time are perfect) or before a punctus. A longa before a whole or composite longa, as here: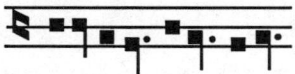

Or before a longa rest, as here: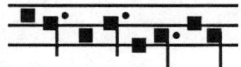

Or before a punctus, as here:

---

[49]These final three examples and their commentary concern how a single *punctus perfectionis* can be used to prevent the imperfection of a note by a figure one level down in the mensural hierarchy that stands before it, thus effectively creating displacement rhythms or syncopations across perfections. For the same configuration with breves and semibreves, see chapter 19 (328.3–8). For similar examples in another treatise of the English tradition involving three figures perfected by puncti mixed among three rests of the next smaller figure that together make a perfection, see Walsingham, *Regulae de musica mensurabili* (ed. Reaney), pp. 94–95: example 94 (longae and brevis-rests) and example 99 (breves and semibrevis-rests). In practice, these *puncti perfectionis* might be hard to distinguish from *puncti divisionis*, with the consequence that someone might mistakenly allow the preceding smaller value to imperfect the larger. To prevent this in an unambiguous manner and according to contemporaneous French practices, the longae in these examples would have to be preceded as well as followed by puncti (*puncti syncopationis*).

Octo semibrevium, quando semibrevis vel valor antecedit longam, ut hic:

Tunc semibrevis vel valor precedens longam imperficit primam brevem. Vel subsequitur, ut hic:

Tunc semibrevis subsequens ultimam brevem imperficit. ‖

Septem semibrevium, quando longa ponitur inter duas semibreves vel inter valorem, ut hic patet in exemplo:

Tunc prima semibrevis vel valor imperficit primam brevem, secunda vero ultimam.

Sex semibrevium, quando brevis perfecta vel valor antecedit longam, ut hic patet in exemplo:

Vel subsequitur, ut hic patet:

Quinque semibrevium, quando semibrevis vel valor antecedit, et brevis vel valor subsequitur:

Tunc semibrevis vel valor precedens longam imperficit primam brevem; brevis vero vel valor sequens longam imperficit eam. Vel quando brevis vel valor precedit longam et semibrevis vel valor subsequitur, ut convenienter patet: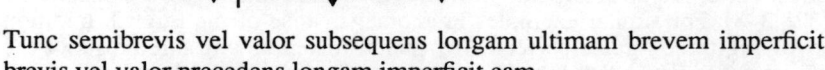

Tunc semibrevis vel valor subsequens longam ultimam brevem imperficit; brevis vel valor precedens longam imperficit eam.

Quatuor semibrevium, quando brevis perfecta cum semibrevi sequente vel valor precedit longam et semibrevis vel valor subsequitur, ut hic patet: ‖

---

23 semibrevis]brevis, semi *in marg., m. sec.* A2 ‖

Eight semibreves when a semibrevis or its value precedes a longa, as here:

Then the semibrevis or value preceding the longa imperfects the first brevis. Or follows, as here:

Then the following semibrevis imperfects the last brevis.

Seven semibreves when the longa is employed between two semibreves or between their value, as is shown here in an example:

Then the first semibrevis or value imperfects the first brevis; the second, the last.

Six semibreves when a perfect brevis or value precedes a longa, as is shown here in an example:

Or follows, as is shown here:

Five semibreves when a semibrevis or its value precedes and a brevis or its value follows:

Then the semibrevis or value preceding the longa imperfects the first brevis; the brevis or value following the longa imperfects it. Or when a brevis or its value precedes the longa and a semibrevis or its value follows, as is appropriately shown:

Then the semibrevis or value following the longa imperfects the last brevis; the brevis or value preceding the longa imperfects it.

Four semibreves when a perfect brevis with a following semibrevis or its value precedes a longa and a semibrevis or its value follows, as is shown here:

Vel quando semibrevis vel valor precedit longam et brevis perfecta cum semibrevi vel cum valore subsequitur, ut hic patet:

Tunc brevis perficitur per punctum; semibrevis precedens longam imperficit primam brevem; semibrevis vero subsequens secundam brevem imperficit.

⟨Vel⟩ si quatuor semibreves vel valor precedunt longam et semibrevis vel valor subsequitur, ut hic:

Tunc tres semibreves precedentes faciunt perfectionem; quarta semibrevis primam brevem imperficit; semibrevis subsequens longam imperficit secundam brevem. ⟨Vel⟩ si semibrevis vel valor precedit longam et quatuor semibreves vel valor sequuntur, ut hic patet in exemplo:

Tunc semibrevis precedens longam primam brevem imperficit; semibrevis vero subsequens imperficit secundam brevem; tres semibreves sequentes faciunt perfectionem.

Vel quando longa constat de duabus brevibus imperfectis:

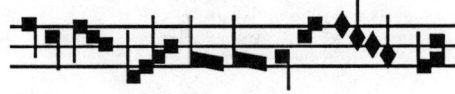

‖ Et sicut longa ante longam vel ante longam pausam de modo perfecto est perfecta, ita longa ante longam ⟨vel ante longam⟩ pausam de modo imperfecto est imperfecta.

Or when a semibrevis or its value precedes a longa and a perfect brevis with a semibrevis or with its value follows, as is shown here:

Then the brevis is perfected by a punctus; the semibrevis preceding the longa imperfects the first brevis; the semibrevis following the longa imperfects the second brevis.

Or if four semibreves or their value precede a longa and a semibrevis or its value follows, as here: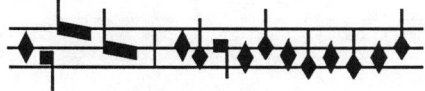

Then the three preceding semibreves make a perfection; the fourth semibrevis imperfects the first brevis;[50] the semibrevis following the longa imperfects the second brevis. Or if a semibrevis or its value precedes a longa and four semibreves or their value follow, as is shown here in an example:

Then the semibrevis preceding the longa imperfects the first brevis; the semibrevis following imperfects the second brevis; the three following semibreves make a perfection.

Or when the longa consists of two imperfect breves:

And just as a longa before a longa or before a longa rest is perfect when the mode is perfect, likewise a longa before a longa or before a longa rest is imperfect when the mode is imperfect.

---

[50]By "the three preceding semibreves," Hanboys clearly means the first three, not the second through fourth; note also the "modern" counting of semibreves by threes rather than the Franconian way of counting them by twos.

## ⟨CAPITULUM IX⟩

Hanboys: Longarum alie recte, alie altere vocantur. Fit autem recta longa tripliciter: ante duplicem longam, post duplicem longam, et inter longas duplices. Ante longam duplicem, ut hic: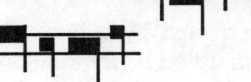

Post duplicem longam, ut hic:

Inter longas duplices, ut hic patet in exemplo:

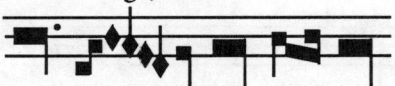

Longa altera est illa que duas longas in se includit in valore, tamen a longa recta non differt in forma. Et fit longa altera tribus modis. Primo modo, quando due longe tantum vel valor unius longe et una longa inveniuntur inter duas duplices longas. Due longe tantum, ut hic:

Vel valor unius longe et una longa, ut hic:

Tunc prima longa recta vocatur, secunda quoque alteratur, nisi per divisionis punctum distinguatur, ut hic: ‖

CS1: 416b

Tunc due longe equales manent, et prima longa vel valor primam duplicem longam imperficit, et secunda ultimam.

Vel quando due longe tantum vel valor unius longe et una longa ante duplicem longam ponuntur. Due longe tantum, ut hic:

Vel valor unius longe et una longa, ut hic patet in exemplo:

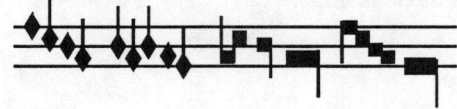

Secundo modo, quando tres longe vel valor duarum longarum et una longa vel valor unius longe et due longe inveniuntur inter duas duplices lon-

---

2 Hanboys *in marg., m. sec.* A2 ‖ 17 longa *m. sec.* A2 ‖ 19 *punctus ult. om.* A2 ‖ 27 valor *in marg., m. sec.* A2 ‖

## CHAPTER 9

Hanboys: Some longae are called rectae, others alterae. The longa recta occurs in three ways: before a duplex longa, after a duplex longa, and between duplex longae. Before a duplex longa, as here: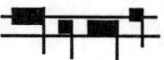

After a duplex longa, as here: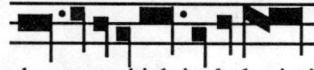

Between duplex longae, as is shown here in an example:

The longa altera is that one which includes in itself two longae in value. Nevertheless, it does not differ from the longa recta in form. And the longa altera occurs in three manners. In the first manner, when just two longae or the value of one longa and one longa are found between two duplex longae. Just two longae, as here:

Or the value of one longa and one longa, as here:

Then the first longa is called recta, and the second is altered, unless they are distinguished by a *punctus divisionis*, as here:

Then the two longae remain equal, and the first longa or value imperfects the first duplex longa, while the second imperfects the last.

Or when just two longae or the value of one longa and one longa are employed before a duplex longa. Just two longae, as here:

Or the value of one longa and one longa, as is shown here in an example:

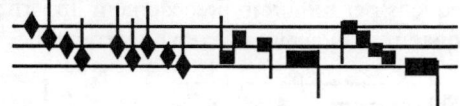

In the second manner, when three longae or the value of two longae and one longa or the value of one longa and two longae are found between two

gas, et si inter primam longam et secundam vel inter valorem sit punctus divisionis appositus, ut hic patet:

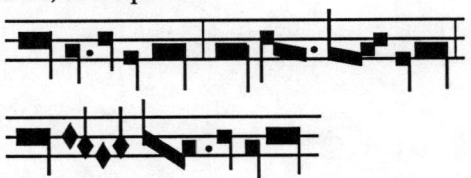

Tunc prima longa vel valor primam duplicem longam imperficit, secunda
5  recta vocatur, tertia quoque alteratur.

Tertio modo, quando plures longe vel valor ante duplicem longam vel post adinvicem inveniuntur. Tres longe vel valor pro perfectione computentur, et si due longe vel valor unius longe et una longa in fine remanserint, prima longa ‖ vel valor pro recta teneatur, secunda quoque alteratur, et punc-
10  tum divisionis ante penultimam vel valorem habere tenetur, ut hic:

CS1: 417a

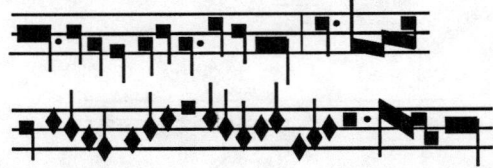

Et si una longa in fine remanserit, recta vocatur et ad perfectionem duplicis longe subsequentis pertinere debet, ut hic:

15  Et potest longa ⟨altera⟩ diminui veluti duplex longa ⟨imperfecta⟩ correspondens sibi, manente alterata.

Et longa, cum sit perfecta ex omnibus perfectis, diminui potest per semibrevem precedentem vel subsequentem, vel per semibrevem precedentem et subsequentem, manente perfecta. Si per semibrevem subsequentem vel per
20  semibrevem precedentem et subsequentem predicta longa diminuatur, semibrevis longam sequens per minorem precedentem imperfici potest, si minor vel valor eam sequatur, ut hic patet in exemplo sequenti:

---

9 et]nisi A2 ‖ 11*punctus ult. om.* A2 ‖ 12 duplicis]dupplicis A2 ‖ 15 et]et ⟦si⟧ A2 ‖ 15–16 correspondens]corespondens A2 ‖ 23 *minor* 23.5 A2 ‖

duplex longae, and if between the first and the second longa or between their values, there is employed a *punctus divisionis*, as is shown here:

Then the first longa or value imperfects the first duplex longa, the second is called normal, the third is altered.

In the third manner, when several longae or their value are found together before or after a duplex longa. Three longae or their value are counted as a perfection, and if two longae or the value of one longa and one longa should remain at the end, the first longa or value is held as recta, the second is altered, and it is held to have a *punctus divisionis* before the penultimate or its value, as here:

And if one longa should remain at the end, it is called recta, and it ought to pertain to the perfection of the subsequent duplex longa, as here:

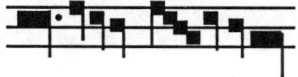

And the longa altera can be diminished like the imperfect duplex longa corresponding to it, remaining altered.

And the longa, if it is perfect on all levels, can be diminished by a preceding or following semibrevis or by a preceding and following semibrevis, remaining perfect. If the aforesaid longa is diminished by a following semibrevis or by a preceding and following semibrevis, the semibrevis following the longa can be imperfected by a preceding minor if a minor or its value follows the longa, as is shown here in the following example:

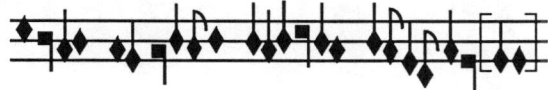

Sed semibrevis utraque, scilicet ante longam et post, imperfici potest per minorem subsequentem, minor autem per semiminorem, et semiminor per minimam, ut hic patet in exemplo:

|| Et longa predicta potest aliter diminui. Nam ultima brevis imperfici potest per semibrevem subsequentem, manente de duabus semibrevibus. Secunda semibrevis imperfici potest per minorem subsequentem, manente de duabus minoribus. Secunda minor imperfici potest per semiminorem subsequentem, manente de duabus semiminoribus. Secunda semiminor imperfici potest per minimam, ⟨manente de duabus minimis⟩, ut hic:

CS1: 417b

Hanboys: Longa, cum sit perfecta ex omnibus perfectis, continet 3 breves, 9 semibreves, 27 minores, 81 semiminores, 243 minimas. Et longa, cum sit imperfecta ex omnibus imperfectis, continet 2 breves, 4 semibreves, 8 minores, 16 semiminores, 32 minimas.

## ⟨CAPITULUM X⟩

Franco: Forma brevium simplicium talis est. Quandocunque invenitur punctus quadratus carens omni tractu, brevis dicitur, ut hic:

Hanboys: Si tractum habeat a parte sinistra solumodo ascendentem, erecta vocatur, ut hic:

Et etiam per semitonium erigitur veluti longa erecta.

Franco: Brevis plicata cum duobus tractibus ascendentibus vel descendentibus sinistra parte longiore dextra, ut hic patet:

|| Hanboys: Sicut erecte longe non plicantur, ita nec erecte breves.

CS1: 418a

---

4 *semiminor* 4.4, 9 A2 || 19 solo modo A2 ||

But each semibrevis (namely, before and after the longa) can be imperfected by a following minor, the minor by a semiminor, and the semiminor by a minima, as shown here in an example:

And the aforesaid longa can be diminished in another way. For its last brevis can be imperfected by a subsequent semibrevis, remaining as two semibreves. The second semibrevis can be imperfected by a following minor, remaining as two minors. The second minor can be imperfected by a following semiminor, remaining as two semiminors. The second semiminor can be imperfected by a minima, remaining as two minimae, as here:

Hanboys: The longa, if it is perfect on all levels, contains 3 breves, 9 semibreves, 27 minors, 81 semiminors, 243 minimae. And the longa, if it is imperfect on all levels, contains 2 breves, 4 semibreves, 8 minors, 16 semiminors, 32 minimae.

## CHAPTER 10

Franco: The form of whole breves is thus. Whenever a square notehead is found lacking any stem, it is said to be a brevis, as here:[51]
Hanboys: If it has an ascending stem on the left side only, it is called erecta, as here:[52]
And it is also raised by a semitone, just as is the longa erecta.[53]
Franco: A brevis plicata has two stems, ascending or descending, with the left one longer than the right, as is shown here:[54]

Hanboys: Just as longae erectae are not plicated, so neither are breves erectae.[55]

---

[51]Handlo, *Regule*, Rubric I, Rule IV (84.13–14).
[52]Handlo, *Regule*, Rubric I, Rule V (84.16–17).
[53]Handlo, *Regule*, Rubric I, Maxim 4 (86.2).
[54]Handlo, *Regule*, Rubric I, Rule VI (86.4–6).
[55]Handlo, *Regule*, Rubric I, Maxim 5 (86.8).

Hanboys: Brevis ante brevem vel ante brevem pausam de tempore perfecto vel ante punctum est perfecta. Brevis ante brevem, ut hic:

Vel ante brevem pausam, ut hic:

Vel ante punctum, ut hic:

Hanboys: Si sit de tempore perfecto vel de tempore imperfecto, brevis ante punctum est perfecta, id est valet tres semibreves. Et imperfici potest per semibrevem precedentem vel sequentem, vel per valorem. ⟨Per semibrevem precedentem⟩, ut hic:

Per semibrevem subsequentem, ut hic:

Brevis aliquando valet novem minores, aliquando octo, aliquando septem, ⟨aliquando sex⟩, aliquando quinque, et aliquando quatuor. Novem minorum, quando ponitur brevis ante brevem vel ante brevem pausam, vel ante punctum, veluti de brevibus et semibrevibus perfectis exemplum supra patet.

Octo minorum, quando minor vel valor antecedit brevem, ut hic: ||

Tunc minor vel valor precedens brevem primam semibrevem imperficit. Vel subsequitur, ut hic:

Tunc minor subsequens brevem ultimam semibrevem imperficit.

---

1 Hanboys]Franco A2 ‖ 8 sit]si[n]t A2 | perfecto][im]perfecto A2 ‖ 14 *semiminor* 14.8 A2 ‖ 19 quando minor *in marg., m. sec.* A2 ‖ 21 semibrevem]brevem A2 ‖ 23 *punctus post* 23.1 A2 ‖

Hanboys:⁵⁶ A brevis before a brevis or before a brevis rest (when the tempus is perfect) or before a punctus is perfect. A brevis before a brevis, as here: 

Or before a brevis rest, as here: 

Or before a punctus, as here: 

Hanboys: Whether the tempus is perfect or imperfect, a brevis before a punctus is perfect, that is, it is worth three semibreves. And it can be imperfected by a preceding or following semibrevis or by its value. By a preceding semibrevis, as here:

By a following semibrevis, as here:

The brevis is sometimes worth nine minors, sometimes eight, sometimes seven, sometimes six, sometimes five, and sometimes four. It is worth nine minors when a brevis is employed before a brevis, before a brevis rest, or before a punctus, just as in the example of perfect breves and semibreves that appears above.

Eight minors when a minor or its value precedes the brevis, as here:

Then the minor or value preceding the brevis imperfects the first semibrevis. Or follows, as here:

Then the minor following the brevis imperfects the last semibrevis.

---

⁵⁶This statement is attributed to Franco in the manuscript, but it is just at this point that the text shifts from quotation of the *Regule* to new material. Two possibilities suggest themselves: either "Franco" is an outright error for "Hanboys," perhaps in an attempt to sustain an alternation of statements by Hanboys with statements by Franco; or Hanboys's exemplar of the *Regule* differed here from the text in **GB-Lbl**, Additional 4909, containing later material that Hanboys, nonetheless, associated with Franco.

240

Septem minorum, quando brevis ponitur inter duas minores vel inter valorem, ut hic patet in exemplo:

Tunc minor vel valor precedens brevem imperficit primam semibrevem;
5 minor vero subsequens ultimam semibrevem imperficit.

Sex minorum, quando semibrevis perfecta vel valor antecedit brevem, ut hic:

Tunc semibrevis vel valor precedens brevem imperficit eam.

10 Quinque minorum, quando minor vel valor antecedit brevem, et semibrevis vel valor subsequitur, ut hic patet:

Tunc minor vel valor precedens brevem imperficit primam semibrevem; semibrevis vel valor subsequens brevem imperficit eam. Vel quando semi-
15 brevis vel valor precedens brevem et minor vel valor subsequitur, ut hic: ‖

CS1: 419a

Tunc minor vel valor subsequens brevem ultimam semibrevem imperficit; semibrevis vel valor precedens brevem imperficit eam.

Quatuor minorum, quando semibrevis perfecta cum minore subsequente
20 vel valor precedit brevem et minor vel valor subsequitur, ut hic patet in exemplo:

Tunc semibrevis perficitur per punctum et brevem imperficit. Minor precedens brevem imperficit primam semibrevem. Minor vero subsequens secun-
25 dam semibrevem imperficit. Vel quando minor valorve precedit brevem et semibrevis perfecta cum minori vel cum valore subsequitur, ut hic:

Tunc semibrevis perficitur per punctum, minor vel valor precedens brevem primam semibrevem imperficit, minor vero vel valor brevem subsequens
30 imperficit secundam semibrevem.

---

3 *punctus post* 3.2 A2 | *minima* 3.11 A2 ‖ 10 vel *bis* A2 ‖ 25 minor]minor ⟦vel⟧ A2 ‖

Seven minors when the brevis is employed between two minors or between their value, as is shown here in an example:

Then the minor or value preceding the brevis imperfects the first semibrevis; the minor following imperfects the last semibrevis.

Six minors when a perfect semibrevis or its value precedes the brevis, as here:

Then the semibrevis or value preceding the brevis imperfects it.

Five minors when a minor or its value precedes the brevis and a semibrevis or its value follows, as is shown here:

Then the minor or value preceding the brevis imperfects the first semibrevis; the semibrevis or value following the brevis imperfects it. Or when a semibrevis or its value precedes the brevis and a minor or its value follows, as here:

Then the minor or value following the brevis imperfects the last semibrevis; the semibrevis or value preceding the brevis imperfects it.

Four minors when a perfect semibrevis with a following minor or its value precedes the brevis and a minor or its value follows, as is shown here in an example:

Then the semibrevis is perfected by a punctus and imperfects the brevis. The minor preceding the brevis imperfects the first semibrevis. The minor following the brevis imperfects the second semibrevis. Or when a minor or its value precedes the brevis and a perfect semibrevis with a minor or with its value follows, as here:

Then the semibrevis is perfected by a punctus, the minor or value preceding the brevis imperfects the first semibrevis, and the minor or value following the brevis imperfects its second semibrevis.

Vel quando quatuor minores valorve precedunt brevem et minor vel valor subsequitur, ut hic patet in exemplo:

Tunc tres minores brevem precedentes faciunt perfectionem, quarta minor primam semilIbrevem imperficit, minor autem brevem subsequens imperficit secundam semibrevem. Vel quando minor vel valor precedit brevem et quatuor minores sequuntur, ut hic patet:

Tunc minor precedens brevem primam semibrevem imperficit, minor vero subsequens imperficit secundam semibrevem, tres minores sequentes faciunt perfectionem.

Vel quando brevis constat de duabus semibrevibus imperfectis, ut hic patet in exemplo:

Et sicut brevis ante brevem vel ante brevem pausam de tempore perfecto est perfecta, ita brevis ante brevem vel ante brevem pausam de tempore imperfecto est imperfecta.

## ⟨CAPITULUM XI⟩

⟨Franco⟩: Brevium alie recte, alie altere nominantur. Recta brevis est illa que non valet nisi unum tempus, quod est minimum in plenitudine vocis. Fit autem recta brevis tripliciter: ante longam, post longam, et inter longas. Ante longam, ut hic:

---

3 *semiminor* 3.6 A2 ‖ 7 sequitur A2 ‖ 14 *brevis* 14.3 A2 ‖

Or when four minors or their value precede the brevis and a minor or its value follows, as is shown here in an example:

Then the three minors preceding the brevis make a perfection, the fourth minor imperfects the first semibrevis, and the minor following the brevis imperfects the second semibrevis. Or when a minor or its value precedes the brevis and four minors follow, as is shown here:

Then the minor preceding the brevis imperfects the first semibrevis, the minor following the brevis imperfects the second semibrevis, and the following three minors make a perfection.

Or when the brevis consists of two imperfect semibreves, as is shown here in an example:

And just as a brevis before a brevis or before a brevis rest is perfect when the tempus is perfect, likewise a brevis before a brevis or before a brevis rest is imperfect when the tempus is imperfect.

## CHAPTER 11[57]

Franco: Some breves are named rectae; others, alterae. The brevis recta is that which has no value other than one tempus, which is the minimum in fullness of voice.[58] The brevis recta occurs in three ways: before a longa, after a longa, and between longae. Before a longa, as here:

---

[57]The beginning of this chapter was not defined by an initial letter. The scribe did, however, leave a space in the writing block, presumably for the name Franco, though the first paragraph surrounds a quotation from Franco with language that is typical of the *Summa*.

[58]Franco, *Ars cantus mensurabilis*, cap. 5, sent. 10 and 12 (ed. Reaney and Gilles) p. 34: "Recta brevis est quae unum solum tempus continet ... Unum tempus appellatur illud quod est mininum in plenitudine vocis (a brevis recta is that which comprises only one tempus ... 'one tempus' is called that which is the minimum in fullness of voice)." A nearly identical statement is found in the inauthentic Parisian version of the first chapter of the

Post longam, ut hic: [musical notation]

Inter longas, ut hic: [musical notation]

‖ Hanboys: Brevium alia perfecta, alia imperfecta. Perfecta brevis est que tres semibreves in se continet; que duas continet, brevis imperfecta vocatur. Et cum brevis recta sit perfecta, imperfici potest per semibrevem precedentem vel subsequentem vel per valorem. Per semibrevem precedentem, ut hic: [musical notation]

Per valorem, ut hic patet:

Per semibrevem subsequentem, ut hic patet: [musical notation]

Per valorem, ut hic patet in exemplo:

Et cum brevis recta sit perfecta ex omnibus perfectis, diminui potest per minorem precedentem vel subsequentem, vel per minorem precedentem et subsequentem, manente perfecta. Si per minorem precedentem vel subsequentem, vel per minorem precedentem et subsequentem predicta brevis diminuatur, minor sequens brevem per semiminorem precedentem imperfici potest, si semiminor vel valor eam sequatur, ut hic patet:

[musical notation]

Et utraque minor, ante brevem et post, per ‖ semiminorem subsequentem imperfici potest, et semiminor per minimam, ut hic patet:

---

4 *brevis post* 4.1 A2 ‖ 10 *ligatura ternaria et punctus post* 10.2 A2 ‖ 12 *semibrevis* 12.4, 6 A2 | *semibrevis, minor, semibrevis, minor, semibrevis* 12.9–13 A2 ‖ 14 *semibrevis, semibrevis, semibrevis, brevis post* 14.2 A2 ‖ 18 ⟦*per minorem*⟧ A2 ‖ 23 *minor* 23.4 A2 | *semiminor* 23.10 A2 ‖

After a longa, as here:

Between longae, as here: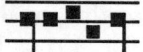

Hanboys: Of the breves, one kind is perfect, the other imperfect. The perfect brevis is that which contains in itself three semibreves; that which contains two is called the imperfect brevis. And if the brevis recta is perfect, it can be imperfected by a preceding or following semibrevis or by its value. By a preceding semibrevis, as here:

By its value, as is shown here: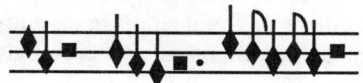

By a following semibrevis, as is shown here:

By its value, as is shown here in an example:

And when the brevis recta is perfect on all levels, it can be diminished by a preceding or following minor or by a preceding and following minor, remaining perfect. If the aforesaid brevis is diminished by a preceding or following minor or by a preceding and following minor, the minor following the brevis can be imperfected by a preceding semiminor if the semiminor or its value follows the brevis, as is shown here:

And each minor (before the brevis and after) can be imperfected by a following semiminor, and the semiminor by a minima, as is shown here:

---

treatise of Johannes de Garlandia as transmitted in the *Tractatus de musica* of Jerome of Moravia. See Simon Cserba, ed., *Hieronymus de Moravia, O.P. Tractatus de musica*, Freiburger Studien zur Musikwissenschaft, no. 2 (Regensburg: Friedrich Pustet, 1935), p. 195; and Johannes de Garlandia, *De Mensurabili Musica* (ed. Reimer), 1:91 [PI, lns. 9-10].

Hanboys: Et potest brevis predicta aliter diminui, quia ultima semibrevis imperfici potest per minorem subsequentem, manente de ⟨duabus minoribus. Secunda minor imperfici potest per semiminorem subsequentem, manente de⟩ duabus semiminoribus. Secunda semiminor imperfici potest per mini-
5   mam, manente de duabus minimis, ut hic:

Hanboys: Valet etiam brevis perfecta ex omnibus perfectis 3 semibreves, 9 minores, 27 semiminores, 81 minimas. Et cum brevis sit imperfecta ex omnibus imperfectis, valet 2 semibreves, 4 minores, 8 semiminores, 16
10  minimas. Dictum est de brevibus rectis.
    Hanboys: Altera brevis includit in se duas breves in valore licet non in forma. Que magis proprie potest dici brevis alterata, quia a sua recta proportione alteratur.
    Franco: Fit etiam altera brevis tribus modis. Primo, quando due breves
15  tantum vel valor unius brevis et una brevis sint inter duas longas. Tunc prima brevis vel valor valet unum tempus, brevis altera valet duo tempora. Longe ambe erunt perfecte, ut hic patet:

Nisi sola brevis precedat vel sequatur.
20      Hanboys: Due breves igitur inequales manent.
    ⟨Franco⟩: Nisi per divisionem modi aliter distinguantur, ut hic: ‖        CS1: 421a

Tunc ambe breves erunt equales, et prima brevis vel valor imperficit primam longam; secunda vero ultimam.
25      Hanboys: Vel quando due breves tantum, vel valor unius brevis et una brevis inveniuntur ante longam, vel ante longam pausam, ut hic:

Tunc prima brevis vel valor pro recta habeatur et secunda alteratur.

---

1 potest]potest ⟦[predictus]⟧ A2 ‖ 4 duabus]duobus A2 ‖ 7 Hanboys]Franco A2 ‖ 12 alterata]altera A2 ‖ 21 distinguatur A2 ‖

Hanboys: And the aforesaid brevis can be diminished another way, because its last semibrevis can be imperfected by a following minor, remaining as two minors. The second minor can be imperfected by a following semiminor, remaining as two semiminors. The second semiminor can be imperfected by a minima, remaining as two minimae, as here:

Hanboys: The brevis perfect on all levels is worth 3 semibreves, 9 minors, 27 semiminors, 81 minimae. And if the brevis is imperfect on all levels, it is worth 2 semibreves, 4 minors, 8 semiminors, 16 minimae. Enough has been said about breves rectae.

Hanboys: The brevis altera includes in itself two breves in value, but not in form. This more properly can be said to be an altered brevis, because it is altered from its normal proportion.[59]

Franco: The brevis altera occurs in three manners. In the first manner, when just two breves or the value of one brevis and one brevis are between two longae. Then the first brevis or its value is worth one tempus, and the brevis altera is worth two tempora.[60] Moreover, both longae will be perfect, as is shown here:[61]

Unless a solitary brevis precedes or follows.[62]

Hanboys: Therefore, two breves remain unequal.[63]

Franco: Unless they are otherwise distinguished by a division of the mode, as here:[64]

Then both breves will be equal, and the first brevis or its value imperfects the first longa, while the second imperfects the last.[65]

Hanboys: Or when just two breves, or the value of one brevis and one brevis, are found before a longa or before a longa rest, as here:

Then the first brevis or value is taken as recta, and the second is altered.

---

[59]Handlo, *Regule*, Rubric III, Maxim 3 (92.24–25).
[60]Handlo, *Regule*, Rubric III, Maxim 2 (92.19–22).
[61]Handlo, *Regule*, Rubric III, Rule IV (94.2–3).
[62]Handlo, *Regule*, Rubric III, Rule V (94.5–6).
[63]Handlo, *Regule*, Rubric III, Maxim 4 (94.8).
[64]Handlo, *Regule*, Rubric III, Rule VI (94.10–11).
[65]Handlo, *Regule*, Rubric III, Maxim 5 (94.13–14).

Franco: Si autem tres breves inveniantur inter duas longas, vel etiam ante longam, omnes erunt equales, ut hic: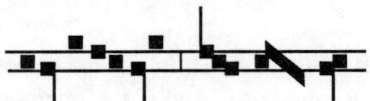

Tunc ambe longe erunt perfecte, nisi predictas longas brevis vel valor pre-
5 cedat vel sequatur, ut hic patet in exemplo sequenti:

Hanboys: Tres igitur breves inter duas longas equales manent.
Franco: Nisi per divisionem modi aliter distinguantur, ut hic:

10 Tunc prima brevis imperficit primam longam; secunda brevis valet unum tempus; tertia valet duo tempora, et erit brevis altera. Et hic modus est secundus quod tres breves fiunt inequales. ‖

Franco: Tertius modus est si plures breves quam tres inveniantur inter duas longas, vel etiam sine prima longa, ita ⟨quod⟩ semper ultima longa
15 remaneat. Computentur ergo tres pro perfectione, et si in fine due breves remaneant, tunc ultima brevis habebit duo tempora, ut hic patet:

CS1:
421b

⟨Hanboys⟩: Questio: sed quid si quatuor breves inter duas longas inveniantur? An manebit prima longa perfecta, et tres breves pro perfectione com-
20 putabuntur, et ultima brevis imperficiet longam ultimam, vel prima brevis primam longam imperficiet et tres breves pro perfectione computabuntur, manente ultima perfecta? Respondeo: prima via questionis abolenda est, ut hic:

---

7 manent *in marg., m. sec.* A2 ‖ 8 distinguatur A2 ‖ 14 defectus? *in marg.* A2 | semper]semper ⟦et⟧ A2 ‖ 18 questio *in marg., m. sec.* A2 ‖ 22 respondeo *in marg., m. sec.* A2 ‖ 24 *brevis post* 24.5 A2 ‖

Franco: If, moreover, three breves are found between two longae or also before a longa, all will be equal, as here:[66]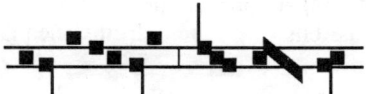

Then both longae will be perfect, unless a brevis or its value precedes or follows the aforesaid longae, as is shown here in the following example:[67]

Hanboys: Three breves, therefore, between two longae remain equal.[68]

Franco: Unless they are otherwise distinguished by a division of the mode, as here:[69]

Then the first brevis imperfects the first longa; the second brevis is worth one tempus; the third is worth two tempora and will be a brevis altera. And this is the second manner that three breves are made unequal.[70]

Franco: The third manner is if more than three breves are found between two longae, or even without the first longa, so that the last longa always remains. They are counted three as a perfection, and if two breves remain at the end, then the last brevis will have two tempora, as is shown here:[71]

Hanboys: Question: but what if four breves are found between two longae? Will the first longa remain perfect, three breves be counted as a perfection, and the last brevis imperfect the last longa? Or will the first brevis imperfect the first longa, and the three breves be counted as a perfection, with the last longa remaining perfect? I answer: the first way of the question must be abolished, as here:[72]

---

[66]Handlo, *Regule*, Rubric III, Rule VII (94.16–18).
[67]Handlo, *Regule*, Rubric III, Rule VIII (96.2–4).
[68]Handlo, *Regule*, Rubric III, Maxim 6 (96.6).
[69]Handlo, *Regule*, Rubric III, Rule IX (96.8–9).
[70]Handlo, *Regule*, Rubric III, Maxim 7 (96.11–13).
[71]Handlo, *Regule*, Rubric III, Rule X (96.15–19).
[72]Handlo, *Regule*, Rubric III, Rule XI (96.21–26).

Fallit tamen modi divisione apposita, ut hic: [musical notation]

Et ⟨tunc⟩ prima tenenda est via.

Si etiam inter duas longas quinque breves inveniantur, recurrendum est ad Franchonem, dicentem longam primam perfectam fieri, manentibus tribus brevibus sequentibus equalibus et duabus ultimis inequalibus, quia ultima brevis alterata manet, ut hic: [musical notation]

Fallit tamen modi divisione apposita, ut hic: [musical notation]

‖ Et tunc prima brevis primam longam imperficit, manentibus tribus brevibus equalibus, et ultima brevi longam ultimam imperficiente.   CS1: 422a

Ad maiorem noticiam quando quinque breves inveniuntur inter duas longas, prima longa habebit punctum postpositum et secunda, seu brevis vel valor ultimam longam sequitur; et punctus divisionis post tertiam brevem apponitur, ut hic: [musical notation]

Tunc prima longa perficitur per punctum; tres breves sequentes vel valor faciunt perfectionem; quarta brevis recta vocatur; quinta quoque alteratur. Secunda quoque longa per punctum perficitur.

Aut ad secundam longam modus imitatur, et tunc secunda longa per colorem differt a prima.

Aut prima longa caret punctu et secunda, ut hic: [musical notation]

Tunc prima longa imperficitur per brevem subsequentem; secunda brevis, tertia et quarta faciunt perfectionem; quinta vero recta vocatur et ad perfectionem longe sequentis pertinet.

---

11 tunc]nunc A2 ‖ 25 secunda brevis ⟦secunda⟧ A2 ‖

Nevertheless, this fails when there is the introduction of a division of the mode, as here:[73]

And then the first way must be held fast.[74]

If five breves are found between two longae, reference must be had to Franco, who says that the first longa is made perfect, with the remaining three following breves equal and the last two unequal, because the last brevis remains altered, as here:[75]

Nevertheless, this fails when there is the introduction of a division of the mode, as here:[76]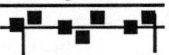

And then the first brevis imperfects the first longa, with the remaining three breves equal and the last brevis imperfecting the last longa.[77]

For greater knowledge when five breves are found between two longae,[78] the first and second longa will have a punctus after it (unless a brevis or its value follows the last longa), and a *punctus divisionis* is employed after the third brevis, as here:

Then the first longa is perfected by the punctus; the three following breves or value make a perfection; the fourth brevis is called recta; and the fifth is altered. The second longa is perfected by the punctus.

Or for the second longa, the manner is imitated, and then the second longa differs from the first by color.

Or else the first and second longae lack a punctus, as here:

Then the first longa is imperfected by the following brevis; the second, third, and fourth breves make a perfection; the fifth is called recta and pertains to the perfection of the following longa.

---

[73]Handlo, *Regule*, Rubric III, Rule XII (98.2).
[74]Handlo, *Regule*, Rubric III, Maxim 8 (98.4).
[75]Handlo, *Regule*, Rubric III, Rule XIII (98.6–10).
[76]Handlo, *Regule*, Rubric III, Rule XIV (98.12–13).
[77]Handlo, *Regule*, Rubric III, Maxim 9 (98.15–16).
[78]The following three paragraphs represent further commentary by Hanboys, not derived from the *Regule*, on the use of the *punctus divisionis* to clarify relationships between longae and breves. See the Introduction, pp. 41–42.

Et si brevis sit perfecta ex omnibus perfectis et alterata, diminui potest per semibrevem precedentem vel subsequentem, vel per semibrevem precedentem et subsequentem, vel per valorem, ⟨manente⟩ alterata.

Si predicta brevis ⟨diminuatur⟩ per semibrevem precedentem vel per valorem, prima brevis illius alterationis per semibrevem vel per valorem imperficitur. Semibrevis autem imperfici ⟨potest⟩ per minorem subsequentem, minor per semiminorem, et semiminor per minimam, ut hic patet:

‖ Si per semibrevem subsequentem vel per valorem diminuatur, secunda brevis illius alterationis per semibrevem subsequentem vel per valorem imperficitur. Semibrevis quoque imperfici potest per minorem, minor per semiminorem, et semiminor per minimam:

CS1: 422b

Si per semibrevem precedentem et subsequentem vel per valorem diminuatur, prima semibrevis vel valor primam brevem imperficit, alteram vero semibrevis subsequens, et utraque semibrevis imperfici potest per minorem subsequentem, minor per semiminorem, et semiminor per minimam, ut hic patet in exemplo:

Et potest predicta brevis altera aliter diminui, manente alterata. Nam secunda brevis imperfici potest per semibrevem subsequentem, manente de duabus semibrevibus. Secunda semibrevis imperfici potest per minorem subsequentem, manente ⟨de⟩ duabus minoribus. Secunda minor imperfici potest per semiminorem subsequentem, manente de duabus semiminoribus. Secunda semiminor imperfici potest per minimam, manente de duabus

---

8 *semiminor* 8.13 A2 | *punctus ult. om.* A2 ‖ 13 *ligatura binaria* 13.5 A2 | *punctus post* 13.17 A2 | *minor* 13.18 A2 ‖ 19 *punctus om.* 19.11 A2 | *minima* 19.14 | *semiminor* 19.15 A2 ‖ 23 duabus]duobus A2 ‖ 24 duabus]duobus A2 ‖

And if the brevis is perfect on all levels and is altered, it can be diminished by a preceding or following semibrevis or by a preceding and following semibrevis or their value, remaining altered.[79]

If the aforesaid brevis is diminished by a preceding semibrevis or its value, the first brevis of the altered note is imperfected by the semibrevis or its value. The semibrevis, moreover, can be imperfected by a following minor, the minor by a semiminor, and the semiminor by a minima, as is shown here:

If it is diminished by a following semibrevis or its value, the second brevis of the altered note is imperfected by the following semibrevis or its value. The semibrevis can be imperfected by a minor, the minor by a semiminor, and the semiminor by a minima:

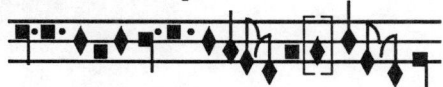

If it is diminished by a preceding and following semibrevis or their value, the first semibrevis or value imperfects its first brevis, the following semibrevis imperfects the other, and each semibrevis can be imperfected by a following minor, the minor by a semiminor, and the semiminor by a minima, as is shown here in an example:

And the aforesaid brevis altera can be diminished in another way, remaining altered. For its second brevis can be imperfected by a following semibrevis, remaining as two semibreves. The second semibrevis can be imperfected by a following minor, remaining as two minors. The second minor can be imperfected by a following semiminor, remaining as two semiminors. The second semiminor can be imperfected by a minima, remaining

---

[79]The following passage represents a new concentration on the subject of the diminishment of an altered note; by contrast, diminishment of the altered duplex longa (chapter 6 [216.4–5]) and altered longa (chapter 9 [234.15–16]) were treated in quite summary fashion. See also the Introduction, pp. 42–46 and table 2.

minimis. Et sicut altera brevis imperfici potest et diminui a parte post, eodem modi diminui potest a parte ante, ut hic:

⟨CAPITULUM XII⟩

5   Franco: Forma semibrevium simplicium talis est. Quandocunque punctus vel nota formatur ad modum losonge sive ad modum grani ordeacei, semibrevis dicitur, ut hic:
‖ Franco: Et plicari non potest, nisi quando tres super unam sillabam ordinantur, ut hic patet:

10  Hanboys: Que quidem sic ordinantur, quodammodo coniunguntur, et plicatur ultima, non obstante sillaba subterposita, ut supra patet. Et nota quod simplices predicte et plicate non differunt in valore.

Hanboys: Semibrevium alia perfecta, alia imperfecta. Perfecta semibrevis est que tres minores in se continet; que dues, semibrevis imperfecta vocatur. Semibrevis ante semibrevem vel ante semibrevem pausam de semibrevibus perfectis est perfecta. Tamen de semibrevibus imperfectis non

CS1: 423a

---

3 *semiminor* 3.13 A2 | *minima* 3.14 A2 ‖ 5 semibrevium]brevium (semi *in marg., m. sec.*) A2 ‖ 6 losonge]losenge A2 ‖ 8 Franco]Hanboys A2 ‖ 11 Hanboys]Franco A2 ‖ 15 que dues]dues (que *in marg., m. sec.*) A2 | semibrevis]brevis A2 ‖

255

as two minimae. And just as the brevis altera can be imperfected and diminished *a parte post*, in the same way it can be diminished *a parte ante*, as here:[80]

## CHAPTER 12

Franco: The form of whole semibreves is thus. Whenever a notehead or note is shaped in the manner of a lozenge or a grain of barley, it is said to be a semibrevis, as here:[81]

Franco: And it cannot be plicated, except when three are ordered above one syllable, as is shown here:[82]

Hanboys: When some of these are so ordered, they are in some sense conjoined and the last is plicated, notwithstanding the syllable placed beneath, as is shown above.[83] And note that the aforesaid whole and plicated semibreves do not differ in value.[84]

Hanboys: Some semibreves are perfect, others imperfect. A perfect semibrevis is that which contains in itself three minors; that which contains two is called an imperfect semibrevis. A semibrevis before a semibrevis or semibrevis rest is perfect when semibreves are perfect. Nevertheless, this

---

[80]Until this point in the discussion of the diminishment of the larga recta, duplex longa, longa, and brevis (i.e., beginning with this paragraph), diminishment *a parte ante* was not mentioned. The corresponding discussion of the diminishment of the semibrevis altera (chapter 15 [294.1–25]) and minor altera (chapter 16 [304.29–306.17]) agree in substance with this passage on the brevis but have slightly different language. See also the Introduction, pp. 42–46 and table 2.

[81]Handlo, *Regule*, Rubric I, Rule VII (86.10–11).

[82]Handlo, *Regule*, Rubric I, Rule VIII (86.13–15).

[83]Handlo, *Regule*, Rubric I, Maxim 6 (86.17–18).

[84]See the anonymous *De valore notularum tam veteris quam novae artis* (ed. Reaney), p. 24: "Et nota quod de plicatis et non plicatis idem est iudicium (And note that the same is true for plicated and non-plicated notes)." See also the similar language of Hanboys, *Summa*, chapter 19 (320.20–21): "Sciendum est quod de ligatis et non ligatis idem est iudicium in valore temporum (It must be known that the same is true for ligated and non-ligated notes in the value of their tempora)."

tenet; sed semibrevis ante punctum perfectionis semper perficitur. Semibrevis ante semibrevem vel ante semibrevem pausam, ut hic:

Vel ante punctum, ut hic:

5  Franco: Quando due semibreves inter duas longas, vel inter longam et brevem, vel inter duas breves, vel inter longam et longam pausam, vel inter brevem et brevem pausam inveniuntur, prima semibrevis habebit unum tempus semibrevis, id est tertiam partem unius temporis, secunda vero duo tempora, ut hic:
10

   ‖ Hanboys: Hodie distinguendum est an sit de brevi perfecta vel de brevi imperfecta. Si sit de brevi perfecta, tenet regula: prima semibrevis erit recta, secunda vero altera. Si sit de brevi imperfecta, ambe erunt equales.   CS1: 423b
   Franco: Si autem tres semibreves inter duas breves, vel inter duas longas,
15 vel inter longam et longam pausam, vel inter brevem et brevem pausam inveniantur, erunt equales, ut hic patet in exemplo:

   ⟨Hanboys⟩: Nisi per divisionem ⟨modi⟩ aliter distinguatur, ut hic patet in exemplo:
20

   Tunc prima semibrevis imperficit brevem precedentem, secunda recta vocatur, tertia quoque alteratur.
   Franco: Semibrevium alia maior, alia minor. Minor autem tertiam partem unius brevis recte valet. Maior autem duas partes unius brevis in se con-
25 tinet. Et plures semibreves quam tres pro uno tempore accipi non possunt de rigore artis, et tunc quelibet semibrevis minor dicatur.

---

1 sed]set A2 ‖ 3 *pausa semibrevis post* 3.2 A2 ‖ 7–9 nota miraculum de alteratione *in marg., m. sec.* A2 ‖ 10 *pausa om.* 10.14, 18 ‖ 11 Hanboys *in marg., m. sec.* A2 ‖ 14 Franco *in marg., m. sec.* A2 ‖ 15 et brevem *in marg., m. sec.* A2 ‖ 17 *semibrevis, semibrevis, semibrevis, divisio post* 17.10 A2 ‖ 21 recta]rcta A2 ‖ 23 Franco *in marg., m. sec.* A2 ‖

does not hold when semibreves are imperfect. But a semibrevis before a *punctus perfectionis* is always perfected. A semibrevis before a semibrevis or semibrevis rest, as here:

Or before a punctus, as here:

Franco: Whenever two semibreves are found between two longae, between a longa and a brevis, between two breves, between a longa and a longa rest, or between a brevis and a brevis rest, the first semibrevis will have one semibrevis tempus, that is, the third part of one tempus; the second will have two, as here:[85]

Hanboys: Today, the distinction must be made whether the brevis is perfect or imperfect. If breves are perfect, the rule holds that the first semibrevis will be recta and the second altera. If the breves are imperfect, both will be equal.

Franco: If, moreover, three semibreves are found between two breves, between two longae, between a longa and a longa rest, or between a brevis and a brevis rest, they will be equal, as is shown here in an example:[86]

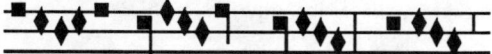

Hanboys: Unless they are otherwise distinguished by a division of the mode, as is shown here in an example:

Then the first semibrevis imperfects the preceding brevis, the second is called recta, and the third is altered.

Franco: Some semibreves are major, others minor.[87] The minor has the value of the third part of one brevis recta. The major comprises in itself two parts of one brevis. And by strict rule of the art, more than three semibreves cannot be accepted as one tempus, and then each and every semibrevis is said to be minor.[88]

---

[85]Handlo, *Regule*, Rubric IV, Rule I (100.4–8).

[86]Handlo, *Regule*, Rubric IV, Rule II (100.10–11), with some straightforward elaboration.

[87]Franco, *Ars cantus mensurabilis*, cap. 4, sent. 15 (ed. Reaney and Gilles), p. 31.

[88]Franco, *Ars cantus mensurabilis*, cap. 5, sent. 22–23 (ed. Reaney and Gilles), pp. 38–39.

258

Hanboys: Equales vocantur, quia tres pro una brevi ponuntur. Et etiam dicuntur minores. Minor vero semibrevis tertiam partem habet unius brevis, ut supra patet.

Franco: Si autem quatuor semibreves inveniantur, tunc due ⟨et due⟩ pro
5  recta brevi computantur, ut hic patet: ‖

CS1: 424a

⟨Hanboys⟩: Hodie tenet ut pro brevi imperfecta, sed pro brevi perfecta nequaquam.

⟨Hanboys⟩: Securius tamen et verius additur punctus inter duas et duas,
10  vel inter tres et tres, vel inter duas et tres, ⟨vel inter tres et duas,⟩ ut ponit Petrus de Cruce. Hoc quod fecerunt antiqui cantores, ut hic:

Franco: Sciendum est quod quando plures semibreves quam tres inveniuntur inter duas longas, vel inter duas breves, vel inter longam et longam
15  pausam, vel inter brevem et brevem pausam, omnes erunt ⟨inequales, nisi tres in fine remaneant. Ille erunt⟩ equales, ut hic:

Nisi per divisionem modi aliter distinguantur, ut hic patet:

---

1 Hanboys *in marg., m. sec.* A2 ‖ 4 Franco *in marg., m. sec.* A2 ‖ 13 Franco *in marg., m. sec.* A2 ‖ 18 distinguatur A2 ‖

Hanboys: They are called equal because three are employed for one brevis. And they are also said to be minor. A minor semibrevis has the third part of one brevis, as is shown above.[89]

Franco: If, moreover, four semibreves are found, then they are counted by twos as a brevis recta, as shown here:[90]

Hanboys: Today, this holds when breves are imperfect, but never when breves are perfect.[91]

Hanboys: It is, nevertheless, safer and more suitable for a punctus to be added between two and two or between three and three or between two and three or between three and two, as Petrus de Cruce employs it. Older singers did this, as here:[92]

Franco: It must be known that when more than three semibreves are found between two longae, between two breves, between a longa and longa rest, or between a brevis and brevis rest, all will be unequal, unless three remain at the end. Those will be equal, as here:[93]

Unless they are otherwise distinguished by a division of the mode, as is shown here:[94]

---

[89]Handlo, *Regule*, Rubric IV, Maxim 1 (100.13–14).

[90]Handlo, *Regule*, Rubric IV, Rule III (100.16–18).

[91]Hanboys returns to this issue according to modern practice in chapter 15 (292.3–10).

[92]Handlo, *Regule*, Rubric IV, Rule IV (100.24–102.3). Handlo distanced himself from Petrus by saying that what Petrus did, the moderns do. Here, however, in a further distancing, Handlo's moderns have become Hanboys's ancients. On Petrus de Cruce, see the Introduction, pp. 17–20.

[93]Handlo, *Regule*, Rubric IV, Rule V (102.5–9).

[94]Handlo, *Regule*, Rubric IV, Rule VI (102.11–12).

⟨Hanboys⟩: Tunc punctus inter tres et tres positus facit eas equales, et si in fine due remanserint, ille erunt inequales.

Petrus de Cruce de semibrevibus verius indicat. Ponit enim, ut prius dictum est, punctum inter duas et duas, et tunc erunt inequales; hoc est prima
5 minor, secunda maior. Et inter tres et tres, et tunc erunt equales; hoc est omnes erunt minores. Vel inter duas et tres, et tunc erunt due inequales et tres equales. Vel inter tres et duas, et tunc erunt tres equales et due inequales, ut in hoc exemplo patet: ‖    CS1: 424b

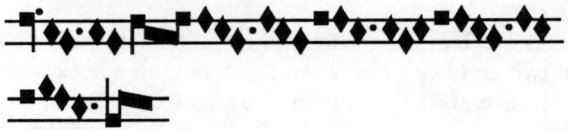

10  Sed si quatuor semibreves sine puncto inveniantur, alterius proportionis erunt quam indicat Francho, quia non important valorem nisi unius brevis. Licet inveniantur quinque vel sex vel septem, et illa patent moteto suo qui vocatur *Aucun ont trouvé chant*:

*Aucun ont trouvé chant par usage*

15  Et quod quatuor semibreves sine puncto brevem unam valeant, patet in moteto qui vocatur ⟨*Novum melos promere*⟩:

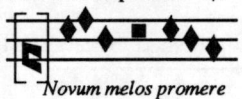

*Novum melos promere*

---

3 Petrus de Cruce *rep. in marg., m. sec.* A2 ‖ 11 valorem *in marg., m. sec.* A2 ‖ 13 Acums ount trone (chant *om.*) A2 (*idem* 14) ‖ 17 promere *sup. lin., m. sec.* A2 ‖

Hanboys: Then the punctus employed between three and three makes them equal, and if two remain at the end, they will be unequal.[95]

Petrus de Cruce more suitably addresses semibreves. As was previously said, he employs a punctus between two and two, and then they will be unequal—that is, the first minor, the second major; and between three and three, and then they will be equal—that is, all will be minors; or between two and three, and then two will be unequal and three equal; or between three and two, and then three will be equal and two unequal, as is shown in this example:[96]

But if four semibreves are found without a punctus, they will be of another proportion than that addressed by Franco, because together they have no other value than that of a brevis. It is permitted for five or six or seven to be found, and these are shown in his motet that is called *Aucun ont trouvé chant*:[97]

*Aucun ont trouvé chant par usage*

And that four semibreves without a punctus may be worth one brevis is shown in the motet that is called *Novum melos promere*:[98]

*Novum melos promere*

---

[95]Handlo, *Regule*, Rubric IV, Maxim 3 (102.14–15).

[96]Handlo, *Regule*, Rubric IV, Rule VII (102.17–104.2).

[97]Handlo, *Regule*, Rubric IV, Rule VIIIa (106.13–20). For bibliography on *Aucun ont trouvé chant*, see the commentary to this rule in the *Regule*.

[98]The example does not bear out what it is intended to exemplify, but at a later point in the motet, one can presumably find four semibreves in the place of a brevis. For bibliography on *Novum melos promere*, see the commentary to Rule VI of Rubric XIII (174.2–4) in the *Regule*. This quotation appears in a context in the *Summa* different from that in the *Regule*; its placement here suggests that the motet may have been written by Petrus de Cruce.

## ⟨CAPITULUM XIII⟩

⟨Hanboys⟩: Johannes de Garlandia aliter de semibrevibus indicat et verissime. Distinguit enim maiorem semibrevem a minori sic: si maior sit, formabitur ad modum losonge habens sub se tractum, ut patet hic:

Si minor sit, modo nudo formabitur ad modum losonge sic:
Maior cum minori sic formatur:

Et ideo aliquando maior precedit minorem, et e contrario, dempto puncto, ut hic patet in exemplo:

Idem valet brevis imperfecta cum semibrevi sequenti.

Johannes de Garlandia dividit semibreves || ulteriores ad quatuor, et ad quinque, et ad sex, et ad septem, et ad octo, et ad novem, et quilibet numerus istorum unam brevem valet. Ideo semibrevis minor valet tres minimas, et brevis habet tres minores. Brevis igitur habet novem minimas et formari debent ut minores semibreves, sed rotundum signum post ⟨se⟩ habent, ut hic:

Hiis novem minimis equepollent novem minores, ut hic:

CS1: 425a

---

4 losonge]losengie A2 || 6 losonge]losengie A2 || 9 dempto]deposito A1 ||

## CHAPTER 13[99]

Hanboys: Johannes de Garlandia addresses semibreves in another and very accurate fashion.[100] He distinguishes the major semibrevis from the minor thus: if the semibrevis is major, it will be formed in the manner of a lozenge having beneath itself a stem, as is shown here:[101]

If it is minor, it will be formed in a plain manner in the manner of a lozenge:

A major with a minor is formed thus:

And sometimes the major precedes the minor (and contrariwise) with the punctus removed, as is shown here in an example:[102]

An imperfect brevis with a following semibrevis has the same value.[103]

Johannes de Garlandia separates semibreves further, up to four, five, six, seven, eight, or nine, and whatever number of these there are, they are worth one brevis.[104] Therefore the minor semibrevis is worth three minimae, and the brevis has three minors. The brevis, therefore, has nine minimae, and they ought to be formed like minor semibreves, but they have a *signum rotundum* after them, as here:[105]

Nine minors are equivalent to these nine minimae, as here:

---

[99]The provision of an initial capital letter indicates that a new chapter was intended at this point. The letter so capitalized (presumably in error), however, was the initial A of *Aucun* from the motet incipit cited at the end of the preceding chapter.

[100]On Johannes de Garlandia, see the Introduction, pp. 24–27.

[101]Handlo, *Regule*, Rubric IV, Rule IX (108.8–110.3), but here modified so that the descending stem on the major is not described as oblique; in the accompanying examples, it is drawn as vertical.

[102]Handlo, *Regule*, Rubric IV, Rule X (110.5–7).

[103]This initiates a series where quotations drawn from Rubric IV are followed by Hanboys's remark describing the up-to-date equivalent.

[104]Handlo, *Regule*, Rubric IV, Maxim 8 (110.9–11).

[105]Handlo, *Regule*, Rubric IV, Rule XI (110.13–16).

Tunc sunt minorate semibreves. Unde minorata duas minimas valet et formatur veluti minima. Naturaliter vero precedit minima minoratam, quando ambe habent post se signum rotundum, ut hic:

5 Hiis tribus minoratis et tribus minimis equepollent tres semibreves cum tribus minoribus, ut hic:

Si autem sola semibrevis habeat post se hoc signum rotundum, minor dicetur, et tunc misceri debet inter minimas et minoratas. Due etiam semi-
10 breves duo signa rotunda habent inter minimas et minoratas, quando tertia deest, ut hic:

Et si inter minimas et minoratas tres semillbreves minores committentur, punctum habebunt post se, ut hic patet:  CS1: 425b
15
Minorata nunquam potest poni, nisi sua minima eam precedente, ut hic patet:

Tot igitur dicuntur semibreves, scilicet maior, minor vel equalis, mino-
20 rata, et minima.
Brevis denique maiorem et minorem valet, vel tres minores, et tunc sunt equales, vel tres minimas et tres minoratas mixtim se habentes, vel novem minimas. Tres breves se habent in perfectione; ergo perfectio habet 27 minimas, vel novem minimas et totidem minoratas mixtim se habentes, vel
25 novem minores, vel tres maiores et totidem minores mixtim se habentes, vel e contrario, ut hic patet:

---

9 due]que A2 ‖ 12 *signum rotundum post* 12.5 A2 ‖ 19 equalis]equales A2 ‖ 27 *sextum signum rotundum om.* lin. 2.24 A2 ǀ *signum rotundum ante longam pr.* lin. 3.27 A2 ‖

Then there are semibreves minoratae, where the minorata is worth two minimae and is formed like the minima. The minima naturally precedes the minorata when the two of them have a *signum rotundum* after themselves, as here:[106]

Three semibreves with three minors are equivalent to these three minoratae and three minimae, as here:

If, moreover, a solitary semibrevis should have after itself a *signum rotundum*, it is said to be a minor, and then it ought to be mixed between minimae and minoratae. Two semibreves have two *signa rotunda* between minimae and minoratae when a third one is lacking, as here:[107]

And if three minor semibreves are combined between minimae and minoratae, they will have a punctus after themselves, as is shown here:[108]

A minorata can never be employed unless it has a minima preceding it, as is shown here:[109]

Therefore, all of these are said to be semibreves, namely, the major, minor or equal, minorata, and minima.

Finally, a brevis is worth a major and a minor, or three minors (and then they are equals), or three minimae mixed with three minoratae, or nine minimae. Three breves are arranged in a perfection; therefore, a perfection has twenty-seven minimae, or nine minimae mixed with just as many minoratae, or nine minors, or three majors mixed with just as many minors (or contrariwise), as is shown here:[110]

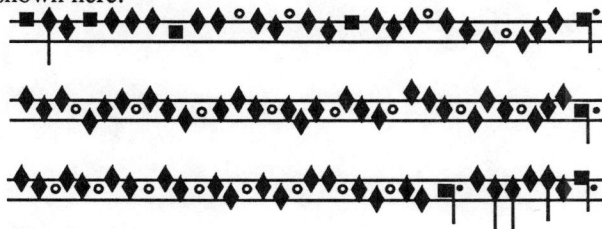

---

[106]Handlo, *Regule*, Rubric IV, Rule XII (110.18–21).
[107]Handlo, *Regule*, Rubric IV, Rule XIII (112.2–6).
[108]Handlo, *Regule*, Rubric IV, Rule XIV (112.8–10).
[109]Handlo, *Regule*, Rubric IV, Rule XV (112.12–14).
[110]Handlo, *Regule*, Rubric IV, Rule XVI (112.16–114.5).

Hic ponitur circulus pro divisione semibrevium ut antiqui solebant. Tamen a modernis circulus tribus modis ponitur: ante notam, sub et supra. Si ante notam, brevem denotat fore perfectam. Si punctus sit in circulo, semibrevis in brevi manet perfecta, ut hic:

5 Carente puncto, in semibrevi non stat perfectio, ut hic:

Si supraponatur, ibi inceptio demonstratur, ut hic:

Si supponatur, finis ibi verificatur, ut hic:
10
Et quando ponitur semicirculus ante notam, brevem denotat imperfectam. Si punctus in eo sit, semibrevis in brevi perfecta manet, ut hic:

Carente puncto, in semibrevi non est perfectio, ut hic:
15 Una vero semibrevis maior inter minores et minoratas comitari potest, ut hic:

A modernis debent sic figurari:

20 Figura quidem habens in se tres quadrangulos, longa triplex dicitur, id est trium perfectionum nota vocatur. Si quatuor, quatuor perfectionum longa dicetur; si quinque, quinque; si sex, sex; si septem, septem; si octo, octo; si novem, novem. Nec ultra debet longa maiorari, quia sicut longa simplex habet in valore novem semibreves minores et non plures, sic nec longa

---

5 punctu A2 (*idem* 14) ‖ 17 *semibrevis* 17.7, 11 A2 ‖

Here the circle is employed for the division of semibreves, as was the custom of the older singers. Nevertheless, the circle is employed in three manners by the moderns: before, above, or below a note.[111] If before a note, it denotes that the brevis will be perfect. If there is a punctus in the circle, the semibrevis in the brevis remains perfect, as here:
Lacking the punctus, there is no perfection in the semibrevis, as here:

If it is placed above, the beginning is shown there, as here:
If it is placed below, the end is verified there, as here:

And when the semicircle is employed before a note, it denotes that the brevis is imperfect. If there is a punctus in it, the semibrevis in the brevis remains perfect, as here:
Lacking a punctus, there is no perfection in the semibrevis, as here:

Indeed, one major semibrevis can be accompanied by minors and minoratae, as here:[112]

By the moderns, these ought to be shaped thus:

That shape having in itself three squares is said to be a triplex longa, that is, it is called a note of three perfections. If four, it is said to be a longa of four perfections; if five, five; if six, six; if seven, seven; if eight, eight; if nine, nine. But the longa ought not to be made larger beyond this, because just as the simplex longa has nine minor semibreves in value and no more,

---

[111]This paragraph on the circle, stimulated by mention of the *signum rotundum*, is an interpolation by Hanboys into a sequence of material drawn from Handlo. Hanboys appears to conflate two separate practices. For one, he describes the familiar use of the circle and semicircle before a note as mensuration signs, which indicates that the brevis is perfect or imperfect; the presence or absence of a punctus inside the circle indicates that the semibrevis is perfect or imperfect as well (there is no mention of the terminology of major and minor prolation). For another, the circle placed above or below a note respectively indicates something about that note's beginning or end. The use of the circle "before, above, or below" recalls Hanboys's fourfold use of the *punctus perfectionis* (chapter 3 [196.2–6]), even to the choice of verbs (*demonstratur, verificatur*). Perhaps Hanboys intended here to explain the indication of perfection of the first or final third of a note by the circle.

[112]Handlo, *Regule*, Rubric IV, Rule XVII (114.7–10). The version notated by the moderns that follows does not quite match, because the minima-minorata pair (1+2) is represented as corresponding to the semibrevis-minima pair (2+1).

novem perfectionum plures quam novem longas habere debet. Ecce omnium istarum longarum figure hic patent: ‖

Talibus vero longis utitur vetus organum purum, sed non formantur sic. Hec itaque sic formantur, ut melius et securius agnoscantur. Hec itaque longe prenotate nunquam imperficiuntur, quia inter breves non ponuntur, nec inter semibreves. Decet enim eas inter longas simplices et duplices et inter se associari.

Longe vero simplices cum brevibus misceri debent, cum semibrevibus vero maioribus et minoribus comitari possunt, sed cum minoratis et minimis nequaquam. Breves vero cum longis duplicibus misceri possunt, et cum semibrevibus ligatis et obliquis, ut convenienter hic patet:

Et ideo duplex longa, id est sex temporum, imperficitur per brevem precedentem vel subsequentem vel per pausam unius temporis, et tunc est quinque temporum, ut hic:

Breves etiam cum semibrevibus maioribus atque minoribus, cum minoratis et minimis associantur. Et si alia mixtura sit, vitiosa est. Patet igitur que note cum quibus mixtim se habere possunt.

Hanboys: Hodie non tenet, quia large, duplices longe, et longe diminui possunt per breves, semibreves, minores, semiminores, et per minimas ut supra dictum est; et cum possint per eas diminui, cum illis possunt comitari. Nam longe quatuor longarum, quinque, ‖ sex, septem, octo, novem large equepollent. Et longe trium longarum valent veluti duplices longe perfecte.

Alio modo differt semibrevis maior a minori, et minorata a minima quam prius dictum est. Unde W. de Doncastre posuit semibrevem maiorem

---

5 hec (*pr.*)]hec ⟦tales⟧ A2 ‖ 6 nunquam]nuncquam A2 ‖ 11 Hanboys *in marg.* A2 ‖ 20 haberi A2 ‖ 21 large]large ⟦hodie⟧ A2 ‖

so the longa of nine perfections ought not to have any more than nine longae. Behold the shapes of all these longae shown here:[113]

The old organum purum uses such longae, but they are not thus formed. And these are thus formed so that they can be better and more safely recognized.[114] The longae just notated are never imperfected because they are not employed between breves or between semibreves. They should be associated between simplex and duplex longae and with others of their kind.[115]

Simplex longae ought to be mixed with breves. They can also be accompanied by semibreves both major and minor, but never by minoratae and minimae. Breves can be mixed with duplex longae and with ligated and oblique semibreves, as is appropriately shown here:[116]

The duplex longa, that is, of six tempora, is imperfected by a preceding or following brevis or by a rest of one tempus, and then it is of five tempora, as here:[117]

Breves are associated with major and minor semibreves, with minoratae and minimae. And if there should be another mixture, it is defective. It is therefore evident which notes can be mixed with which.[118]

Hanboys: Today, this does not hold, because largae, duplex longae, and longae can be diminished by breves, semibreves, minors, semiminors, and minimae, as has already been said. And since they can be diminished by these, they can be accompanied by these.[119] For a longa of four, five, six, seven, eight, or nine longae is equivalent to a larga, and longae of three longae are worth just as much as perfect duplex longae.

In another manner than has been previously said, the major semibrevis differs from the minor, and the minorata from the minima. For W. de Doncastre[120] posited a major semibrevis with a short descending stem, the rea-

---

[113]Handlo, *Regule*, Rubric V, Rule I (116.4–15).

[114]Handlo, *Regule*, Rubric V, Maxim 1 (116.17–18).

[115]Handlo, *Regule*, Rubric V, Maxim 2 (116.20–118.2).

[116]Handlo, *Regule*, Rubric V, Rule II (118.4–8).

[117]Handlo, *Regule*, Rubric V, Rule III (118.10–13).

[118]Handlo, *Regule*, Rubric V, Maxim 3 (118.15–18).

[119]On the mixing of note values, see also chapters 7 (224.13–226.10) and 19 (328.3–8).

[120]W. de Doncastre is not otherwise known, unless he may possibly be

cum tractulo descendente, cuius ratio est talis: nam unum quodque tendens ad suum originale principium activum et in media, tamen adquirit perfectionem. Sed ⟨maior⟩ semibrevis sic figurata: ✦

5   Est huiusmodi, ergo talis est perfecta. Minor probatur: nam ad tenorem tendit, a quo in cantando originatur inesse perfectio.
   Minor semibrevis sic figuratur: ✦

Cuius ratio probatur: contrariorum contrarie sunt conditiones, sed contra
10 semibrevem, tractus ascendens et descendens sunt contrariantes. Ergo opposite sunt eorum conditiones. Sed tractus descendens directe perficit semibrevem. Ergo directe ascendens inducet imperfectionem, et per consequens semibrevis efficiet minorem.
   Minorata semibrevis sic portionatur: ✦
15
Cuius ratio declaratur sic: nam medium inter contraria duplex potest esse, aut extremorum per participationem, vel per utriusque extremi abnegatio-

---

2 in media]*fort.* immedia *vel* immediatum A2 ‖ 5–6 hic deficit *in marg.* A2 ‖

son for which is this: anything reaching toward its original active principle nevertheless acquires perfection at the center.[121] But the major semibrevis is shaped thus:

As it is of such kind, therefore it is perfect. The minor premise was proven: for it reaches toward the tenor, from which perfection begins to inhere in singing.

The minor semibrevis is shaped thus:

The reason for this was proven: the conditions of contraries are contrary,[122] but against the semibrevis, ascending and descending stems are contraries. Therefore their conditions are opposed. But the directly descending stem perfects the semibrevis; therefore the one that directly ascends induces imperfection and, as a consequence, makes the semibrevis minor.

The semibrevis minorata is thus proportioned:

The reason for this is declared thus: for the mean between contraries can be twofold, either through participation of the extremes or through negation of

---

identified with a Dominican priest traceable in Cambridge in the 1340s (see the Introduction, pp. 60–61). His notation, based on that of Johannes de Garlandia but giving distinct shapes to each of the four kinds of semibrevis, is found in one fragmentary motet, *Beatus vir-Benedicamus Domino*, preserved in London, Westminster Abbey, 12185, f. 2 (for a transcription, see appendix II). The very different tone of language here, with its scholastic and heavily Aristotelian manner of argumentation, suggests that Doncastre is a man of the schools or university and that Hanboys is quoting or closely paraphrasing him, either from lecture notes or a treatise now lost.

[121]This seems not to be an exact quotation of Aristotle, but see the passages in *Metaphysics* 9.8 (1050a4–16) arguing that actuality is prior to potentiality: "Everything that comes to be moves toward principle, i.e. an end. For that for the sake of which a thing is, is its principle, and the becoming is for the sake of the end; and the actuality is the end; and it is for the sake of this that the potentiality is acquired" (Jonathan Barnes, ed., *The Complete Works of Aristotle: The Revised Oxford Translation*, 2 vols., Bollingen Series, LXXI/1–2 [Princeton: Princeton University Press, 1984], 2:1658–59).

[122]Again this statement cannot be found in Aristotle; its neat assonance in Latin suggests that it is a scholastic paraphrase (similar locutions are used frequently by Aquinas). Doncastre employs the Aristotelian doctrine on opposition in fashioning syllogisms to justify the following three figures. Of the four kinds of opposition (contradictory, contrary, relative, and possessive/privative), he relies on contrariety for his proofs. Contraries are diametrically opposed, but if they lie along the same line, then there can be intermediates, or means, between the extremes; in another formulation, they are

nem. Sed habens tractum a parte sinistra obliquum, participatione est medium ad extrema, nam deficit a perfectione extremorum. Ergo figura sic prolata:

5  Recte semibrevis nuncupabitur minorata.
   Minima vero carebit omni tractu, ut hic:
Et huius est ratio: nam cuius oppositio creat de necessitate aliquam proprietatem seu perfectionem, eiusdem ablatio imperfectionis est declaratio. Sed tractus descendens indirecte seu oblique, vel ascendens super semibrevem
10 directe aliquam ‖ creat perfectionem. Ergo eius totaliter remotio a figura tollit virtutem. Nam secundum Philosophum: eadem est disciplina oppositorum. Ergo illa ⟨figura⟩:
Ergo illa sortitur nominem semibrevis minime.
   Continet igitur semibrevis maior duas minores. Minor vero minoratam
15 continet et minimam. Minorata autem duas continet minimas.
   Robertus Trowell aliter figuravit minorem, minoratam, et minimam, sic dicendo: maior caudam deprimit, ut hic:

   Minor tractum perimit, ut hic:
20
   Minorata dirigitur, ut hic:

   Minima sed flectitur, ut hic:

25 Hiis maioribus, minoribus, minoratis, et minimis equepollent iste figure modernis, scilicet brevis imperfecta cum semibrevi perfecta, semibrevis imperfecta cum minori recta, ut hic:

CS1: 427b

---

5 nunctupabitur A2 ‖ 9 indirecto seu obliquo A2 ‖

each extreme.[123] But having an oblique stem from the left side, the mean is in a participation toward the extremes, for it is lacking in the perfection of the extremes. Hence the figure is brought forth this way:
It will correctly be referred to as the semibrevis minorata.

The minima will lack any stem, as here:
And this is the reason: since its opposition necessarily creates some propriety or perfection, its ablation is a declaration of imperfection. But the stem descending indirectly or obliquely, or ascending directly above the semibrevis, creates some perfection. Therefore, its removal from the figure takes away virtue. For according to the Philosopher: "the discipline of opposites is the same."[124] Therefore this shape:
Therefore this shape is allotted the name of semibrevis minima.

The major semibrevis therefore comprises two minors. The minor, indeed, comprises a minorata and a minima. The minorata, moreover, comprises two minimae.

Robert Trowell[125] shaped the minor, minorata, and minima in another way, saying: the major draws down a stem, as here:

The minor does away with the stem, as here:

The minorata is written straight, as here:

But the minima is bent, as here:

To these majors, minors, minoratae, and minimae are equivalent the shapes employed by the moderns, namely, the imperfect brevis with the perfect semibrevis and the imperfect semibrevis with the minor recta, as here:

---

those things in the same genus most distant from one another. For a thorough treatment of the different kinds of opposites, see *Categories* 10 (11b17)–11 (14a25).

[123]See Aristotle, *Categories* 10 (12a24): "it is by the negation of each of the extremes that the intermediate is marked off" (Ackrill, *Aristotle's Categories*, p. 33).

[124]Aristotle frequently mentions the claim that the knowledge (or science) of contraries is the same. See *Topics* 2.3 (110b16–21), *Physics* 8.1 (251a30), *Metaphysics* 13.4 (1078b25–27), etc.

[125]Neither Trowell nor his notation are otherwise known aside from this reference; like Doncastre, he is an Englishman working in the post-Garlandian tradition.

## ⟨CAPITULUM XIV⟩

Hanboys: Antiqui siquidem aliquando pro brevi perfecta tres semibreves posuerunt, ut prius dictum est, aliquando quatuor, aliquando quinque, aliquando sex. Si tres, formantur ut prius dictum est.

Si quatuor, aut prima maior et secunda, et due equales, aut prima et secunda equales, et tertia maior atque quarta, aut prima maior et quarta et due equales, ut hic:

A modernis sic debent figurari:

Si quinque, aut prima maior et quatuor equales; aut quatuor equales et quinta maior; aut due ‖ prime et due ultime equales, et tertia maior, ut hic:

Hodie debent sic figurari:

Si sex, omnes erunt equales, ut hic:

Tamen de novo modo debent sic figurari:

Et quando tres semibreves pro brevi imperfecta ponuntur, aut prima maior et due equales, aut due equales et tertia maior erit, ut hic:

Hodie distinguendum ⟨est⟩ an sit de semibrevi perfecta vel de semibrevi imperfecta. Si sit de semibrevi perfecta, sic debent figurari:

---

4 si]sed A2 ‖ 5 et (*pr.*)][aut] (*corr. sup. lin., m. sec.*) A2 | secunda [minor] A2 ‖ 15 *minor, semibrevis, semibrevis, semibrevis, semibrevis* 15.1–5 A2 ‖

## CHAPTER 14

Hanboys: Sometimes, to be sure, the older singers employed three semibreves for a perfect brevis, as was said above, sometimes four, sometimes five, and sometimes six.[126] If three, they were formed as was said above.

If four, either the first and second were major, and two equals; or the first and second were equals and the third and fourth were major; or the first and fourth were major, and two equals, as here:

They ought to be shaped by the moderns thus:

If five, either the first is major and four equals; or four equals and the fifth major; or the first two and the last two equals and the third major, as here:

Today, they ought to be shaped thus:

If six, all will be equal, as here: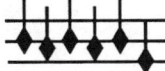

Nevertheless, in the new fashion, they ought to be shaped thus:

And when three semibreves are employed as an imperfect brevis, either the first is major and two equals, or two are equals and the third will be major, as here:

Today, the distinction must be made whether the semibrevis is perfect or imperfect. When the semibrevis is perfect, they must be shaped thus:

---

[126]The mensuration described is akin to de Vitry's tempus perfectum minor or Marchetto's senaria perfecta, with a fundamentally ternary brevis divisible into from three to six smaller values, all of which are varieties of

Si sit de semibrevi imperfecta, distinguendum est an sit de curta mensura, quatuor equales pro brevi, vel de longa mensura, videlicet octo equales pro brevi. Si de curta mensura, tunc prima erit semibrevis, secunda et tertia minores equales; aut due prime minores equales, et tertia semibrevis, ut hic: ‖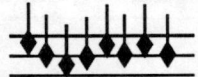

Si quatuor semibreves pro brevi imperfecta inveniantur, ut de curta mensura, omnes erunt equales, ut hic:

Hodie debent sic figurari, ut hic:

Si sit de longa mensura, debent formari veluti de curta.

Hodie non differunt de forma, tamen differunt de valore, quia quatuor semibreves pro duabus brevibus ponuntur. Aut prima maior, secunda minor,

---

13 brevibus]semibrevibus A2 ‖

If the semibrevis is imperfect, the distinction must be made whether it is of *curta mensura* (four equals to the brevis) or *longa mensura* (eight equals to the brevis). If it is of *curta mensura*, then the first will be a semibrevis and the second and third equal minors; or the first two equal minors and the third a semibrevis, as here:[127]

If four semibreves are found for an imperfect brevis in *curta mensura*, all will be equals, as here:

Today, they ought to be shaped thus, as here:

If in *longa mensura*, they ought to be formed just as if in *curta mensura*.

Today, they do not differ in form, but they do differ in value because four semibreves are employed as two breves.[128] Either the first is a major, the second a minor, and two equals; or two will be equals, the third a major,

---

semibrevis. If replaced by four or five, the larger values are "majors" and the smaller ones are "equals."

[127]At first, this example looks wrong because it appears to have a brevis where the text calls for a semibrevis. But the possibility must be considered that the square figure is a variant form of the major semibrevis, a shape reported in both versions of the *Quatuor principalia* (CS, 3:337a; CS, 4:257a): "Dividebat enim Franco longam in tres breves, et brevem in tres semibreves, sed non minus quam in duas semibreves, quarum prima major, secunda minor semibrevis ab eo nominatur, vel e contrario. Major autem semibrevis pro tanto dicitur, quia duas minores includit, et figurari debet ut brevis recta, quia aequipollet brevi imperfecte. Minor semibrevis figurari debet ad modum losongae, ut supra (Franco divided the longa into three breves and the brevis into three semibreves, but not into less than two semibreves, of which the first was named by him the major and the second the minor semibrevis, or contrariwise. The semibrevis is said to be major on account of its size, because it includes two minor semibreves, and it ought to be shaped like a brevis recta because it is equivalent to an imperfect brevis. The minor semibrevis ought to be shaped in the manner of a lozenge, as above)." If the variant (square) form of major semibrevis indeed is being used by Hanboys here, it perhaps replaces the down-stemmed form in order to distinguish the "semibrevis plus two minor equals" in *curta mensura* from the "major plus two equals" of the ancients. See Lefferts, *The Motet in England*, p. 132, for the square form of the major semibrevis in fourteenth-century musical sources.

[128]In this paragraph, Hanboys discusses the situation where *longa mensura* is understood to pertain and four semibreves not all equal are used in place of the brevis; patterns are therefore more complex. The comparable solutions of the moderns are worth, in modern values, two breves, not one.

et due equales; aut due equales, tertia maior, quartaque minor erit; aut prima et quarta erunt equales, secunda maior, et minor tertia erit, ut hic:

A modernis prima erit semibrevis perfecta per punctum, secunda minor, ter-
5 tia et quarta equales erunt; aut due prime equales et tertia semibrevis per punctum perficitur, et quarta minor erit; aut prima et quarta erunt equales, et secunda semibrevis perficitur per punctum, tertiaque minor erit, ut hic:

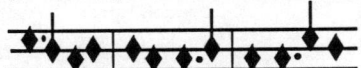

Si quinque pro brevi inveniantur, aut prima maior erit, secunda et tertia
10 minores, quarta et || quinta semibreves equales erunt; aut due prime minores et tertia maior, quarta et quinta semibreves equales erunt. Aut prima et secunda semibreves erunt equales, tertia et quarta minores, quintaque maior erit, ut hic patet:

CS1: 429a

15 Hodie tamen prima erit semibrevis, secunda et tertia minores erunt, quarta et quinta erunt semibreves. Aut due prime minores, et tertia, quarta et quinta semibreves erunt; aut due prime erunt semibreves, tertia et quarta minores, et quinta semibrevis, ut hic:

20 Si sex pro brevi inveniantur, aut prima maior erit et secunda; et tertia, quarta et quinta et sexta equales erunt. Aut prima maior erit et sexta; secunda, tertia, quarta et quinta erunt equales. Aut quatuor equales erunt, et quinta erit maior et sexta. Aut prima maior erit et quarta; secunda et tertia, quinta et sexta equales, ut hic:

25

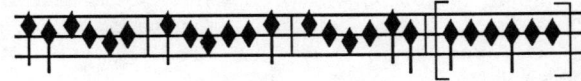

---

2 secunda]secunda et A2 ‖ 3 *tractus om.* 3.1 A2 ‖ 8 *minores* 8.4–5, 7–8, 13, 17 A2 ‖ 10–11 aut due prime ... equales erunt *bis* A2 ‖ 14 *semibrevis* 14.8, 17 A2 ǀ *minima* 14.5 A2 ‖ 15 Hodie]⟦Si sex pro brevi inveniantur⟧ hodie A2 ǀ tamen]tamen ⟦fallit⟧ A2 ǀ ⟦minores erunt⟧ A2 ‖ 15–19 vacat *in marg.* A2 ‖ 16 tertia]tertia ⟦maior⟧ A2 ‖ 25 *fig.* 25.15–21 *ante* 25.1 A2 ‖

and the fourth will be a minor; or the first and the fourth will be equals, the second a major, and the third will be a minor, as here:

According to the moderns, the first will be a semibrevis perfected by a punctus, the second a minor, the third and fourth will be equals; or the first two will be equals, the third a semibrevis perfected by a punctus, and the fourth a minor; or the first and fourth will be equals, the second a semibrevis perfected by a punctus, and the third will be a minor, as here:

If five are found for a brevis, either the first will be a major, the second and third minors, and the fourth and fifth will be equal semibreves; or the first two will be minors, the third a major, and the fourth and fifth will be equal semibreves; or the first and second semibreves will be equals, the third and fourth minors, and the fifth will be a major, as is shown here:[129]

Today, nevertheless, the first will be a semibrevis, the second and third will be minors, and the fourth and fifth will be semibreves; or the first two will be minors, and the third, fourth, and fifth will be semibreves; or the first two will be semibreves, the third and fourth minors, and the fifth a semibrevis, as here:[130]

If six are found for a brevis, either the first and second will be majors, and the third, fourth, fifth, and sixth will be equals; or the first and sixth will be majors, and the second, third, fourth, and fifth will be equals; or four will be equals, and the fifth and sixth will be majors; or the first and fourth will be majors, and the second, third, fifth, and sixth will be equals, as here:

---

[129]The major has the same value as the equals but is distinguished by a (redundant) downstem so as to make clear the grouping of a major-plus-two-minors.

[130]This entire paragraph is marked "vacat" in the manuscript because the scribe at first skipped over it and started to copy out the following para-

A modernis, prima et secunda semibreves erunt; tertia, quarta, quinta, et sexta erunt minores. Aut prima erit semibrevis et sexta; secunda, tertia, quarta et quinta minores erunt. Aut prima ⟨et secunda⟩ et tertia et quarta erunt minores; quinta et sexta semibreves erunt. Aut prima semibrevis erit et quarta; secunda, tertia, quinta et sexta minores erunt, ut hic:

Si septem pro brevi inveniantur, aut prima maior ‖ erit; secunda, tertia, quarta, quinta, et sexta et septima erunt equales. Aut tertia maior; prima, secunda, quarta, quinta, sexta et septima erunt equales. Aut quinta maior; prima, secunda, tertia, quarta, sexta et septima equales erunt. Aut septima maior erit; prima, secunda, tertia, quarta, quinta, et sexta equales, ut hic:

Hodie tamen prima erit semibrevis; secunda, tertia, quarta, quinta, sexta et septima minores erunt. Aut tertia erit semibrevis; prima, secunda, quarta, quinta, sexta et septima minores erunt. Aut quinta erit semibrevis; prima, secunda, tertia, quarta, sexta et septima minores erunt. Aut septima semibrevis; prima, secunda, tertia, quarta, quinta et sexta minores erunt, ut hic:

Si octo pro brevi inveniantur, omnes erunt equales, ut hic patet:

A modernis tamen sic debent figurari:

‖ Et sciendum est quod maior ante capitulum antiqui siquidem semper equepollet brevi, et post illud capitulum maior equepollet semibrevi, si sit de

---

1 semibreve⟦i⟧s A2 ‖ 4 erit]erunt *ante corr.* A2 ‖ 15 erunt]erunt m A2 erunt secundum naturam CS ‖ 24 equepollent A2 ‖

According to the moderns, the first and second will be semibreves, and the third, fourth, fifth, and sixth will be minors; or the first and sixth will be semibreves, and the second, third, fourth, and fifth will be minors; or the first, second, third, and fourth will be minors, and the fifth and sixth will be semibreves; or the first and fourth will be semibreves, and the second, third, fifth, and sixth will be minors, as here:

If seven are found for a brevis, either the first will be a major, and the second, third, fourth, fifth, sixth, and seventh will be equals; or the third will be a major, and the first, second, fourth, fifth, sixth, and seventh will be equals; or the fifth will be a major, and the first, second, third, fourth, sixth, and seventh will be equals; or the seventh will be a major, and the first, second, third, fourth, fifth, and sixth will be equals, as here:

Today, nevertheless, the first will be a semibrevis, and the second, third, fourth, fifth, sixth, and seventh will be minors; or the third will be a semibrevis, and the first, second, fourth, fifth, sixth, and seventh will be minors; or the fifth will be a semibrevis, and the first, second, third, fourth, sixth, and seventh will be minors; or the seventh will be a semibrevis, and the first, second, third, fourth, fifth, and sixth will be minors, as here:

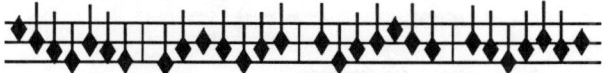

If eight are found for a brevis, all will be equals, as is shown here:

According to the moderns, nevertheless, they ought to be shaped thus:

And it must be known that before this chapter, the major of old indeed is always equivalent to a brevis, and after this chapter, the major is equivalent

---

graph; he discovered the error and stopped, correcting himself, a fact not observed by the proofreader who wrote the cancellation.

brevi perfecta vel imperfecta. Et cum sit de longa mensura, quod pro brevi ponitur, valorem longe continet.

Dictum est de semibrevibus secundum antiquos, iam dicendum est de illis secundum modernos.

⟨CAPITULUM XV⟩

Hanboys: Semibrevium alie recte, alie altere nominantur. Recta semibrevis est que ⟨tertiam⟩ partem brevis perfecte continet, ut supra patet per Franchonem. Fit autem semibrevis recta tripliciter: ante brevem, post brevem, et inter breves. Ante brevem, ut hic patet:

Post brevem, ut hic:

Inter breves, ut hic:

Semibrevium alia perfecta, alia imperfecta. Perfecta semibrevis est que tres minores in se continet. Et si duas in se continet, semibrevis imperfecta manet. Potest etiam semibrevis recta, cum sit ex semibrevibus perfectis, imperfici per minorem precedentem vel subsequentem, vel per valorem. Per minorem precedentem, ut hic:

Per valorem, ut hic: ‖

Per minorem subsequentem, ut hic:

Per valorem, ut hic:

CS1: 430b

---

6 Hanboys *in marg., m. sec.* A2 ‖ 12 *brevis om.* 12.5, 11 A2 ‖ 16 recta]rcta A2 ‖

to a semibrevis, whether breves are perfect or imperfect. And when in *longa mensura*, that which is employed for a brevis comprises the value of a longa.[131]

Enough has been said concerning semibreves according to the older singers; now something must be said concerning them according to the moderns.

## CHAPTER 15

Hanboys: Some semibreves are named rectae; others, alterae. The semibrevis recta is that which comprises the third part of a perfect brevis, as was shown above with reference to Franco.[132] Moreover, the semibrevis recta occurs three ways: before a brevis, after a brevis, and between breves. Before a brevis, as is shown here: 
After a brevis, as here: 

Between breves, as here: 

Some semibreves are perfect, others imperfect. A perfect semibrevis comprises within itself three minors. And if it comprises in itself two, it remains an imperfect semibrevis. The semibrevis recta (when semibreves are perfect) can be imperfected by a preceding or following minor or its value. By a preceding minor, as here: 

By its value, as here: 

By a following minor, as here: 

By its value, as here: 

---

[131]This paragraph is undoubtedly a vestige of an earlier version of its material that lacked Hanboys's interpolations about the most up-to-date practice. Despite the present tense of its verbs, it describes the past in respect to Hanboys's position, as can be seen by the following sentence and chapter 15. In essence, this paragraph observes that in the preceding chapter (i.e., chapter 13—and chapter 12, too), the term "major semibrevis" was assigned a value worth two semibreves rectae (two-thirds of a brevis recta), hence equivalent to what is called in the present chapter (chapter 14) an imperfect brevis. In chapter 14, the major semibrevis is equivalent to some large fraction of a semibrevis. The terminology of major, equal, and minor semibreves is abandoned by Hanboys in chapter 15.

[132]See chapter 12 (256.23–24).

Et cum semibrevis sit perfecta ex omnibus perfectis, diminui potest per semiminorem precedentem vel subsequentem, vel per semiminorem precedentem et subsequentem, vel per valorem, manente perfecta.

Si per semiminorem precedentem vel subsequentem, vel per semiminorem precedentem et subsequentem, predicta semibrevis diminuatur, semiminor subsequens semibrevem imperfici potest per minimam precedentem, si minima eam sequatur, ut hic:

Et utraque semiminor, ante semibrevem et post, per minimam subsequentem imperfici potest, ut hic:

Et predicta potest semibrevis alio modo diminui, quia ultima minor imperfici potest per semiminorem subsequentem, manente de duabus semiminoribus. Secunda semiminor imperfici potest per minimam, ⟨manente de duabus minimis,⟩ ut hic:

‖ Continet etiam semibrevis perfecta ex omnibus perfectis 3 minores, 9 semiminores, 27 minimas. Et cum sit imperfecta ex omnibus imperfectis, valet 2 minores, 4 semiminores, 8 minimas.

CS1: 431a

Semibrevis alterata duas semibreves in valore in se continet, licet non in forma. Et fit semibrevis alterata tribus modis. Primo, quando due semibreves tantum vel valor unius semibrevis et semibrevis sint inter duas breves, ut hic: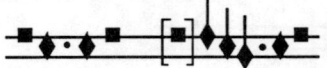

Tunc prima semibrevis vel valor pro recta habeatur, secunda vero alteratur, nisi per divisionem modi aliter distinguatur, ut hic:

Tunc due semibreves equales manent, et prima semibrevis vel valor primam brevem imperficit, et secunda ultimam. Vel quando due semibreves tantum vel valor unius semibrevis et semibrevis inveniuntur ante brevem, ut hic patet:

Tunc prima semibrevis vel valor recta vocatur, et secunda alteratur.

---

6 subsequens *in marg., m. sec.* A2 | ⟦semibrevis⟧ semibrevem A2 | imperficere A2 ‖ 8 *minima post* 8.3 A2 ‖ 9 et]si A2 ‖ 11 *semiminor* 11.5 A2 ‖ 13 duabus]duobus A2 ‖ 16 *punctus post* 16.1 A2 | *punctus om.* 16.3 A2 ‖ 20 in (*pr.*) *sup. lin.* A2 ‖ 21 fit *in marg., m. sec.* A2 | alterata]altera A2 ‖ 25 pro recta *m. sec.* A2 ‖

And when the semibrevis is perfect on all levels, it can be diminished by a preceding or following semiminor or by a preceding and following semiminor or by their value, remaining perfect.

If the aforesaid semibrevis is diminished by a preceding or following semiminor or by a preceding and following semiminor, the semiminor following the semibrevis can be imperfected by a preceding minima if the minima follows the semibrevis, as here:

And each semiminor (before and after the semibrevis) can be imperfected by a following minima, as here:

And the aforesaid semibrevis can be diminished in another manner, because its last minor can be imperfected by a following semiminor, remaining as two semiminors. The second semiminor can be imperfected by a minima, remaining as two minimae, as here:

When the semibrevis is perfect on all levels, it comprises three minors, nine semiminors, twenty-seven minimae. And when the semibrevis is imperfect on all levels, it is worth two minors, four semiminors, eight minimae.

The altered semibrevis comprises within itself two semibreves in value, although not in form. And an altered semibrevis occurs in three manners. In the first, when two semibreves or the value of one semibrevis and a semibrevis are between two breves, as here:

Then the first semibrevis or its value is taken as recta, and the second is altered, unless they are otherwise distinguished by a division of the mode, as here:

Then the two semibreves remain equal, and the first semibrevis or value imperfects the first brevis, and the second the last. Or when only two semibreves or the value of one semibrevis and one semibrevis are found before a brevis, as is shown here:

Then the first semibrevis or value is called recta, and the second is altered.

Secundo modo, quando tres semibreves, vel valor duarum semibrevium et una semibrevis inveniuntur inter duas breves, et si inter primam brevem et secundam vel inter valorem sit punctus divisionis appositus, ut hic:

5 ‖ Tunc prima semibrevis vel valor primam brevem imperficit, secunda erit recta, et tertia altera manet.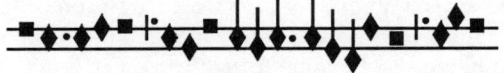

Tertio modo, quando plures semibreves ⟨quam tres⟩ adinvicem inveniuntur. Computentur semper tres pro perfectione, et si due semibreves vel valor unius semibrevis et semibrevis in fine remanserint, prima erit recta, et
10 secunda alterata; et punctus divisionis ante semibrevem penultimam vel ante valorem apponitur, ut hic:

Alio modo assignatur alteratio in semibrevibus ligatis. Unde Robertus de Brunham posuit duas notas cum opposita proprietate, quarum secunda nota
15 descendit quadrata, ut hic:

Nam vitiose ponitur, quia contradicit regulas magistri Franchonis, qui dicit: Omnis ligatura cuius ultimus punctus descendit quadratus, et cetera.

---

4 *minor, minor, minor, punctus post* 4.15 A2 ‖

In the second manner, when three semibreves or the value of two semibreves and a semibrevis are found between two breves, and if between the first brevis and the second or between their values there is introduced a *punctus divisionis*, as here:

Then the first semibrevis or value imperfects the first brevis, the second will be recta, and the third remains altera.

In the third manner, when more than three semibreves are found together. Three are always counted as a perfection, and if two semibreves or the value of one semibrevis and a semibrevis should remain at the end, the first will be recta and the second altered; and a *punctus divisionis* is introduced before the penultimate semibrevis or value, as here:

In another manner, alteration is assigned in ligated semibreves.[133] For Robert of Brunham has posited two notes with opposite propriety, of which the second square note descends, as here:

But this is employed defectively because it contradicts the rules of Master Franco, who says: "Every ligature whose last square notehead descends etc."[134]

---

[133] For each of Robertus's four ways of indicating alteration, Hanboys raises an objection, quoting Franco; these citations match the doctrines of "Franco" as quoted in the *Summa* while not agreeing as closely with the corresponding passages in the *Regule* as edited above. About Robertus of Brunham, see the Introduction, pp. 62–63; and Lefferts, *The Motet in England*, p. 138 and figure 40, for further discussion and examples of his note forms in the practical sources. Ligature shapes like those proposed by Robertus also are discussed in Walsingham, *Regulae de musica mensurabili* (ed. Reaney), p. 80: "Sequitur: quod quando semibreves habeas, et si ultima formatur ad modum longae, quod prima est recta et secunda est altera, ut hic: [ex. 35 follows] (It follows that when you have semibreves, and if the last is formed in the manner of a longa, then the first is recta and the second is altera)." And they receive the attention of at least one disapproving continental theorist, in *De musica mensurabili* (ed. Sweeney), p. 49: "Sunt etiam aliqui qui ponunt pro uno tempore duas notulas copulatas quadratas et descendentes sic appropriatas: (ex. sequitur), quod est contra regulam nisi ultima sit longa per naturam artis (there are some who employ two square, descending, ligated notes so arranged [example follows] as one tempus, which is against the rule unless the last is a longa by the nature of the art)."

[134] Chapter 20 (330.1–3). See also Handlo, *Regule*, Rule II of Rubric VIII (136.8–10).

Et in ligatura ascendente secunda nota ponitur adverso capite, ut patet hic:

Ad oppositum est Francho, dicens: Omnis ligatura cuius ultimus punctus recte stat supra penultimam, et cetera.

Alio modo in ligatura ascendente idem Robertus alterationem assignavit. Posuit enim secundam notam ascendentem cum tractulo a parte dextra, ut hic:

‖ Ad oppositum est Francho, dicens: quandocunque in fine ligaturarum punctus quadratus ascendendo vel descendendo, et cetera.

CS1: 432a

Quarto modo idem Robertus assignavit alterationem per duos tractulos ad similitudinem caude yrundinis sub nota vel supra notam positos, ut hic:

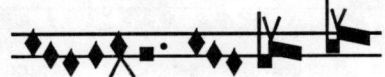

And in an ascending ligature, the second note is employed with its head turned the other way, as is shown here:

Opposed to this is Franco, saying: "Every ligature whose last punctus stands normally above the penultimate etc."[135]

The same Robert assigns alteration to an ascending ligature in another manner. He also posits a second note ascending with a little stem from its right side, as here:

Opposed to this is Franco, saying: "Whenever at the end of ligatures there is a square notehead ascending or descending etc."[136]

The same Robert assigns alteration in a fourth manner by two little stems similar to a swallow's tail employed under or over a note, as here:[137]

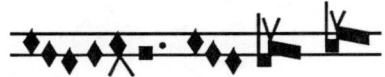

---

[135]Chapter 20 (328.19–21). See also Handlo, *Regule*, Rule I of Rubric VIII (136.4–6). One might suppose that "turned the other way" means "stands indirectly," in which case the quotation and example do not fit. But Hanboys appears to have in mind that the step-wise ascending ligature with opposite propriety should normally lack perfection, so "the other way" in this case means "stands directly over."

[136]Chapter 20 (332.4–6). See also Handlo, *Regule*, Rule I of Rubric X (152.9–10).

[137]The swallow's tail likely owes its existence to the variable tradition of alteration in England, i.e., 1+2 and 2+1. On the extensive appearances of the *cauda yrundinis* in the practical sources, see Lefferts, *The Motet in England*, pp. 138–41 and table 21, to which can be added now the musical examples in item 2 of **GB-Lbl**, Additional 21455, f. 5v. The *cauda* is also mentioned in both versions of the *Quatuor principalia* (quartum principale [CS, 3:349; CS, 4:271]), where its use is also deplored. Version A reads: "Ceterum qui per punctum aut per caudam hirundinis aut quoquomodo alterationem supradictis regulis repugnantem faciunt, errant et viam veritatis hujus artis ignorant ... Tamen figure ad placitum sunt ponende: unde modernis temporibus aliqui semiminimam, id est crochutam, et aliqui dragmam posuerunt; aliqui vero per caudam hirundinis alterationem fecerunt; et punctum pausis dederunt; et nulla talia invenerunt, et novas produxerunt figuras. Que tamen dictis antiquorum repugnant." A reference in Walsingham, *Regulae de musica mensurabili* (ed. Reaney), p. 86, that survives without its intended music example probably also shows he had in mind the *cauda* on account of its negative reference to the use of a sign to show alteration: "de semibrevibus et brevibus alteratis per signa per ignorantiam (semibreves and breves altered by a sign out of ignorance)."

Quod hoc sit vitiosum. Probatio: frustra fit per plura quod fieri potest per pauciora. Sed alteratio potest assignari per punctum, et assignatur per duos tractulos, ergo et cetera. Maior patet per Philosophum. Minor patet per Franchonem in secundo modo de alterationibus, ubi ipse dicit: nisi per divisio-

But this is defective. The proof: it is bad to do with more what can be done with less.[138] But alteration can be assigned by a punctus, and it is assigned by two little stems, therefore, etc. The major premise is shown by the Philosopher. The minor premise is shown by Franco in the second mode of altera-

---

[138]Hanboy's major premise, "Frustra fit per plura ...," is better known as Ockham's razor because of its association with the influential English Franciscan theologian and philosopher William of Ockham (ca. 1285–1349). Hanboys's wording is identical to its formulation in multiple citations by Ockham, particularly in the early projects of his Oxford years around 1320, from the *Commentary on the Sentences* (finished by 1319) to the *Summa logicae* (finished by 1323). For the dating of these early treatises, see Ockham's *Summa logicae, Opera philosophica*, vol. 1, ed. P. Boehner, G. Gab, and S. Brown (St. Bonaventure, N.Y.: Franciscan Institute, 1974), pp. 50*–56*.

While Ockham's novel and extensive use of the razor is noteworthy, he did not coin the expression, which may have had fairly general currency at the time he wrote. Though the gist of the "principle of economy" goes back to Aristotle, its particular language here can be traced back no farther than Odo of Rigaldus (d. 1275), the student of Alexander of Hales and teacher of Bonaventure: "frustra fit per plura quod potest fieri per unum." It is found in related language in the works of the English Franciscan philosopher Johannes Duns Scotus (ca. 1265–1308) and others of his era. In the exact words of Ockham, the principle is also cited in two Parisian scholastic treatises of the early 1320s: Book IV of the *Commentary on the Sentences of Franciscus de Marchia* (1320) and Book 7 of the *Speculum musicae* of Jacques de Liège, of 1323–1324/5 (for the citation, see Book 7, cap. I, sent. 4 [ed. Bragard], 7:5; for the dating of the *Speculum*, see the Introduction, p. 1, n. 2).

Hanboys credits the maxim to the Philosopher, presumably Aristotle, and it is conceivable that he learned it from a florilegium such as the *Auctoritates Aristoteles* (ed. Hamesse, p. 141), a Parisian work of the early fourteenth century, where it is cited in reference to the *Physics* (188a17-18): "Melius est ponere principia finita quam infinita ex quo habetur quod peccatum est fieri per plura quod potest fieri per pauciora (It is better to use finite principles than infinite, from which we have that it is a sin to do with more what can be done with less)."

On Ockham's razor in general, see H. J. Cloeren, "Ockham's razor," *Historisches Wörterbuch der Philosophie* 6 (1984): 1094–96; Armand Maurer, "Ockam's Razor and Chatton's Anti-Razor," *Mediaeval Studies* 46 (1984): 463–75; the section on "Ockham's Rasiermesser" in Jüngen Miethke, *Ockhams Weg zur Sozialphilosophie* (Berlin: Walter de Gruyter & Co., 1969), pp. 238–44; and C. K. Brampton, "Nominalism and the Law of Parsimony," *The Modern Schoolman* 41 (1963-64): 273–81.

nem modi aliter distinguatur, et cetera. Ergo vitiose assignatur alteratio quando assignatur per duos tractulos et potest assignari per punctum.

Si quatuor semibreves vel plures, ita quod unitas transit tertiarium, inveniantur inter duas breves, prima brevis imperficitur per semibrevem sub-
5 sequentem, ut hic:

Nisi punctus perfectionis post primam brevem apponatur, ut hic:

Tunc prima brevis perficitur per punctum, ultima semibrevis ad perfectio-
10 nem brevis subsequentis pertinet, si sit de brevibus perfectis.

Tamen de brevibus imperfectis, si tres semibreves vel plures, ita quod unitas transit dualitatem, inveniantur inter duas breves et prima brevis punctum habet post se positum, semibrevis subsequens brevem ad eam pertinet et ita brevis cum puncto || et semibrevi subsequente duas breves continet, ut
15 hic:

Si secunda brevis punctum habeat postpositum, semibrevis precedens brevem ad eam pertinet et brevis cum puncto et semibrevi precedente duas breves valet, ut hic:
20

Et si unica semibrevis inveniatur inter duas breves et prima brevis vel secunda habet punctum postpositum, brevis cum puncto et semibrevi duas breves valet, ut hic:

25 Si utraque brevis careat puncto, et prima brevis vel secunda ponitur inter duas semibreves, utraque brevis imperfecta manet, et due semibreves pro brevi imperfecta ponuntur, ut hic manifestissime apparet:

---

14 punctu A2 (*idem* 18, 22) ||

CS1: 432b

tions, where he says: "Unless they are otherwise distinguished by a division of the mode, etc."[139] Therefore, alteration is defectively assigned when it is assigned by two little stems and can be assigned by a punctus.

If four or more semibreves are found between two breves, so that unity exceeds a grouping by threes, the first brevis is imperfected by the following semibrevis, as here:

Unless a *punctus perfectionis* is introduced after the first brevis, as here:

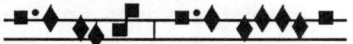

Then the first brevis is perfected by the punctus, and the last semibrevis pertains to the perfection of the following brevis, if the breves are perfect.

Nevertheless, when the breves are imperfect, if three or more semibreves are found between two breves, so that unity exceeds a grouping by twos, and the first brevis has a punctus employed after it,[140] the semibrevis following the brevis pertains to it, and thus the brevis with the punctus and the following semibrevis comprises two breves, as here:

If the second brevis has a punctus employed after it, the semibrevis preceding this brevis pertains to it, and the brevis with the punctus and the preceding semibrevis is worth two breves, as here:

And if one semibrevis is found between two breves and the first or second brevis has a punctus employed after it, the brevis with the punctus and the semibrevis is worth two breves, as here:

And if each brevis lacks a punctus, and the first or second brevis is employed between two semibreves, each brevis remains imperfect, and the two semibreves are employed as an imperfect brevis, as appears most clearly here:

---

[139]Chapter 11 (248.8–9). See also Handlo, *Regule*, Rule IX of Rubric III (96.8–9).

[140]There are parallel passages for the minor (chapter 16 [304.10–28]), semiminor (chapter 17 [314.7–19]), and minima (chapter 18 [320.1–14]), but not for the larger four of Hanboys's eight figures. This punctus is, in effect, a *punctus additionis* in imperfect mensuration, though Hanboys does not call it that. He regards it as a *punctus perfectionis* (chapter 3 [194.12 *et passim*]).

Et si semibrevis sit perfecta ex omnibus ⟨perfectis⟩ et alterata, diminui potest per minorem precedentem vel subsequentem, vel per minorem precedentem et subsequentem, manente alterata. Si predicta semibrevis diminuatur per minorem precedentem vel per valorem, prima semibrevis illius alterationis per minorem vel per valorem imperficitur, minor etiam imperfici potest per semiminorem et semiminor per minimam, ut hic patet: ‖

CS1: 433a

Si diminuatur per minorem subsequentem vel per valorem, secunda semibrevis illius alterationis per minorem vel per valorem imperficitur, minor autem imperfici potest per semiminorem, et semiminorem per minimam, ut hic patet:

Si per minorem precedentem et subsequentem vel per valorem diminuatur, prima minor vel valor primam semibrevem imperficit, et secunda alteram, et utraque minor imperfici potest per semiminorem et semiminor per minimam, ut hic:

Potest etiam semibrevis alterata alio modo diminui. Nam secunda semibrevis imperfici potest per ⟨minorem subsequentem, manente de duabus minoribus. Secunda minor imperfici potest per⟩ semiminorem subsequentem, manente de duabus semiminoribus. Secunda semiminor imperfici potest per minimam ⟨subsequentem, manente de duabus minimis⟩. Et semibrevis alterata imperfici potest et diminui a parte post; eodem modo imperfici potest et diminui a parte ante, ut hic:

Semibrevis recta de semibrevibus perfectis aliquando valet novem semiminores, aliquando octo, aliquando septem, aliquando sex, aliquando quinque, aliquando quatuor. Novem semiminorum, quando ponitur semibre-

---

3 si]sed A2 ‖ 8 per ⟦valorem⟧ minorem A2 ‖ 21 duabus]duobus A2 ‖ 25 *semibrevis* 25.13 A2 ‖

And if the semibrevis is perfect on all levels and is altered, it can be diminished by a preceding or following minor or by a preceding and following minor, remaining altered. If the aforesaid semibrevis is diminished by a preceding minor or its value, the first semibrevis of this alteration is imperfected by the minor or its value. The minor also can be imperfected by a semiminor and the semiminor by a minima, as shown here:

If it is diminished by a following minor or its value, the second semibrevis of this alteration is imperfected by the minor or its value. The minor also can be imperfected by a semiminor, and the semiminor by a minima, as shown here:

If it is diminished by a preceding and following minor or by their value, the first minor or value imperfects the first semibrevis, and the second the other, and each minor can be imperfected by a semiminor and the semiminor by a minima, as here:

The altered semibrevis can also be diminished in another manner. The second semibrevis can be imperfected by a following minor, remaining as two minors. The second minor can be imperfected by a following semiminor, remaining as two semiminors. The second semiminor can be imperfected by a following minima, remaining as two minimae. And the altered semibrevis can be imperfected and diminished *a parte post*; in the same manner, it can be imperfected and diminished *a parte ante*, as here:

When semibreves are perfect, the semibrevis recta sometimes is worth nine semiminors, sometimes eight, sometimes seven, sometimes six, sometimes five, sometimes four.[141] It is worth nine semiminors when the semi-

---

[141]In respect to the parallelism (or variation) in the exposition of similar material for different figures, it can be observed that in discussions of the semibrevis, minor, and semiminor, the following paragraphs or their equivalent follow rather than precede the discussion of the diminishment of the altered value.

vis ante semibrevem, vel ante semibrevem pausam, vel ante punctum, veluti de semibrevibus et minoribus perfectis, ut supra.

Octo semiminorum, quando semiminor vel valor antecedit semibrevem, ut hic patet:

Vel subsequitur, ut hic:

‖ Septem semiminorum, quando semibrevis ponitur inter duas semimi- nores vel inter valorem, ut hic patet:

CS1: 433b

Tunc prima semiminor vel valor imperficit primam minorem, secunda vero ultimam.

Sex semiminorum, quando minor vel valor antecedit semibrevem, ut hic:

Vel subsequitur, ut hic:

Quinque semiminorum, quando semiminor vel valor antecedit semibrevem et minor vel valor subsequitur, ut hic:

Tunc semiminor precedens semibrevem primam minorem imperficit. Minor vero vel valor subsequens semibrevem imperficit eam.

Quatuor semiminorum, quando minor perfecta cum semiminore sequente vel valor precedit semibrevem, et semiminor vel valor subsequitur, ut hic:

Vel quando semiminor vel valor precedit semibrevem, et minor perfecta cum semiminore vel cum valore subsequuntur, ut hic: ‖

CS1: 434a

Tunc minor perficitur per punctum, semiminor vel valor precedens semibrevem primam minorem imperficit, alteramque semiminor subsequens.

---

7 *punctus post* 7.1, 3 A2 ‖ 10 *punctus post* 10.2 A2 | *punctus om.* 10.4 A2 | *semiminor, minor, minor* 10.5–7 A2 ‖ 13 semiminorum]minorum A2 ‖ 20 semiminor]semibrevis A2 ‖ 23 valor ⟦subsequens semibrevem⟧ precedit A2 ‖ 25 *semiminor, minor* 25.10–11 A2 | *semiminor* 25.13, 20–22 A2 ‖

brevis is employed before a semibrevis, before a semibrevis rest, or before a punctus, just as for perfect semibreves and minors, as above.

Eight semiminors when a semiminor or its value precedes the semibrevis, as is shown here:

Or follows, as here:

Seven semiminors when the semibrevis is employed between two semiminors or their value, as is shown here:

Then the first semiminor or its value imperfects the first minor; the second, the last.

Six semiminors when a minor or its value precedes the semibrevis, as here:

Or follows, as here:

Five semiminors when a semiminor or its value precedes the semibrevis and a minor or its value follows, as here:

Then the semiminor preceding the semibrevis imperfects the first minor; the minor or its value following the semibrevis imperfects it.

Four semiminors when a perfect minor with a following semiminor or its value precedes the semibrevis, and a semiminor or its value follows, as here:

Or when a semiminor or its value precedes the semibrevis, and a perfect minor with a semiminor or its value follows, as here:

Then the minor is perfected by a punctus, the semiminor or value preceding the semibrevis imperfects the first minor, and the following semiminor imperfects the other.

Vel quando quatuor semiminores vel valor precedunt semibrevem et semiminor vel ⟨valor⟩ subsequitur, ut hic:

Tunc tres semiminores semibrevem precedentem faciunt perfectionem, quarta semiminor primam minorem imperficit, semiminor autem vel valor subsequens semibrevem secundam minorem imperficit. Vel quando semiminor vel valor precedit semibrevem, et quatuor semiminores sequuntur, ut hic:

Tunc semiminor precedens semibrevem primam minorem imperficit, semiminor vero subsequens imperficit secundam minorem, tres semiminores sequentes faciunt perfectionem.

Vel quando semibrevis constat de duabus minoribus imperfectis, ut hic:

Et sicut semibrevis ante semibrevem vel ante semibrevem pausam de semibrevibus perfectis est perfecta, ita semibrevis ante semibrevem vel ante semibrevem pausam de semibrevibus imperfectis est imperfecta.

## ⟨CAPITULUM XVI⟩

Hanboys: Forma minorum talis est. Quando||cunque semibrevis habet tractulum directe ascendentem, minor dicitur, ut hic: CS1: 434b

Et simplex est, quia ligari non potest. Sed perfici potest, id est potest continere in se tres semiminores, ut minor ante minorem, vel ante minorem pausam de minoribus perfectis est perfecta; sed de minoribus imperfectis nequaquam. Sed minor ante punctum perfectionis, si sit de minoribus perfectis vel imperfectis, semper perficitur. Minor ante minorem, ut hic:
Vel ante minorem pausam, ut hic:

Vel ante punctum, ut hic:
Minor tamen imperfecta duas semiminores equales continet.

---

3 *semiminor* 3.12 A2 ‖ 7 semibreves secuntur A2 ‖ 9 *semiminor* 9.9, 13 A2 ‖ 11 minorem]semiminorem A2 ‖ 13 duabus]duobus A2 ‖ 24 imperfectis] perfectis (im *in marg., m. sec.*) A2 ‖ 27 ut hic ⟦vel ante puncti ut hic, vel ante puncti ut⟧ hic A2 ǀ ante pausam *in marg., m. sec.* A2 ‖

Or when four semiminors or their value precede the semibrevis and a semiminor or its value follows, as here:

Then three semiminors preceding the semibrevis make a perfection, the fourth semiminor imperfects the first minor, and the semiminor or its value following the semibrevis imperfects the second minor. Or when a semiminor or its value precedes the semibrevis, and four semiminors follow, as here:

Then the semiminor preceding the semibrevis imperfects the first minor, the semiminor following imperfects the second minor, and the following three semiminors make a perfection.

Or when the semibrevis consists of two imperfect minors, as here:

And just as a semibrevis before a semibrevis or before a semibrevis rest is perfect when semibreves are perfect, likewise a semibrevis before a semibrevis or before a semibrevis rest is imperfect when semibreves are imperfect.

## CHAPTER 16

Hanboys: The form of minors is thus. Whenever a semibrevis has a little stem directly ascending, it is called a minor, as here:

And it is whole, because it cannot be ligated. But it can be perfected, that is, it can comprise in itself three semiminors, as a minor before a minor or before a minor rest is perfect when minors are perfect, but never when they are imperfect. But a minor before a *punctus perfectionis*, whether minors are perfect or imperfect, is always perfected. A minor before a minor, as here:

Or before a minor rest, as here:

Or before a punctus, as here:
An imperfect minor nevertheless comprises two equal semiminors.

Minorum autem alie recte, alie alterate nominantur. Recta minor est que tertiam partem semibrevis perfecte in se continet. Fit etiam recta minor tribus modis: ante semibrevem, post semibrevem, et inter semibreves. Ante semibrevem, ut hic:

Post semibrevem, ut hic:

Inter semibreves, ut hic: 

CS1: 435a

Minor recta de minoribus perfectis et perfecta imperfici potest per semiminorem precedentem vel subsequentem. Per semiminorem precedentem, ut hic:

Per semiminorem subsequentem, ut hic:

Minor, si sit perfecta ex omnibus perfectis, diminui potest per minimam precedentem vel subsequentem, vel per minimam precedentem et subsequentem, manente perfecta. Per minimam precedentem, ut hic:

Per minimam subsequentem, ut hic:

Per minimam precedentem et subsequentem, ut hic patet:

Tunc prima minima primam semiminorem imperficit, secunda vero ultimam.

Valet minor perfecta ex omnibus perfectis tres semiminores et novem minimas. Imperfecta tamen ex omnibus imperfectis duas semiminores in se continet, et utraque semiminor duas minimas.

Altera minor duas minores in se continet in valore, non tamen in forma. Fit autem minor altera tribus modis. Primo modo, quando due minores tantum vel valor unius minoris et minor inveniuntur inter duas semibreves, vel inter semibrevem et semibrevem pausam, ut hic:

CS1: 435b

---

13 *seminimor post* 13.2 A2 ǁ 19 *seminimor, semibrevis, punctus, seminimor, seminimor, semibrevis* A2 ǁ 21 *seminimor* 21.2 A2 ǁ 23 *seminimor* 23.1 A2 ǀ *punctus post* 23.2 A2 ǁ

Some minors are named rectae; others altered. A minor recta is that which comprises in itself the third part of a perfect semibrevis. The minor recta occurs in three manners: before a semibrevis, after a semibrevis, and between semibreves. Before a semibrevis, as here:

After a semibrevis, as here:

Between semibreves, as here:

The minor recta and perfect (consisting of perfect minors) can be imperfected by a preceding or following semiminor. By a preceding semiminor, as here:

By a following semiminor, as here:

The minor, if it is perfect on all levels, can be diminished by a preceding or following minima or by a preceding and a following minima, remaining perfect. By a preceding minima, as here:

By a following minima, as here:

By a preceding and a following minima, as is shown here:

Then the first minima imperfects the first semiminor, and the second imperfects the last.

The minor perfect on all levels is worth three semiminors and nine minimae. The one imperfect on all levels nevertheless comprises in itself two semiminors; and each semiminor, two minimae.

The minor altera comprises in itself two minors in value but not in form. The minor altera occurs in three manners. In the first manner, when just two minors or the value of one minor and a minor are found between two semibreves or between a semibrevis and a semibrevis rest, as here:

Tunc prima minor recta vocatur, et secunda alteratur. Nisi per divisionem modi aliter distinguatur, ut hic:

Tunc due minores manent equales, et prima minor primam semibrevem imperficit, secunda vero ultimam. Vel quando due minores tantum vel valor unius minoris et minor inveniuntur ante semibrevem, ut hic patet:

Tunc prima minor vel valor pro recta teneatur, secunda quoque alteratur.

Secundo modo, quando tres minores vel valor duarum minorum et una minor inveniuntur inter duas semibreves, vel inter semibrevem et semibrevem pausam, et si inter primam minorem et secundam vel inter valorem punctus divisionis sit appositus, ut hic:

Tunc prima minor vel valor semibrevem precedentem imperficit, secunda recta vocatur, tertia quoque alteratur.

Tertio modo, si plures minores quam tres inveniantur inter duas semibreves vel ante unam semibrevem. Tres pro perfectione computentur; si due in fine remanserint, vel valor unius minoris et una minor, prima erit recta et secunda alterata, et punctus alterationis ante minorem penultimam vel ante valorem appositus erit, ut hic:

CS1: 436a

Et si una minor in fine remanserit, recta vocatur, et semibrevem subsequentem imperficit, ut hic:

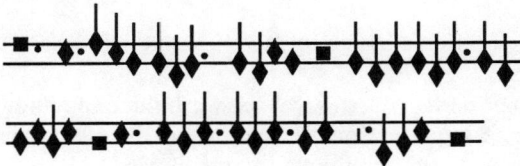

---

3 *punctus om.* 3.3 A2 ‖ 7 *minor* 7.7 A2 ‖ 8 quoque]quidem A2 ‖ 9 duarum]duorum A2 ‖ 13 *exemplum ut in* 302.7 A2 ‖

Then the first minor is called recta, and the second is altered, unless they are otherwise distinguished by a division of the mode, as here:

Then the two minors remain equal, the first minor imperfects the first semibrevis, and the second imperfects the last. Or when just two minors or the value of one minor and a minor are found before a semibrevis, as is shown here:

Then the first minor or its value is held as a recta, while the second is altered.

In the second manner, when three minors or the value of two minors and one minor are found between two semibreves or between a semibrevis and a semibrevis rest, and if between the first and the second minor or between their values a *punctus divisionis* is introduced, as here:

Then the first minor or value imperfects the preceding semibrevis, the second is called recta, and the third is altered.

In the third manner, when more than three minors are found between two semibreves or before one semibrevis. Three are counted as a perfection; if two should remain at the end or the value of one minor and one minor, the first will be recta and the second altered, and a *punctus alterationis*[142] will be introduced before the penultimate minor or its value, as here:

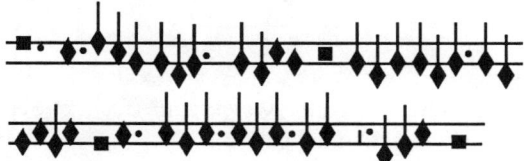

And if one minor should remain at the end, is is called recta and imperfects the following semibrevis, as here:

---

[142]Heretofore called a *punctus divisionis*.

Et si quatuor minores vel plures inveniantur inter duas semibreves, ita quod tres pro perfectione semper computentur, et si una minor in fine remanserit, prima semibrevis per minorem subsequentem imperficitur, ut hic patet:

Nisi punctus perfectionis post primam semibrevem apponatur, ut hic:

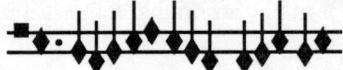

Tunc semibrevis prima per punctum perficitur. Ultima minor ad perfectionem semibrevis subsequentis pertinet, si de semibrevibus perfectis constet. ‖ Si de semibrevibus imperfectis tres minores vel plures inveniantur inter duas semibreves, ita quod una minor post numerum binarium remaneat, computando due minores pro semibrevi et prima semibrevis punctum perfectionis habet postpositum, minor subsequens semibrevem ad eam pertinet, et semibrevis cum puncto et minore subsequente duas semibreves valet, ut hic:

CS1: 436b

Si secunda semibrevis punctum habeat postpositum, minor precedens ad eam pertinet, et semibrevis cum puncto et minore precedente duas semibreves valet, ut hic:

Et si una minor inveniatur inter duas semibreves et prima semibrevis vel secunda habeat punctum postpositum, semibrevis cum puncto et minore duas semibreves valet, ut hic:

Si utraque semibrevis careat puncto, et prima semibrevis vel secunda ponitur inter duas minores, utraque semibrevis est imperfecta et due minores semibrevem imperfectam valent, ut hic patet:

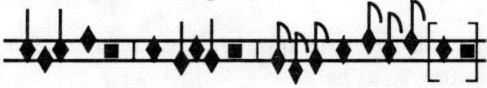

Si minor sit perfecta ex omnibus perfectis et alterata, diminui potest per seminiorem precedentem vel subsequentem, vel per seminiorem precedentem et subsequentem, manente alterata. Si predicta minor diminuatur per semi‖minorem precedentem vel per valorem, imperficitur minor prima illius

CS1: 437a

---

26 imperfecta]perfecta A2 ‖ 26–27 semibrevem]brevem A2 ‖ 28 *exemplum in marg., m. sec.* A2 ‖ 29 omnibus]semiminoribus A2 ‖

And if four or more minors are found between two semibreves—so that three are always counted as a perfection—and if one minor should remain at the end, the first semibrevis is imperfected by the following minor, as is shown here:

Unless a *punctus perfectionis* is introduced after the first semibrevis, as here:

Then the first semibrevis is perfected by the punctus; the last minor pertains to the perfection of the following semibrevis if they should consist of perfect semibreves.

If when semibreves are imperfect, three or more minors are found between two semibreves, so that one minor remains beyond the pairs (when counting two minors as a semibrevis) and the first semibrevis has a *punctus perfectionis* employed after it, the minor following the semibrevis pertains to it, and the semibrevis with the punctus and the following minor is worth two semibreves, as here:

If the second semibrevis has a punctus employed after it, the preceding minor pertains to it, and the semibrevis with the punctus and the preceding minor is worth two semibreves, as here:

And if one minor is found between two semibreves and the first or second semibrevis has a punctus employed after it, the semibrevis with the punctus and the minor is worth two semibreves, as here:

If each semibrevis lacks a punctus and the first or second semibrevis is employed between two minors, each semibrevis is imperfect and the two minors are worth an imperfect semibrevis, as is shown here:

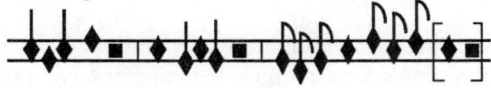

If the minor is perfect and altered (when minors are perfect), it can be diminished by a preceding or following semiminor or by a preceding and following semiminor, remaining altered. If the aforesaid minor is diminished by a preceding semiminor or its value, the first minor of the alteration is

illius alterationis per semiminorem vel per valorem. Semiminor etiam imperfici potest per minimam, ut hic:

Si diminuatur per semiminorem subsequentem vel per valorem, secunda
5    minor illius alterationis per semiminorem vel per valorem imperficitur. Et semiminor per minimam imperfici potest:

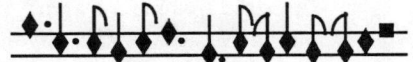

Si diminuatur per semiminorem precedentem et subsequentem vel per valorem, prima semiminor vel valor primam minorem imperficit, secunda
10    quoque alteram, et utraque semiminor imperfici potest per minimam, ut hic:

Potest etiam minor alterata aliter diminui, quia secunda minor imperfici potest per semiminorem subsequentem, manente de duabus semiminoribus. Secunda semiminor imperfici potest per minimam, ⟨manente de duabus min-
15    imis⟩. Et sicut minor alterata imperfici potest et diminui a parte post, illa imperfici potest ⟨et diminui⟩ a parte ante, ut hic patet:

Minor recta de minoribus perfectis aliquando valet novem minimas, aliquando octo, aliquando septem, aliquando sex, aliquando quinque, ali-
20    quando quatuor. Novem minimarum, quando ponitur minor ante minorem vel minorem pausam, ‖ vel ante punctum, ut de minoribus et semiminoribus perfectis, ut supra.

CS1: 437b

Octo minimarum, quando minima antecedit minorem, ut hic:
Vel subsequitur, ut hic:
25

Septem minimarum, quando minor ponitur inter duas minimas, ut hic patet:

Tunc prima minima primam semiminorem imperficit, et secunda ultimam.
30    Sex minimarum, quando semiminor vel valor antecedit minorem, ut hic:

---

3 *semiminores* 3.13, 19–21 A2 ‖ 7 *punctus ante* 7.1 A2 ‖ 17 *punctus om.* 17.6 A2 ‖ 23 *punctus post* 23.2 A2 ‖ 25 *punctus post* 25.1 A2 ‖ 28 *punctus post* 28.2 A2 ‖

imperfected by the semiminor or its value. The semiminor can be imperfected by a minima, as here:

If it is diminished by a following semiminor or its value, the second minor of the alteration is imperfected by the semiminor or by its value. And the semiminor can be imperfected by a minima:

If it is diminished by preceding and following semiminors or their value, the first semiminor or value imperfects the first minor, the second imperfects the other, and each semiminor can be imperfected by a minima, as here:

The altered minor can be diminished in another way, because the second minor can be imperfected by a following semiminor, remaining as two semiminors. The second semiminor can be imperfected by a minima, remaining as two minimae. And just as the altered minor can be imperfected and diminished *a parte post*, so it can be imperfected and diminished *a parte ante*, as is shown here:

The minor recta (when minors are perfect) is worth sometimes nine minimae, sometimes eight, sometimes seven, sometimes six, sometimes five, sometimes four. It is worth nine minimae when the minor is employed before a minor or a minor rest or before a punctus, just as for perfect minors and semiminors, as above.

Eight minimae when a minima precedes the minor, as here:
Or follows, as here: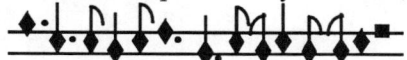

Seven minimae when a minor is employed between two minimae, as is shown here:

Then the first minima imperfects the first semiminor, and the second imperfects the last.

Six minimae when a semiminor or its value precedes the minor, as here:

Vel subsequitur, ut hic: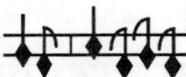

Quinque minimarum, quando minima antecedit minorem et semiminor vel valor subsequitur, ut hic:

Tunc minima antecedens minorem primam semiminorem imperficit. Semiminor vel valor subsequens minorem imperficit eam.

Quatuor minimarum, quando semiminor per||fecta cum minima vel valor precedit minorem et minima subsequitur, ut hic:    CS1: 438a

Vel quando minima precedit minorem et semiminor perfecta cum minima vel valor subsequitur, ut hic:

Tunc semiminor perficitur per punctum; minima precedens minorem primam semiminorem imperficit; minima vero subsequens semiminorem imperficit secundam.

Vel quando quatuor minime precedunt minorem et minima subsequitur, ut hic:

Tunc tres minime minorem precedentes faciunt perfectionem. Quarta minima primam semiminorem imperficit. Minima autem minorem sequens secundam semiminorem imperficit. Vel quando minima precedit minorem et quatuor minime sequuntur, ut hic:

Tunc minima precedens minorem primam semiminorem imperficit, minima subsequens semiminorem vero imperficit secundam. Tres minime sequentes faciunt perfectionem.

Vel quando minor constat de duabus semiminoribus imperfectis, ut hic: ||   CS1: 438b

Et sicut minor ante minorem vel ante minorem pausam de minoribus perfectis est perfecta, ita minor ante minorem vel ante minorem pausam de minoribus imperfectis est imperfecta.

---

13 *punctus om.* 13.5 A2 | *minima post* 13.9 A2 || 15 primam minorem A2 || 29 *semibrevis, semiminima* 29.1–2 A2 ||

Or follows, as here:

Five minimae when a minima precedes the minor and a semiminor or its value follows, as here:

Then the minima preceding the minor imperfects its first semiminor. The semiminor or value following the minor imperfects it.

Four minimae when a perfect semiminor with a minima or its value precedes the minor, and a minima follows, as here:

Or when a minima precedes the minor, and a perfect semiminor with a minima or its value follows, as here:

Then the semiminor is perfected by the punctus; the minima preceding the minor imperfects the first semiminor; the minima following imperfects the second semiminor.

Or when four minimae precede the minor, and a minima follows, as here:

Then three minimae preceding the minor make a perfection; the fourth minima imperfects the first semiminor. The minima following the minor imperfects its second semiminor. Or when a minima precedes the minor, and four minimae follow, as here:

Then the minima preceding the minor imperfects the first semiminor; the minima following imperfects the second semiminor; the three following minimae make a perfection.

Or when the minor consists of two imperfect semiminors, as here:

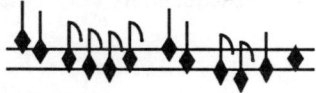

And just as a minor before a minor or before a minor rest is perfect when minors are perfect, likewise a minor before a minor or before a minor rest is imperfect when minors are imperfect.

### ⟨CAPITULUM XVII⟩

Hanboys: Forma semiminorum talis est. Quandocunque semibrevis habet tractum ascendentem retortum a dextra parte, semiminor dicitur, ut hic:

Et simplex est, quia ligari non potest. Sed perfici potest, id est potest continere in se tres minimas, ut semiminor ante semiminorem, vel ante semiminorem pausam de semiminoribus perfectis est perfecta. Tamen de semiminoribus imperfectis non tenet.

Si sit de semiminoribus perfectis vel imperfectis, semiminor ante punctum perfectionis semper perficitur. Semiminor ante semiminorem, ut hic patet:

Vel ante semiminorem pausam, ut hic:

Vel ante punctum, ut hic:

Semiminor tamen imperfecta duas ⟨minimas⟩ equales in se continet.

Semiminorum alie recte, alie altere vocantur. Semiminor recta est que tertiam partem minoris perfecte in se continet, et fit tribus modis. ‖ Primo modo, quando ponitur semiminor ante minorem, ut hic:

CS1: 439a

Secundo modo, quando ponitur semiminor post minorem, ut hic:

Tertio modo, ⟨quando⟩ ponitur semiminor inter minores, ut hic:

Semiminor recta de semiminoribus perfectis et perfecta imperfici potest per minimam precedentem vel subsequentem. Per minimam precedentem, ut hic:

Per minimam subsequentem, ut hic:

---

24 *exemplum in marg., m. sec.* A2 ‖ 26 *exemplum in marg.* A2 ‖

# CHAPTER 17

Hanboys: The form of semiminors is thus. Whenever a semibrevis has an ascending stem bent over to the right side, it is called a semiminor, as here:

And it is whole because it cannot be ligated. But it can be perfected, that is, it can comprise in itself three minimae, as a semiminor before a semiminor or before a semiminor rest is perfect when semiminors are perfect. Nevertheless, this does not hold when semiminors are imperfect.

If semiminors are perfect or imperfect, a semiminor is always perfected before a *punctus perfectionis*. A semiminor before a semiminor, as is shown here:

Or before a semiminor rest, as here:

Or before a punctus, as here:

An imperfect semiminor nevertheless comprises in itself two equal minimae.

Some semiminors are recta, others are called alterae. The semiminor recta is that which comprises in itself one third of a perfect minor, and it occurs in three manners. In the first manner, when a semiminor is employed before a minor, as here:

In the second manner, when a semiminor is employed after a minor, as here:

In the third manner, when a semiminor is employed between minors, as here:

A semiminor recta and perfect (consisting of perfect semiminors) can be imperfected by a preceding or a following minima. By a preceding minima, as here:

By a following minima, as here:

Semiminor alterata duas seminimores in se continet in valore licet non in forma. Fit autem semiminor ⟨alterata⟩ tribus modis. Primo modo, quando due semiminores tantum vel valor unius semiminoris et una semiminor inveniuntur inter duas minores, vel inter minorem et minorem pausam, ut hic patet:

‖ Tunc prima semiminor recta vocatur, secunda vero alteratur, nisi per divisionem modi aliter distinguatur, ut hic:  CS1: 439b

Tunc prima semiminor vel valor primam minorem imperficit, et secunda ultimam. Vel quando due semiminores tantum vel valor unius semiminoris et una semiminor inveniuntur ante minorem, ut hic:

Tunc prima semiminor vel valor pro recta vocatur, et secunda alteratur.

Secundo modo, quando tres semiminores inveniuntur inter duas minores vel inter minorem et minorem pausam, et si inter primam semiminorem et secundam, vel inter valorem, sit punctus divisionis appositus, ut hic patet:

Tunc prima semiminor vel valor primam minorem imperficit, secunda vel valor ponitur pro recta, et tertia erit alterata.

Tertio ⟨modo⟩, quando plures semiminores inveniuntur inter duas minores. Computentur semper tres pro perfectione, et si due in fine remanserint, vel valor unius semiminoris et una semiminor, prima erit recta, secunda vero altera, et punctus alterationis ante semiminorem penultimam, vel ante valorem apponitur, ut hic patet in exemplo:

‖ Et si una semiminor in fine remanserit, vocatur recta, et ad perfectionem minoris subsequentis pertinet, ut hic: CS1: 440a

Si quatuor semiminores vel plures inveniantur inter duas minores, computentur semper tres pro perfectione, et si una in fine remanserit, recta voca-

---

1 semiminores]semiminor (es *in marg., m. sec.*) A2 ‖ 4 minores][⟦semi⟧minores A2 ‖ 6 *minor* 6.9 A2 ǀ *semiminor* 6.10 A2 ǀ *pausa semiminoris* 6.13 A2 ‖ 7 alterateratur A2 ‖ 9 *punctus om.* 9.12 A2 ‖ 18 *punctus om.* 18.10 A2 ‖ 26 *punctus om.* 26.11, 20 A2 ǀ *semiminor* 26.14 A2 ‖

An altered semiminor comprises in itself two semiminors in value but not in form. The altered semiminor occurs in three manners. In the first manner, when just two semiminors or the value of one semiminor and a semiminor are found between two minors or between a minor and a minor rest, as is shown here:

Then the first semiminor is called recta, while the second is altered, unless they are otherwise distinguished by a division of the mode, as here:

Then the first semiminor or its value imperfects the first minor; the second, the last. Or when just two semiminors or the value of one semiminor and a semiminor are found before a minor, as here: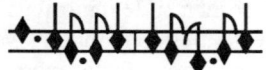

Then the first semiminor or its value is called recta, and the second is altered.

In the second manner, when three semiminors are found between two minors or between a minor and a minor rest, and if between the first and the second semiminor or between their values, a *punctus divisionis* is introduced, as is shown here:

Then the first semiminor or its value imperfects the first minor, the second or its value is employed as a recta, and the third will be altered.

In the third manner, when several semiminors are found between two minors. Three are always counted as a perfection, and if two should remain at the end or the value of one semiminor and one semiminor, the first will be recta, the second is altera, and a *punctus alterationis* is introduced before the penultimate semiminor or its value, as is shown here in an example:

And if one semiminor should remain at the end, it is called recta and pertains to the perfection of the following minor, as here:

If four or more semiminors are found between two minors, three are always counted as a perfection, and if one should remain at the end, it is

tur, et prima minor per semiminorem subsequentem imperficitur, ut hic:

Nisi punctus perfectionis post minorem sit appositus, ut hic patet:

5  Tunc prima minor per punctum perficitur, ultima semiminor ad perfectionem minoris subsequentis pertinet, si de minoribus perfectis sit.

Si de minoribus imperfectis tres semiminores vel plures inveniantur inter duas minores, computentur semper due semiminores pro minore. Si una in fine remanserit, et prima minor punctum perfectionis habeat postpositum, minor
10  cum puncto et semiminore sequente duas minores valet, ut hic:

Si secunda minor punctum perfectionis habeat postpositum, semiminor precedens ad eam pertinet, et minor cum puncto et semiminore precedente duas minores valet, ut hic: ‖
15

CS1:
440b

Et si una semiminor inveniatur inter duas minores et prima minor vel secunda punctum habeat postpositum, minor cum puncto et semiminore duas minores continet, ut hic:

20  Si utraque minor careat puncto et prima minor vel secunda ponitur inter duas semiminores, utraque minor est imperfecta et due semiminores minorem imperfectam valent, ut hic:

Si semiminor sit perfecta et alterata, diminui potest per minimam prece-
25  dentem vel subsequentem, vel per minimam precedentem et subsequentem, manente alterata. Si predicta semiminor diminuatur per minimam precedentem, prima semiminor illius alterationis per minimam imperficitur, ut hic:

---

2 *minor* 2.6, 11 A2 ‖ 3 punctus ⟦divisionis⟧ perfectionis A2 ‖ 4 *punctus ante* 4.1 A2 | *minor* 4.7 A2 ‖ 7 semiminores]semiminoribus A2 ‖ 8 minore brevi A2 ‖ 13 semiminori A2 (*idem* 17) ‖ 14 semiminores A2 ‖ 19 *punctus om.* 19.9 A2 ‖ 20 punctu A2 ‖

called recta, and the first minor is imperfected by the following semiminor, as here: [music notation]

Unless a *punctus perfectionis* is introduced after the minor, as is shown here:

Then the first minor is perfected by the punctus, and the last semiminor pertains to the perfection of the following minor if it should consist of perfect minors.

If when the minors are imperfect, three or more semiminors are found between two minors, two semiminors are always counted as a minor. If one should remain at the end and the first minor has a *punctus perfectionis* employed after it, the minor with the punctus and the following semiminor is worth two minors, as here: [music notation]

If the second minor has a *punctus perfectionis* employed after it, the preceding semiminor pertains to it, and the minor with the punctus and the preceding semiminor is worth two minors, as here: [music notation]

And if one semiminor is found between two minors and the first or the second minor has a *punctus perfectionis* employed after it, the minor with the punctus and the semiminor comprises two minors, as here: [music notation]

If each minor lacks a punctus and the first or the second minor is employed between two semiminors, each minor is imperfect, and the two semiminors are worth an imperfect minor, as here: [music notation]

If the semiminor is perfect and altered, it can be diminished by a preceding or following minima or by a preceding and following minima, remaining altered. If the aforesaid semiminor is diminished by a preceding minima, the first semiminor of the alteration is imperfected by the minima, as here:

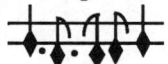

Si diminuatur per minimam subsequentem, secunda semiminor per minimam imperficitur:

Si diminuatur per minimam precedentem et subsequentem, prima minima primam semiminorem illius alterationis imperficit, secunda vero ultimam, ut hic: ‖

Et sicut semiminor ante semiminorem vel ante semiminorem pausam de semiminoribus perfectis est perfecta, ita semiminor ante semiminorem vel ante semiminorem pausam de semiminoribus imperfectis est imperfecta.

⟨CAPITULUM XVIII⟩

Hanboys: Forma minimarum talis est. Quandocunque nota formatur ad modum semibrevis habens tractum ascendentem retortum a parte sinistra, minima dicitur, ut hic:

Hac ratione: nam nota quadrata habens tractum a parte dextra descendentem vel ascendentem, longa dicitur, ut supra patet. Si habeat tractum ascendentem vel descendentem ex parte sinistra, brevis dicitur, ut supra patet. Ergo nota quadrata habens tractum a parte sinistra minor est nota quadrata tractum habente ex parte dextra. Sic in proposito nota formata ad modum losonge habens tractum ascendentem retortum a parte dextra semiminor dicitur. Et nota formata ad modum losonge habens tractum ascendentem retortum a parte sinistra, minor est ea, sicut brevis ad longam. Ergo talis figura dicitur minima. Et simplex est, quia ligari non potest. Nam quid individuum est.

Minimarum alie recte, alie altere nominantur. Minima recta tertia pars est semiminoris perfecte, et fit tribus modis. Primo modo, quando ponitur minima ante semiminorem, ut hic:

Secundo modo, quando ponitur minima post semiminorem, ut hic:

‖ Tertio modo, quando ponitur minima inter semiminores, ut hic:

---

4 prima seminimor minima A2 ‖ 18 parte ⟦dextra⟧ sinistra A2 ‖ 21 losensge A2 ‖ 22 losengie A2 ‖ 33 *minor* 33.6 A2 ‖

If it is diminished by a following minima, the second semiminor is imperfected by the minima:

If it is diminished by a preceding and following minima, the first minima imperfects the first semiminor of the alteration, and the second imperfects the last, as here:

And just as a semiminor before a semiminor or before a semiminor rest is perfect when semiminors are perfect, likewise a semiminor before a semiminor or before a semiminor rest is imperfect when semiminors are imperfect.

## CHAPTER 18

Hanboys: The form of minimae is thus. Whenever a note is formed in the manner of a semibrevis having an ascending stem bent over to the left side, it is called a minima, as here:

For this reason: for a square note having a descending or ascending stem on the right side is said to be a long, as is shown above. If it has a stem ascending or descending from the left side, it is said to be a brevis, as shown above. Therefore, a square note having a stem from the left side is smaller than a square note having its stem from the right side. So in the present instance, a note formed in the manner of a lozenge having an ascending stem bent over to the right side is said to be a semiminor. And a note formed in the manner of a lozenge having an ascending stem bent over to the left side is smaller than it, just as is the brevis in relation to the longa. Therefore, such a figure is said to be the minima. And it is whole because it cannot be ligated. Moreover, it is indivisible.

Some minimae are named rectae, others alterae. The minima recta is one third of a perfect semiminor, and it occurs in three manners. In the first manner, when a minima is employed before a semiminor, as here:

In the second manner, when a minima is employed after a semiminor, as here:

In the third manner, when a minima is employed between semiminors, as here:

Minima alterata duas minimas continet in valore, non tamen in forma. Et fit tribus modis. Primo modo, quando due minime tantum inveniuntur inter duas seminimores, vel inter seminimorem et seminimorem pausam, ut hic:

Tunc prima minima recta vocatur, secunda quoque alteratur, nisi per divisionem modi aliter distinguatur, ut hic patet:

Tunc prima minima primam seminimorem imperficit, secunda vero ultimam. Vel quando due minime tantum inveniuntur ante seminimorem, ut hic patet:

Tunc prima minima recta vocatur et secunda alteratur.

Secundo modo, quando tres minime ponuntur inter duas seminimores, et si inter primam minimam et secundam punctus divisionis sit appositus, ut hic:

Tunc prima primam seminimorem imperficit, secunda recta vocatur, et tertia alteratur. ‖

Tertio modo, quando plures minime inveniuntur inter duas seminimores. Computentur ergo tres semper pro perfectione, et si due minime in fine remanserint, prima erit recta, secunda vero altera, et punctus alterationis ante minimam penultimam apponitur, ut hic:

CS1: 442a

Et si una minima in fine remanserit, recta vocatur, et ad perfectionem seminoris subsequentis pertinet, ut hic:

Si quatuor minime vel plures inveniantur inter duas seminimores, computentur semper tres pro perfectione, et si una in fine remanserit, vocatur recta, et prima seminimor per minimam subsequentem imperficitur, ut hic patet:

Nisi punctus perfectionis post primam seminimorem apponitur, ut hic:

---

7 *punctus om.* 7.5 A2 ‖ 11 *exemplum ut in* 318.16 A2 ‖

The altered minima comprises two minimae in value but not in form. And it occurs in three manners. In the first manner, when just two minimae are found between two semiminors or between a semiminor and a semiminor rest, as here:

Then the first minima is called recta, and the second is altered, unless they are otherwise distinguished by a division of the mode, as is shown here:

Then the first minima imperfects the first semiminor, while the second imperfects the last. Or when just two minimae are found before a semiminor, as is shown here:

Then the first minima is called recta, and the second is altered.

In the second manner, when three minimae are employed between two semiminors and if between the first and the second minima a *punctus divisionis* is employed, as here:

Then the first imperfects the first semiminor, the second is called recta, and the third is altered.

In the third manner, when several minimae are found between two semiminors. Three are always counted as a perfection. And if two minimae should remain at the end, the first will be recta, the second altera, and a *punctus alterationis* is introduced before the penultimate minima, as here:

And if one minima should remain at the end, it is called recta, and it pertains to the perfection of the following semiminor, as here:

If four or more minimae are found between two semiminors, three are always counted as a perfection, and if one should remain at the end, it is called recta, and the first semiminor is imperfected by the following minima, as is shown here:

Unless a *punctus perfectionis* is introduced after the first semiminor, as here:

Tunc prima semiminor per punctum perficitur, ultima minima ad perfectionem semiminoris subsequentis pertinet, si sit de semiminoribus perfectis.

Si de semiminoribus imperfectis tres minime vel plures inveniuntur inter duas semiminores, computentur ergo semper due minime pro semiminore et
5 si una in fine remanserit, et prima semiminor punctum perfectionis habeat  ||  CS1: postpositum, semiminor cum puncto et minima sequente duas semiminores  442b valet, ut hic:

Si secunda semiminor punctum perfectionis habeat postpositum, minima
10 precedens ad eam pertinet, et semiminor cum puncto et minima precedente duas semiminores valet, ut hic:

Si una minima inveniatur inter duas semiminores, et prima semiminor vel secunda punctum perfectionis habeat postpositum, semiminor cum puncto et
15 minima duas valet semiminores, ut hic:

Si utraque semiminor careat puncto, et prima semiminor vel secunda ponitur inter duas minimas, utraque semiminor est imperfecta, et due minime semiminorem imperfectam valent, ut hic:
20

### ⟨CAPITULUM XIX⟩

⟨Hanboys⟩: Sciendum est quod de ligatis et non ligatis idem est iudicium in valore temporum.

Franco: Sciendum est quod quilibet modus acceptus sine ligabilis littera
25 est, excepto illo qui procedit ex omnibus longis. ⟨Hanboys⟩: Omnes note que super unam sillabam seu dictionem ponuntur in sillabam ligari debent si commode possent.

---

4 semiminore]semiminori A2 || 6 punctu A2 || 16 *punctus om.* 16.9 A2 || 20 *fig. bis* 20.1–4 A2 || 24 Franco *in marg., m. sec.* A2 ||

Then the first semiminor is perfected by the punctus, and the last minima pertains to the perfection of the following semiminor, if it should consist of perfect semiminors.

If when the semiminors are imperfect, three minimae or more are found between two semiminors, two minimae are therefore always counted as a semiminor, and if one should remain at the end and the first semiminor has a *punctus perfectionis* employed after it, the semiminor with the punctus and the following minima is worth two semiminors, as here:

If the second semiminor has a *punctus perfectionis* employed after it, the preceding minima pertains to it, and the semiminor with the punctus and the preceding minima is worth two semiminors, as here:

If one minima is found between two semiminors, and the first semiminor or the second has a *punctus perfectionis* employed after it, the semiminor with the punctus and the minima is worth two semiminors, as here:

If both semiminors lack a punctus, and the first or the second semiminor is employed between two minimae, each semiminor is imperfect, and the two minimae are worth an imperfect semiminor, as here:

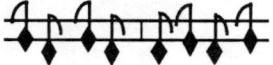

## CHAPTER 19

Hanboys: It must be known that the same is true for ligated and non-ligated notes, in the value of their tempora.

Franco: It must be known that any accepted mode can be ligated without words, except the one that proceeds exclusively by longs.[143] Hanboys: All notes that are employed over one syllable or utterance ought to be ligated in the syllable, if it can be easily done.

---

[143]Franco, *Ars cantus mensurabilis*, cap. 10, sent. 8 (ed. Reaney and Gilles), p. 60.

⟨Franco⟩: Ligaturarum alia cum proprietate, alia sine proprietate, alia cum ‖ opposita proprietate. ⟨Hanboys⟩: Hiis enim tribus principia omnium ligaturarum cognoscuntur.

⟨Franco⟩: Proprietas est nota primarie inventionis ligature, a plana musica data, in principio illius.

Omnis ligatura cuius secundus punctus altior est primus, carens omni tractu a primo puncto, cum proprietate dicitur, et est prima brevis, ut hic patet: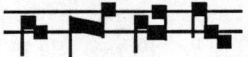

Omnis ligatura cuius primus punctus altior est secundo, tractum gerens a primo puncto descendentem, cum proprietate dicitur, ut hic:

Omnis ligatura cum proprietate primam facit brevem.

⟨Hanboys⟩: Tenet regula si ligatura sit descendens ut per punctos quadratos vel per obliquitatem, habens in principio sui tractum descendentem, ut supra patet.

⟨Hanboys⟩: Nulla nuda obliquitas per se ligatura dici potest. Et est ratio, quia oblique breves dummodo in sola obliquitate manent, vel semibreves non sunt nisi in uno corpore. Inconveniens igitur est directe eas ligare, ex quo ligatura duo corpora ad minus requirit. Maneat igitur obliquitas per se simplex in qua breves et semibreves obliquantur, non ligantur. Plures tamen obliquitates ligate ligaturam adinvicem ut hic constituunt:

---

7 cum]sine A2 ‖ 11 cum *bis* A2 ‖

Franco: Some ligatures are said to be with propriety, others are without propriety, others are with opposite propriety.[144] Hanboys: The beginnings of all ligatures are understood in these three ways.

Franco: Propriety is the note first encountered at the beginning in a ligature, as given by plainchant.[145]

Every ligature whose second notehead is higher than the first, lacking any stem on the first notehead, is said to be with propriety, and the first note is a brevis, as is shown here:[146]

Every ligature whose first notehead is higher than the second, with a descending stem on the first notehead, is said to be with propriety, as here:[147]

Every ligature with propriety makes the first note a brevis.[148]

Hanboys: This rule holds whether the ligature descends by square noteheads or an oblique figure, when it has a descending stem at the beginning, as is shown above.[149]

Hanboys: A plain oblique figure cannot in itself be said to be a ligature. And this is the reason: because oblique breves and semibreves—as long as they remain in a solitary oblique figure—cannot exist except in one body. It is therefore inappropriate to ligate them directly, because a ligature requires at least two bodies.[150] An oblique figure in which there are oblique breves or semibreves therefore remains whole, not ligated.[151] Nevertheless, several oblique figures ligated to each other constitute a ligature, as here:[152]

---

[144]Franco, *Ars cantus mensurabilis*, cap. 7, sent. 6 (ed. Reaney and Gilles), p. 44; see also Handlo, *Regule*, Rubric VI, Maxim 1 (120.5–6).

[145]Franco, *Ars cantus mensurabilis*, cap. 7, sent. 15 (ed. Reaney and Gilles), p. 45.

[146]Handlo, *Regule*, Rubric VI, Rule I (120.8–10).

[147]Handlo, Rub. VI, Rule III (120.17–20) and Rule V (122.20–24).

[148]Franco, *Ars cantus mensurabilis*, cap. 7, sent. 26 (ed. Reaney and Gilles), p. 50; see also Handlo, *Regule*, Rubric VI, Maxim (122.10).

[149]Handlo, *Regule*, Rubric VI, Maxim 6 (122.12–13).

[150]Two breves or two semibreves that are joined in descent must be in an oblique figure.

[151]Handlo, *Regule*, Rubric VI, Maxim 7 (124.2–6).

[152]Handlo, *Regule*, Rubric VI, Rule VI (124.8–10).

Obliquitas sola descendens habens in principio tractum descendentem, cum proprietate obliquitas dici debet, ut hic: ‖

⟨Franco⟩: Omnis ligatura cuius secundus punctus est altior primo, tractum habens a primo puncto descendentem a parte sinistra vel a parte dextra, quod magis proprium est, sine proprietate dicitur, ut hic:

⟨Hanboys⟩: Licet supra primum punctum ligetur obliquitas ascendens vel descendens, ut hic:

⟨Franco⟩: Omnis ligatura cuius primus punctus altior est secundo, et primus punctus caret omni tractu, id est proprietate, dicitur longa, ut hic patet in sequenti exemplo:

⟨Hanboys⟩: Si etiam descendendo plures puncti primum punctum sequantur in ligatura vel obliquitas, et primus omni tractu caret, ligatura sine proprietate dicitur, ut supra patet.

⟨Franco⟩: Omnis ligatura sine proprietate primam facit longam.

⟨Hanboys⟩: Tenet regula, si ligatura sit descendens, ut per punctos quadratos sive per punctum quadratum, vel per obliquitatem, in principio sui tractulo carente, ut supra patet.

Post obliquitatem ⟨ascendentem⟩ nichil potest ei ligari, nec adiungi, nisi plica. Superfluum vero est imponere obliquitatem ascendentem, plica carente.

A solitary descending oblique figure having a descending stem at the beginning ought to be said to be an oblique figure with propriety, as here:[153]

Franco: Every ligature whose second notehead is higher than the first, having a stem on the first notehead descending from the left or from the right side, which is more normal, is said to be without propriety, as here:[154]

Hanboys: It is permitted to ligate an ascending or descending oblique figure above the first notehead, as here:[155]

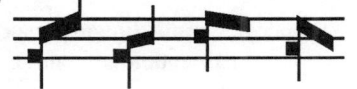

Franco: Every ligature whose first notehead is higher than the second and the first notehead lacks any stem, that is, propriety, is said to be a longa, as is shown in the following example:[156]

Hanboys: If in descending, several noteheads follow the first notehead, whether in ligature or as an oblique figure, and the first lacks any stem, the ligature is said to be without propriety, as shown above.[157]

Franco: Every ligature without propriety makes the first note a longa.[158]

Hanboys: The rule holds if the ligature, lacking a stem at its beginning, descends either by square noteheads or by a square notehead or by an oblique figure, as shown above.[159]

After an ascending oblique figure, nothing can be ligated or added to it except a plica. It is superfluous to employ an ascending oblique figure lacking a plica.[160]

---

[153]Handlo, *Regule*, Rubric VI, Rule VII (124.12–15).
[154]Handlo, *Regule*, Rubric VI, Maxim 7a (124.17–19).
[155]Handlo, *Regule*, Rubric VI, Rule VIII (124.21–23).
[156]Handlo, *Regule*, Rubric VI, Rule IX (126.2–4).
[157]Handlo, *Regule*, Rubric VI, Rule X (126.6–9).
[158]Handlo, *Regule*, Rubric VI, Maxim 8 (126.11).
[159]Handlo, *Regule*, Rubric VI, Rule XIV (126.25–128.5).
[160]Handlo, *Regule*, Rubric VI, Maxim 9 (128.11–13).

Ante obliquitatem ascendentem vel descendentem plicatam potest nota
ligari, ut hic: ‖

CS1: 444a

Et post, ut hic:

Obliquitas quoque descendens, si sola sit, cum plica vel sine, semper potest poni, ut hic:

⟨Franco⟩: Omnis ligatura ascendens vel descendens tractum gerens a primo puncto ascendentem, cum opposita proprietate dicitur, ut hic patet:

Omnis ligatura cum opposita proprietate dat duas primas semibreves. Omnes medie sunt breves, nisi per oppositam proprietatem defendantur, ut hic:

Tunc prima de mediis est semibrevis. Et ratio est, quia nulla semibrevis potest esse sola.

⟨Franco⟩: Unde notandum quod plures longe ligari non possunt, nisi in binaria ligatura que est sine proprietate et cum perfectione. Nec adhuc in tali loco sunt vitiose si non ligentur, eo quod longa nunquam alibi cum longa ligabilis invenitur. Ex quo sequitur quod vehementer errant qui tres longas aliqua oratione, ut in tenoribus, adinvicem ligant. Sed et plus qui inter duas

---

2 ligari]plicari A2 ‖ 20 nunquam]nuncquam A2 ‖ 22 tenoribus [[ut]] A2 ‖

A note can be ligated before an ascending or descending plicated oblique figure, as here:[161]

And after,[162] as here: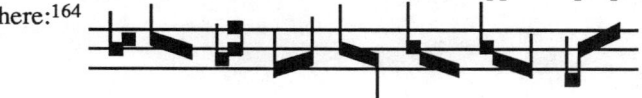

A descending oblique figure, if it is solitary, always can be employed with or without a plica, as here:[163]

Franco: Every ascending or descending ligature with a stem ascending from the first notehead is said to be with opposite propriety, as is shown here:[164]

Every ligature with opposite propriety gives the first two notes as semibreves.[165] All middle notes are breves, unless this is prevented by opposite propriety, as here:[166]

Then the first of the middle notes is a semibrevis, and the reason is because no semibrevis can be solitary.[167]

Franco: On which account, it must be noted that several longae cannot be ligated except in a binary ligature that is without propriety and with perfection. Nor in such a place are they defective if they are not ligated, because in no other place is a longa found ligated with a longa. From which it follows that those who ligate together three longae in some phrase, as in tenors, err exceedingly—and even more so those who ligate a longa between

---

[161]Handlo, *Regule*, Rubric VI, Rule XV (128.7–9).

[162]Placing anything except a plica after an ascending oblique ligature has just been forbidden by Hanboys (quoting Handlo) but, in clear contradiction, it is permitted by this rule and example.

[163]Handlo, *Regule*, Rubric VI, Rule XVIII (130.2–4), with the excision of a phrase about the ascending form.

[164]Handlo, *Regule*, Rubric VI, Rule XIX (130.6–8).

[165]Handlo, *Regule*, Rubric VI, Maxim 11 (132.11).

[166]Handlo, *Regule*, Rubric VII, Rule I (134.3–5).

[167]Handlo, *Regule*, Rubric VII, Maxim 1 (134.10).

breves longam ligant, || cum in dispositione mediarum visum sit prius quod omnes medie brevientur.  CS1: 444b

⟨Hanboys⟩: Ista regula—"Nulla semibrevis" et cetera—habet intelligi de semibrevibus ligatis, sed de ⟨non⟩ ligatis nequaquam, quia tres semibreves cum tribus brevibus misceri possunt et quelibet harum trium brevium per punctum perfectionis perfici potest, et tunc tres semibreves faciunt perfectionem, ut hic: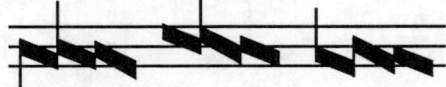

Vel potest illa regula alio modo intelligi. Nulla semibrevis potest esse sola, id est nulla semibrevis potest esse quin pertinet ad perfectionem alicuius brevis, vel pertinet ad aliam semibrevem sequentem, et sic hee due semibreves brevem perfectam valent, ut supra patet.

Ligature obliquitatum sic formantur, ut patet:

Obliquitas in medio ligature descendens semper erit, non ascendens, ut supra patet.

### ⟨CAPITULUM XX⟩

⟨Franco⟩: Finis ligaturarum alia cum perfectione, alia sine perfectione dicitur. Omnis ligatura cuius ultimus punctus recte stat supra penultimum cum perfectione dicitur, ut hic:

---

1 longam⟦t⟧ A2 || 3 semibrevis ⟦habet⟧ A2 || 12 imperfectam A2 ||

two breves, since in regard to the disposition of middle notes, it has been previously seen that all middle notes are made breves.[168]

Hanboys: This rule, "No semibrevis et cetera," has to be observed for ligated semibreves but never for unligated ones, because three semibreves can be mixed with three breves, and any one of these three breves can be perfected by a *punctus perfectionis*, and then three semibreves make a perfection, as here:[169]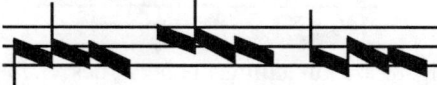

Or that rule can be observed in another manner. No semibrevis can be solitary, that is, there can be no semibrevis that does not pertain to the perfection of some brevis or pertain to some following semibrevis, and these two semibreves are worth a perfect brevis, as shown above.

Ligatures of oblique figures are formed thus, as is shown:[170]

An oblique figure in the middle of a ligature will always be descending, not ascending, as is shown above.[171]

## CHAPTER 20

Franco: The ends of some ligatures are said to be with perfection, others without perfection.[172] Every ligature whose last notehead stands normally above the penultimate is said to be with perfection, as here:[173]

---

[168]Franco, *Ars cantus mensurabilis*, cap. 10, sent. 2–5 (ed. Reaney and Gilles), p. 59; see also Handlo, *Regule*, Rubric VI, Rule XI (126.13–15).

[169]Hanboys continues here as if the preceding paragraph from the *Ars cantus mensurabilis* had not been interpolated. In light of *ars nova* practice, he makes an essential correction to the fundamental *ars antiqua* rule forbidding the use of a single semibrevis not immediately paired with another. For the corresponding passage concerned with the longa and brevis, see the final three examples of chapter 7 (224.13–226.5).

[170]Handlo, *Regule*, Rubric VII, Rule III (134.12–13).

[171]Handlo, *Regule*, Rubric VII, Maxim 2 (134.19–20).

[172]Franco, *Ars cantus mensurabilis*, cap. 7, sent. 7 (ed. Reaney and Gilles), p. 44.

[173]Handlo, *Regule*, Rubric VIII, Rule I (136.4–6).

Omnis ligatura cuius ultimus punctus descendit quadratus in fine ligature sub penultimam cum perfectione dicitur, ut hic patet in exemplo:

‖ Omnis ligatura cuius ultimus punctus stat directo capite, sine perfectione dicitur, ut hic patet:

Omnis ligatura cum perfectione ultimam facit longam. Omnis ligatura sine perfectione ultimam facit brevem, nisi per oppositam proprietatem defendatur.

⟨Hanboys⟩: In fine etiam cuiuslibet ligature vel obliquitatis semibreves due coniungi deorsum possunt, absente plica, ut hic patet:

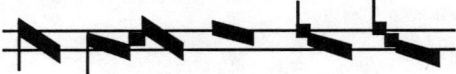

Franco: Omnis ligatura cuius ultimus punctus descendit in obliquo sine perfectione dicitur, ut hic patet in exemplo:

⟨Hanboys⟩: Si due ultime plane note in uno corpore obliquo, tam ascendentes quam descendentes inveniuntur, sine perfectione dicuntur, ut hic patet:

Hanboys: Denique vitiosum est ligabiles notas non ligari, nonligabilesque ligari.

⟨Hanboys⟩: In ligaturis nunquam est plica, nisi in fine.

Every ligature whose last square notehead descends at the end of the ligature below the penultimate is said to be with perfection, as is shown here in an example:[174]

Every ligature whose last notehead stands with its head turned is said to be without perfection, as is shown here:[175]

Every ligature with perfection makes its last notehead a longa.[176] Every ligature without perfection makes its last notehead a brevis, unless it is prevented by opposite propriety.

Hanboys: At the end of any ligature or oblique figure, two semibreves can be conjoined downwards, lacking a plica, as is shown here:[177]

Franco: Every ligature whose last notehead descends obliquely is said to be without perfection, as is shown here in an example:[178]

Hanboys: If the last two distinct notes are found in one oblique body, whether ascending or descending, they are said to be without perfection, as this shows:

Hanboys: Finally, it is defective not to ligate notes that can be ligated or to ligate notes that cannot be ligated.[179]

Hanboys: In ligatures there is never a plica except at the end.[180]

---

[174]Handlo, *Regule*, Rubric VIII, Rule II (136.8–10) and Rule IV (136.19–22).

[175]Handlo, *Regule*, Rubric VIII, Rule V (136.24–26).

[176]Handlo, *Regule*, Rubric VIII, Maxim 1 (136.17).

[177]Handlo, *Regule*, Rubric VI, Rule XXI (130.17–19) and Rubric IX, Rule VI (142.22–144.2), where two or more semibreves may be conjoined downward or upward.

[178]For this paragraph and the following, see Handlo, *Regule*, Rubric VIII, Rule VI (138.2–4).

[179]Handlo, *Regule*, Rubric VIII, Maxim 2 (140.2–3); see also Franco, *Ars cantus mensurabilis*, cap. 10, sent. 1 (ed. Reaney and Gilles), p. 59.

[180]Handlo, *Regule*, Rubric X, Maxim 1 (152.6–7).

Franco: Quandocunque in fine ligaturarum punctus quadratus ascendendo vel descendendo plicatur, pro longa habetur, ut hic patet:

‖ Quandocunque due note tam ascendendo quam descendendo uno corpore plicantur, pro brevibus dicuntur:

⟨Hanboys⟩: Tunc tenet ista regula in ligaturis ascendentibus cum tractulo ex parte sinistra descendente, ut supra. Fallit tamen cum opposita proprietate, ut hic patet plane:

Et in ligatura descendente, prima nota tractu carente, ut in sequentibus patet figuris manifeste hic:

⟨Hanboys⟩: In ligatura ascendente duplex longa cum longa ligari potest, ut hic:

Et potest longa plicari ascendendo et duplex longa descendendo, ut hic patet:

Longa cum duplice longa, ut hic:

---

1–2 ascendendendo A2 ‖ 3 *tractus pr. om.* 3.3. A2 ‖ 20 duplice]2ª A2 ‖

Franco: Whenever at the end of ligatures a square notehead, ascending or descending, is plicated, it is taken as a longa, as is shown here:[181]

Whenever two notes in one body, whether ascending or descending, are plicated, they are said to be breves:[182]

Hanboys: This rule holds in ascending ligatures with a little stem descending from the left side, as above. It fails, nevertheless, with opposite propriety, as is plainly shown here:

Nor in descending ligatures when the first note lacks a stem, as is clearly shown here in the following shapes:

Hanboys: In an ascending ligature, a duplex longa can be ligated with a longa, as here:[183]

And the longa can be plicated when ascending, and the duplex longa when descending, as is shown here:[184]

A longa with a duplex longa, as here:[185]

---

[181]Handlo, *Regule*, Rubric X, Rule I (152.9–10).

[182]Handlo, *Regule*, Rubric X, Rule II (152.15–18).

[183]Handlo, *Regule*, Rubric VI, Rule XIII (126.21–23).

[184]According to Handlo in Rule VII of Rubric X (154.10–14), there are circumstances in which the ascending longa with plica at the end of this ligature would be converted into a longa erecta; one suspects that would not have been true here, where the longa has a short stem of plication on the left.

[185]This form is not allowed by Handlo, *Regule*, Rubric VI, Rule XIII (126.22).

Et potest longa plicari descendendo et duplex longa ascendendo: || 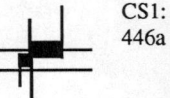 CS1: 446a

    In ligatura descendente, duplex longa cum longa ligari potest, ut hic patet:
5 Longa cum duplice longa, ut hic:
    In ligatura ascendente duplex longa cum brevibus et semibrevibus ligari potest, ut hic patet:

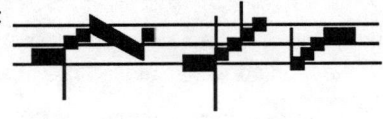

    Et in ligatura descendente, ut hic patet:
10 Item, sic:

⟨CAPITULUM XXI⟩

    ⟨Franco⟩: Pausa est omissio vocis in debita quantitate alicuius modi
15 facta. Pausationum sex sunt species. Prima pausa est trium temporum, id est trium brevium, que longam perfectam valet. Secunda vero duorum, id est longa valet imperfectam. Tertia unius temporis, id est valet brevem perfectam. Hodie et imperfectam, quia cuiusmodi mensure est brevis, eiusmodi mensure est sua pausa. Quarta duarum partium unius temporis, id est valet
20 semi||brevem maiorem, que brevem imperfectam valet. Quinta tertie partis unius temporis, ⟨id est valet semibrevem minorem⟩, que semibrevem valet

CS1: 446b

---

3 ligari]plicari A2 || 5 duplice]2ª A2 || 8 *duplex longa*]*obliquitas descendens* 8.3 A2 || 10 *duplex longa ult.*]*obliquitas descendens* A2 || 21 semibrevem (*sec.*)]brevem A2 ||

And the longa can be plicated when descending, and the duplex longa when ascending:[186]

In a descending ligature, the duplex longa can be ligated with a longa, as is shown here:[187]
The longa with a duplex longa, as here:[188]
In an ascending ligature, a duplex longa can be ligated with breves and semibreves, as is shown here:[189]

And in a descending ligature, as is shown here:[190]

The same, thus:[191]

## CHAPTER 21

Franco: A rest is the withholding of voice in a due quantity made according to some mode.[192] There are six types of rests. The first rest is of three tempora, that is, of three breves that are worth a perfect longa. The second is of two; that is, it is worth an imperfect longa. The third is of one tempus; that is, it is worth a perfect brevis. Today, it is also worth an imperfect brevis because however the brevis is measured, its rest is measured the same way. The fourth is of two thirds of one tempus; that is, it is worth a major semibrevis, which is worth an imperfect brevis. The fifth is worth the third part of one tempus; that is, it is worth a minor semibrevis, which is worth a

---

[186]Handlo, *Regule*, Rubric X, Rule VI (154.6–8).

[187]Handlo, *Regule*, Rubric VI, Rule XII (126.17–19).

[188]Handlo, *Regule*, Rubric VI, Rule XII (126.17–19).

[189]Handlo, *Regule*, Rubric VIII, Rule IX (138.13–15), only in respect to duplex longae and breves, and only with the duplex longa first.

[190]Handlo, *Regule*, Rubric VIII, Rule X (138.13–15), and see also the more limited Rule VII (138.6–8).

[191]That is, as in the preceding example but now including semibreves.

[192]Franco, *Ars cantus mensurabilis*, cap. 9, sent. 2 (ed. Reaney and Gilles), p. 54.

perfectam. Sexta et ultima nullius temporis, sed potius immensurabilis appellatur. Causa inventionis cuius fuit ut ubicunque inveniretur, penultimam notam designaret esse longam, licet penultima brevis vel semibrevis foret.

5  ⟨Franco⟩: Pausa trium temporum, id est longe perfecte, quatuor lineas tangit, tria spatia occupans. Pausa vero duorum temporum, id est longe imperfecte, tres lineas tangit, duo spatia occupans. ⟨Pausa unius temporis, id est brevis, duo lineas tangit, unum spatium occupans.⟩ Pausa duarum partium unius temporis, id est semibrevis maioris, duas partes unius spatii tan-
10 git. Idem valet hodie pausa brevis imperfecte. Pausa vero tertie partis unius temporis, id est semibrevis minoris, tertiam partem unius spatii tangit. Idem valet a modernis semibrevis perfecta. Pausa vero que immensurabilis dicitur, id est finis punctorum, omnes lineas et omnia spatia tangit. Forme hic earum convenienter apparent:
15

⟨Hanboys⟩: Ab antiquis talis modus utebatur pausarum. A modernis aliquantulum differt. Nam pause longe perfecte et longe imperfecte atque brevis ut supra. Pausa tamen semibrevis perfecte unam lineam tangit, dimidiam partem spatii sub et supra occupans. Pausa vero semibrevis imperfecte unam
20 lineam tangit dimidiam partem spatii sub occupans. Pausa etiam minoris unam lineam tangit dimidiam partem spatii supra occupans. Pausa vero semiminoris tangit unam lineam dimidiam partem spatii supra occupans et est retorta a parte dextra. Pausa etiam minime tangit unam lineam dimidiam

---

1 inmensurabilis A2 ‖ 15   A2 ‖

perfect semibrevis. The sixth and last is of no tempus, but rather is called immensurable. The reason for its invention came about because wherever it is found, it designates the penultimate note to be a longa, although the penultimate may be a brevis or semibrevis.[193]

Franco: The rest of three tempora, that is, of a perfect longa, touches four lines, occupying three spaces. The rest of two tempora, that is, of the imperfect longa, touches three lines, occupying two spaces. The rest of one tempus, that is, of a brevis, touches two lines, occupying one space. The rest of two thirds of a tempus, that is, of a major semibrevis, touches two thirds of a space. Today, the rest of an imperfect brevis is the same. The rest of a third part of one tempus, that is, of a minor semibrevis, touches the third part of one space. For the moderns, the rest of a perfect semibrevis is worth the same. The rest that is called immensurable, that is, the endline, touches all lines and spaces. The forms of these appropriately appear here:[194]

Hanboys: This manner of rests was used by the older singers. For the moderns, it differs slightly.[195] The rests of the perfect long, imperfect long, and brevis are as above. Nevertheless, the rest of a perfect semibrevis touches one line, occupying one half of a space above and below. The rest of an imperfect semibrevis touches one line, occupying one half of the space below. The rest of a minor touches one line, occupying half of the space above. The rest of a semiminor touches one line, occupying half of the space above and bent over to the right side. The rest of a minima touches one line,

---

[193]Handlo, *Regule*, Rubric XII, Maxim 1 (160.3–11). Hanboys inserts a comment concerning modern practice after the statements about the third, fourth, and fifth kinds of rest.

[194]Handlo, *Regule*, Rubric XII, Rule I (160.16–162.2). Hanboys inserts a comment concerning modern practice after the descriptions of the fourth and fifth kinds of rest.

[195]Hanboys describes eight rests according to the moderns, which pertain to a six-figure system descending from the longa to a minima three levels below the semibrevis. Six of the rests are entirely conventional, including the form of the semiminima (i.e., Hanboys's semiminor), with its hook to the right. The rest of smallest value (Hanboys's minima) has a hook to the left.

Hanboys gives a distinctive form extending both above and below the line to the perfect semibrevis, while the standard semibrevis rest is given to the imperfect semibrevis. This form of perfect semibrevis rest, while apparently not unique to England, is prevalent there. While not appearing in Handlo's treatise (the illustration in CS, 1:400b is in error), it is found in the *Quatuor principalia* (CS, 3:350a; CS, 4:272b); the anonymous English

partem spatii supra occupans et est retorta a parte sinistra. Pausa vero finis punctorum omnes lineas et omnia spatia tangit, ut supra. Forme earum hic convenienter patent: ||

5   Adhuc alias pausas composuit frater Robertus de Brunham sic dicendo: pausa large perfecte quatuor lineas tangit, tria spatia occupans et dimidiam partem spatii supra quartam lineam. Pausa large imperfecte quatuor lineas tangit, tria spatia occupans. Pausa longe perfecte tres lineas tangit, duo spatia occupans et dimidiam partem spatii supra tertiam lineam. Pausa longe
10  imperfecte tangit tres lineas, duo spatia occupans. Pausa brevis perfecte tangit duas lineas, unum spatium occupans et dimidiam partem spatii supra secundam lineam. Pausa brevis imperfecte tangit duas lineas, unum spatium

---

1 octupans A2 || 4 *fine punctorum om.* A2 || 7 pause A2 ||

occupying half of the space above and bent over to the left side. The rest of an endline touches all lines and spaces, as above. The forms of these are appropriately shown here:

Also, Brother Robert of Brunham composed other rests,[196] speaking thus: the rest of a perfect larga touches four lines, occupying three spaces and half of the space above the fourth line. The rest of an imperfect larga touches four lines, occupying three spaces. The rest of a perfect longa touches three lines, occupying two spaces and half of the space above the third line. The rest of an imperfect longa touches three lines, occupying two spaces. The rest of a perfect brevis touches two lines, occupying one space and half of the space above the second line. The rest of an imperfect brevis

---

*Tractatus de figuris* (ed. Gilles and Reaney), p. 49; item 2 of **GB**-Lbl, Additional 21455 (*Ars nova* [ed. Reaney et al.], p. 77; see also the Introduction, pp. 2–3, n. 6); and also in an anonymous compilation of unknown origin that is transmitted with Petrus de Sancto Dionysio, *Tractatus de musica* (ed. Michels), p. 163. The same form is found in the anonymous *De musica mensurabili* (ed. Sweeney), p. 48, representing the value of two-thirds of a perfect brevis. See also Sweeney's discussion (p. 21) of the shape; and Lefferts, *The Motet in England*, pp. 151–52.

[196]From this discussion of rests, it is apparent that Brunham's mensural system employed six figures: the larga, longa, brevis, semibrevis, minor, and semiminor. Although Hanboys says that the rests prescribed by Brunham for perfect and imperfect semibreves, minors, and semiminors are just "as above," the context does not establish that minor and semiminor are Brunham's preferred terminology for his two smallest figures; he is likely to have called them simpla or crocheta (see chapter 2 [188.1] and the Introduction, pp. 54–55 and 63). Brunham's forms for rests of a perfect larga, longa, and brevis are distinctive in their extension half a space above the imperfect form; he may have derived these from the corresponding (and more widespread) English relationship of perfect to imperfect semibrevis rest. The *Tractatus de figuris* (ed. Gilles and Reaney), p. 49, and item 2 of **GB**-Lbl, Additional 21455 (*Ars nova* [ed. Reaney et al.], p. 77; see also the Introduction, pp. 2–3, n. 6) offer a similar form for the rest of a perfect brevis, although in the *Tractatus* the extension is in the opposite direction, halfway into the space below. The *Tractatus* (ed. Gilles and Reaney), p. 49, observes that "De pausis brevium est sciendum quod pausa brevis perfectae in utroque modo perfecto continet unum spatium et medietatem alterius secundum figurantes modernos (Concerning the rest of a brevis, it must be known that the rest of a perfect brevis in either perfect mode comprises one space and half of another according to modern notators)." For examples of Brunham's rests in the practical sources, see Lefferts, *The Motet in England*, p. 152.

occupans. Pausa semibrevis imperfecte et perfecte, minoris et semiminoris, ut supra. Forme earum convenienter hic patent: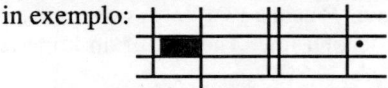

Adhuc alio modo restat dicere de pausis, quia quelibet nota pausam sibi
5 correspondentem non habet. Nam pausa large tangit quatuor lineas, tria spatia occupans et dimidiam partem spatii supra quartam lineam, et perfici et imperfici potest veluti larga, quia large correspondet. Ergo cuiusmodi nature est large, huiusmodi nature est sua pausa. Ergo pausa perfici potest et imperfici atque diminui, veluti larga cui correspondet. Potest etiam pausa large
10 perfici, ut pausa ante largam vel ante largam pausam, vel ante punctum, ut hic patet in exemplo:

‖ Et imperfici potest atque diminui veluti larga, ut supra dictum est.
Pausa duplicis longe tangit quatuor lineas, tria spatia occupans et perfici
15 potest et imperfici, alterari atque diminui, veluti duplex longa cui correspondet. Nam perfici potest ut pausa ante duplicem longam vel ante duplicem longam pausam, vel ante punctum, ut hic patet:

CS1: 447b

Pausa longe tangit tres lineas, duo spatia occupans. Et perfici potest et
20 imperfici, alterari atque diminui, veluti longa cui correspondet longa pausa. Potest etiam perfici ut pausa ante longam, vel ante longam pausam, vel ante punctum, ut hic patet:

Pausa brevis tangit duas lineas, unum spatium occupans. Et perfici potest
25 atque imperfici, alterari atque diminui, veluti brevis cui correspondet. Et potest pausa brevis perfici, ut pausa ante brevem, vel ante pausam brevem, vel ante punctum, ut hic:

---

3 *pausa om.* 3.1, 3 A2 ‖ 5 corespondentem A2 ‖ 9 corespondet A2 ‖ 12 *duplex longa* 12.2 A2 ‖ 20 longa (*pr.*)]lon⟦r⟧ga A2 ‖ 26 ut]vel A2 ‖

touches two lines, occupying one space. The rests of perfect and imperfect semibreves, minors and seminimors, are as above. The forms of these are appropriately shown here: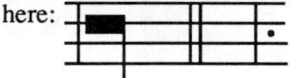

Also, it remains to speak of rests in another manner,[197] for not every note has a corresponding rest. The rest of a larga touches four lines, occupying three spaces and half the space above the fourth line, and it can be perfected and imperfected like a larga, because it corresponds to a larga. Therefore, whatever is the nature of the larga, such is the nature of its rest: therefore, the rest can be perfected and imperfected and diminished, just like the larga to which it corresponds. The rest of a larga can be perfected as a rest before a larga or before a larga rest or before a punctus, as here in an example: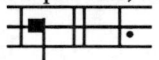

And it can be imperfected and diminished like a larga, as was said above.

The rest of a double longa touches four lines, occupying three spaces, and it can be perfected and imperfected, altered and diminished, like the double longa to which it corresponds. It can be perfected as a rest before a double longa or before a double longa rest or before a punctus, as is shown here: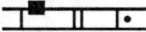

The rest of a longa touches three lines, occupying two spaces, and it can be perfected and imperfected, altered and diminished, like the longa to which this longa rest corresponds. It can be perfected as a rest before a longa or before a longa rest or before a punctus, as is shown here:

The rest of a brevis touches two lines, occupying one space, and it can be perfected and imperfected, altered and diminished, like the brevis to which it corresponds. And the rest of a brevis can be perfected as a rest before a brevis or before a brevis rest or before a punctus, as here:

---

[197]This appears to be Hanboys's own series of rests, providing one for each of his eight figures. The radical doctrine is espoused that these rests can be perfected and imperfected, altered and diminished, just like the figures to which they correspond.

Pausa vero semibrevis tangit unam lineam, dimidiam partem spatii sub occupans. Et perfici potest et imperfici, alterari atque diminui, veluti semibrevis cui correspondet. Potest etiam pausa semibrevis perfici, ut pausa ante semibrevem, vel ante semibrevem pausam, vel ante punctum, ut hic:

‖ Pausa minoris tangit unam lineam, dimidiam partem spatii supra occupans. Et perfici potest et imperfici, alterari atque diminui, veluti minor cui correspondet. Potest vero pausa minoris perfici ut pausa ante minorem, vel ante minorem pausam, vel ante punctum, ut hic:

Pausa semiminoris tangit unam lineam, dimidiam partem spatii supra occupans, et est retorta a parte dextera. Et perfici potest et imperfici, alterari atque diminui, veluti semiminor cui correspondet. Potest etiam semiminor pausa perfici ut pausa ante semiminorem, vel ante semiminorem pausam, vel ante punctum, ut hic patet:

Pausa vero minime tangit unam lineam, dimidiam partem spatii supra occupans, et est retorta a parte sinistra. Alterari potest, non tamen perfici neque diminui, quia correspondet minima que quidem individua est. Alterari tamen potest, ut hic:

⟨CAPITULUM XXII⟩

⟨Franco⟩: Sciendum est quod quinque sunt modi, quorum primus constat ex omnibus longis perfectis, ut hic patet in exemplo:

Vel ex longa imperfecta et brevi recta, ut hic:

‖ Secundus modus constat ex brevi recta et longa imperfecta, ut hic:

---

4 semibrevem (*pr.*) *m. sec.* A2 ‖ 7–9 Et perfici ... ut hic *in marg.* A2 ‖ 10 *exemplum cum exemplo* 342.16, *corr. in marg., m. sec.* A2 ‖ 11 minoris (semi *sup. lin., m. sec.*) A2 ‖ 12 ⟦et est retorta a parte dextra⟧ A2 ‖ 19 minime A2 | Alterari ⟦non⟧ A2 ‖ 21 *minor, semibrevis, semiminor, semiminor, semiminor, punctus, semiminor, semibrevis, minor* A2 ‖ 29 *longa* 29.6 A2 ‖

The rest of a semibrevis touches one line, occupying half of the space beneath, and it can be perfected and imperfected, altered and diminished, like the semibrevis to which it corresponds. The rest of a semibrevis can be perfected as a rest before a semibrevis or before a semibrevis rest or before a punctus, as here:

The rest of a minor touches one line, occupying half of the space above, and it can be perfected and imperfected, altered and diminished, like the minor to which it corresponds. The rest of a minor can be perfected as a rest before a minor or before a minor rest or before a punctus, as here:

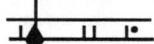

The rest of a semiminor touches one line, occupying half of the space above and bent over to the right side. And it can be perfected and imperfected, altered and diminished, like the semiminor to which it corresponds. The semiminor rest can be perfected as a rest before a semiminor or before a semiminor rest or before a punctus, as is shown here:

The rest of a minima touches one line, occupying half the space above and bent over to the left side. It can be altered but cannot be perfected or diminished, because it corresponds to the minima, which is indivisible. Nevertheless, it can be altered, as here:

## CHAPTER 22

Franco: It must be known that there are five modes, of which the first consists of all perfect longae, as is shown here in an example:[198]

Or of an imperfect longa and brevis recta, as here:[199]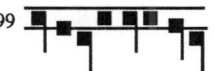

The second mode consists of a brevis recta and an imperfect longa, as here:[200]

---

[198]Handlo, *Regule*, Rubric XIII, Maxim 1 and Rule I (166.4–8).
[199]Handlo, *Regule*, Rubric XIII, Rule II (168.2–4).
[200]Handlo, *Regule*, Rubric XIII, Rule III (168.17–19).

Tertius modus constat ex longa et duabus brevibus quarum secunda alteratur, ut hic:

Quartus modus constat ex duabus brevibus unaque longa, quarum secunda alteratur, ut hic patet:

Quintus modus constat ex brevibus et semibrevibus universis, ut hic patet in exemplo:

Sciendum est quod modus est representatio soni longis brevibusque temporibus mensurati.

Explicit summa magistri Johannis Hanboys, doctoris musice reverendi, super musicam continuam et discretam.

The third mode consists of a longa and two breves, of which the second is altered, as here:[201]

The fourth mode consists of two breves and a longa, of which the second brevis is altered, as is shown here:[202]

The fifth mode consists of all sorts of breves and semibreves, as is shown here in an example:[203]

It must be known that mode is the representation of sound measured in long and short tempora.[204]

Here ends the Summa of Master John Hanboys, venerable teacher of music, concerning continuous and discrete music.[205]

---

[201]Handlo, *Regule*, Rubric XIII, Rule IV (170.11–13).

[202]Handlo, *Regule*, Rubric XIII, Rule V (172.2–4).

[203]Handlo, *Regule*, Rubric XIII, Rule VI (174.2–4).

[204]Franco, *Ars cantus mensurabilis*, cap. 3, sent. 1 (ed. Reaney and Gilles), p. 26.

[205]The explicit is entered below the main text by the primary scribe. The reference to "continuous and discrete music" obviously recalls the *Quatuor principalia*, where these terms identify plainsong and mensural music, respectively (see CS, 3:335 and CS, 4:254, for instance). There is, however, nothing about plainsong in the *Summa*, and the passage from Franco's *Ars cantus mensurabilis* with which it begins clearly states an intention to deal only with mensural music. Nonetheless, if a reference on f. 64r of **GB**-Lbl, Additional 8866 is being interpreted correctly (see the Introduction, pp. 33 and 38), then Hanboys was the author of a larger treatise. It may be either that the *Summa* in its present form is the last part of that work (corresponding to the *quartum principale* of the *Quatuor principalia*, for instance) or else that the explicit was mistakenly intended to label the entire contents of **GB**-Lbl, Additional 8866 as the work of Hanboys.

8

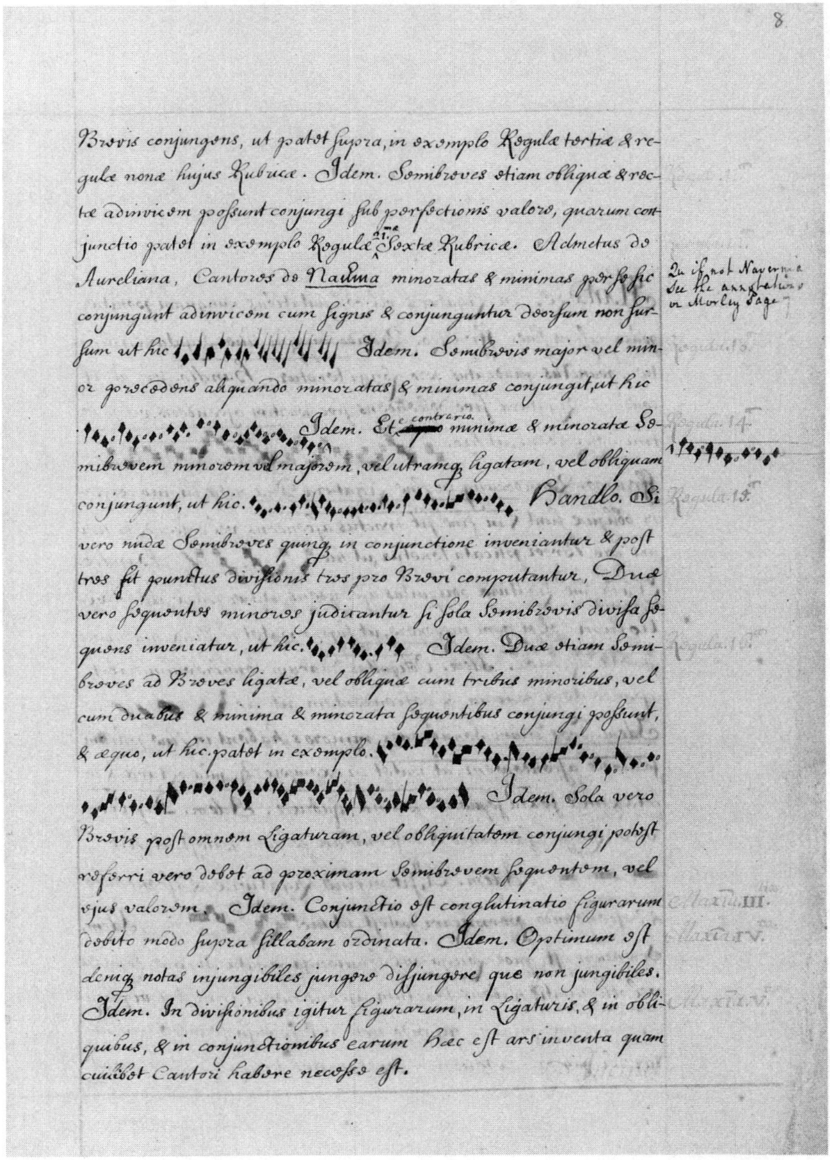

Brevis conjungens, ut patet supra, in exemplo Regulæ tertiæ & regulæ nonæ hujus Rubricæ. Idem. Semibreves etiam obliquæ & rectæ adinvicem possunt conjungi sub perfectionis valore, quarum conjunctio patet in exemplo Regulæ 21mæ Sextæ Rubricæ. Admetus de Aureliana, Cantores de Nauma minoratas & minimas per se sic conjungunt adinvicem cum signis & conjunguntur deorsum non sursum ut hic Idem. Semibrevis major vel minor precedens aliquando minoratas & minimas conjungit, ut hic Idem. Et e contrario minimæ & minoratæ Semibrevem minorem vel majorem, vel utramque ligatam, vel obliquam conjungunt, ut hic. Handlo. Si vero nudæ Semibreves quinque in conjunctione inveniantur & post tres sit punctus divisionis tres pro Brevi computantur, Duæ vero sequentes minores judicantur si sola Semibrevis divisa sequens inveniatur, ut hic. Idem. Duæ etiam Semibreves ad Breves ligatæ, vel obliquæ cum tribus minoribus, vel cum duabus & minima & minorata sequentibus conjungi possunt, & æquo, ut hic. patet in exemplo. Idem. Sola vero Brevis post omnem Ligaturam, vel obliquitatem conjungi potest referri vero debet ad proximam Semibrevem sequentem, vel ejus valorem. Idem. Conjunctio est conglutinatio figurarum debito modo supra sillabam ordinata. Idem. Optimum est demum notas injungibiles jungere & disjungere que non jungibiles. Idem. In divisionibus igitur figurarum, in Ligaturis, & in obliquibus, & in conjunctionibus earum hæc est ars inventa quam cuilibet Cantori habere necesse est.

Qu. if not Navarra See the annotation in Morley Page

Plate 1. London, British Library, Additional 4909, f. 8r.
By permission of the British Library.

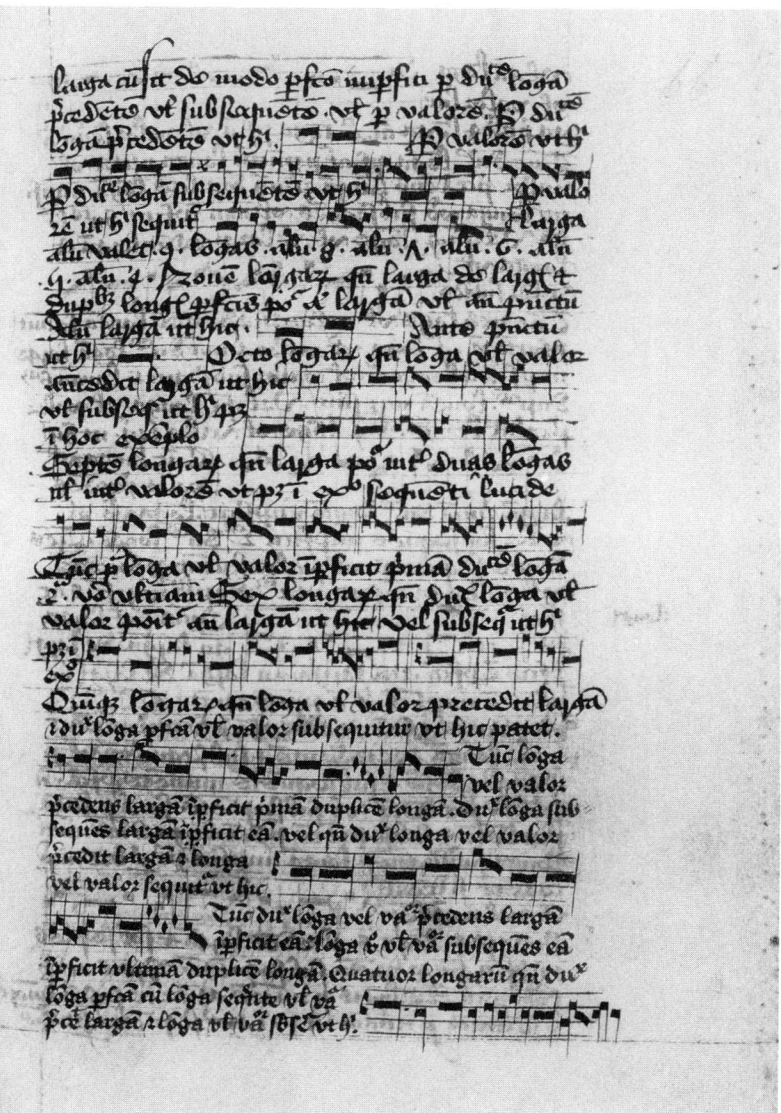

Plate 2. London, British Library, Additional 8866, f. 66r.
By permission of the British Library.

# APPENDIX I

## EXAMPLES FROM THE *REGULE* IN THE *SUMMA*

This concordance of the music examples in the *Regule* with their equivalents in the *Summa* provides an overview of related passages and an additional means of access to them. Each example is identified by an ordinal number (i.e., example 1.1 is the first example in the first rubric or chapter) and then by page and line number from the present edition.

| Handlo, *Regule* | | Hanboys, *Summa* | |
|---|---|---|---|
| 1.1 | (82.2) | 7.1 | (220.8) |
| 1.2 | (82.6) | 7.2 | (220.10) |
| 1.3 | (84.8) | 7.3 | (222.3) |
| 1.4 | (84.14) | 10.1 | (236.18) |
| 1.5 | (84.18) | 10.2 | (236.21) |
| 1.6 | (86.6) | 10.3 | (236.25) |
| 1.7 | (86.11) | 12.1 | (254.7) |
| 1.8 | (86.15) | 12.2 | (254.10) |
| | | | |
| 2.1 | (88.5) | 7.4 | (222.10) |
| 2.2 | (88.15) | 7.8 | (222.23) |
| 2.3 | (88.18) | 7.9 | (222.24) |
| 2.4 | (90.3) | 5.1 | (206.5) |
| | | +6.15 | (218.4) |
| | | | |
| 3.1 | (92.7) | 7.12 | (224.12) |
| 3.2 | (92.11) | 7.10 | (224.3) |
| 3.3 | (92.14) | 7.11 | (224.5) |
| 3.4 | (94.3) | 11.11 | (246.18) |
| 3.5 | (94.6) | no example | |
| 3.6 | (94.11) | 11.12 | (246.22) |
| 3.7 | (94.18) | 11.14 | (248.3) |
| 3.8 | (96.4) | 11.15 | (248.6) |
| 3.9 | (96.9) | 11.16 | (248.9) |
| 3.10 | (96.19) | 11.17 | (248.17) |
| 3.11 | (96.26) | 11.18 | (248.24) |
| 3.12 | (98.2) | 11.19 | (250.2) |
| 3.13 | (98.10) | 11.20 | (250.8) |
| 3.14 | (98.13) | 11.21 | (250.10) |
| 3.15 | (98.20) | no example | |
| | | | |
| 4.1 | (100.8) | 12.5 | (256.10) |
| 4.2 | (100.11) | 12.6 | (256.17) |
| 4.3 | (100.18) | 12.8 | (258.6) |
| 4.4 | (102.3) | 12.9 | (258.12) |
| 4.5 | (102.9) | 12.10 | (258.17) |
| 4.6 | (102.12) | 12.11 | (258.19) |
| 4.7 | (104.2) | 12.12 | (260.9) |
| 4.8 | (106.20) | 12.13 | (260.14) |
| 4.9 | (110.3) | 13.1 | (262.5) |
| | | +13.2 | (262.6) |
| | | +13.3 | (262.8) |
| 4.10 | (110.7) | 13.4 | (262.11) |
| 4.11 | (110.16) | 13.5 | (262.18) |
| 4.12 | (110.21) | 13.7 | (264.4) |
| 4.13 | (112.6) | 13.9 | (264.7) |
| 4.14 | (112.10) | 13.10 | (264.15) |
| 4.15 | (112.14) | 13.11 | (264.18) |
| 4.16 | (114.5) | 13.12 | (264.27) |
| 4.17 | (114.10) | 13.19 | (266.17) |
| | | | |
| 5.1 | (116.15) | 13.21 | (268.3) |
| 5.2 | (118.8) | 13.22 | (268.13) |
| 5.3 | (118.13) | 13.23 | (268.17) |
| | | | |
| 6.1 | (120.10) | 19.1 | (322.9) |
| 6.2 | (120.15) | no example | |
| 6.3 | (120.20) | 19.2 | (322.12) |
| 6.4 | (122.23) | 19.2 | (322.12) |
| 6.5 | (124.10) | 19.3 | (322.23) |
| 6.6 | (124.15) | 19.4 | (324.3) |
| 6.7 | (124.23) | 19.5 | (324.7) |
| | | +19.6 | (324.10) |
| 6.8 | (126.4) | 19.7 | (324.14) |

| | | | | | | | |
|---|---|---|---|---|---|---|---|
| 6.9 | (126.9) | 19.7 | (324.14) | 10.3 | (152.25) | 20.9 | (332.10) |
| 6.10 | (126.15) | no example | | 10.4 | (154.4) | no example | |
| 6.11 | (126.19) | 20.15 | (334.4) | 10.5 | (154.8) | 20.12 | (332.19) |
| | | +20.16 | (334.5) | | | +20.14 | (334.2) |
| 6.12 | (126.23) | 20.11 | (332.16) | 10.6 | (154.14) | no example | |
| 6.13 | (128.5) | no example | | | | | |
| 6.14 | (128.9) | 19.8 | (326.3) | 12.1 | (162.2) | 21.1 | (336.15) |
| 6.15 | (128.17) | no example | | | | | |
| 6.16 | (128.21) | no example | | 13.1 | (166.8) | 22.1 | (342.25) |
| 6.17 | (130.4) | 19.10 | (326.8) | 13.2 | (168.4) | 22.2 | (342.27) |
| 6.18 | (130.8) | 19.11 | (326.11) | 13.3 | (168.19) | 22.3 | (342.29) |
| 6.19 | (130.15) | no example | | 13.4 | (170.13) | 22.4 | (334.3) |
| 6.20 | (130.19) | 20.4 | (330.12) | 13.5 | (172.4) | 12.14 | (260.17) |
| 6.21 | (132.4) | no example | | | | +22.5 | (334.6) |
| 6.22 | (132.9) | no example | | 13.6 | (174.4) | 22.6 | (334.9) |
| | | | | | | | |
| 7.1 | (134.5) | 19.12 | (326.15) | | | | |
| 7.2 | (134.13) | 19.14 | (328.14) | | | | |
| 7.3 | (134.17) | no example | | | | | |
| | | | | | | | |
| 8.1 | (136.6) | 20.1 | (328.21) | | | | |
| 8.2 | (136.10) | 20.2 | (330.3) | | | | |
| 8.3 | (136.15) | no example | | | | | |
| 8.4 | (136.17) | 20.2 | (330.3) | | | | |
| 8.5 | (136.26) | 20.3 | (330.6) | | | | |
| 8.6 | (138.4) | 20.5 | (330.15) | | | | |
| | | +20.6 | (330.19) | | | | |
| 8.7 | (138.8) | no example | | | | | |
| 8.8 | (138.15) | no example | | | | | |
| 8.9 | (138.19) | 20.18 | (334.10) | | | | |
| 8.10 | (138.23) | no example | | | | | |
| | | | | | | | |
| 9.1 | (142.6) | no example | | | | | |
| 9.2 | (142.10) | no example | | | | | |
| 9.3 | (142.13) | no example | | | | | |
| 9.4 | (142.20) | no example | | | | | |
| 9.5 | (144.2) | 20.4 | (330.12) | | | | |
| 9.6 | (144.6) | no example | | | | | |
| 9.7 | (144.9) | no example | | | | | |
| 9.8 | (144.17) | no example | | | | | |
| 9.9 | (146.11) | no example | | | | | |
| 9.10 | (146.15) | no example | | | | | |
| 9.11 | (148.4) | no example | | | | | |
| 9.12 | (148.10) | no example | | | | | |
| 9.13 | (148.15) | no example | | | | | |
| | | | | | | | |
| 10.1 | (152.13) | 20.7 | (332.3) | | | | |
| 10.2 | (152.18) | 20.8 | (332.6) | | | | |

## APPENDIX II

## TWO MOTET FRAGMENTS IN INSULAR NOTATIONS

London, Westminster Abbey, 12185 (**GB**-Lwa 12185) is a fragmentary source of fourteenth-century English motets.[1] It is remarkable for the fact that each of its five surviving pieces is notated in a different style. The first follows Franco of Cologne; the second follows Johannes de Garlandia as described in the *Regule* (and *Summa*); the third follows W. de Doncastre as described in the *Summa*; the fourth is in an insular, ternary breve-semibreve notation;[2] and the fifth follows Petrus de Cruce. Presented here are transcriptions of the second and third motets.

**GB**-Lwa 12185, f. 1v (RISM no. 2): *Hac a valle-Hostem vicit*

Two upper voices of a motet a4, for St. Nicholas. Published facsimiles appear in *Fourteenth-Century English Polyphony: A Selection of Facsimiles*, ed. Frank Ll. Harrison and Roger Wibberley, Early English Church Music, vol. 26 (London: Stainer and Bell, 1981), pls. 170 and 171; and Margaret Bent, "A Preliminary Assessment of the Independence of English Trecento Notations," in *L'Ars nova italiana del Trecento IV (1975)*, ed. Agostino Ziino (Certaldo: Centro di studi sull'Ars nova italiana del Trecento, 1978), p. 81. The notation is that of Johannes de Garlandia (*Regule*, Rubric IV [108.5–114.10]; *Summa*, chapter 13 [262.2–266.17]). This transcription bars the brevis; the longa is perfect, with the underlying impress of second mode. The stem on the major semibrevis descends vertically beneath the notehead. For further commentary, see Peter M. Lefferts, *The Motet in England in the Fourteenth Century* (Ann Arbor, MI: UMI Research Press, 1986), pp. 126–27 and 270.

---

[1] See Gilbert Reaney, ed., *Manuscripts of Polyphonic Music (c. 1320–1400)*, Répertoire international des sources musicales, BIV/2 (München-Duisberg: G. Henle, 1969), pp. 245–46; and Peter M. Lefferts, *The Motet in England in the Fourteenth Century* (Ann Arbor, MI: UMI Research Press, 1986), pp. 269–71.

[2] See Lefferts, *The Motet in England*, pp. 130–42.

## GB-Lwa 12185, f. 2 (RISM no. 3):  Beatus vir-T.[Benedicamus Domino]

Tenor and lowest voice of a duet motet a3 with medius cantus, for Trinity Sunday. Published facsimiles include Early English Church Music, vol. 26, pls. 172 and 173; and Luther Dittmer, trans. and ed., *Robert de Handlo, Music Theorists in Translation*, vol. 2 (Brooklyn, NY: Institute of Medieval Music, 1959), p. 21 (with an unreliable edition on pp. 22–24). The notation follows that of W. de Doncastre (*Summa*, chapter 13 [268.26–272.15]). This transcription bars the brevis; longa and brevis are normally both perfect, with the underlying impress of second mode. Red coloration is used in both surviving parts to imperfect the longa and brevis. The semiminima is introduced, in effect, in two configurations taking the place of a minor semibrevis: a minorata followed by two minimae (mm. 12 and 58), and groups of four minimae (mm. 6, 12, 66, and 78). Following the pattern of subdivision evidently intended in the first configuration, the groups of four are transcribed as if the last two are semiminimae. Plain, tailless semibreves are presumed to need tails in three instances (mm. 55.5, 66.5, and 78.6). For further commentary, see Lefferts, *The Motet in England*, pp. 127–29 and 270–71.

## APPENDIX III

## TEXT POSSIBLY FROM A LARGER TREATISE BY HANBOYS

The following text is the second item in **GB**-Lbl, Additional 8866. It occupies the lower half of f. 64r, where the main scribe has used it to fill out the remainder of the page following the explicit of the *Quatuor principalia*; the *Summa* begins in the same hand on the verso of the same leaf.[1] This brief text consists of two parts. The first is a compact "pars metrica"[2] in which designations for metrical feet and line have been applied to figures from plainchant notation.

The material on metrics is not entirely clear, though its purpose is straightforward. That is, neums are put into correspondence with the names of metrical feet (e.g., dactyl or iamb). Distinctions—in grammar a term referring to signs of division such as the colon and comma, or to sections defined by such markers, but here evidently a musical term referring to larger or more complex neums—are put into correspondence with the names of verse meters (e.g., pentameter or tetrameter). And because classical versification involves designations of "long" and "short" syllables, the caution is necessary that in plainchant all notes are actually given the same length.

The second part of this passage is a sentence on "sinemmenon," which may have been appended simply because of its use of a Greek term. Concluding this sentence is a reference to a volume by Hanboys that corresponds neither to the *Quatuor principalia* nor to the *Summa* in its present form. This citation suggests that the *Summa* was once part of a larger and more comprehensive survey in several books. If so, the material on notation would correspond to the first half of the *Quartum principale* of the *Quatuor principalia*, or to the material on mensural notation within the framework of the treatises by Odington and Willelmus.

A minimum of punctuation has been added to the Latin text, whose parsing by the editor is clear from the parallel English translation.

---

[1] See the Introduction, pp. 38 and 76.

[2] For an example of a more traditional *pars metrica* in an English music treatise, see Part IV of Walter Odington, *Summa de speculatione musicae*, ed. Frederick Hammond, Corpus scriptorum de musica, no. 14 ([Rome]: American Institute of Musicology, 1970), pp. 89–91; the discussion there is based upon the *Etymologiarum* of Isidore of Seville.

Sciendum est tamen et neupme loco sunt pedum et distinctiones loco versuum utpote ista neupma Dactilico alia iambico more decrerat et distinctionem tetrametram nunc pentametram alias quas exametras trinas et multa alia ad hunc modum.

5 Dactilus unam habet longam et duas breves sic:

Geminos vel dupla sic:

aut sic:

10 Pentametrum hoc modo:

Anapestus est repercussio sic:

Trimetrum vel Trametrum vel Trocheus vero dictus est eo quod celerem
15 facit conversionem cantilene hoc modo:

Tribracus dictus est ex tribus brevibus hoc modo:

Figura vero molosus qui a saltacione dictus est hoc modo:
20
Fictilos hoc modo facimus:

Ternarios hoc modo:

25 Triplus dictus est quia maior pars ter continent totam minorem id est tria et unum sic:

Exametros vel epitriti vocati sunt quia semper tres longas habent et unam brevem sic:
30
Licet enim longas et breves nominemus non sic tenentur in plana musica sicut et in organo sed omnes note preter pausaciones equaliter canentur ita ut

---

14 Trochaeus 〚Tr〛 ‖ 28 quia]quod 〚uod〛

It must be known that neums correspond to feet, as distinctions correspond to verses, inasmuch as this neum is determined to be in the dactylic manner, another in the iambic manner; and a distinction now tetrameter, now pentameter, [and there are] others that [are called] hexameters, trinas, and many others [that belong] to this manner.

A dactyl has one long and two short, thus:

Geminos or duples, thus:

or thus:

A pentameter, in this manner:

An anapest is a repercussion, thus:

A trimeter or trametrum, or trochee, correctly said, is that which makes the quick turning round of a song, in this manner:

A tribrach is said to be from three shorts, in this manner:

The figure of the molossus, which is said to be from dancing, in this manner:

We make fictilos in this manner:

Ternaries, in this manner:

A triple is so called because the greater part contains three all minor, that is, three and one, thus:

Hexameters or epitriti are so called, because they always have three longs and one short, thus:

It is permitted that we call them longs and shorts, [but] they are not held out in plain chant as they are in organum. Rather, all notes except rests are

in unum terminentur partes et distinctiones neupmarum atque verborum et cetera.

Sinemmenon est figura quedam et dicitur commutacio sive defectio tonorum vel semitoniorum et est in alphabeto 2 ut dicit Hanboys libro primo capitulo sexto.

sung equally, thus as in one.[1] Here are ended the passages concerning the distinctions of neums and words and so on.[2]

Sinemmenon is a certain figure and it is said to be a commutation or defect of tones or semitones, and it is the second in the alphabet,[3] as Hanboys says in Book I, chapter 6.

---

[1] The expression "as in one (ut in unum)" is reminiscent of the expression "on one meter (super unum metrum)" in the definition of conductus in the second part of the *Discantus positio vulgaris* (1270s); see the discussion in Ernest Sanders, "Conductus and Modal Rhythm," *Journal of the American Musicological Society* 38 (1985): 439–69, especially 444–45.

[2] Alternatively, "Here end the parts and distinctions of neums and words, etc."

[3] That is, it is the letter "b," which in musical notation can change a tone into a semitone and a semitone into a tone.

# INDEX VERBORUM
# TRACTATUS ROBERTI DE HANDLO

abolenda, 96.25
addere, 100.25; 176.23
additio, 80.2
adinvicem, 116.2; 124.8; 130.18; 144.4; 146.4, 9
adiungi, 128.12; 162.7, 11; 164.2
Admetus de Aureliana, 146.8
affirmare, 106.3
Agmina fidelium Katerina, 174.4
agnoscere, 110.13; 116.18
aliter, 92.13; 94.10; 96.8; 102.11; 152.20
alius, 80.2–3; 100.24; 118.17;122.20; 142.16; 176.23
alter, 142.19; *v.* brevis altera
alterari, 92.25
alteratus, *v.* brevis alterata
altior, 120.8, 17; 124.17; 126.2
ambe, 94.2, 13, 17; 106.5, 8; 110.20
animadvertere, 122.15
annexio solida, 120.23
annus Dominus, 178.16
apparere, 162.1
appellari, 160.10, 24
appositus, 92.2; 98.2, 12
apte, 120.22
ars, 150.13
ascendere, 82.4; 84.16; 120.12–13; 122.16; 124.13, 21; 126.14, 26; 128.7, 11, 12, 15; 130.3, 7, 13–14; 132.6; 134.19–20; 136.12; 138.13; 152.11, 11–12, 16, 20, 23, 28; 154.2, 6, 11
ascensus, 126.21
associari, 116.2; 118.16
attributus, 164.4
Aureliana, *v.* Admetus de Aureliana
ballada, 176.8–9

bonus, 108.6
brevis, 80.4; 84.14; 86.4; 90.8 (bis); 92.2, 3, 5, 9, 16, 19, 20, 21 (bis); 94.5, 8, 13, 16 (bis); 96.2, 6, 11 (bis), 13, 18, 21, 22, 23 (bis); 98.6, 8, 15; 100.2, 4, 5, 13, 14, 16, 21; 102.6 (bis); 104.4, 8, 10 (bis), 18, 22 (bis); 106.3, 4, 7, 8, 10, 13, 14 (bis), 17; 110.9, 11, 14 (bis); 112.18; 144.1; 166.20; 188.4, 6, 10, 15; 122.10; 124.3, 6; 128.8 (bis); 134.3, 12, 15; 136.12, 13, 20 (bis), 25; 138.3, 6, 14, 17; 142.12; 144.5, 11, 15; 148.7, 12; 154.16; 158.7; 160.11; 162.11; 168.2, 7, 12, 14, 17 (bis); 170.2, 5, 11; 172.2, 3; 174.2; 176.4, 9, 10, 12, 14; brevis altera, 92.3, 22; 96.12; 106.2; 138.21; 176.15; brevis alterata, 92.24; 98.8–9, 18; 156.2; 158.7; brevis coniungens, 146.1; brevis erecta, 84.16–17; 86.8; brevis plicata, 86.5; 152.16; brevis recta, 98.18–19; 100.17; 132.2; 134.15; 138.22
brevitas, 80.7
cantor, 150.13; 178.10; cantores de Navernia, 146.8; cantores moderni, 102.2
cantus, 100.24; 166.1, 4; 178.2
cantusfractus, 176.9
carere, 84.13; 120.9, 13; 126.3, 7; 128.2, 3, 13, 15
causa, 160.10
causare, 132.6; causari, 162.7
celum, 176.10
cernere, 178.9
ceterum, 80.7; 178.16
Christus, 178.14
circulus parvulus, 164.8
cognosci, 92.1; 120.1; 134.1; 136.1
compilatus, 80.2
comprehendi, 176.11
computari, 96.17, 22, 24; 100.17; 144.11; 148.7; 176.12, 14
computatio, 176.16
concomitari, 114.8; 118.5
congeries figurarum, 120.22
conglutinatio figurarum, 150.6
coniunctim, 114.8
coniunctio, 142.1, 15; 144.20; 146.5; 148.6; 150.6, 13; 168.12, 15; 170.6, 9
coniunctus, 106.13
coniungere, 146.1, 9, 14; 148.3; coniungi, 86.17; 104.11; 130.18; 142.2, 4–5, 8, 12; 144.1, 4, 15; 146.4, 9; 150.3
consequenter, 118.7; 126.8
constare, 166.6; 168.2, 17; 170.11; 172.2; 174.2
constitutus, 154.17

constituere, 124.8
contineri, 112.8–9; 164.13
contrarium, 114.4; 148.2; *v.* conversus
convenienter, 170.7; 176.19
conversus, 92.2; 100.5; 102.6; 110.5; 126.18, 22; 138.7; 144.16; 148.14; 162.12; 164.2; *v.* contrarium
Copais, *v.* Copiiis
Copiiis, 164.6
corea, 176.9
corpus, 124.4, 5; corpus obliquum, 130.7; 138.2; 152.15
correspondens, 160.13–14
Cruce, vide Petrus de Cruce
curari, 122.2
currere, 100.21; 164.6, 11
curtus, 132.7
debere, 100.2; 104.11; 110.15; 112.3; 116.2, 10. 12; 118.4, 16; 124.2; 142.2; 150.3; 172.8; deberi, 150.6
decet, 118.1; 142.12; 154.25
defendi, 134.4
deleri, 164.9
demum, 176.23
denegare, 106.2, 5
denique, 112.18; 140.2; 150.9
deorsum, 86.18; 138.10; 142.5, 23 (bis); 146.9; 154.18, 21
depositus, 110.6
descendere, 82.1; 120.13, 18; 122.13, 20, 21; 124.12 (bis), 14, 18, 22; 126.6, 14; 128.1 (bis), 3, 15; 130.2, 14; 134.19; 136.14, 19; 138.6; 146.1; 152.11, 12, 16, 24; 154.2, 6
descensus, 126.18
describi, 104.8
deservire, 106.11
designare, 160.11
desinere, 136.19
dexter, 82.1, 4; 84.6; 86.5; 124.18; 126.26
dicere, 98.7; 124.4; 126.14; dici, 84.14; 86.17–18; 88.11, 17; 92.24; 100.14; 102.18; 106.18; 112.3, 16; 116.7; 120.9, 13, 18; 122.7, 12, 22; 124.2, 13, 14, 19; 126.3, 8; 128.1, 3, 16; 136.5, 9; 146.1; 154.12; 160.24; 168.13, 15; 170.7, 9
dies Veneris, 178.15
differencia, 84.2
differe, 178.5

difficilis, 164.4
disiungere, 150.9
dissimilis, 88.13
dissimilitudo, 142.19
distinguere, 122.4; distingui, 108.9; 110.16; distingui aliter per divisionem modi, 92.13; 94.10; 96.8; 102.11
diversificari, 162.10
dividi, 104.11 (bis)
divisim, 114.8
divisio, 80.5; 150.12; divisio modi, 92.13; 94.10; 96.8; 98.2, 12; 100.2; 102.11; 106.16 (bis); 144.8; *v.* punctus divisionis
divisus, 104.12, 19; 106.13; 144.12; 148.8; 156.3; 168.13, 14; 170.6
Dominus, *v.* annus Dominus
equalis, 94.13. 17; 96.6; 98.8, 16; 100.10, 13; 102.8, 14, 20; 104.1 (bis), 14, 15; 106.4, 10; 112.17, 19
equalitas, 92.2; 100.1; 104.16; 106.3
equivocari, 152.4; 156.5
erectus, 82.4; 84.2, 3, 10, 16; 86.2, 8 (bis); 88.17; 90.5; 98.18; 152.2; 154.11, 13
erigi, 84.4; 86.2
estampeta, 176.9
evidens, 102.17; 176.16
excedere, 116.1; 154.23
exemplum, 90.9; 122.17; 128.4; 130.3; 134.8; 138.11; 142.16; 146.2, 5; 148.14; 152.28; 154.13; 168.3, 18; 174.3; 178.5, 6
exhibens, 178.7
explicere, 178.15
exprimeri, 172.9
facere, 102.2, 14; 160.1; 178.8
fallacia, 164.8
fallere, 98.2, 12; 144.8
figura, 88.13; 108.8; 116.2, 4, 14; 120.22; 142.2; 150.6, 12; 168.11; 170.8; figura rotunda, 142.8; *v.* signum rotundum
figurari, 116.18
finis, 178.8; finis obliquitatis, 128.20; finis punctorum, 160.24
finitus, 178.13, 15
floritura, 176.9
foret, 160.11
forma, 162.1
formari, 86.10; 90.2; 108.9; 110.1–2, 15, 19; 116.17–18; 134.12
formatus, 120.23

Franco, 80.2; 98.7; 100.20; 176.16; *et passim*
Garlandia, *v.* Johannes de Garlandia
gaudere, 80.7
gloria, 178.14
habere, 82.1, 4; 84.16; 86.4; 92.16; 96.18; 100.5, 14, 21; 104.17, 25; 106.6, 17; 108.9; 110.20; 112.2, 4, 9; 114.1; 116.4, 6, 11, 12; 120.12, 18; 122.13, 21; 124.12, 13, 18; 126.26; 136.19; 144.5; 146.1; 150.13; 152.23, 27; 154.11; 158.4, 7; 160.13; 164.8, 12; 176.19; 178.3; habere se, 80.5; 112.19; 114.2, 3; 118.18; 120.2–3; 144.20; 152.1; 176.21, 22
Handlo, *v.* Robertus de Handlo
hoketus, 100.22; 162.9, 10; 164.6, 12 (bis), 12–13; 176.8; hocketus lascivus, 104.24
immensurabilis, *v.* pausa immensurabilis
impedimentum, 142.18
imperfectio, 152.3; 156.6
imperfectus, 84.10; 88.7, 10; 106.5
imperficere, 92.5–6, 9, 17; 94.13–14; 96.11, 23, 24; 98.15; imperfici, 90.7; 116.20; 118.10
imperficiens, 98.16
imponere, 128.12; 152.21
In Bethleem, 166.8
incipere, 80.2, 80.2, 4; 88.1; 92.1; 100.1; 116.1; 120.1; 128.2; 134.1; 136.1; 142.1; 152.1; 158.1; 160.1
inconsonus, 118.17
inconveniens, 124.4
indirecte, 136.24
inequalis, 92.19; 94.8; 96.13; 98.8; 102.7, 15, 18; 104.1, 2, 14–15, 15
inequalitas, 100.1–2; 104.16; 106.3
integer, 160.17, 18
intelligi, 178.6
intentio, 102.17; 176.16
intentus, 178.12
inveniri, 84.3, 13; 92.20–21; 94.16; 96.15, 21; 98.6; 100.5, 10, 16–17; 102.5–6; 104.21; 106.7–8, 16, 18; 120.23–122.1; 122.17; 130.7; 136.9, 21; 138.3; 148.6, 8; 154.12; 160.10
inventio, 160.10
inventus, 150.13
iocundus, 164.7
iudicari, 148.8
iudicium, 108.5
iungere, 150.9

iungibilis, 150.9
Jacobus de Navernia, 162.10
Johannes de Garlandia, 108.5; 110.9, 13; 114.7; 162.6; 164.11
karus, 178.9
lascivus, 104.6, 18, 24; 106.7; 172.8
latere, 138.21
liber, 178.13
licet, 160.11
ligabilis, 140.2
ligare, 140.2 (bis); ligari, 124.4, 6; 126.13, 14, 18; 128.11; 130.11, 13, 17; 132.2; 134.15; 138.7, 10, 13, 17; 154.24
ligatura, 120.1, 2, 5, 22; 122.4, 8, 10, 15, 16, 20; 124.2, 4–5, 8; 126.6–7, 7, 11, 13, 25, 26; 128.1, 2, 3; 130.6; 132.7; 134.1, 12, 19; 136.1, 8, 14, 19; 138.2, 6, 13, 21; 142.2, 22; 144.1; 150.2, 12; 152.1, 6, 9, 11, 15, 20; 154.6, 10, 16; 156.2; 168.11, 14; 170.5, 8
ligatus, 104.19; 106.15; 122.8, 12; 124.8; 148.3, 12; 154.10; 158.11
locum habere, 100.21; 104.17, 25; 106.6
longa, 80.4; 82.1; 84.6; 88.1, 4 (bis), 7, 11, 13; 92.1, 5, 9, 16, 17, 20; 94.8, 13, 16; 96.2, 6, 11, 16 (ter), 21, 22, 23, 23–24; 98.6, 15, 16; 100.2, 4, 5, 16; 102.6 (bis); 104.4, 7, 10, 18, 21; 106.4, 7, 10, 14; 116.1, 4, 10, 11, 12 (bis), 14, 17, 20; 118.12; 126.11, 13; 128.7, 16; 132.3; 136.12 (bis), 17, 20 (bis); 142.3; 144.15; 152.3, 10; 154.10, 16, 23; 156.3, 5, 6; 160.11; 168.2 (bis), 6, 17; 170.11 (bis), 16; 172.2; 176.3, 10; longa erecta, 82.4–5; 84.2, 10; 86.2, 8; 88.17; 90.5; 152.2–3; 154.11, 13; longa plicata, 84.7; 152.2; longa perfecta, 88.7, 11; 94.2, 17; 98.7; 106.8; 166.6; longa imperfecta, 88.7, 10; 106.5; longa simplex, 90.5; 116.11; 118.1, 4; 126.17, 21; 152.2; 158.5; longa duarum perfectionum, 126.17; 126.21–22; 138.6; longa duplex, 88.2; 90.2, 7; 104.20; 116.1; 118.2, 6, 10; 138.10, 13, 17; 154.2, 23; 158.3; longa recta, 84.2–3; *v.* semilonga
longus, 84.6; 86.4; 104.5, 7, 15; 106.6; 108.2; *v.* mos longus
losonga, 86.10, 108.9; 110.1
Magister Franco, 80.2; *v.* Franco
magnus, 154.23
maior, *v.* semibrevis maior
maiorari, 116.10
Mane prima sabbati surgens dei filius, 168.19
manere, 86.18; 94.8, 96.6, 22, 24; 98.7–8, 9, 15; 124.3, 5; 128.7; 168.13; 170.7
maxima, 80.2; 104.25; 122.7; 152.21, 28; 156.7; 172.9; 178.5, 6, 8; *et passim*
media [figura], 134.3, 4, 12, 15

mediale, 134.1
mediocris, *v.* mos mediocris
medium, 122.2; 134.19
melius, 116.18; 176.23
mensura, 154.23; 166.1; 176.19; 178.2 (bis)
mensurabilis, *v.* modus mensurabilis
minima, 110.13, 14, 15. 18–19, 19 (bis); 112.3, 4, 8, 11, 17, 19, 20; 114.1–2, 8; 118.5, 16; 142.8; 146.8, 14; 148.2, 13; 154.21; 158.10, 11; 160.13; 164.11
minor [semibrevis], 100.14; 102.19, 20; 108.9; 110.1, 5, 110.14, 15; 112.2, 18 (bis); 114.3 (bis); 148.8, 13; 176.6; *v.* semibrevis minor
minorata, 110.13, 18 (bis), 20; 112.4–5; 8, 12, 17, 19; 114.2, 8; 118.6, 16; 142.8; 146.8, 13; 148.2, 13; 154.21; 158.7, 9, 11; 160.13; 164.11
minus, 124.5
misceri, 112.3; 118.4, 6
mixtim, 112.19; 114.2, 3; 118.18; 176.21
mixtura, 118.17; 176.24
modernus, 80.7; 102.2; 166.4
modicum, *v.* volumen modicum
modus, 86.10, 17; 92.19; 96.12, 15; 108.9; 110.1; 112.16; 120.5; 122.7, 15, 16, 20; 126.25; 142.8; 150.6; 154.25; 162.11; 164.1, 3, 4; 166.1, 4, 6, 10 (bis); 168.2, 6, 11, 13, 17; 170.2, 5, 7, 11, 15; 172.2, 6, 8; 174.2; 176.2, 8, 11, 12, 18 (bis), 21, 22, 23, 24; 178.2, 3; 178.6; modus mensurabilis, 166.10–11; *v.* divisio modi
mos, 104.4, 14, 21, 25; 106.2, 4; mos longus, 104.5, 7, 15; 106.6; 108.2; mos mediocris, 104.5, 9, 17; mos lascivus, 104.5–6, 18; 106.7; 172.8
motetus, 100.22, 24; 106.19; 166.7; 170.12
musicus, 80.3
natura, 164.12
naturaliter, 110.19
Navernia, *v.* Jacobus de Navernia
necesse, 142.5; 150.14
nichil, 122.2; 128.11
noniungibilis, 150.10
nonligabilis, 140.3
nosci, 120.5; 126.25; 176.23–24
nota, 116.5, 6; 140.2; 150.9; 154.12; 160.11; nota quadrata, 80.9
notari, 142.4
notitia, 178.6
Novum melos promere, 174.4
nudus, 110.1; 122.8, 12; 124.2, 5; 144.20; 148.6; 178.6

O Maria maris stella plena gratie, 168.4
obliqua [figura], 118.7
obliquari, 124.6; 130.11, 17
obliquitas, 120.1–2, 2 (bis), 12, 23; 122.4, 8, 12, 21; 124.2, 3, 5, 8, 12, 14, 21; 126.7; 128.3, 7, 8 (bis), 11, 12, 15, 19; 130.2; 132.7; 134.12, 19; 136.13; 138.22; 142.22; 144.1; 150.2, 12; 152.2, 6, 20, 23; 154.11, 17; 156.2; 168.12, 14–15; 170.5, 8
obliquum, 110.1
obliquus, 104.19; 106.15; 120.22; 124.3; 130.7; 132.2, 3; 138.2; 142.18; 146.4; 148.3, 12; 152.15
omitti, 104.21, 22; 160.1
oportet, 88.11; 104.11; 110.13; 122.4; 168.13; 170.7
oppositus, 144.8; *v.* proprietas opposita
optimum, 150.9
opus, 108.6
orare, 178.12
ordinari, 86.14, 17
ordinatim, 150.7
ordinatus, 142.4
organum purum, 116.17
os, 88.14
pars, 100.6, 14; 160.7, 8, 20 (bis), 22 (bis); 162.6, 7; 164.1, 3, 7; 176.4, 5; pars dextra, 82.1, 4; 124.18; 126.26; pars sinistra, 84.16; 120.18; 122.13, 16–17; 128.15; 144.20–146.1
partim, 142.23 (bis); 152.9, 10
parvulus, *v.* circulus parvulus
pausa, 92.2; 118.11; 154.12; 160.1, 9, 13, 16, 17, 19, 20, 22, 24; 162.6, 11; 164.1, 3, 7 (bis), 8, 12; 168.5, 6 (bis), 7 (bis), 12, 15; 170.2, 3 (bis), 6, 9, 15; 172.6; 176.2, 3 (bis), 4, 5; pausa immensurabilis, 160.9, 24
pausatio, 160.3
penitus, 136.13
Pentecoste, 178.16
penultimus, 136.4, 9, 24; 160.10, 11
perfectio, 96.17, 22, 24; 114.1 (bis); 116.5, 6, 12; 126.17, 21–22; 136.5, 9, 14; 138.6; 146.5; 152.3; 156.5; 176.12, 14, 22
perfectus, 136.17; 166.10; *v.* longa perfecta
perfici, 128.19
perplicari, 154.6, 20–21, 24; 156.2; 158.11; *v.* plicari
pertinere, 110.9–10; 128.20; 144.12; 168.6; 170.2, 15; 172.6; 176.2
Petrus de Cruce, 102.1, 17; 106.13
Petrus le Viser, 104.4; 108.2

plica, 128.12, 13; 130.2; 152.6, 20, 23, 27; 154.11, 12; 158.1, 3, 5, 7, 8, 9
plicari, 84.10; 86.8, 13; 152.9; 154.2, 17; *v.* perplicari
plicatus, 84.7; 86.5, 18; 152.2, 16
ponere, 102.1, 17; poni, 84.2; 100.13; 112.12; 118.1, 2; 130.3; 152.6; 166.4
positus, 102.14; 106.4, 10, 15
possedens, 84.6
potius, 160.9
precedere, 84.2–3; 90.8; 92.5; 94.5; 96.2; 100.20; 104.16; 106.8; 110.5, 19; 112.12; 118.11; 122.7; 126.17; 128.7; 130.10, 13; 132.8; 138.11, 13; 144.19; 146.13; 168.7 (bis), 8, 9; 170.2–3, 3, 14–15; 176.2–3, 3, 4, 4–5, 5, 6, 18
predictus, 94.16; 96.2; 102.7
prefatus, 176.21; 178.2
prefiguratus, 116.20
principium, 120.1, 5; 122.1, 8, 12, 21; 124.12, 13; 128.19
prius, 102.18
proferri, 104.5, 8, 9, 18, 20, 22; 108.3
pronunciari, 154.25
proportio, 88.14; 92.25; 100.21; 110.11
proprietas: cum proprietate, 120.5–6, 9, 13, 18; 122.10, 16, 17, 21–22; 124.13, 14; sine proprietate, 120.6, 124.18; 126.3, 7–8, 11, 25; 128.3–4, 19; proprietas opposita, 120.6; 130.6; 132.6, 11; 134.3
provenire, 104.24; 176.8
proximus, 138.11; 144.12; 150.3; 178.15
punctus [divisionis], 100.25; 102.14, 17; 106.17, 19; 110.6; 112.9; punctus divisionis, 142.5; 148.7; 176.23; *et v.* divisio modi; punctus [perfectionis], 128.20; punctus [quadratus], 120.8, 9, 12, 17; 122.17; 124.17, 18, 21; 126.2, 3, 6, 7, 26; 128.2; 130.6, 24; 136.4; punctus quadratus, 80.9; 84.13; 122.20; 136.8; 152.9; finis punctorum, 160.24
purum organum vetus, 116.17
quadrangulum, 116.4
quadratus, 136.19; *v.* nota quadrata, punctus quadratus
quadruplex, 116.6
Quid miraris partum virgineum, 170.13
ratio, 124.2; 134.7, 10
recte, *v.* stare recte, stari recte
rectus, 84.3; 92.24; 98.19; 100.17; 130.13; 132.2; 134.15; 138.22; 146.4; 158.11
recurri, 98.6–7
reddari, 178.14
reduci habere, 176.19; 178.3

referri, 92.17; 150.3
Regina regni glorie, 174.4
regula, 80.1, 2; 90.9; 100.20; 104.16, 25; 106.5, 9, 11; 122.18; 134.8; 138.11; 142.16; 146.2 (bis), 5; 152.28; 156.7; 178.5 (bis), 6–7, 8, 15; *et passim*
remanere, 96.16, 17; 102.7, 15
respondere, 96.25
requirere, 124.5
Robertus de Handlo, 80.1, 3; *et passim*
Rosula primula salve Jesse virgula, 172.4
Rota versatilis rubens versucia, 188.8
rotundus, *v.* signum rotundum
rubrica, 80.4; 88.1; 90.9; 92.1; 100.1; 100.20; 104.25; 106.5, 9, 11; 116.1; 120.1; 122.7, 18; 134.1, 8; 136.1; 142.1, 16; 146.2, 6; 152.1, 21, 29; 156.8; 158.1; 160.1; 166.1; 172.9
rundellus, 176.8
sciri, 92.19; 98.18; 102.5; 138.21; 154.10; 158.3
scriptor, 178.11
securius, 100.24; 116.18
semibrevis, 80.4; 86.10; semibrevis maior, 102.19; 104.19; 108.8, 9; 110.5; 112.16, 18; 114.3, 7; 118.5, 15; 130.10; 132.7; 142.16, 19; 146.13; 148.3; 158.4, 9; 162.7; 176.5; semibrevis minor, 100.14, 104.19; 110.14–15; 112.4, 8, 16; 114.7, 116.11; 118.5, 15; 130.10; 132.7; 142.4, 16, 19; 146.13; 148.2; 152.27; 154.20; 158.5, 8, 10; 162.7; 164.1, 2, 6, 8; 176.4; semibrevis plicata, 86.18; *v.* equalis, minor [semibrevis], minorata, minima
semibrevitas, 132.11
semilonga, 88.1, 10, 13; 92.1; 104.4, 7, 10, 18, 21; 132.3; 154.10; 156.3, 6; 158.5; 168.8, 9, 11; 170.3, 6, 8; 176.3; semilonga erecta, 88.17
semitonium, 84.4; 86.2
semper, 96.16; 100.17; 130.2–3; 134.19
sepius, 162.6
sequi, 90.8; 92.9, 16; 94.5; 96.2; 104.26; 106.8–9, 17, 19; 108.6; 126.6; 128.20; 134.7; 144.11–12; 148.8 (bis), 13; 150.3; 152.28; 154.12; 156.3; 168.13; 170.6; 174.3; 176.22; *v.* subsequi
servare, 178.9
signum, 108.8; 132.11; 144.4; 146.9; signum rotundum, 110.15–16, 20; 112.2; 112.4
sillaba, 86.13; 150.6–7
similis, 88.13; 142.8, 15
similiter, 138.10; 154.17

simplex, 124.5–6; *v.* longa simplex
sinister, 84.7, 16; 86.4; 120.18; 122.13, 16; 128.15; 146.1
Sola salve singularis gratie, 174.4
solidus modus, 154.25; *v.* annexio solida
solus, 92.5, 9; 94.5; 112.2; 122.5; 124.3; 128.7; 130.2; 134.10; 148.8
spatium, 160.16, 18, 19, 20, 22, 25
species pausationum, 160.3
stare recte, 126.22; 136.4; stare indirecte, 136.24; stari recte, 136.14
subintelligi, 122.1
subsequi, 96.2; 118.11; *v.* sequi
substantia, 168.13; 170.7
subtus, 110.1
sumi, 100.2; 110.9; 156.7
superfluus, 128.12
sursum, 86.18; 142.5, 23; 144.1; 146.9–10; 154.17, 21
tangens, 104.16
tegere, 160.16, 18, 19, 21, 23, 25
tempus, 88.4, 6; 90.2, 7; 92.16, 21, 21–22; 96.12 (bis), 18; 100.6 (bis)
    118.10, 11, 12; 160.4, 9, 16, 17, 19, 20, 22; 168.6, 7; 170.15; 172.6;
    176.2
tendere, 154.12
teneri, 96.25; 98.4; 152.10, 17
terminatio, 136.1–2
terminus, 156.5
teste, 104.25
tractus, 84.6, 84.14; 86.4; 110.1; 120.9, 13; 122.17; 126.3, 7; 128.2, 3, 16;
    142.18; tractus ascendens, 82.4; 84.16; 130.7; 132.6; 152.16; 154.11;
    tractus descendens, 82.1; 120.18; 122.13, 21; 124.12, 13–14, 18;
    126.26–128.1; 144.20–146.1; 152.16
transire, 152.2; 154.11
transmutari, 172.8
triplex, 116.4–5
ultra, 116.10
universus, 176.9
uti, 178.6
valere, 88.4; 90.2; 92.21 (bis); 96.12; 106.14; 110.14 (bis), 15, 19; 112.18
valor, 88.1; 90.8; 92.5, 9, 16, 21; 94.5; 96.2; 100.21; 106.8, 17; 110.9;
    116.1, 11, 12; 144.4, 13; 146.5; 150.4; 158.1, 3, 6, 7, 8, 9; 160.16;
    176.13
Veneris, *v.* dies Veneris,
verumtamen, 178.8–9

vestigium, 178.9
vetus organum purum, 116.17
Viser, *v.* Petrus le Viser
vita, 178.11
vitiosum, 140.2; 152.21
vocari, 82.1, 5; 84.3, 6, 17; 86.5; 88.7; 92.22; 100.13; 116.5
vocatus, 104.18
volumen modicum, 178.9
vox, 88.14; 104.5; 120.23; 172.9; vox omissa, 160.1

# INDEX VERBORUM
## TRACTATUS JOHANNIS HANBOYS

ablatio, 272.8
abnegatio, 270.17–272.1
aboleri, 248.22
absens, 330.11
acceptus, 320.24
accidens, 180.17–18
accipi, 256.25
activus, *v.* principium activum
addere, 186.5; addi, 258.9
additio, 180.2
adequari, 182.27–28
adinvicem, 182.15, 28; 214.19; 234.7; 286.7; 322.22; 326.22
adiungi, 324.22
adquirere, 270.2
adversus, *v.* caput adversus
agnosci, 268.5
alibi, 326.20
aliter, 182.14; 214.2; 224.4; 236.5; 246.1, 21; 248.8; 252.20; 262.2; 272.16
alter, 212.6, 14, 17; 232.2, 10, 11; 234.15; 242.19; 246.11, 14, 16; 248.11; 252.15, 20; 254.1; 256.13; 260.10; 282.6; 286.6; 294.14; 296.30; 300.29, 30; 306.10; 310.19; 312.23; 316.26; 318.21; *v.* alteratus
alterari, 212.7, 15, 21; 214.2, 18, 23; 232.17; 234.5, 9; 246.13, 28; 250.19; 256.22; 284.25, 33; 302.1, 8, 15; 312.7, 14; 318.5, 12, 18; 340.15, 20, 25; 342.2, 7, 12, 18, 19; 344.1–2, 5
alteratio, 196.8; 212.16; 252.5, 10; 286.13; 288.6, 12; 290.2, 4; 292.1; 294.4–5, 9; 306.1, 5; 314.27; 316.5
alteratus, 216.4, 5; 234.16; 246.12; 250.7; 252.1, 3, 20; 284.20, 21; 286.10; 294.1, 3, 18, 23; 300.1; 302.19; 304.29, 31; 306.12, 15; 312.1, 2, 20; 314.24, 26; 318.1; *v.* alterus
altus, 322.6, 10; 324.4, 11
ambe, 246.17, 23; 248.4; 256.13; 264.3
an, 248.19; 256.11; 274.23; 276.1

antecedere, 198.20; 208.8; 218.16; 228.1, 13, 18; 238.19; 240.6, 10; 296.3, 13, 17; 306.23, 30; 308.3, 6; *v.* precedere
antiquus, 180.16; 266.1; 274.2; 280.23; 282.3; 336.16; antiqui cantores, 258.11
apertissime, 204.12
apparere, 292.27; 336.14
appellari, 182.13, 22, 23; 336.2
apponi, 250.16; 286.11; 292.7; 304.6; 312.24–25; 318.22, 32; *v.* poni
appositus, 234.2; 250.1, 9; 286.3; 302.12, 20; 312.17; 314.3; 318.14; *v.* positus
apprehensio, 180.14
arrogantia, 180.12
ars, 256.26; ars de mensurabili musica, 180.16; ars liberalis, 186.2
ascendere, 194.3; 220.9; 222.1; 236.19, 23; 270.10, 12; 272.9; 288.1, 6, 7, 11; 298.20; 310.3; 316.13, 17, 18, 21, 22–23; 324.8, 22, 23; 326.1, 9, 10; 328.15; 330.16–17; 332.1–2, 4, 7, 14, 17; 334.1, 6
assignare, 288.6, 12; assignari, 286.13; 290.2 (bis); 292.1, 2 (bis)
associari, 268.8, 19
attendi, 182.12
Aucun ont trouvé chant, 260.13, 14
auditor, 180.14
binarius numerus, 304.11; binaria ligatura, 326.19
Boetius, 180.7
bonus, 182.5
breviari, 328.2
brevis (adj.), 182.8, 27; 192.6; brevis (n.), 186.1; 192.6; 204.6 (bis), 10 (bis), 16, 17 (bis), 25, 27; 208.1, 3, 8 (bis), 11 (bis), 14, 16, 18, 28 (bis); 210.1, 3, 6, 8 (bis), 9, 11 (bis), 14, 15, 17, 17–18, 20 (bis), 21, 22, 23, 25, 26, 27; 216.6, 7 (bis), 8, 9, 12, 17 (bis), 17–18, 26, 28; 218.16; 220.1; 222.8, 18; 224.1, 6, 10 (bis), 13, 16, 18, 19 (bis); 226.4 (bis), 7, 9; 228.4, 7, 11, 13, 18; 21, 22 (bis), 26, 27, 28; 230.1, 4, 5 (bis), 10, 11, 14, 15, 17; 236.5, 13, 14; 236–54, Cap. X–XI (de brevibus) *passim*; 256.6 (bis), 7 (bis), 11 (bis), 12, 13, 14, 15 (bis), 21, 24 (bis); 258.1, 2, 5, 7 (bis), 14, 15 (bis); 260.11, 15; 262.12, 15, 16 (bis); 264.21, 23; 266.3, 4, 11, 12; 268.6, 9, 11, 14, 18, 22; 272.26; 274.2, 20; 276.2, 3, 6, 13; 278.9, 20; 280.7, 19, 24; 282.1 (bis), 7, 8 (bis), 9 (bis), 10, 12; 284.22, 29, 30; 286.2 (bis), 5; 292.4 (bis), 7, 9, 10 (bis), 11, 12 (bis), 13, 14 (bis), 17, 17–18, 18, 19, 21 (bis), 22, 23, 25 (bis), 26, 27; 316.18, 23; 322.7, 13, 18, 21; 326.13; 328.1, 5 (bis), 11, 12; 330.8; 332.5; 334.6, 16, 17, 18, 20; 226.3, 8, 10, 17–18; 338.10, 12; 340.24, 25, 26 (ter); 342.26, 28; 344.1, 4, 7, 10; brevis erecta, 236.20, 26

brevitas, 182.10
Brunham, *v.* Robertus de Brunham
cani, 182.15
cantare, 270.6
cantor, 186.4; cantores antiqui, 258.11
cantus, 182.8, 11, 14, 26, 27; cantus ecclesiasticus, 182.23
capitulum, 182.7; 184.12; 194.1; 204.1; 206.1; 212.4; 220.3; 226.11; 232.1; 236.16; 242.18; 254.4; 262.1; 274.1; 280.23, 24; 282.5; 298.18; 310.1; 316.11; 320.21; 328.17; 334.13; 342.22
caput adversus, 288.1; caput directus, 330.4
carere, 202.27; 212.3; 236.18; 250.23; 266.5, 14; 272.6; 292.25; 304.25; 314.20; 320.17; 322.6; 324.12, 16, 21, 24; 332.11
cauda, 272.17; cauda yrundinis, 288.13
causa, 336.2
ceterum, 286.18; 288.5, 11; 290.3; 292.1; 328.3
circulus, 266.1, 2, 3
coequari, 182.16
cognosci, 322.3
color, 250.21–22
comitari, 266.15; 268.10, 23
committi, 264.13
commode, 320.27
commoditas, 180.13
communiter, 182.13, 21, 22
compendium, 182.3
componere, 186.3; 338.5
compositor, 186.4
compositus, 182.24; 184.13, 14; 206.7, 8; 222.6, 9; 226.16
computari, 214.20; 234.7–8; 248.15, 19–20, 21; 258.5; 286.8; 302.17; 304.2, 12; 312.22, 30–31; 314.8; 318.20, 27–28; 320.4
conditio, 270.9, 11
coniungi, 254.11; 330.11
consequens, 270.12
consonantia, 182.26
constare, 202.23; 210.28; 212.16; 230.17; 242.12; 298.13; 304.9; 308.28; 342.23, 28; 344.1, 4, 7
constituere, 322.22
continere, 194.7; 204.24, 26; 206.2; 236.12, 14; 244.6 (bis); 254.15; 256.24–25; 272.14, 15 (bis); 282.2, 7, 15 (bis); 284.17, 20; 292.14; 298.22–23, 30; 300.2, 28, 29; 310.6–7, 18–20; 312.1; 314.18; 318.1
continuus, 334.13

contra, 188.8; 270.9
contradicere, 286.17
contrariantes, 270.10
contrarium, 180.17; 182.13; 184.9; 262.9; 264.26; 270.9, 16
contrarius, 270.9
convenienter, 228.23; 268.12; 336.14; 338.3; 340.2
copula, 184.2
copulatus, 184.2
corpus, 322.19, 20; 332.4; corpus obliquum, 330.16; [corpus] obliquum, 330.13
correspondere, 216.4–5; 234.15–16; 340.5, 7, 9, 15, 16, 20, 25; 342.3, 8, 13, 19
creare, 272.7, 10
crocheta, 188.1, 5, 6, 7; 190.1, 2; 192.2
curtus, v. mensura curta
dare, 326.12
datus, 322.5
debere, 184.9; 234.13; 262.18; 264.9; 266.18, 23; 268.1, 9; 274.9, 14, 18, 24; 276.9, 11; 280.21; 320.26; 324.2
debitus, 182.28; 186.1; 334.14
decet, 186.3; 268.7
declarare, 182.3–4; declarari, 270.16
declaratio, 272.8
deesse, 264.11
defectum, 182.1
defendi, 326.13; 330.9
deficere, 180.18; 272.2
demonstrari, 196.6; 266.7
demptus, 262.9
denotare, 196.5, 9; 266.3, 11
deorsum, 330.11
deprimere, 272.17
descendere, 194.3; 220.7; 222.1–2, 22; 236.23–24; 270.1, 10, 11; 272.9; 286.15, 18; 288.11; 316.16–17, 18; 322.11, 14, 15; 324.1 (bis), 5, 9, 15, 19; 326.1, 6, 9; 328.15; 330.1, 17; 332.2, 4, 8, 11, 17; 334.1, 3, 9
designare, 336.3; designari, 182.28–184.1
destruere, 182.4; 186.5
detrimentum, 182.2
dexter, v. pars dextra
dicere, 180.12, 17; 182.11, 14; 188.8; 250.5; 272.17; 288.10; 338.5; 340.4; dicere Francho, 186.3; 286.17; 290.4; dici, 182.19, 21, 24; 184.6; 192.3;

194.4; 196.1, 2, 7; 204.29 (bis); 206.4; 220.7; 236.18; 246.12; 254.7; 256.26; 258.2; 260.3–4; 264.9, 19; 266.20, 22; 268.23, 27; 274.3, 4; 282.3 (bis); 298.20; 310.3; 316.14, 17, 18, 22, 24; 322.7, 11, 17; 324.2, 6, 12, 17; 326.10; 328.19, 20; 330.2, 5, 14, 17; 332.5; 336.12; 340.13
dictio, 320.26
dictum, 182.2, 4
differe, 232.11; 250.22; 254.13; 268.26; 276.12 (bis); 336.17
differentia, 220.11
diffinitio, 182.9
dimidius, *v.* pars dimidia
diminui, 204.2, 5, 14; 216.4, 6, 8–9, 16; 234.15, 17, 20; 236.5; 244.17, 21; 246.1; 252.1, 4, 9, 14–15; 20; 254.1, 2; 268.21, 23; 284.1, 5, 12; 294.1, 3–4, 8, 13, 18, 23, 24; 300.16; 304.29, 31; 306.4, 8, 12, 15, 16; 314.24, 26; 316.1, 4; 340.9, 13, 15, 20, 25; 342.2, 7, 13, 19
directe, 270.11, 12; 272.10; 298.20; 322.19
directus, *v.* caput directus
dirigi, 272.21
discantus, 182.18, 24, 26; 184.1 (bis), 3
disciplina, 272.11
discretus, 334.13
dispositio, 328.1
distinguere, 262.3; distingui, 256.11; 274.23; 276.1; distingui aliter per punctum divisionis, 214.2; distingui aliter per divisionem modi, 224.4; 232.17–18; 246.21; 248.8; 256.18; 258.18; 284.26; 292.1; 302.2; 312.8; 318.6
diversus, 180.3; 182.14, 26, 27; 184.4 (ter), 5
dividere, 196.7; 262.13
dividi, 182.17; 184.1
divisio, 196.10; divisio modi, 224.4; 246.21; 248.8; 250.1, 9; 256.18; 258.18; 266.1; 284.26; 290.4–292.1; 302.1–2; 312.7–8; 318.5–6; *v.* punctus divisionis
doctor, 186.2 (Franco); 334.12 (Hanboys)
Doncastre, *v.* W. de Doncastre
dualitas, 292.12
duplex, 270.16
duplex longa, 192.6; 194.3, 7–8, 15; 198.3–4, 4, 9, 15; 200.4, 6, 11–12, 14, 15 (bis); 202.1, 2, 3, 6, 9, 10, 11, 16, 17, 20, 21, 23; 204.15, 24, 26–27, 29; 206–220, Cap. V–VI (de duplicis longis) *passim*; 226.8 (bis); 232.3 (bis), 3–4, 4, 6, 8, 13, 20–21, 23, 27, 28–234.1; 234.4, 6, 12–13, 15; 268.7, 11, 14, 21, 25; 332.14, 17, 20; 334.1, 3, 5, 6; 340.14, 15, 16, 16–17; duplex longa composita, 206.7, 8; longa duplex imperfecta, 202.23;

longa duplex perfecta, 200.11–12; 202.3, 6–7; duplex longa simplex, 206.6–7, 8;
duplicari, 212.15
dupliciter, 182.20–21; 196.1, 7
duplum, *v.* organum duplum
ecclesiasticus, *v.* cantus ecclesiasticus, tropus ecclesiasticus
efficaciter, 180.6
efficere, 270.13
effugare, 182.4
equalis (adj.), 214.5; 232.20; 246.23; 248.2, 7; 250.6, 12; 256.13, 16; 258.16; 260.1, 5, 7 (bis); 284.28; 298.30; 302.4; 310.18; equalis (n., vel tertia pars brevis), 258.1; 264.19, 22; *v.* minor semibrevis; equalis (de quibusdam antiquis), 274.5, 6, 7, 11 (bis), 12, 16, 21 (bis); 276.2 (bis), 7; 278.1 (bis), 2, 5 (bis), 6, 10, 11, 12, 21, 22 (bis), 24; 280.8, 9, 10, 11, 19; minor equalis, 276.4 (bis)
equepollere, 262.19; 264.5; 268.25; 272.25; 280.24 (bis)
erectus, *v.* brevis erecta, longa erecta
erigi, 220.13; 236.22
errare, 180.18; 326.21
error, 182.1, 4; 186.4, 5
estimare, 182.1
evidens, 180.13
exceptus, 320.25
exemplum, 200.2, 9; 204.12; 208.29; 210.18, 23, 29; 212.12; 214.3, 10; 216.10, 14, 23; *et passim*
explicere, 344.12
extra, 188.2
extremum, 270.17 (bis); 272.2 (bis)
facere, 194.6; 258.11; 260.1; 322.13; 324.18; 330.7, 8; facere perfectionem, 202.15, 22; 210.20, 27; 224.16; 226.1, 5; 230.9, 16; 242.4, 10–11; 250.19, 26; 298.4, 12; 308.23, 27; 328.6–7
facillimam, 180.14
factus, 334.15
fallere, 224.13; 250.1, 9; 332.8
figura, 182.28; 184.6, 8, 9, 13; 186.3, 5; 188.1, 2; 192.5; 194.15; 196.5; 222.21; 266.20; 268.2; 272.2, 10, 12, 25; 316.24; 332.12
figurare, 272.16; figurari, 266.18; 270.7; 274.9, 14, 18, 24; 276.9; 280.21
figuratus, 270.3
finis, 214.21; 216.1; 234.8, 12; 248.15; 258.16; 260.2; 266.9; 286.9; 302.18, 22; 304.2; 312.22, 27, 31; 314.8; 318.20, 24, 28; 320.5; finis ligature, 288.10; 328.18; 330.1, 10, 22; 332.1; finis punctorum, 336.13; 338.1–2

flecti, 272.23
fore, 266.3
foret, 336.4
forma, 194.2; 206.2; 212.15; 220.5; 232.11; 236.17; 246.12; 254.5; 276.12; 284.21; 298.19; 300.29; 318.1; 310.2; 312.2; 316.12; 336.13; 338.2; 340.2
formaliter, 192.2
formari, 188.3, 5; 194.2; 218.3; 254.6; 262.3–4, 6, 7, 16; 264.1–2; 268.4, 5; 274.4; 276.11; 316.12; 328.13
formatus, 316.20; 318.1
formula, 216.2
forte, 180.12, 18; 182, 1
Francho, 186.2; 218.2–3; 250.5; 260.11; 282.7–8; 288.4, 10; 290.3–4; Magister Francho, 286.17; *v.* Franco
Franco, 180.2; *et passim*; *v.* Francho
frater Robertus de Brunham, 338.5; *v.* Robertus de Brunham
frustrare, 290.1
Garlandia, *v.* Johannes de Garlandia
gerens, 322.10; 326.9
gradus, 188.2; 192.1, 3
granum ordeacei, 254.6
gratia, 182.9
Gregorius, 180.8
grossus punctus, 206.2
Guydo monachus, 180.7
habere, *v.* teneri habere; se habere, 268.20; haberi pro longa, 332.2; haberi pro recta, 214.1, 18; 246.28; 284.25
habitudo quantitativa, 182.10
habitus, 184.5
Hanboys, *v.* Johannes Hanboys
hodie, 218.1; 224.13; 256.11; 258.7; 268.21; 274.14, 23; 276.9, 12; 278.15; 280.13; 334.18; 336.10
hoketus, 184.2
ibi, 266.7, 9
illucidare, 180.6–7
imitari, 250.21
immediate, 224.15
immensurabilis, 336.1, 12
imperfectio, 270.12; 272.8
imperfectus, 192.4; 202.27 (bis); 210.28; 212.3 (bis); 216.4; 218.2; 222.4; 230.17, 21; 234.15; 242.12, 17; 244.5, 6; imperfecta ex omnibus imper-

fectis, 204.26; 216.27; 236.14; 246.8–9; 254.14, 15, 17; 256.12, 13; 258.7; 262.12; 266.11–12; 272.26, 27; 274.20, 24; 276.1, 6; 282.1, 14, 15; 284.18; 292.11, 26, 27; 298.13, 17 (bis), 24, 26, 30; 300.27; 304.10, 26, 27; 308.28, 32 (bis); 310.9, 10, 18; 314.7, 21, 22; 316.10 (bis); 320.3, 18, 19; 334.17, 18, 20; 336.7, 10, 17, 19; 338.7, 10, 12; 340.1; 342.26, 28; *v.* modus imperfectus

imperficere, 192.4; 200.4, 14, 15; 202.1, 2, 10, 11, 16, 17, 20, 21; 208.16; 210.1–2, 2, 6–7, 7, 15, 16, 21 (bis), 25, 26; 214.6, 17; 224.1, 11, 19; 226.4; 228.4, 7, 11, 21, 22, 26, 27; 230.4, 5, 10 (bis), 14, 15; 232.21; 234.4; 238.21, 24; 240.4, 5, 9, 13, 14, 17, 18, 23, 24, 25, 29, 30; 242.5, 5–6, 9, 10; 246.23; 248.10, 20, 21; 250.11, 12; 252.15, 16; 256.21; 284.29; 286.5; 294.14; 296.20, 21, 30; 298.5, 6, 10, 11; 300.24; 302.5, 14, 23; 306.9, 29; 308.6, 7, 15, 16, 21, 22, 25, 26; 312.10, 19; 316.5; 318.8, 17; imperfici, 198.1, 2; 204.6, 9, 15, 16, 17, 18, 20, 21; 206.6, 12; 208.26; 216.9, 12, 16, 18, 19, 20, 22; 218.1; 234.21; 236.1, 5, 7, 8, 9–10; 238.9; 244.7, 21, 25; 246.2, 3, 4; 250.25; 252.5–6, 6, 11 (bis), 21, 22, 23, 25; 254.1; 268.6, 14; 282.17; 284.6, 10, 13, 14; 292.4; 294.5 (bis), 9, 10, 15, 19, 20, 21, 23 (bis); 300.10; 304.3, 32; 306.1–2, 5, 6, 10, 12, 14, 16; 310.27; 314.1, 27; 316.2; 318.29; 340.7, 8–9, 13, 15, 20, 25; 342.2, 7, 12; *v.* perficere; perfici

imponere, 324.23

importare, 260.11

impossibile, 188.8

inceptio, 266.7

incipere, 180.2, 13

includere, 212.14; 218.5, 16–17; 232.10; 246.11

inconveniens, 322.19

indicare, 260.3, 11; 262.2

indirectus seu obliquus, 272.9

individuus, 316.24–25; 342.19

inducere, 270.12

inequalis, 246.20; 248.12; 250.6; 258.15; 260.2, 4, 6, 7–8

inesse, 270.6

instructio, 180.15

intelligi, 224.8; 328.3, 9

interponere, 182.4

inveni, 206.2–3; 212.19; 214.8, 13, 19–20; 220.12; 232.12–13, 28; 234.7; 236.17; 246.26; 248.1, 13, 18–19; 250.3, 4; 256.7, 16; 258.4, 13–14; 260.10, 12; 276.6; 278.9, 20; 280.7, 19; 284.30; 286.2; 286.7–8; 292.4, 12, 21; 300.31; 302.6, 10, 16; 304.1, 10, 21; 312.3–4, 12, 15, 21, 30; 314.7, 16; 318.2, 9, 19, 27; 320.3, 13; 326.21; 330.17; 336.2

inventio, 322.4; 336.2
inventus, 182.5
iudicium, 222.24; 320.22
Johannes de Garlandia, 262.2, 13
Johannes Hanboys, 180.1; 344.12; *et passim*
larga [de novem bis quatuor longis], 192.6; 194–204, Cap. III–IV (de largis) *passim*; 212.8 (quater), 10, 12, 19; 214.5–6, 8, 13, 17; 216.2, 4; 226.8; 268.21, 24; 340.5, 7 (bis), 8, 9 (bis), 10 (bis), 13; larga [de novem vel sex bis quatuor brevibus], 186.5; 218.2; 338.6, 7
liberali, 186.2
licet, 212.14; 246.11; 260.12; 284.20; 312.1; 324.8; 336.3
ligabilis, 320.24; 330.20; 326.21
ligare, 322.19; 326.22; 328.1; ligari, 184.14 (bis); 194.6; 298.22; 310.6; 316.24; 320.26; 322.21; 324.8, 22; 326.2, 18, 20; 330.20, 21; 332.14; 334.3, 6
ligatura, 286.286.18; 288.1288.1, 4, 6, 10; 322.1, 3, 4, 6, 10, 13, 14, 17, 20, 22; 324.4, 11, 16 (bis), 18, 19; 326.9, 12, 19; 328.13, 15, 18, 19; 330.1 (bis), 4, 7 (bis), 10, 13, 22; 332.1, 7, 11, 14; 334.3, 6, 9
ligatus, 268.12; 286.13; 320.22 (bis); 322.22; 328.4 (bis)
linea, 336.5, 7, 8, 13, 18, 20, 21, 22, 23; 338.2, 6, 7 (bis), 8, 9, 10, 11, 12 (bis); 340.5, 6, 14, 19, 24; 342.1, 6, 11, 17
littera, 320.24
locus, 326.20
longus (adj.), 182.8, 27; 222.2; 236.24; longa mensura, 276.2, 11; 282.1; longa (n.), 186.1; 192.6; 198.13, 14, 20 (bis); 200.1 (bis), 4, 6, 12 (bis), 14, 16; 202.1, 3 (bis), 4, 6 (bis), 10, 12 (bis), 15, 16 (bis), 18 (bis), 20, 21, 22; 204.2–3, 3, 4, 5, 6, 9, 15, 16 (bis), 25, 27; 206.3, 12, 13; 17; 208.3, 16, 18, 22, 26, 29; 210.1, 2, 3, 6, 7, 8, 11, 14, 15, 16, 21, 22, 25–26, 26; 216.16, 25, 27; 218.5, 10, 12, 14, 16 (bis); 220–236, Cap. VII–IX (de longis) *passim*; 242.21 (ter), 22; 244.1, 3; 246.15, 17, 26 (bis); 248.1, 2, 4 (bis), 7, 10, 14 (ter), 18, 19, 20; 250.4, 5, 11, 12, 14 (bis), 15, 18, 20, 21 (bis), 23, 25, 27; 256.5 (bis), 6 (bis), 14, 15 (bis); 266.20, 21, 23 (bis), 24; 268.1, 2, 4, 6, 7, 9, 21, 24, 25 (bis); 282.2; 316.17, 23; 320.25; 324.12, 18; 326.18, 20 (bis), 21; 328.1; 330.7; 332.2, 14, 17, 20; 334.1, 3, 5, 16, 17; 336.3, 5, 6, 17(bis); 338.8, 9; 340.19, 20 (bis), 21 (bis); 342.24, 26, 28; 344.1, 4, 10; longa erecta, 220.9, 11, 12; 222.4, 24; 236.22, 26
longitudinis, 182.10
losonga, *v*. modus losonge
lucide, 200.2
magis proprie, 246.12; magis proprium, 324.6

magister Johannes Hanboys, 180.1; 334.12; magister Franco, 180.2; magister Francho, 286.17; *v.* Johannes Hanboys, Francho
magnus, 180.10; 186.4; punctus magnus et grossus, 206.2
maior, 188.8; maior [nota], 212.16; maior nota, 194.16; maior noticia, 250.13; maior semibrevis [vel brevis imperfecta], 262.3; 266.15; 268.9–10, 18, 26, 27; 270.3; 272.14; 334.20; maior [semibrevis, vel brevis imperfecta], 256.23, 24; 260.5; 262.3, 7, 9; 264.19, 21, 25; 272.17, 25; maior [semibrevis, de quibusdam antiquis], 274.5, 6 (bis), 11, 12 (bis), 21 (bis); 276.13; 278.1, 2, 9, 11, 12, 20, 21, 23 (bis); 280.7, 8, 9, 11, 23, 24; maior [propositum], 290.3
maiorari, 266.23
manere, 192.1, 3; 204.4, 14, 15, 16, 18, 19, 20, 22; 216.5, 17, 18, 20, 21, 22; 226.5, 7; 232.20; 234.16, 19; 236.6, 7, 9, 10; 244.19; 246.2, 3, 5, 20; 248.7, 19, 22; 250.5, 7, 11; 252.3, 20, 21, 23, 24, 25; 266.4, 12; 282.16; 284.3, 13, 14, 28; 286.6; 294.3, 19, 21, 22; 300.18; 302.4; 304.31; 306.13, 14; 314.26; 322.18, 20
manifesta, 190.1
manifestans, 182.11
manifeste, 332.12
manifestissime, 292.27
maxime, 180.7, 17
media, 270.2; media [nota], 326.13, 16; 328.1, 2
medietas, 196.9
medium, 198.2; 270.16; 272.2; 328.15
melius, 268.5
mensura, 182.9, 10; 182.12 (bis); 334.18, 19; mensura curta, 276.1, 3, 6–7, 11; mensura longa, 276.2, 11; 282.1
mensurabilis, 182.11 (bis), 17, 18, 19; *v.* musica mensurabilis
mensurari, 182.14, 19, 20
mensuratus, 182.9, 23; sonus mensuratus, 344.11
minima (n., de figuris Johannis Hanboys), 192.6; 204.11, 21, 22, 25–26, 28; 216.14, 22 (bis), 26, 28; 226.9–10; 236.3, 10 (bis), 13, 15; 244.25; 246.4–5, 5, 8, 9–10; 252.7, 12, 17, 25; 254.1; 268.22; 284.6, 7, 9, 14, 15, 18, 19; 294.6, 10, 15–16, 22 (bis); 300.16, 17, 18, 20, 22, 24, 27, 28; 306.2, 6, 10, 14, 14–15, 18, 20, 23 (bis), 26 (bis), 29, 30; 308.3 (bis), 6, 8 (bis), 9, 11 (bis), 14, 16 (bis), 20, 20–21, 21, 22, 23, 25 (bis), 26; 310.7, 18, 28 (bis), 31; 314.24, 25, 26, 27; 316.1, 1–2, 4 (bis); 316–20, Cap. XVIII (de minimis) *passim*; 336.23; 342.17, 19; minima (de figuris Johannis de Garlandia et aliorum), 186.5; 188.1, 3, 6, 7; 190.1, 2; 192.1
minimum, 188.8; 242.20
minor, 188.6, 7 (bis); 190.1, 2; 192.2; 212.7; 316.19, 23; minor semibrevis

[vel tertia pars brevis], 256.26; 258.2; 262.15, 17; 264.13; 266.24; 268.9–10, 18; 270.7; 334.21; 336.11; minor [semibrevis, vel tertia pars brevis], 256.23 (bis); 260.5, 6; 262.3, 6, 7, 9, 16; 264.8, 19, 21 (bis), 25 (bis); 266.15; 268.26; 270.13; 272.14 (bis), 16, 19, 25; *v.* equalis; minor [semibrevis, de quibusdam antiquis], 276.13; 278.1, 2, 4, 6, 7, 10 (bis), 12, 15, 16, 17; 280.2, 3, 4, 5, 14, 15, 16, 17; minor equalis, 276.4 (bis); minor [propositum], 270.5; 290.3; minor (n., de figuris Johannis Hanboys), 192.1, 2, 4, 6; 204.11 (bis), 19 (bis), 20, 25, 27; 216.13 (bis), 19, 20 (bis), 26, 28; 226.9 (bis); 234.21 (bis); 236.2 (bis), 7, 8 (bis), 13, 15; 238.15, 16–17, 19 (bis), 21, 24; 240.1 (bis), 4, 5, 6, 10, 13, 15, 17, 19 (bis), 20, 23, 24, 25, 26, 28, 29; 242.1 (bis), 4 (bis), 5, 6, 7, 9 (bis), 10; 244.18 (bis), 19, 20, 21, 24; 246.2 (bis), 3, 8, 9; 252.6, 7, 11 (bis), 16, 17, 22, 23 (bis); 254.15; 262.19; 264.6; 268.22; 272.27; 282.15, 17, 18, 22; 284.12, 17, 19; 294.2 (bis), 4, 5 (bis), 8, 9 (bis), 13, 14, 15, 19, 20 (bis); 296.2, 11, 13, 18, 20 (bis), 22, 26, 29, 30; 298.5, 6, 10, 11, 13; 298–308, Cap. XVI (de minoribus) *passim*; 310.20, 21, 23, 25; 312.4 (ter), 10, 12, 15, 16 (bis), 19, 21, 28, 30; 314.1, 3, 5, 6 (bis), 7, 8 (bis), 9 (bis), 10, 12, 13, 14; 16 (bis), 17, 18, 20 (bis), 21, 21–22; 336.20; 340.1; 342.6, 7, 8 (bis), 9

minorata, 264.1, 2, 5, 9, 10, 13, 16, 19–20, 22, 24; 266.15; 268.10, 18–19, 26; 272.5, 14, 15, 16, 21, 25; minorata semibrevis, 264.1; 270.14

minus, 188.8; 322.20

misceri, 224.14; 226.7; 264.9; 268.9, 11; 328.5

mixtim, 224.18; 264.22, 24, 25; 268.20

mixtura, 268.19

moderatio, 224.8

modernus, 266.2, 18; 272.26; 274.9; 278.4; 280.1, 21; 282.4; 336.12, 16

modus, 184.8, 9; 192.5; 194.3; 198.2; 204.14; 212.17 (bis); 214.12, 19; 216.16; 232.11, 12, 27; 234.6; 246.14; 248.11, 13; 250.21; 254.2; 266.2; 268.26; 284.12, 21; 286.1, 7, 13; 288.6, 12; 290.4; 293.23; 294.18; 300.3, 30 (bis); 302.9, 16; 310.20, 21, 23, 25; 312.2 (bis), 15, 21; 316.27 (bis), 30, 32; 318.2 (bis), 13, 19; 328.9; 334.10; 336.16; 340.4; modus [mensurabilis], 196.7 (bis); 320.24; 334.14; 342.23, 28; 344.1, 4, 7, 10; modus grani ordeacei, 254.6; modus losonge, 254.6; 262.4, 6; 316.21, 22; modus novus, 274.18; modus nudus, 262.6; modus perfectus, 194.11, 12; 198.3; 222.8, 17; 226.15; 230.19; modus imperfectus, 194.11, 12–13; 222.17; 230.20–21; modus semibrevis, 316.13; *v.* divisio modi

motetus, 260.12, 16

musica, 180.2; musica continua et discreta, 334.12, 13; musica mensurabilis, 180.8, 15, 16–17; 182.3, 8, 17; musica plana, 180.5; 182.11–12; 322.4–5

mutare, 188.1, 2; mutari, 190.2
mutatus, 192.1, 3
natura, 340.7, 8
naturaliter, 264.2
necessitas, 180.14; 272.7
nomen, 188.1, 2; 190.2; 192.1, 3; 272.13
nominari, 184.13; 212.6; 242.19; 282.6; 300.1; 316.26
nonligabilis, 330.20–21
nota, 194.2, 16; 196.3, 4; 212.7, 15; 254.6; 266.2, 3, 11; 268.20; 286.14; 288.1, 7, 13 (bis); 316.12, 20, 22; 320.25; 322.4; 326.1; 330.20; 332.4, 11; 336.3; nota plana, 330.16; nota quadrata, 220.6; 286.14–15; 316.16, 19, 19–20; *v.* punctus quadratus
notare, 194.16; 198.1; 212.6, 15; 254.12; notari, 326.18
notator, 180.15
noticia, 250.13
novus, 180.16; 182.5
Novum melos promere, 260.16, 17
nudus, 262.6; 322.17
numerus, 262.14; numerus binarius, 304.11; numerus tertius, 214.20
nuncupari, 184.2; 272.5
obliquari, 322.21
obliquus, 268.12; 322.18; 330.13, 16; tractus obliquum, 272.1
obliquitas, 322.15, 17, 18, 20, 22; 324.1, 2, 8, 16, 20, 22, 23; 326.1, 6; 328.13, 15; 330.10
obstante, 254.12
occupans, 336.7, 8, 19, 20, 21, 22; 338.1, 6, 8, 9, 10, 11; 340.1, 6, 14, 19, 24; 342.2, 6–7, 12, 18
olim, 218.2
omissio, 334.14
omissus, 182.13; 184.3, 5, 7
opinio, 180.2, 18
oppositio, 272.7
oppositus, 270.10–11; 272.11–12; 288.4, 10
opus, 180.12
oratio, 326.22
ordeacei, *v.* granum ordeacei
ordinari, 254.9, 11
ordinatus, 184.8
ordo, 180.10
organum, 182.19, 20, 21, 23; organum duplum, 182.22; organum purum, 182.22; 268.4

originale, 270.2
originari, 270.6
pars, 182.18, 20; 188.7 (bis); 190.1; 194.3; 198.1, 2; 256.8, 23–24; 258.2; 282.7; 334.19, 20; 336.8–9, 9, 10, 11; pars dextra, 194.3–4; 220.6, 9; 222.2, 22; 236.24; 288.7; 300.2; 310.20; 316.26; 310.3; 316.16, 20, 21; 324.5; 336.23; 342.12; pars dimidia, 190.1; 336.18–19, 20, 21, 22, 23–338.1; 338.6–7, 9, 11; 340.6; 342.1, 6, 11, 17; pars sinistra, 222.2; 236.19, 24; 272.1; 316.13, 18, 19, 23; 324.5; 332.8; 338.1; 342.18; diminui a parte ante, 254.2; 294.24; 306.16; diminui a parte post, 254.1; 294.23; 306.15
participatio, 270.17; 272.1
partim, 182.17–18, 19
patere, 202.7, 24; 204.12, 22; 208.22, 29; 210.9, 12, 18, 23, 29; 212.10; 214.2, 10; 216.10, 14, 22; 218.2, 6, 14, 17; 222.2, 22; 224.4, 11; 226.2; 228.9, 14, 24, 29; 230.2, 12; 232.8, 25; *et passim*; pateri, 182.2
pauciora, 290.2
pausa, 182.13, 14, 15 (bis); 184.7; 218.14; 222.7, 13; 226.15, 18; 230.19, 20; 238.1, 4, 17; 242.15, 16; 246.26; 254.16; 256.2, 6, 7, 15 (bis); 258.15 (bis); 268.15; 296.1; 298.15, 17, 23–24, 27; 300.32; 302.11; 306.21; 308.30, 31; 310.8, 14; 312.4, 16; 316.8, 10; 318.3; 334.14, 15, 19; 336.5, 6, 7, 8, 10 (bis), 12, 16, 17, 18, 19, 20, 21, 23; 338.1, 5, 6, 7, 8, 9, 10, 12; 340.1, 4 (bis), 5, 8 (bis), 9, 10 (bis), 14, 16, 17, 19, 20, 21 (bis), 24, 26 (ter); 342.1, 3 (bis), 4, 6, 8 (bis), 9, 11, 14 (ter), 16
pausatio, 334.15
penultimus, 336.2–3, 3
perfectio, 196.5, 6, 7–8, 9; 202.15, 22; 210.20, 27; 212.16; 214.20; 216.1; 224.16; 226.1, 5; 230.9, 16; 234.7, 12; 242.4, 11; 248.15, 19, 21; 250.19, 26, 26–27; 264.23 (bis); 266.5, 14, 21 (bis); 268.1; 270.2, 3, 6; 272.2, 8, 10; 286.8; 292.9, 10; 298.4, 12; 302.17; 304.2, 8–9; 308.20, 27; 310.11; 312.22, 27, 31; 314.4–5; 318.20, 24, 28; 320.1–2; 326.19; 328.6–7, 10; cum perfectione, 326.19; 328.18, 20; 330.2, 7; sine perfectione, 328.18; 330.4, 8, 13–14, 17; *v.* punctus perfectionis
perfectissime, 180.11
perfectissimus, 180.15
perfectus, 194.7, 8; 196.5; 198.1 (bis); 202.26 (bis); 204.4, 14; 208.3 (bis, 18, 22, 29; 210.3, 8, 12; 212.1–2, 2; 222.4, 18, 19; 224.15; 226.1, 5, 7; 228.13, 28; 230.1, 20; 234.19; 238.2, 9, 18; 240.6, 19, 26; 242.16; 244.5 (bis), 7, 19; 246.17; 248.4, 19, 22; 250.5; 254.14 (bis), 17 (bis); 256.11, 12; 258.7; 266.3, 4, 12; 268.25; 270.5; 272.26; 274.2, 23, 24; 278.4; 282.1, 7, 14 (bis), 16; 284.3; 292.10; 294.26; 296.2, 22, 26; 298.16 (bis), 24 (bis), 25; 300.2, 10 (bis), 18; 304.9, 29 (bis); 306.18, 22; 308.8, 11,

31 (bis); 310.8 (bis), 10, 20, 27 (bis); 314.6, 24; 316.9 (bis), 27; 320.2; 328.12; 334.16, 17–18; 336.1, 5, 12, 17, 18; 338.6, 8, 10; 340.1; 342.23; perfecta ex omnibus perfectis, 204.2, 24; 216.6, 25; 234.17; 236.12; 244.17; 246.7; 252.1; 284.1, 17; 294.1; 300.16, 26; 304.29; *v.* modus perfectus

perficere, 196.4; 270.11; perfici, 194.6, 13, 15, 16; 202.9; 206.6 (bis); 210.14; 218.1; 230.4; 240.23, 28; 250.18, 20; 256.1; 270.11; 278.6, 7; 292.9; 296.29; 298.22, 26; 304.8; 308.14; 310.6, 11; 314.5; 320.1; 328.6; 340.6, 8, 10, 14, 16, 19, 21, 24, 26; 342.2, 3, 7, 8, 12, 14, 18; *v.* imperficere, imperfici

perimere, 272.19

pertinere, 216.2; 234.13; 250.27; 292.10, 13, 18; 304.9, 13, 18; 312.28; 314.6, 13; 318.25; 320.10; 328.10, 11

pervertere, 180.10

Petrus de Cruce, 258.11; 260.3

philosophus, 180.5, 11; 188.8; 272.11; 290.3

plane, 332.9

planus, *v.* nota plana, musica plana

plenitudo vocis, 242.20

plica, 324.23 (bis); 326.6; 330.11, 22

plicatus, 222.1; 236.23; 254.13; 326.1

plicari, 218.5; 222.4; 236.26; 254.8, 12; 332.2, 5, 17; 334.1

ponere, 184.10; 188.2; 258.10; 260.3; 268.27; 274.3; 286.14; 288.7; poni, 196.5, 9; 198.15; 200.1, 6; 208.3, 11; 220.11; 224.18; 226.14; 228.8; 232.23; 238.17; 240.1; 258.1; 264.16; 266.1, 2, 11; 268.6; 274.20; 276.13; 282.2; 286.17; 288.1; 292.25, 27; 294.28; 296.8; 304.25; 306.26; 310.21, 23, 25; 312.20; 314.20; 316.27, 30, 32; 318.13; 320.17, 26; 326.7; *v.* apponi

portionari, 270.14

positus, 260.1; 288.13; 292.13; *v.* appositus

postpositus, 196.4; 224.15; 250.14; 292.17, 22; 304.13, 17, 22; 314.9, 12, 17; 320.6, 9, 14

potius, 336.1

practice, 180.6, 7

precedere, 180.9; 182.24; 184.5; 196.4; 198.4–5; 200.11, 14, 16; 202.1, 4, 6, 9, 12, 15, 18, 20; 204.3 (bis), 4, 5, 6, 9; 206.12, 13; 208.18, 22, 26, 28; 210.1, 3, 7, 9, 11, 14, 17, 20, 22, 25; 216.7 (bis), 8, 9; 220.11; 224.10; 226.4–5; 228.4, 21, 23, 27, 29; 230.1, 4, 6, 9, 11, 14; 234.18 (bis), 20, 21; 238.10, 11, 21; 240.4, 9, 13, 15, 18, 20, 23–24, 25, 28; 242.1, 4, 6, 9; 244.7–8, 8, 18 (bis), 19, 20, 21; 246.19; 248.4–5; 252.2, 2–3, 4, 14; 256.21; 262.9; 264.2, 16; 268.14–15; 282.17, 18; 284.2, 2–3, 4, 5, 6;

292.17, 18; 294.2, 2–3, 4, 13; 296.20, 23, 26, 29; 298.1, 4, 7, 10; 300.11 (bis), 17 (bis), 18, 22; 302.14; 304.17, 18, 30, 30–31, 32; 306.8; 308.9, 11, 14, 17, 20, 22, 25; 310.28 (bis); 314.12–13, 13, 24–25, 25, 26–27; 316.4; 320.10 (bis); v. antecedere
preces, 180.9
precise, 180.7
predictus, 180.11; 182.1–2; 204.5, 14; 216.8, 16; 218.1; 224.8; 234.20; 236.5; 244.20; 246.1; 248.4; 252.4, 20; 254.13; 284.5, 12; 294.3; 304.31; 314.26
prenotatus, 268.6
primarius, 322.4
principalis, 180.9
principium, 322.2, 5, 15; 324.1, 20; principium activum, 270.2
prius, 184.5; 192.1, 3; 260.3; 268.27; 274.3, 4; 328.1
privatio, 184.6
probare, 182.6; probari, 270.5, 9
probatio, 290.1
procedere, 320.25
prohemium, 180.4
prolatus, 182.12; 184.1; 272.3
propalatam, 180.11
proponere, 180.10; 182.3
proportio recta, 246.12–13; proportio altera, 260.10
proportionaliter, 182.27
proportionari, 182.28
propositum, 316.20; [propositum] maior, 290.3; [propositum] minor, 270.5; 290.3
proprie, 182.21 (bis); 246.12;
proprietas, 272.7–8; 322.4; 324.12; cum proprietate, 322.1, 7, 11, 13; sine proprietate, 322.1; 324.6, 16–17, 18; 326.19; proprietas opposita, 286.14; 322.2; 326.10, 12, 13; 330.8; 332.8–9
proprium, 324.6
proximus, 196.4
punctus [alterationis], 290.2; punctus alterationis, 302.19, 312.24; 318.21; punctus [divisionis], 258.9; 260.1, 4, 10, 15; 262.9; 264.14; 292.2; punctus divisionis, 196.2, 7; 214.2, 15, 23; 232.17–18; 234.2–3, 9–10; 250.15; 286.3, 10; 302.12; 312.17; 318.14; v. divisio modi; punctus [perfectionis], 194.8; 196.4, 9; 198.16, 18; 202.9, 27; 206.7, 10; 208.4, 6; 210.14; 212.3; 222.7, 15, 18; 226.15, 20; 230.4; 238.2, 6, 9, 18; 240.23, 28; 250.14, 18, 20, 23; 256.4; 266.3, 5, 12, 14; 278.4, 6, 7; 292.9, 12–13, 14, 17, 18, 22 (bis), 25; 296.1, 29; 298.29; 304.8, 14, 17, 18, 22 (bis),

25; 306.21; 308.14; 310.16; 314.5, 10, 13, 17 (bis), 20; 320.1, 6, 10, 14, 16; 340.10, 17, 22, 27; 342.4, 9, 15; punctus perfectionis, 194.12; 196.1–2, 2, 3; 224.15; 226.2; 256.1; 292.7; 298.25; 304.6, 12–13; 310.10–11; 314.3, 9, 12; 318.32; 320.5, 9, 14; 328.6; punctus [quadratus], 254.5–6; 288.4; 322.6, 7, 10, 11; 324.4, 5, 8, 11, 12, 15; 326.10; 328.19; 330.4, 13; punctus quadratus, 220.5–6, 21; 236.18; 286.18; 288.11; 322.14–15; 324.19–10, 20; 330.1; 332.1; punctus magnus et grossus, 206.2; *v.* nota quadrata, finis punctorum

purus, *v.* organum purum

quadrangulum, 266.20

quadratus, *v.* nota quadrata, punctus quadratus

quantitas, 206.2; 334.14

quantitativa, *v.* habitudo quantitativa

quatripliciter, 196.3

questio, 248.22

ratio, 182.5–6; 270.1, 9, 16; 272.7; 316.16; 322.17; 326.16

recte, 272.5; recte stare, 288.5; 328.19

rectus, 212.5, 7, 21; 214.1, 18, 22; 216.1; 220.12; 232.2 (bis), 11, 17; 234.5, 9, 12; 242.19 (bis); 244.7, 17; 246.10, 12, 28; 250.19, 26; 256.12, 21, 24; 258.5; 272.27; 282.6 (bis), 8, 16; 284.25, 33; 286.6, 9; 294.26; 300.1 (bis), 2, 10; 302.1, 8, 15, 19, 22; 306.18; 310.19 (bis), 27; 312.7, 14, 20, 23, 27, 31; 316.26 (bis); 318.5, 12, 17, 21, 24, 29; 342.26, 28; vox recta, 184.3, 5, 6

recurri, 250.4

recusare, 182.4

referri, 224.6

regula, 186.3; 194.11; 224.8, 9, 13; 256.12; 322.14; 324.19; 328.3, 9; 332.7; regulas Magistri Franchonis, 286.17

regulari, 184.3

remanere, 214.22; 216.1; 234.8, 12; 248.15, 16; 258.16; 260.2; 286.9; 302.18, 22; 304.3, 11; 312.22, 27, 31; 314.9; 318.21, 24, 28; 320.5

remotio, 272.10

representatio, 184.8; 334.10

require, 322.20

respondere, 248.22

restare, 340.4

retortus, 310.3; 316.13, 21, 23; 336.23; 338.1; 342.12, 18

reverendus, 334.12

rigor, 256.26

Robertus de Brunham, 286.13–14; frater Robertus de Brunham, 338.5; Robertus [de Brunham], 288.6, 12

Robertus Trowell, 272.16
rotundus, *v.* signum rotundum
salvari, 224.9
sciendum est quod, 182.20; 196.1; 218.5, 8; 258.13; 280.23; 320.22, 24; 342.23; 344.10
scientia, 182.2
scriptus, 182.28
secundum, 196.2; 272.11; 282.3, 4
securius, 258.9; 268.5
semibrevis, 182.27; 186.1; 192.2, 6; 204.10 (bis), 12, 13 (bis), 25, 27; 216.9, 10, 13 (bis), 18, 18–19, 19, 26, 28; 226.8, 9, 12, 14; 228.1 (bis), 4, 7, 8 (bis), 11, 13, 18 (bis), 21, 23, 26, 28 (bis), 29; 230.1, 2, 4, 5, 6 (bis), 9 (bis), 10, 11, 11–12, 14 (bis), 15; 234.17–18, 18, 19, 20, 20–21; 236.1, 6 (bis), 7, 13, 14; 238.9, 10, 10–11, 13, 18, 21, 24; 240.4, 5, 6, 9, 10–11, 13, 14, 14–15, 17, 18, 19, 23, 24, 25, 26, 28, 29, 30; 242.5, 6, 9, 10, 12; 244.6, 7, 8, 13; 246.1, 7, 9; 252.2 (bis), 4, 5, 6, 9, 10, 11, 14, 15, 16 (bis), 21, 22 (bis); 254–98, Cap. XII–XV (de semibrevibus) *passim*; 298.19; 300.2, 3 (ter), 4, 6, 8, 31, 32 (bis); 302.4, 6, 10 (bis), 10–11, 14, 16–17, 17, 22; 304.1, 3, 6, 8, 9 (bis), 10, 11, 12 (bis), 13, 14 (bis), 17, 18, 18–19, 21 (bis), 22, 23, 25 (bis), 26, 26–27; 310.2; 316.13; 322.18, 21; 326.12, 16 (bis); 328.3, 4 (bis), 6, 9, 10, 11, 11–12; 330.10; 334.6, 20, 21 (bis); 336.3, 12, 18, 19; 340.1; 342.1, 2–3, 3, 4 (bis); 344.7; semibrevis maior, 262.3; 266.15; 268.9–10, 18, 26, 27; 336.9; semibrevis minor, 256.26; 258.2; 262.15, 17; 264.13; 266.24; 268.9–10, 18; 270.7; 334.21; 336.11; semibrevis minorata, 264.1; 270.14; *v.* maior, minor, equalis, minorata
semicirculus, 266.11
semiminor, 192.3, 4, 6; 204.11 (bis), 20, 21 (bis), 25, 27; 216.13–14; 14, 20–21, 21 (bis), 26, 28; 226.9–10; 236.2 (bis), 8, 9 (bis), 13, 15; 244.21, 22, 24, 25; 246.3, 4 (bis), 8, 9; 252.7 (bis), 12 (bis), 17 (bis), 24 (bis), 25; 268.22; 284.2 (bis), 4, 4–5, 5–6, 9, 13, 13–14, 14, 18, 19; 294.6 (bis), 10 (bis), 15 (bis), 20, 21 (bis), 26–27, 29; 296.3, 8, 8–9, 11, 13, 17 (bis), 20, 22 (bis), 23, 26, 27, 29, 30; 298.1, 2, 4, 5, 6–7, 7, 10, 10–11, 11, 23, 30; 300.10–11, 11, 14, 24, 26, 27, 28; 304.30 (bis), 32; 306.1 (bis, 4, 5, 6, 8, 9, 10, 13 (bis), 14, 21, 29, 30; 308.3, 6, 6–7, 8, 11, 14, 15 (bis), 21, 22, 25, 26, 28; 310–16, Cap. XVII (de semiminoribus) *passim*; 316.21–22, 27, 28, 30, 32; 318.3 (ter), 8, 9, 13, 17, 19, 24–25, 27, 29, 32; 320.1, 2 (bis), 3, 4 (bis), 5, 6 (bis), 9, 10, 11, 13 (bis), 14, 15, 17 (bis), 18, 18–19; 336.21–22; 340.1; 342.11, 13 (bis), 14 (bis)
semis, 192.4
semitonium, 220.12–13; 236.22

sequi, 200.2, 16; 202.3, 7, 18, 22; 204.7, 12; 208.24, 29; 210.8, 23, 27; 216.2 (bis), 9, 10; 220.4; 224.1, 6, 7, 19; 228.22, 28; 230.12, 15; 234.21, 22 (bis); 238.10; 242.7; 244.21, 22; 246.19; 248.5 (bis); 250.6, 15, 18, 27; 262.12; 284.7; 296.23; 308.21, 23, 26; 314.10; 320.6; 324.13, 15–16; 326.21; 328.11; 332.11; *v.* subsequi

significancia, 184.4

significare, 184.6, 7, 9

signum, 184.4; signum rotundum, 262.17; 264.3, 8, 10

sillaba, 254.8, 12; 320.26 (bis)

similitudinis, 288.13

simplex, 182.24; 184.13, 14; 194.6; 220.5; 222.6, 9; 226.16; 236.17; 254.5, 13; 266.23; 268.7, 9; 298.22; 310.6; 316.24; 322.21

simpliciter, 182.17, 18; 184.1

sinister, *v.* pars sinistra

solus, 224.1, 10; 246.19; 264.8; 322.18; 324.1; 326.6, 17; 328.9

solere, 266.1

sonus, 184.8; sonus mensuratus, 344.11

sorti, 272.13

spatia, 336.7, 8, 9, 11, 13, 19, 20, 21, 22; 338.1, 2, 6, 7, 8, 8–9, 9, 10, 11 (bis), 12; 340.5–6, 6, 14, 19, 24; 342.1, 6, 11, 17

species, 186.1; 192.5; 196.5; 334.15

stare, 218.9; 220.1; 266.5; recte stare, 288.5; 328.19

subalternam, 180.9

subsequi, 198.4, 9, 22; 200.9, 12, 15; 202.2, 4, 10, 13, 17, 21; 204.3, 3–4, 4, 5, 6, 9, 10, 15, 16, 17–18, 19, 20, 21–22; 206.12, 17; 208.9, 20, 26, 29; 210.2, 4, 6, 9, 12, 15, 18, 21, 26; 214.1; 216.2, 7, 8, 13, 17, 18, 19, 21; 218.19; 228.5, 7, 16, 19, 23, 26, 29; 230.2, 5, 7, 10, 15; 234.13, 18, 19 (bis), 20; 236.2, 6, 7, 7–8; 238.13, 22, 24; 240.5, 11, 14, 15, 17, 19, 20, 24, 26, 29; 242.2, 5, 10 (bis); 244.8, 13, 18, 19, 19–20, 20, 24; 246.2, 3; 250.25; 252.2, 3, 6, 9, 10, 14, 16, 17, 21, 23, 24; 268.15; 282.17, 22; 284.2, 3, 4, 5, 6, 9, 13; 292.4–5, 10, 13, 14; 294.2, 3, 8, 13, 19, 20–21, 22; 296.6, 15, 18, 21, 23, 27, 30; 298.2, 6, 7, 11, 12; 300.11, 14, 17, 17–18, 20, 22; 302.22–23; 304.3, 9, 13, 14, 30, 31; 306.4, 8, 13, 24; 308.1, 4, 7, 9, 12, 15, 17, 26; 310.28, 31; 312.28; 314.1, 6, 25 (bis); 316.1, 4; 318.25, 29; 320.2; *v.* sequi

subterpositus, 254.12

succurrendum, 182.1; 186.4

sufficienter, 180.5; 186.3

summa, 180.1; 334.12

sumptum, 182.22

superfluum, 324.23

supponere, 180.11; supponi, 266.9
suppositus, 196.6
supraponi, 266.7
suprapositus, 196.4
sustinere, 182.6
tangere, 336.6, 7, 8, 9–10, 11, 13, 18, 20, 21, 22, 23; 338.2, 6, 8 (bis), 10, 10–11, 12; 340.5, 14, 19, 24; 342.1, 6, 11, 17
tempus, 182.8, 10, 12, 14, 18–19, 20, 23; 218.8, 9, 16; 220.1; 222.7, 19; 224.6; 242.20; 246.16 (bis); 248.11 (bis), 16; 256.8, 25; 268.14, 15, 16; 320.23; 334.15, 17, 19, 21; 336.1, 5, 6, 7, 9, 11; 344.10–11; tempus perfectum, 226.15; 238.1–2, 8; 242.15; tempus imperfectum, 238.8; 242.16–17; tempus semibrevis, 256.7–8; tempus [semibrevis], 256.8–9
tendere, 270.1, 5, 6
tenere, 256.1, 12; 258.7; 268.21; 310.9; tenere regula, 194.11; 322.14; 324.19; 332.7; teneri, 250.3; teneri pro recta, 214.22; 234.9; teneri habere, 214.24; 224.15; 226.2; 234.10; 302.8
tenor, 270.5; 326.22
tertiarium, 292.3
theorice, 180.6, 7
tollere, 272.9–10
tonus, 192.5
totaliter, 272.10
tractare, 180.5–6, 10
tractulus, 270.1; 288.7, 12; 290.3; 292.2; 298.20; 324.20–21; 332.7; *v.* tractus, cauda
tractus, 184.14; 194.3; 220.6, 9; 222.1, 22; 270.10, 11; 272.1, 6, 9, 19; 236.18, 19, 23; 262.4; 310.3; 316.13, 16, 17, 19, 20, 21, 22; 322.7, 10, 15; 324.1, 4–5, 12, 16; 326.9; 332.11; *v.* tractulus, cauda
transire, 292.3, 12
trinitas perfecta, 194.7
triplex, 266.20
tripliciter, 212.7; 232.3; 242.21; 282.8
tropus ecclesiasticus, 180.8
Trowell, *v.* Robertus Trowell
truncatus, 184.2
ulterior, 262.13
unicus, 292.21
unitas, 292.3, 12
universus, 344.7
uterque, 216.12; 236.1; 244.24; 252.16; 270.17; 284.9; 292.26; 294.15; 300.28; 304.25, 26; 306.10; 314.20, 21; 320.17, 18

uti, 268.4; 336.16
valere, 208.1; 216.25, 27; 222.18; 226.12; 238.9, 15; 246.7, 9; 242.20; 246.16 (bis); 248.10; 256.24; 260.15; 262.15; 264.1; 268.25; 284.19; 293.26; 300.26; 304.14, 19, 23, 27; 306.18; 314.10, 14, 22; 320.7, 11, 15, 19; 328.12; 334.16, 17 (bis), 19, 20, 21 (bis); 336.10, 12
valor, 198.4, 7, 11, 20; 200.1, 2, 4, 6, 11, 12, 14, 16 (bis); 202.1, 2, 4 (bis), 6, 7, 9, 12 (bis), 15, 16, 17, 18 (bis), 20, 21, 22; 204.7; 206.14, 16, 27, 28, 29; 208.22; 210.1, 2, 3, 4, 6, 7, 8, 9, 11, 12, 14, 17, 18, 22, 23, 25, 26, 27; 212.14, 15, 18, 21; 214.1, 5, 7, 10, 12, 14, 17, 18, 19, 20, 21, 22, 24; 216.10; 222.6–7, 11; 224.1, 10, 13, 16, 18, 19; 228.1, 4, 9, 11, 13, 18, 19, 21, 22, 23 (bis), 26, 27, 29 (bis); 230.1, 2, 6, 7, 11, 12; 232.10, 12, 15, 20, 22, 25, 27, 28; 234.1; *et passim*
vehementer, 326.21
velle, 188.1
venerabilis, 186.2
verificari, 196.6; 266.9
verissime, 262.2–3
verius, 258.9; 260.3
vetus organum purum, 268.4
via, 248.22; 250.3
videre, 180.16; vidi, 182.9; 328.1
virtus, 272.8
vitiosum, 188.6; 290.1; 330.20
vitiose, 286.17; 292.1; 326.20
vitiosus, 268.19
vocari, 192.1–2, 2, 3; 218.2; 220.12; 222.19; 236.20; 244.6–7; 254.15–16; 258.1; 260.13, 16; 266.21; recta vocari, 212.5–6, 21; 216.1; 232.2, 17; 234.5, 12; 250.19, 26; 256.21–22; 284.33; 302.1, 15, 22; 310.19; 312.7, 14, 27, 31–314.1; 318.5, 12, 17, 24, 28–9
vox, 182.12, 13, 27; 184.3, 5, 6, 7, 8; 242.20; 334.14
W. de Doncastre, 268.27
yrundinis, *v.* cauda yrundinis

## INDEX NOMINUM ET RERUM

Admetus de Aureliana, 12–13, 20, 26, 27–28, 39, 146–49
*Agmina fidelium Katerina*, 16–17, 28, 174–75
alteration, 40–42, 92–93, 212–13; of semibreves according to Robertus de Brunham, 62–63, 286–93
Anonymous IV, 21, 23, 68–69, 74
Anonymous OP: *Tractatus de musica*, 48
antiquarians: interest of in Hanboys, 32–37
Aristotle, 185n.7, 189n.15; 269.n120–273n.124
*Ars cantus mensurabilis*: *see* Franco
*Aucun ont trouvé chant*, 18n.53, 106–7, 260–61
Bale, John: *Illustrium maioris britanniae scriptorum*, 33–35; 36, 37
*Beatus vir*: English motet in the notation of Doncastre, 60–61; transcribed, 356–59
binary mensuration, 62, 64
*Breviarium regulare musicae*: *see* Willelmus
brevis, 11–12; brevis erecta, 6, 11–12, 39
Brunham: *see* Robertus de Brunham
Burney, Charles, 32–33, 37n.102
Carpenter, Nan Cooke, 20, 38
*circulum parvulum*, 21, 164–65
*Compendium musicae practice*: *see* Johannes de Muris
*coniunctura*: *see* conjunctions of semibreves
conjunctions of semibreves, 39, 142–51
Copais, 21–22; 164–65
Corbe, J. de (John de Corby), 32, 65
Cottonian manuscripts, 6–7, 69–71
counterpoint, 1n.1
*crocheta*, 47, 54, 188–93
*Cum de mensurabili musica*, 2, 2n.6
*currentes*: *see* conjunctions of semibreves
*curta* and *longa mensura*, 62, 64, 276–83
dances, 15–16, 176–77
de Muris: *see* Johannes de Muris

*De origine et effectu musicae*: *see* Wylde anonymous
*Declaratio trianguli et scuti*: *see* Torkesey
Dee, John, 5, 6, 69–71
diminishment: in the *Summa*, 42–46
diminution: *see* diminishment
*divisio modi*, 14, 19
Doncastre, W. de, 26, 39, 60, 268–73; his notation in *Beatus vir*, 60–61, 351, 356
dot (of division, of perfection, etc.): *see punctus*
duplex longa, 11, 59, 206–17, 218–21
extended longa, 10–11, 53
*figura* and *signum* in the *Regule*, 29–30
figures, notational, in the *Summa*: larga, 194–205, duplex longa, 206–21, longa, 220–37, brevis, 236–55, semibrevis, 254–99, minor, 298–309, semiminor, 310–17, minima, 316–21, ligatures, 320–35, rests, 334–43
Franco of Cologne: *Ars cantus mensurabilis*, 1, 8, 38, 39, 46; quoted at length, 180–87
*Gaudent brevitate moderni*, 8–9, 40
genres of mensurable music, 15–16; 176–77
gradus system, expansion of, 46–58
*Hac a valle*: English motet in the tradition of Garlandia, 26–27; transcribed, 351–55
Hanboys: *see* Johannes Hanboys
Handlo: *see* Robertus de Handlo
Hawkins, Sir John, 32–33, 37n.102, 75
hockets, 15, 21–22, 23–24, 28, 162–65
Holinshed, Raphael: *Chronicles of England, Scotland, and Ireland*, 36
Hothby, Johannes, 37
imperfection in the *Summa*, 40–42
*In Bethleem*, 166–67
Jacobus de Navernia, 20–21
Jacques de Liège: *Speculum musicae*, 1n.2, 9, 17, 22, 25–26
Johannes de Garlandia, 12, 13, 14, 24–27, 59–60, 108–15, 262–67; his notation in *Hac a valle*, 26–27, 351
Johannes de Muris: *Notitia artis musicae*, 48–51; *Compendium musicae practice*, 55; *Libellus cantus mensurabilis*, 49, 58
Johannes Hanboys: identity, 30–38, 64–66; an earlier work by, 47, 283n.131; a larger work by, 33, 38, 64–65, 185n.9; contents of the *Summa*, 38–64; gradus system of, 57–58; his rests, 64; musical works cited by: *see Aucun ont trouvé chant*, *Novum melos promere*; authorities mentioned or cited: *see* Franco of Cologne, Johannes de Garlandia,

Petrus de Cruce, Robertus de Brunham, [Robertus de Handlo], Robertus Trowell, W. de Doncastre
Koller, Oswald, 38
Leland, John, 33
*Libellus cantus mensurabilis*: see Johannes de Muris
longa, 11–12, 220–237; longa erecta, 6, 11–12, 39
*Mane prima sabbati surgens dei filius*, 168–69
Marchetto da Padova: his divisions of the semibrevis compared to English practice, 26, 61–62
manuscripts: London, British Library, Cotton Tiberius B.IX, 66–71; London, British Library, Additional 4909, 71–75; London, British Library, Additional 8866, 76–77; London, British Library, Additional 21455, 2–3n.6, 12; London, Westminster Abbey, 12185, 26–27, 60–61, 351
Martini, G. (Gilbert Martyn?), 32, 65
mensuration signs, 266–67
modes, rhythmic, 166–79, 342–45; mixture of modes, 176–77, 196–97; transmutation of the third and fourth modes, 172–73
Morley, Thomas: *A Plaine and Easy Introduction to Practicall Musicke*, 5–6
Navarre, 20–21, 26, 27–28
Navernia: *see* Jacobus de Navernia
*Nobilis humilis*: see *Rosula primula*
*Notitia artis musicae*: see Johannes de Muris
*Novum melos promere*, 18n.53; 174–75; 260–61
Ockham's razor, 62–63, 290–91
*O Maria maris stella plena gratia*, 168–69
Odington, Walter: *Summa de speculacione musicae*, 2, 28, 75; and the mixture of modes, 15; and the *Agmina* triplum, 17; and hockets, 21; and the transmutation of modes, 23
Pepusch, Dr. Johann Christoph, 7, 69, 75
Petrus de Cruce, 12, 14–15, 17–20, 25, 59, 100–107, 260–61; *Tractatus de tonis*, 18; his mensural treatise, 19
Petrus de Sancto Dionysio: *Tractatus de musica*, 53
Petrus le Viser, 12, 20, 22–24, 39, 59, 102–9
Petrus Picardus: *Ars motettorum*, 19
Philippe de Vitry, theoretical tradition of, 3n.6, 22–23, 27, 47, 48–49, 51n.130, 61–62; his mensurations compared with English practices, 26, 61–62
Phillipotus, 50, 53–54, 53–54n.135
Pits, John: *De Illustribus Angliae Scriptoribus*, 36
*Plaine and Easy Introduction to Practicall Musicke*: see Morley
plica, 14, 39, 152–57, 158–59

punctus (alterationis, divisionis, perfectionis, quadratus, etc.), 14–15, 41–42, 58–59, 128–29, 196–97, 224–27, 250–51; in mensuration signs, 266–67

*Quatuor principalia*: both versions, 33–37, 51–53, 63; Version A, 3, 67–68, 72–73; Version B, 3, 38, 76;

*Quid miraris partum virgineum*, 170–71

Reaney, Gilbert, 19, 27, 38

*Regina regni glorie*, 174–75

*Regulae de musica mensurabili*: see Walsingham, Thomas

*Regule*: see Robertus de Handlo

rests, 63–64, 160–65, 334–43

Robertus de Brunham, 39, 46n.118, 62–63; ligature forms of, 62, 286–89; *cauda yrundinis* of, 62–63, 288–93; rests of, 64, 338–41; mensural system of, 339n.196

Robertus de Handlo: identity of, 4–8; an earlier work by, 29–30; contents of the *Regule*, 8–28; English origin of the *Regule*, 28; musical works cited by: see *Aucun ont trouvé chant*, *Agmina fidelium*, *In Bethleem*, *Mane prima sabbati*, *Novum melos promere*, *O Maria maris stella*, *Quid miraris*, *Regina regni glorie*, *Rosula primula*, *Rota versatilis*, *Sola salve singularis*; authorities cited by: see Admetus de Aureliana, Copais, Jacobus de Navernia, Johannes de Garlandia, Petrus de Cruce, Petrus le Viser

*Rosula primula salve Jesse virgula*, 172–73; contrafact of *Nobilis humilis*, 16, 28

*Rota versatilis rubens versucia*, 17, 28, 118–19

*Sciendum est tamen et neupme loco*, 38n.104, 76; edited and translated, 361–65

semibrevis, 12–13, 59–63, 254–99

*signum perfectionis*, 14

*signum rotundum*, 12, 26

*Sola salve singularis gratie*, 174–75

*Speculum musicae*: see Jacques de Liège

*Sub arturo plebs*, 31–32, 65–66

*Summa*: see Johannes Hanboys

*Summa de speculacione musicae*: see Odington, Walter

syllogism, 40, 60, 65

syncopation, 64, 292–93 *et passim*

Tanner, Thomas: *Bibliotheca Britannico–Hibernica*, 7, 37

Torkesey, Johannes: *Declaratio trianguli et scuti*, 3, 46n.118, 54–56, 58

*Tractatus de figuris sive de notis*, 3, 53–54, 339n.196

*Tractatus de tonis*: see Petrus de Cruce

*Tractatus figurarum*, 67, 71–72

transmutation of modes, 23, 28, 29, 172–73

Trowell, Brian, 30–32
Trowell, Robertus, 26, 39, 60, 272–73
Tunstede, Simon, 33, 35, 37
*vox* in the *Regule*, 28–29
Walsingham, Thomas: *Regulae de musica mensurabili*, 4, 53–54, 55; transmitting the notations of Brunham, 63
Willelmus: *Breviarium regulare musicae*, 3, 56–57
Wylde anonymous: *De origine et effectu musicae*, 4, 53–54, 57